ELEMENTARY SOCIAL STUDIES:

A Whole Language Approach

P A M E L A   J .   F A R R I S

NORTHERN ILLINOIS UNIVERSITY

S U S A N   M .   C O O P E R

CALIFORNIA STATE UNIVERSITY at SAN BERNARDINO

WCB Brown & Benchmark
PUBLISHERS

Madison, Wisconsin • Dubuque, Iowa

Book Team
Executive Editor *Stan Stoga*
Editor *Paul L. Tavenner*
Developmental Editor *Sue Pulvermacher-Alt*
Production Editor *Deborah J. Donner*
Photo Editor *Carol A. Judge*
Visuals/Design Developmental Consultant *Marilyn A. Phelps*
Visuals/Design Freelance Specialist *Mary L. Christianson*
Publishing Services Specialist *Sherry Padden*
Marketing Manager *Pamela S. Cooper*
Advertising Manager *Jodi Rymer*

WCB Brown & Benchmark
A Division of Wm. C. Brown Communications, Inc.
Executive Vice President/General Manager *Thomas E. Doran*
Vice President/Editor in Chief *Edgar J. Laube*
Vice President/Sales and Marketing *Eric Ziegler*
Director of Production *Vickie Putman Caughron*
Director of Custom and Electronic Publishing *Chris Rogers*

Wm. C. Brown Communications, Inc.
President and Chief Executive Officer *G. Franklin Lewis*
Corporate Senior Vice President and Chief Financial Officer *Robert Chesterman*
Corporate Senior Vice President and President of Manufacturing *Roger Meyer*

Cover and interior designs by Katherine M. Wagenknecht, National Graphics, Inc.
Illustrations by Katherine M. Wagenknecht, National Graphics, Inc. with the assistance of
Mrs. Karen Seban and her fifth grade class, Immanuel Lutheran School unless noted otherwise.

Cover image © C. Jeffrey Myers/FPG International; cover inset © Telegraph Colour
Library/FPG International.

Copyedited by Marie Enders

A Times Mirror Company

Library of Congress Catalog Card Number: 92–82969

ISBN 0–697–16198–6

Printed in the United States of America by Wm. C. Brown Communications, Inc.,
2460 Kerper Boulevard, Dubuque, IA 52001

10 9 8 7 6 5 4 3 2 1

DEDICATION

To my parents,
Edgar and Fay Farris,
and my brothers,
Greg and Eddie,
who continue to offer
support and encouragement

–PJF

■

To William and Dorothy Cooper,
who guided my youth;
and to their grandchildren
who will influence our future

–SMC

■

CONTENTS

Reading, Writing, and Discussing: Communicating in Social Studies

Another Time, Another Place: Bringing Social Studies to Life Through Literature

Facilitating Learning: Strategic Instruction in Social Studies

Drama in the Social Studies:
Gateway to the Past, Pathway to the Future

Civic Education: Building Participation
Skills in a Democratic Society

Moving Beyond Indoor Classrooms: Outdoor Education and the Social Studies

It All Depends on Your Point of View: Multicultural Education in the Social Studies

Social Studies, Bilingualism, Respect,
and Understanding: Making the Connections

Immersing Learning Disabled Students in History:
Traveling Back in Time

13

The Interactive Technology Environment

14

Assessing Social Studies in Whole Language Classrooms

PREFACE

Social studies and whole language are a natural fit. Both can offer the student meaningful, relevant, and above all, authentic learning. Language acquisition itself occurs through social interaction. That is why nearly every 4-year-old in America can identify a McDonald's restaurant; they have been there and talked about it. Those golden arches are a giant written symbol that they readily recognize.

The basic tenets of social studies are virtually identical to those of the whole language approach:

■

CHILDREN should be actively involved in their learning.

■

CHILDREN should be given opportunities to make decisions
and become decision makers.

■

CHILDREN need to use their previously gained knowledge
and experiences as a learning scaffold.

■

CHILDREN need to develop a positive self-concept in which they
feel secure, effective, competent, and capable.

■

CHILDREN need to develop an appreciation for the aesthetics of a subject.

■

CHILDREN need to be productive, contributing citizens.

■

Elementary Social Studies: A Whole Language Approach was developed on the basis of these tenets. The book provides the "theory into practice" that preservice and in-service teachers can both understand and appreciate.

After a few years of teaching undergraduates about the whole language philosophy and sharing anecdotes about my former elementary students, I decided that teachers needed a textbook on how to teach social studies according to the whole language philosophy. I contacted Susan M. Cooper, who has taught both social studies and instructional technology, and asked her if she would coedit such a book with me. She readily agreed. Thus, *Elementary Social Studies: A Whole Language Approach* was created.

Both Susan and I believed that the book's chapters should be written by individuals who are experts in their field rather than by two people who are strongly interested in teaching social studies through a whole language approach. By availing themselves of a number of highly qualified authors, the readers of the book would be getting the "best of the best." Therefore, we invited classroom teachers and university faculty members well-known for their expertise in specific social studies areas to contribute chapters to the book.

The book's opening chapter, "Bringing Together Social Studies and Whole Language: A Look at Social Studies," was coauthored by myself and Terry Whealon, who teaches social studies methods at the undergraduate and graduate levels. This chapter provides an overview of the social studies: anthropology, economics, geography, history, political science (civic education), and sociology. In it, the authors also present current recommendations from the National Commission on the Social Studies, the Bradley Commission, and others on how social studies is best taught. Examples of ways to link social studies instruction and whole language are provided.

Chapter 2, "Bringing Together Social Studies and Whole Language: A Look at Whole Language," of which I am the author, provides the reader with insights into the whole language philosophy, its rationale, and goals. The latter part of the chapter describes how social studies and whole language can be integrated in the elementary classroom.

Chapter 3, "Early Childhood Social Studies: Doing the Whole Thing in Whole Language," by Billie J. Thomas, a noted early childhood specialist, continues the linkage between social studies instruction and whole language. Focusing on the child's widening awareness of the social studies environment, Thomas elaborates on how the child moves from viewing self to family to neighborhood to community to state to nation to world and finally to the universe itself. In so doing, she presents numerous examples of how whole language activities can be used to teach basic social studies concepts.

Teaching social studies concepts through reading, writing, and discussing is the focus of Chapter 4, "Reading, Writing, and Discussing: Communicating in the Social Studies," which I wrote. This chapter further elaborates on and extends the ideas presented in Chapter 3. The inclusion of children's literature as reading material for social studies instruction is examined. The stages of the writing process are presented, along with suggestions for different types of writing in social studies (narrative, expository, and poetic). In addition, the importance of discussion is considered, and the use of strategic learning strategies and cooperative learning is highlighted.

In Chapter 5, "Another Time, Another Place: Bringing Social Studies to Life Through Literature," Marjorie R. Hancock explores in further depth the use of children's literature to teach history and geography in particular. Hancock, who teaches language arts and children's literature at the undergraduate and graduate levels, weaves the social studies curriculum with a cloth of quality children's books on geographic and historical themes. She presents an example of using thematic units of study in social studies instruction as a way to provide choices, thus enabling children to select areas of study in social studies in which they have a personal interest.

Personalizing instruction in social studies is significant, as is activating students' prior knowledge of concepts. In Chapter 6, "Facilitating Learning: Strategic Instruction in Social Studies," Bonnie L. Kuhrt, a classroom teacher, and I examine a variety of ways that teachers can assist students in acquiring and extending their knowledge of social studies through learning strategies.

The personalizing of instruction is further examined in Chapter 7, "Drama in the Social Studies: Gateway to the Past, Pathway to the Future." The author, Pamela A. Nelson, is a noted authority on historical museums and how teachers can use drama as "living history" lessons. Nelson points out that social studies develops children's attitudes, values, and perspectives. By combining drama and social studies, the aesthetic is awakened in students and becomes part of their vision of social studies. A list of living history museums is provided in the appendix.

Active participation is essential in civic education. In Chapter 8, "Civic Education: Building Participation Skills in a Democratic Society," Phyllis Maxey-Fernlund, a renowned expert on political science and civic education for children, discusses democratic ideals and core values of a democratic society. She provides examples of how case studies, role playing, and simulations can contribute to the development of children's democratic skills. Maxey-Fernlund emphasizes the need for the teacher to be a positive role model by creating a trusting and secure classroom environment, a priority of both social studies and whole language instruction.

Moving social studies instruction outside the classroom is the theme of Clifford E. Knapp in Chapter 9, "Moving Beyond Indoor Classrooms: Outdoor Education and the Social Studies." Knapp, an internationally recognized leader in outdoor education, presents a case for teaching children social studies through the whole language approach. He suggests a wide variety of activities to help children learn more about the world outside the classroom, including their own community.

Community is also the focus of Chapter 10, "It All Depends on Your Point of View: The Role of Multicultural Education in Social Studies," authored by Carla Cooper Shaw, an expert in multicultural studies. Shaw describes how children develop prejudices and what the classroom teacher can do to foster the acceptance of other cultures and beliefs. She suggests activities for multicultural education and includes a list of suggested multicultural literature for children.

Chapter 11, "Social Studies, Bilingualism, Respect, and Understanding: Making the Connection," by Mary Louise Ginejko, a junior high school principal and teacher of a Hispanic drop-out prevention program, continues the multicultural theme. Ginejko discusses cultural awareness in terms of Hispanic children and provides a vast array of whole language, social studies activities for bilingual students.

Like bilingual students, students with learning disabilities typically have difficulty in acquiring social studies concepts. In Chapter 12, "Immersing Learning Disabled Students in History: Travels Back in Time," Carol J. Fuhler, who teaches language arts to students with disabilities, presents an overview of the learning disabled student and explains how whole language can be used successfully with children who have learning disabilities. Fuhler provides thematic units on the Revolutionary War and the Civil War for middle and upper elementary students and a unit on Native Americans for younger children.

Technology has become important in the teaching of social studies, as explained in Chapter 13, "The Interactive Technology Environment," by Susan M. Cooper, coeditor of this book. Cooper has worked extensively with teachers throughout the South and the West in applications of instructional technology. In this chapter, she presents an overview of computer-aided instruction and various types of educational software. She examines telecommunications, laser videodiscs, and hypermedia and describes the changing role of the classroom teacher in a whole language, technologically integrated classroom.

Chapter 14, "Assessing Social Studies in Whole Language Classrooms," by Margaret A. Atwell, provides an overview of evaluation in a whole language, social studies program. An expert on psycholinguistics, Atwell discusses the need for authentic assessment so that the teacher can discover what students really know and understand about social studies.

This book offers the shared belief of thirteen educators that by linking social studies instruction with the whole language approach, children will develop and maintain a lifelong interest in social studies that will result in their making positive contributions as responsible citizens in our democratic society. We hope you share that same belief.

The authors of the various chapters were selected on the basis of their individual area of expertise. All begin their chapters by delineating the various theories and concepts and follow up with suggested activities.

On behalf of all the authors, we would like to gratefully acknowledge the significant assistance and encouragement we received from pre-service and in-service teachers. Many of the ideas presented in this book either came from their suggestions or were field tested in their classrooms. For this we are indebted to them.

Having a large number of authors requires substantial assistance and review. We would like to thank the following individuals, who served as reviewers of the manuscript. Their insights, suggestions, and honest critical comments have greatly improved this book.

ANN SMITH
KENNESAW STATE COLLEGE

GEORGE CHILCOAT
BRIGHAM YOUNG UNIVERSITY

JENNIFER J. ROBINSON
TEACHERS COLLEGE, COLUMBIA UNIVERSITY

SHEILA J. DRAKE
KANSAS WESLEYAN UNIVERSITY

GERALD R. BARKHOLZ
UNIVERSITY OF SOUTH FLORIDA

RICHARD SWERDLIN
UNIVERSITY OF NORTH TEXAS

TIMOTHY L. HEATON
CEDARVILLE COLLEGE

M. BETSY BERGEN
KANSAS STATE UNIVERSITY

MARILYN M. STUBER
MEREDITH COLLEGE

SANDRA L. CARON
UNIVERSITY OF MAINE

DEBORAH GENTRY
ILLINOIS STATE UNIVERSITY

SUSAN S. COADY
OHIO STATE UNIVERSITY

MARION E. BIHM
McNEESE STATE UNIVERSITY

LARRY D. HALL
SPRING HILL COLLEGE

ARNOLD KAHN
BURLINGTON COUNTY COLLEGE

ESTHER HOGANS
SIERRA COLLEGE

To help you in teaching your course, we've written an *Instructor's Mannual and Evaluation Items.* This supplement includes lecture notes, suggested activities, discussion questions, a portfolio assessment checklist, transparency masters, and evaluation questions. We hope you find it useful.

In addition, we would like to express our appreciation to the following individuals for their guidance and assistance throughout the editorial process: Paul Tavenner, senior editor; Sue Pulvermacher-Alt, managing developmental editor; Michelle Campbell, production editor; and Carol Judge, photo editor.

We hope that you share the belief of all the authors of *Elementary Social Studies: A Whole Language Approach:* that children can better develop and understand social studies concepts by reading, writing, and discussing children's literature with social studies themes.

PAMELA J. FARRIS

FOREWORD

Books have always played an important part in my life; my world has been opened to new wonders because of them. Reading historical fiction as a child opened my eyes to the life and times of other people. From reading a series of biographies about Annie Oakley, Buffalo Bill, Chief Crazy Horse, Geronimo, General George Custer, and Wild Bill Hickock, I learned about our nation's westward movement, discovering some folk heroes in the process. The battle of Little Big Horn, the deeds of the young riders of the Pony Express, the injustice of the U.S. government repeatedly breaking treaties with Native Americans all made an impact on me as I read and reread books about them in our classroom library's meager collection. It is important to note, however, that most of the biographies to which I had access were heavily biased in regard to their main character. In those days, no character flaws were permitted in biographies or social studies textbooks.

I read the *Little House* books and discovered the hardships and joys of pioneer life as viewed through the eyes of Laura Ingalls Wilder. While social studies was taught daily by my elementary teachers, it was really Laura Ingalls Wilder who taught me social studies. From her books about pioneer life in the 1800s, I learned about the difficulties of growing up and getting along with others. I also learned about geography from her *Little House in the Big Woods, On the Banks of Plum Creek,* and *Little House on the Prairie.* Her discussions of how her father worked as a laborer to earn money to buy seed and tools while her mother sold eggs to the general store taught me rudimentary economics. The need to be a good citizen was often pointed out by good deeds done to help neighbors during trying times. Laura Ingalls Wilder painted a vivid historical picture for me as well as for the millions of other children who have read and loved her reflections on her childhood and young adulthood.

As a young elementary teacher, I recalled my enthusiasm for the *Little House* and other books. My students often found our social studies textbooks too difficult, or they lost interest because the material was presented in a dry, unengaging manner. Their interest was aroused when I read about the American Revolutionary War in Esther Forbes's classic Newbery Medal winner, *Johnny Tremain.* We talked about the Sons of Liberty and Paul Revere, as well as the suffering that Johnny experienced as a child with a handicap. The students were deeply moved by the book. Later that same year, while I read about the poverty of an African American family in the South in the stirring book *Sounder,* my class, composed entirely of white students, developed empathy for others. The students wondered why only the dog and the white characters had names and whether this had something to do with slavery and discrimination. On the day I read of the death of the wonderful dog Sounder, who had been so loyal and faithful to the family, there was not a dry eye in the classroom.

Perhaps it was a fifth-grade student named Donnie and an elderly school custodian named Smokey who finally opened my eyes to the value of children's literature in social studies. Donnie came from a low socioeconomic background. His oldest brother was in prison for committing a robbery. His father was a truck driver. Donnie had a great sense of humor and was popular with his classmates. But Donnie didn't like to read and write. He tended to disrupt the class whenever an opportunity arose.

Smokey was an institution at the school in which I taught. In this small, rural community, Smokey knew the first names of all of the children's parents and most of their grandparents because he had been a janitor at the building for over 40 years. Smokey was a hard worker who always smelled of Camel cigarettes. During his breaks, Smokey read books. Donnie, as well as the other boys, loved to visit Smokey down in his "office," also known as the furnace room. Smokey would tell the boys about the book he was currently reading, typically a Louis L'Amour western or a novel about World War II.

To Donnie, Smokey's tales were wonderful! He couldn't get enough of them. So Donnie began borrowing some of Smokey's old paperbacks to read. Though limited in his reading ability, Donnie struggled through book after book. He was no longer a discipline problem in social studies; he was too busy raising his hand to contribute to the class discussion. His social studies projects ranged from a model Sioux Indian village to an audiotape of a commercial he had made (complete with sound effects) about a book portraying a professional baseball player who became a fighter pilot in World War II. When I asked him to write down something about parts of the books he liked best, he created a file so other students might discover "really good stuff in some books."

Today, the whole language approach explains Donnie's reaction to Smokey and his books. What Smokey did was to share material that Donnie found relevant and meaningful. By reading the same books Smokey read and then discussing them with him, Donnie learned about social studies. When he was allowed to read children's literature and other books, Donnie found he knew things that his peers didn't and that he could teach them new things. Thus, his motivation and self-concept improved. As was true of my earlier encounter with Laura Ingalls Wilder, Donnie, too, had discovered the rewards and values of reading, discussing, and writing about literature relevant to social studies.

PAMELA J. FARRIS

Bringing Together Social Studies and Whole Language: A Look at Social Studies

PAMELA J. FARRIS AND TERRY WHEALON
NORTHERN ILLINOIS UNIVERSITY

Social studies should be the study

of how citizens in a society

make personal and public decisions

on issues that affect their destiny.

JEFFREY LINN

"Whole Language in Social Studies"

Introduction

The fresh smells of a new school year permeate the air—newly waxed floors, freshly painted rooms, chalk on the chalkrail. Marty Hammond's first graders are already engaged in learning an economic lesson about corn. On the first day of school Marty, a teacher in rural Illinois, asked her students several questions about their interests, what they liked, and what they didn't like. When she asked what their favorite food was, most of the children responded, "Sweet corn." She wasn't surprised since sweet corn is a common favorite; it is locally grown and very plentiful during August and September. Marty decided that since her students liked to eat sweet corn, she would take the opportunity to use corn as a social studies lesson.

Marty found several picture books about corn and maize that she read to her students. Then they talked about the importance of corn. Afterward, they drew pictures about corn: planting, tending, harvesting, and, of course, eating it. During the first week of school, the class went to a nearby grocery store and purchased sweet corn. They cooked the corn in a big pot on a portable electric burner in their classroom and ate it for lunch. The next day, a farmer who grows sweet corn visited the class and brought some cornstalks with him. He told the students about how he tills the soil and plants the corn and explained the measures he takes to prevent soil erosion. He showed pictures of the harvesting equipment used to pick sweet corn. The farmer also talked about how the corn must be harvested at just the right time so that the kernels don't get too hard for people to eat. He told the students that corn must be eaten soon after it is picked or it will spoil. If the corn doesn't quickly reach the people who buy it or the factories that can it, the farmer loses money. The following day the first graders toured a local factory that cans corn and peas. Later, the class will visit a farm that is harvesting corn for livestock feed. In the spring, Marty's class will plant corn in a small garden plot on the school playground.

John Salter and his fourth-grade teaching partner, Sue Kissinger, devoted several weeks of their summer vacation to putting together their social studies units for the year. In addition to covering the exploration and development of the United States, they plan to focus on four major cultural studies during the year: African American, Asian, Jewish, and Native American.

Beginning the year with the discovery of America, John shares children's literature about Native Americans with his students. His students read and discuss Lynne Cherry's (1992) *A River Ran Wild*, a picture book about how the Nashua Indians respected nature and the environment. Through reading and talking about the book, students gain a better understanding of the anthropological and ecological history of the Nashua River Valley in what is now lower New Hampshire and upper Massachusetts. Other picture books are also available for the students to read, for instance, Rafe Martin's (1992) *The Rough-Face Girl* which is the Algonquin Indian version of Cinderella. In addition, each student selects one of four historical novels about Native Americans: Jean Fritz's (1983) *The Double Life of Pocahontas,* Paul Goble's (1990) *Dream Wolf,* Scott O'Dell's (1988) *Black Star, Bright Dawn,* or Elizabeth George Speare's (1983) *The Sign of the Beaver.* Then each student reads the chosen book and writes about his or her reactions in a literature response journal. Every day, the students give their journals to John, who in turn reads the journals and writes comments and questions for the students to read and react to. In addition, students discuss the books with peers who are also reading the same selection.

In addition to the picture books and novel studies, John has selected Gary Paulsen's (1988) *Dogsong* to read aloud to his students, while Sue has chosen Ken Kesey's (1991) *The Sea Lion* to read aloud to her students. Both teachers have elected to use Virginia Sneve's (1989) *Dancing Teepees: Poems of American Indian Youth* to incorporate poetry and dance in their unit.

Since John and Sue's school has a limited number of books for each unit, their classes will take turns studying the different cultures. While John's class starts with Native Americans, Sue's begins with the Asian culture. Her students will read Momoko Ishii's (1987) *The Tongue-Cut Sparrow* (translated by Katherine Paterson), a Japanese folktale about a kind old man and his greedy wife, as a class discussion book. They will also read *El Chino* (Say, 1990), a true story of a Chinese boy who became a famous bullfighter, and *The Land I Lost* (Nhuong, 1982), which depicts daily life in Vietnam prior to the Vietnam War. Sue has chosen *How the Ox Star Fell from Heaven* (Hong, 1991) to read aloud because it is one of her favorite stories. She has also invited members of the Asian community to speak to her class about their countries' customs and traditions.

Sherry Klindera, a fourth-grade teacher in another school district, also likes to incorporate children's literature and writing in her social studies units. Like Marty, John, and Sue, Sherry believes that through reading historical novels and nonfiction children's literature, students develop empathy for and a better understanding of the people, places, and events they study. In addition, Sherry has discovered that her students maintain a higher degree of interest in social studies when she uses children's literature to teach social studies. This allows students to become more personally involved with social studies because they can discuss or write about

■ Children get a better understanding of what life is like for other
people by studying different cultures from throughout the world.

their own reactions to different events or aspects of social studies. This is integrating the elementary curriculum through the whole language approach, using meaningful, relevant materials for instruction.

For her unit on Native Americans, Sherry focuses on the Plains Indians. Books shared include Russell Freedman's (1988) *Buffalo Hunt,* a pictorial portrayal of how buffalo herds were hunted to supply meat. She also shares books about Plains Indian leaders, tribes, and legends. Students work together in groups to create dramas based on books they have read.

One of the activities Sherry's students engage in is making their own buffalo robe stories. Sherry uses this project to get students to think about the importance of their own lives and interests. The students cut brown paper grocery bags into 10-inch strips, soak the strips a few minutes in water before wadding them into balls to give them a leathery look, and then stretch them out on a table to dry. The next day, each student uses crayons or felt-tipped markers to draw four major events, one from each of the last four years of his or her life. Sherry also makes her own buffalo robe story, selecting as her four major events her first teaching position, marriage to her husband, their first house, and the completion of her master's degree. After all the stories are finished, the students sit Indian fashion around an unlit campfire made of sticks found on the playground during recess. The students then share the stories behind each picture on their buffalo robes. This enables the students, as well as Sherry, to get to know each other better.

Teaching Social Studies

When children enter school, they bring with them a wealth of knowledge that they have gleaned through informal schooling. They have likes and dislikes, opinions and beliefs. Research about learning suggests that the "kinds and amounts of knowledge one has before encountering a given topic (i.e., the state of Michigan) in a discipline (i.e., social studies) affect how one constructs meaning. The impact of prior knowledge is not a matter of 'readiness,' component skills, or exhaustiveness; it is an issue of depth, interconnectedness, and access" (Leinhardt, 1992, p. 21).

Learning is largely social in nature. Children learn from others: parents, siblings, relatives, friends, and other significant individuals in their lives. Thus, social studies instruction naturally lends itself to an integrated curriculum based on the personal and social aspects of learning. Social studies is more than a collection of facts for children to memorize; it is an understanding of how people, places, and events came about and how people can relate and respond to each other's needs and desires, as well as how to develop respect for different viewpoints and cultural beliefs. In short, social studies is the study of cultural, economic, geographic, and political aspects of past, current, and future societies.

Social studies at the elementary and middle school levels is usually taught by means of an integrated approach that combines two or more of the social sciences for instructional purposes. This book describes the components of social studies and outlines how the whole language approach can be incorporated into social studies instruction. This chapter focuses on social studies instruction and the social sciences (anthropology, economics, geography, history, political science, and sociology). Chapter 2 describes how the whole language approach lends itself to social studies instruction.

The Social Sciences

To integrate the social sciences fully, it is important that the teacher understand each of the six social sciences listed above, which constitute social studies at the elementary and middle school levels. Each of these is described in this section.

Anthropology

Anthropology is the field of study concerned with the discovery of what people were like from earliest existence. Considered as part of this study are the how, what, and why people change over the years. Typically, an anthropologist conducts an on-site study. That is, an anthropologist actually visits and investigates the locale where the people lived or continue to live. This kind of research enables the anthropologist to better understand and appreciate the people and their culture by living with them and recording their actions and comments.

■ Firsthand experiences with elements from different historical
periods enable children to better understand and appreciate other

Culture is a significant factor in anthropology. Thus, anthropologists study a people's contributions in terms of language, music, art, literature, religion, law, and so on. Artifacts, such as cooking utensils and weapons, also provide insight into a people's culture. Anthropologists analyze the data, then compare and contrast the culture with other cultures either of the same time period or throughout the ages.

Economics

Economics is the field of study concerned with the production, distribution, exchange, and consumption of products. An economist analyzes these four concepts and suggests ways to improve the distribution or production of various products or the economy in general. These basic concepts can be readily taught to elementary and middle school students. For instance, first or second graders can analyze *production* as they compare the goods and services provided by businesses in their community. They might visit a local manufacturer of mattresses, hot dogs, or yarn. The product doesn't matter; it needs to be some type of goods. Students could observe a service business by visiting a fast-food restaurant or a pizza parlor and watching how hamburgers or pizzas are made or by going to a local printing shop and observing brochures being printed to promote sales of an item or upcoming event.

■ To become wise consumers, children must understand basic economic concepts.

In a unit on the *distribution* of products third or fourth graders can study how goods and services are made available to consumers through advertising, selling, and shipping. For instance, they might visit a local shoe store to learn how the manager selects and orders sneakers and how the sneakers are shipped. By looking through newspapers and magazines and watching television advertisements, the students can compare how sneakers are promoted.

The third topic of economics, *exchange,* involves the study of money. While this topic is introduced in kindergarten, it is typically studied in depth in the first through fourth grades. A visit to a local bank after a class discussion about currency and how checks and credit cards are used for exchange is an appropriate activity for this topic.

It is important for children to understand that *consumption* is determined by the needs and wants of the buyer. In addition, older children need to become familiar with federal and state agencies that protect the buyer from fraud or other illegal acts. For instance, most children are familiar with the FBI warning on videotapes that prohibits the duplication of copyrighted movies.

History

History is the study of how people lived in the past. This may include how people lived in the local community, the United States, or the world. The Bradley Commission (1988) identified the following six organizational themes for elementary level students.

- The first theme is *conflict and cooperation*. This includes the causes of war and approaches to peace. Relations between domestic affairs of a country and dealing with other countries also fits into this theme.

- Next is *comparative history of major developments*. Characteristics of revolutionary, reactionary, and reform periods are included here as well as the comparative instances of slavery and emancipation, feudalism and centralization.

- The third theme is that of *patterns of social and political interaction*. Changing patterns of class, ethnic, racial, and gender structures and relations are considered as well as immigration, migration, and social mobility. Multicultural societies also fit into this theme.

- The fourth theme is *civilization, cultural diffusion, and innovation*. The evolution of human skills is noted along with the rise, interaction, and decline of centers of skills and power. The cultural development of major civilizations is an important element of this theme.

- The fifth theme is that of *human interaction with the environment*. Included in this area are relationships among geography, technology, and culture as well as their effects on economic, social, and political developments.

- The sixth and final theme is that of *values, beliefs, political ideas, and institutions*. Origins of political, social, and religious institutions are explored in this theme.

Upper-elementary students might, for instance, compare the major breakthroughs in medical science that have taken place as a result of wars (examples: triage from the Vietnam War, nurses at battlefield sites from the Civil War) or the use of specific weaponry (examples: aircraft carriers during World War II, targeted missiles during the Persian Gulf War).

Geography

Geography is the study of the earth, including its features and the distribution of its human inhabitants and other life. Children should become familiar with five geography themes: location, place, relationships within places, movement, and regions (Joint Committee on Geographic Education, 1984). Children are first introduced to these topics in terms of their own homes and neighborhoods.

The first geography theme, that of *location,* describes where specific places or points are on a map or on the earth's surface. It also describes the relationship between places—for example, the number of miles between San Diego and Phoenix.

The second theme, that of *place,* describes the unique or distinct characteristics of a place. This includes both physical and human characteristics. For instance, the flat land and fertile soil of the prairies of Illinois and Iowa allow for the production of large corn and soybean crops. On the other hand, the cool summers and acid soil of Maine provide the perfect combination for growing blueberries.

The third geography theme, *relationships within places,* describes how people react to their environment and the changes they may make. Examples include preserving the wood owl by not cutting down a forest of trees for lumber and not allowing a company to build a plant on a river that would pollute the water and kill the fish.

Movement is the fourth geography theme. In a highly mobile society such as ours, movement is a very important topic in that it characterizes how people travel from place to place, how they communicate with each other, and how they depend on products (such as oil from the Middle East and auto parts made in Mexico) and information from other areas.

The last geography theme, that of *regions,* involves categorizing areas according to their features: climate, landform, land use, natural vegetation, culture, and so forth. For instance, the Midwest is the biggest beef-producing region in the United States, and the South is the largest producer of tobacco in the world.

A geography activity for third graders might be to have them visit a state park and make a map of the park. They could indicate where people stay (in the park lodge) and eat (in the park restaurant) as well as illustrate the hills and meadows. Major hiking trails could be depicted along with paved and gravel roads.

Political Science

Political science, also referred to as civics, is the study of how people govern themselves. It includes the analysis of governing institutions, processes, and laws. The structure of government and the responsibilities and duties of elected and appointed government officials are all part of political science.

In elementary school, the examination of the political system is important so that children gain an understanding of how government works. By creating a democratic classroom that allows for open discussion

■ Through social interaction, children learn not only about their
immediate world, but about the global society as well.

of issues and voting on those issues, the teacher can begin to set the stage
for the students to become active participants in the democratic process.
Later, such involvement will lead to active and concerned citizenship.

A good year-long political science activity is to create a self-
governing board for the class. Members of the class should be elected to
the governing board. Whenever disciplinary or other problems arise, the
board can hold a hearing on the case and make a judgment. This may be
as simple as a decision to request that pizza be served more frequently in
the cafeteria or that measures be taken to recycle used paper in the
classroom.

Sociology

Sociology is the study of humans and their interactions in groups. Groups may be as small as a nuclear family or as large as the AFL-CIO union or the Catholic church. Sociologists look for common values and beliefs. Unlike the *field study* of anthropologists, sociologists tend to conduct *case studies* of either individuals or a group over a period of time. A case study usually consists of information pertaining to the daily routine of the individuals or the group.

For children, the study of sociology may begin with the study of families, followed by the study of neighborhoods and communities, and on to the study of larger groups. Sociology also involves the study of people from different cultures.

Integrating the Social Sciences

At the elementary level, the six social sciences can be interpreted as part of a unit of study. The social sciences are listed in Table 1.1 along with examples of questions social scientists from each of these six areas of study would ask about a topic such as the Civil War.

The elementary classroom teacher should incorporate all of the social sciences in social studies instruction because all are important in a democratic society. In addition, it is crucial that the teacher create a classroom environment that will help students become good citizens.

Skills Needed to Become a Good Citizen Actor

One of the goals of social studies is to produce "citizen actors." That is, students must learn "how citizens in a society make personal and public decisions on issues that affect their destiny" (Linn, 1990, pp. 49–50). Children need to learn how to make good decisions. Unfortunately, too often children are not given the opportunity to demonstrate or even practice decision making. Parents, other adults, or even peers often make decisions for children that the children themselves should make. This is not to say that children should be permitted to make adult decisions. For example, an eight-year-old should not be asked whether her mother or father should take job A or job B. However, children should be allowed to have some options; this is essential in creating a learning environment that offers relevant and meaningful study material. For instance, in a whole language classroom in which students are studying the topic of pioneer life, the students may work in small groups on projects. The grouping may be based entirely on the students' own selection of which project they would like to work on. In addition, the students can be given the option of selecting which of five or six books about pioneer life they would like to read and discuss in another small group. Students may individually prepare oral or written reports or write poems, or they may work with others to create a drama about a specific aspect of pioneer life and present it to the class.

T A B L E   1 . 1

■

THE SOCIAL SCIENCES THAT COMPRISE ELEMENTARY SOCIAL STUDIES

Social Science	Definition	Type of Question Asked about the Civil War
ANTHROPOLOGY	The study of human beings in terms of race, culture, physical characteristics, and environmental and social relations	What type of medical care was provided to wounded soldiers? How did the ratio of whites to African Americans differ between the North and the South? How did the two armies use African Americans during the war?
ECONOMICS	The study of the production, distribution, exchange, and consumption of goods and services	What were the primary products of the North? Of the South? Why was it important to the South to sell goods to England? What kind of bartering occurred between the soldiers?
GEOGRAPHY	The study of land, sea, and air and the distribution of animal and plant life, including human beings and their industries	Compare the types of agriculture used on Southern plantations with those of the western states of the Union. How did the type of land influence the crops that were raised by each? Why was it important for the North to control the Mississippi River?
HISTORY	The study and recording of important events that may include an explanation of their causes	What was the significance of John Brown's raid and his later hanging? Why did the Union Army under Sherman try to destroy everything they encountered on their way to Atlanta? Why did President Lincoln appoint U. S. Grant to command the Union Army?

■

THE SOCIAL SCIENCES THAT COMPRISE ELEMENTARY SOCIAL STUDIES

Social Science	Definition	Type of Question Asked about the Civil War
POLITICAL SCIENCE (CIVICS)	The study of governmental institutions and processes	What was the significance of having Richmond, Virginia, the capital of the South rather than New Orleans or some other city? How was the government of the Confederate States similar in structure to that of the United States?
SOCIOLOGY	The study of people, their institutions and processes	In both armies, men joined regiments named for the state in which they lived. Why was this important? Compare the life-style of a freed slave living in the North with that of a slave in the South. Compare the culture of the agrarian South with that of the industrialized North.

In the field of social studies, one of the most basic documents for guiding curriculum development was presented by the National Council for the Social Studies (NCSS) in 1989. In its position statement, the NCSS reiterates the point that one of the major goals of social studies is to produce citizen actors through civic participation.

The NCSS statement further expands this concept: "Social studies programs have a responsibility to prepare our people to identify, understand, and work to solve the problems that face our increasingly diverse nation and interdependent world. . . . [P]rograms that combine that acquisition of knowledge and skills with the application of democratic values to life through social participation present an ideal balance in social studies" (National Council for the Social Studies, 1989, p. 377).

The NCSS states (p. 378) that "skills essential to citizen participation in civic affairs can be grouped in a problem-solving/decision-making sequence in the following major categories":

Skills Related to Acquiring Information

Reading skills
Study skills
Reference and information search skills
Technical skills unique to the use of electronic devices

Skills Related to Organizing and Using Information

Thinking skills
Decision-making skills
Metacognitive skills

Skills Related to Interpersonal Relationships and Social Participation

Personal skills
Group interaction skills
Social and political participation skills

Teachers need to consider these skills when creating an integrated whole language/social studies curriculum for elementary students.

Building a Curriculum for Whole Language and Social Studies Integration

The National Commission on the Social Studies (1990), in its highly publicized document *Charting a Course: Social Studies for the 21st Century,* identifies a set of characteristics for the social studies curriculum that establish exemplary guidelines for the integration of whole language and civil participation. Among those characteristics, the following seem particularly relevant. Social studies provides the obvious connection between the humanities and the natural and physical sciences. To assist students to see the interrelationships among branches of "knowledge, *integration of other subject matter with social studies should be encouraged whenever possible*" (National Commission on the Social Studies, 1990, p. 3).

Central to social studies instruction should be observing, role playing, reading, and writing. Students must use creative and critical thinking skills for problem solving, decision making, and resolving differences. Students must also develop and use strategies that help them to be independent learners and responsible citizens. They must learn to work together with their peers through cooperative and collaborative efforts.

The study of social studies should avail itself of a wide variety of learning materials, not only textbooks but children's literature (picture books, historical fiction, nonfiction, poetry, contemporary fiction) that can be incorporated into the curriculum. For instance, Tomasino (1993, p.7) believes that "Good cultural literature and relevant social studies activities reveal people's similarities as well as differences and develop cultural literacy in young students." In addition, children should be able to examine original materials or sources whenever possible. For example, artifacts, documents, and maps available from local libraries and historical museums add relevance and meaning to children's discovery of social studies. Working with U.S. Census Bureau statistics can provide children with insights into demographic data and help them understand the role of mathematics in the study of social studies. Examining the effects of industrialization on the environment brings science into social studies. Media in the form of

■ Through discussion groups, new understandings and concepts are acquired by students.

films, videotapes, interactive video, overhead transparencies, paintings, sculptures, quilts, and so on offer enrichment for social studies topics at all grade levels.

Hennings (1990, p. 8) adds to the rationale for combining whole language and social studies instruction in the following statement regarding the goals of whole language: "Communication is central to learning . . . . Today's teachers are unleashing the power of communication by introducing learning strategies that rely on *social interaction* [italics added]. Oral modeling of reading and writing, collaborative reading and writing, dialogue, and peer journals are just a few of these strategies."

Social studies and whole language studies both suggest that social interaction is essential if children are to become responsible and literate citizen actors. Thus, a literate person does not become literate (acquire literacy skills) or use literacy in isolation. In fact, all literate people must use their literacy in a *social context* in which they interact with others in groups. Concurrently, people do not learn to become good citizen actors unless they engage in purposeful activities in which they *interact and communicate* with others in group situations. When asked why people need to be able to read and communicate, most pragmatists would say, so that people can solve the everyday problems they encounter as members of society. Good citizens encounter problems that require the use of literacy skills to make wise decisions in consort with others for the good of society. In the next section we develop a curricular context for bringing together whole language and social studies.

Banks (1985) developed a model for curriculum integration that involves the decision-making process. This process can be integrated into the curriculum at all levels and provides an ideal opportunity for whole language activities in social studies. The following section breaks down the various parts of the process and gives examples of the kinds of whole language activities that can occur during each step.

The Decision-Making Process

Before describing the decision-making process, it is important to note that issues should be at the heart of the social studies curriculum. Banks (1985, p. 187) supports this notion this way: "[M]aking decisions can be one of the most interesting and important components of the social studies curriculum. It adds vitality to the curriculum and helps make it significant to both students and teachers. The study of social issues gives students an opportunity to get a better understanding of the dynamic and changing nature of our society, their responsibilities as citizens in a democracy, and the importance of concepts such as equality and human dignity in maintaining a democracy." Shirley Engle (1985, p. 265) states the case even more strongly: "The failure to deal in a rigorous and uncluttered way with current social problems is one of the most unconscionable defects of the social studies today. . . . The direct study of social problems has been proposed as a cornerstone of our specialty by social studies reformers over and over again, beginning as early as the recommendations of the Committee on the Social Studies in 1916."

Defining the Process

Step One: Deriving an Issue

In step one students read and discuss ideas presented in myriad sources. This provides them with sufficient background information to see the issue, the dilemma it poses to society, and its relevance to them as members of society.

In this step students might read basic documents such as the Constitution, bills, laws, and so forth. They might also read journal, magazine, and newspaper articles, as well as literature in the form of biographies, other nonfiction, and fiction. They then might be asked to interpret and discuss in group situations both the implications and interconnectiveness of what they have read.

Step Two: Expressing Tentative Choices Based on Tentative Values

In step two students engage in group interaction activities in which they communicate alternate choices and explain and test the values that are driving their choices as they relate to the issue. This might include collaborative writing and analytical and synthesis writing, among other whole language activities.

Step Three: Gathering Information to Test Choices

Students acquire research techniques that enable them to interact with primary documents such as bills, laws, the Constitution, personal journals, primary and secondary sources, and so on. They develop skills of oral inquiry through interviewing authoritative people on their topic. Students engage in analytical and synthesis writing as they organize the data presented. They also interpret data presented and use maps and graphs to find answers to their questions. As members of groups, they use collaborative reading and writing as they write drafts of positions based on their research.

Step Four: Evaluating Data and Identifying Tested Choices

Students master communication skills through debates and persuasive speaking and writing as they move toward group and individual choices on the issue. They evaluate their choices and values expressed earlier in light of their newly acquired knowledge. They arrive at choices on which they will act.

Step Five: Acting on Choices in Society

Students act on the choices agreed upon by the group. They engage in purposeful and meaningful communication, both written and oral, as they become civic actors in trying to resolve the issue. They evaluate the impact of their decisions as they interpret the ramifications of their civic participation and realize the importance of their roles as citizen actors. They might conduct surveys, write letters to politicians proposing legislation, make posters, deliver talks and speeches, canvass people, and write journals.

It should be apparent that the process just outlined lends itself beautifully to the acquisition of literacy skills and citizen actor skills in an integrated fashion. Next we turn to more concrete examples of activities and units at various elementary levels that follow the steps of the decision-making process.

■ In early childhood, students develop meaningful understandings
through sharing and discussion.

Illustrative Examples of Whole Language and Social Studies Activities

The National Commission on the Social Studies (1990) provides examples of integrating activities that can serve as a stimulating springboard to more in-depth units of instruction. The commission suggests that at the kindergarten level, children explore their own immediate environment as well as environments far distant in time and space. Meaningful understandings can be achieved through the use of songs, stories (including children's own pictures), artifacts, overhead transparencies, map making, slide-tape or videotape presentations of a drama, and model building. All of these activities are rich in whole language pedagogy.

In the remaining grades of early childhood education, grades 1 through 3, the commission suggests, children can readily understand the concepts of communities past and present and how laws and individual behavior have an impact on the nature of communities. A literature-based reading program affords students the opportunity to explore these concepts by reading stories about and description of different kinds of people living under different conditions—for example, hunters in tropical rain forests, farmers in European villages, pioneers and immigrant settlers in the United States, Native Americans, urban and rural dwellers. Such a program gives children an opportunity to expand their awareness. At this level, literature should be selected to provide children with insights into the diversity of people and social divisions that make up the multicultural community we call earth. At this level, children's understanding should not come solely from printed material; drawing, building, quilt making, singing, and acting out parts can also be used to expand their consciousness of the variety of human social experience.

The commission suggests that in middle childhood education, grades 4 through 6, the content should focus on United States history, world history, and geography, both physical and cultural. In the reading program, teachers should draw from literature that provides stories about Native Americans, early European explorers and settlers, the nation's founders, populists, suffragists, inventors, activists, business and labor leaders, and other political, economic, and cultural figures to demonstrate the diversity and historical complexity of American society. In addition, children should study in depth the basic documents that provide the foundation of our democratic society. This same approach can be used to engage children in learning about world history as well.

At the upper-intermediate or early adolescent level, the commission (1990) suggests, students should study local and national social, political, and economic relationships and patterns of behavior in depth. When exploring local history, children might study old buildings and successive architectural styles to discover how people in the area have made their living, displayed their idealism, and organized and lived within their private spaces. Conducting oral interviews with older neighborhood residents and different cultural groups, analyzing historical census data, studying old photographs, and consulting newspaper files can introduce students to active historical and geographic research.

Finally, the commission suggests that the ability to look carefully and productively at the worlds we have created in our neighborhoods, towns, cities, and countryside is a major goal of effective social studies education *at all levels*. This requires that related issues be critically examined throughout the elementary years. In fact, such noted authorities on social studies as Shirley Engle (1989) suggest that each school should devote part of its academic year to the exploration of an identified issue at all grade levels.

By now it should be clear that social studies and whole language can work hand in hand to achieve one of the primary goals of education, that of producing good citizens. The chapters that follow expand on the broad examples of how the two fit into the integrated curriculum. Chapter 2 describes in more detail the different aspects of the whole language approach.

Summary

Social studies is the study of the cultural, economic, geographic, and political aspects of past, current, and future societies. When the whole language approach is incorporated with social studies in an integrated curriculum, children are allowed to make decisions about what they want to learn and how they will learn it. Through the use of children's literature, writing, and discussion, students discover concepts in anthropology, economics, geography, history, political science, and sociology. Because self-selection of reading materials in children's literature and activities allows for personalization of learning, children become more fully engaged and interested in social studies learning than they would with teacher-assigned textbook readings. Students also learn to become decision makers.

The decision-making process consists of five steps: (1) deriving an issue, (2) expressing tentative choices based on tentative values, (3) gathering information to test choices, (4) evaluating data and identifying tested choices, and (5) acting on choices in society. Through active participation, children learn to become decision makers and responsible citizen actors. They also learn to be independent learners and thinkers.

By examining the development of their immediate and surrounding worlds, children gain insight into each of the social sciences that make up social studies. In so doing, they better understand the interdependency of people both locally and in the global society.

Children's Books

Cherry, L. (1992). *A river ran wild.* Orlando, FL: Harcourt Brace Jovanovich.

> In this true story of the Nashua River, the author describes the environmental damage caused by civilization.

Freedman, R. (1988). *Buffalo hunt.* New York: Holiday House.

> This book describes how buffalo herds were hunted to provide meat during the 1800s.

Fritz, J. (1983). *The double life of Pocahontas.* New York: Putnam.

> A historical nonfiction account of Indian Princess Pocahontas.

Goble, P. (1988). *Dream wolf.* New York: Bradbury.

> A beautifully illustrated book about a Native American legend.

Hong, L. T. (1991). *How the ox star fell from heaven.* New York: Whitman.

> A novel about an Asian legend.

Ishii, M. (1987). *The tongue-cut sparrow.* (K. Paterson, Trans.; S. Akabar, Illus.). New York: Lodestar, Dutton.

> A Japanese version of the well-known folktale of the fisherman and his wife, who is never satisfied with the gifts she receives.

Kesey, K. (1991). *The sea lion* (N. Waldman, Illus.). New York: Viking.

> One of the few books about the Pacific Northwest Indians, this book depicts the legend of the sea lion.

Martin, R. (1992). *The rough-face girl* (D. Shannon, Illus.). New York: Putman.

> This is the Algonquin Indian version of the Cinderella tale. It is one of the most haunting and beautiful of the over 1,500 versions of Cinderella.

Nhuong, H. Q. (1982). *The land I lost: Adventures of a boy in Vietnam.* New York: Harper & Row.

> Describes daily life in Vietnam prior to the war, including the duties of parents and children.

O'Dell, S. (1988). *Black star, bright dawn.* Boston: Houghton Mifflin.

> A compelling Native American story told by master storyteller Scott O'Dell.

Paulsen, G. (1988). *Dogsong.* New York: Bradbury.

> The story of a Native American boy growing up.

Say, A. (1990). *El chino.* Boston: Houghton Mifflin.

> The true story of a Chinese boy who grew up to be the top bullfighter in Spain.

Sneve, V. (1989). *Dancing teepees: Poems of American Indian youth.* New York: Holiday House.

> A collection of poetry written by Native American children.

Speare, E. G. (1983). *The sign of the beaver.* Boston: Houghton Mifflin.

> A young boy becomes lost in the forest and is stung by a swarm of bees. An Indian chief rescues him, and in turn the boy teaches the chief's grandson how to read.

References

Banks, J. A. (1985). *Teaching strategies for the social studies.* New York: Longman.

Bradley Commission on History in Schools. (1988). *Building a history curriculum.* Washington, DC: Educational Excellence Network.

Engle, S. H. (1985). A social studies imperative. *Social Education, 49,* 264-265.

Hennings, D. G. (1990). *Communication, language and literacy learning.* Boston: Houghton Mifflin Educators' Forum, 8.

Joint Committee on Geographic Education (1984). *Guidelines for geographic education.* Washington, DC: Association of American Geographers.

Leinhardt, G. (1992). What research on learning tells us about teaching. *Educational Leadership, 49*(7), 20-27.

Linn, J. B. (1990). Whole language in social studies. *Social Science Record, 27*(2), 49-55.

National Commission on the Social Studies (1990). *Charting a course: Social studies for the 21st century.* Washington, DC: National Council for the Social Studies.

National Council for the Social Studies (1989). In search of a scope and sequence for social studies. *Social Education, 53*(6), 376-379.

Tomasino, K. (1993). Literature and social studies: A spicy mix for fifth graders. *Social Studies and the Young Learner, 5,* 7-10.

Bringing Together Social Studies and Whole Language: A Look at Whole Language

PAMELA J. FARRIS
NORTHERN ILLINOIS UNIVERSITY

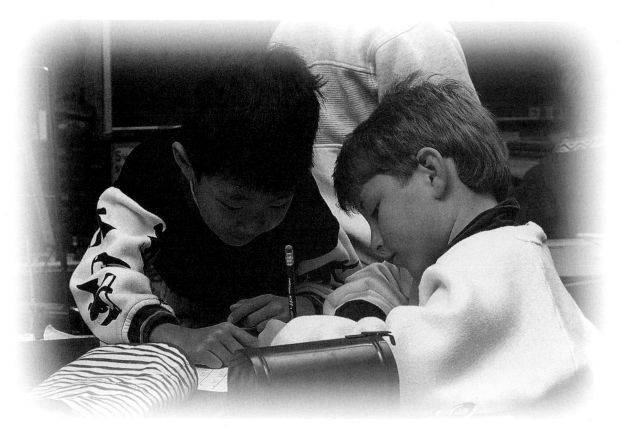

Students do not merely passively receive or copy input from teachers,

but instead actively mediate it by trying to make sense of it

and to relate it to what they already know

(or think they know) about the topic.

JERE BROPHY
"Probing the Subtleties of Subject-Matter Teaching"

Introduction

Social studies serves as an integration of the social sciences: anthropology, economics, geography, history, political science, and sociology. In addition, social studies promotes the development of critical and creative thinking as children learn to assume their role as responsible citizens in a democratic society. According to Brophy (1992, p. 8),

> In social studies, students are challenged to engage in higher-order thinking by interpreting, analyzing, or manipulating information in response to questions or problems that cannot be resolved through routine application of previously learned knowledge. Students focus on networks of connected content structured around powerful ideas rather than long lists of disconnected facts, and they consider the implications of what they are learning for social and civic decision making.

In order for this to occur, learning must be both meaningful and relevant to students.

Like social studies, the whole language approach assumes that learning is "easy when it's whole, real, and relevant; when it makes sense and is functional; when it's encountered in the context of its use; when the learner chooses to use it" (Goodman, 1986, p. 26). While the primary focus of the whole language approach is language or literacy learning, it shares many of the same basic principles of social studies, including (1) respect for the learner and the teacher, (2) belief in the role of the teacher as a facilitator of learning, and (3) encouragement of learners to take risks. Moreover, like language learning (listening, speaking, reading, and writing), social studies is both personal and social. Both social studies and language learning are "driven from the inside by the need to communicate and shaped from the outside toward the norms of society" (Goodman, 1986, p. 26).

With these shared principles, it is appropriate that whole language play a major role in the social studies curriculum. This chapter outlines the whole language approach, including its essential elements. The chapters that follow describe how the whole language approach can be effectively incorporated in the social studies curriculum.

Whole Language as an Approach to Learning

The whole language approach has been traced back to the late 1890s and early 1900s, to John Dewey and his mentor, Francis Parker, founders of the progressive education movement. Their work at the University of Chicago's famous laboratory school encouraged teachers to provide more opportunities for hands-on instruction. Dewey promoted "learning by doing," the belief that children learn best when they are active participants in the learning process.

In the early 1970s, Marie Clay of New Zealand developed the whole language approach. In essence, it focuses on allowing children to be active participants in learning to read and write. The underlying assumption is quite simple and direct: Children learn to read by reading and learn to write by writing. Ken and Yetta Goodman, Donald Graves, Jerry Harste, and others embraced the whole language approach and championed its virtues in the United States. Soon a grass roots movement began in the United States, with individual teachers adopting the whole language approach followed by entire schools and school districts. As McCarty (1991, p. 73) writes, "The whole language approach is one of the most widely acclaimed and popular grass roots movements among teachers . . . in the 1990s. The movement has established itself and grown because of increasing doubts that traditional teaching practices are producing citizens who can read and write effectively."

Rationale for Whole Language Instruction

The whole language approach emphasizes that skills cannot be taught in isolation, by giving children meaningless drill and practice sheets. Skills are best taught when the opportunities arise naturally and in a timely manner. Thus, a whole language teacher is ever aware of a "teachable moment." For instance, a child may ask a question. Instead of responding with the answer, the teacher may respond with another question so that the child can resolve the problem or find the answer through his or her own thinking and initiative. As a follower of the whole language approach, a teacher must be alert to the student's interests, wants, and needs and react to them.

Traditional Versus Whole Language Instruction: Philosophical and Psychological Underpinnings

The traditional instructional approach is the skill-based, behaviorist approach. The whole language approach has its roots in the progressive education, constructionist approach. These approaches differ in terms of views of knowing, learning, and motivation. Behaviorists believe that

■ Children must feel free to ask questions as well as to seek their
own answers.

knowledge is present outside oneself and that it can be broken down into
tiny, discrete units. Constructionists believe that knowledge develops from
within as the individual attempts to "construct" meaning out of experience, both firsthand and vicarious (McCarty, 1991).

Behaviorists believe that learning takes place *only* within the context of appropriately reinforced responses to events (or stimuli). These
may be simple responses (one specific unit of behavior) or complex responses (a series of behaviors) (Joyce & Weil, 1986). On the other hand,
constructionists believe that learning takes place in the flow of daily
human experiences and is an ongoing process. Thus, all individuals are
learners and all are teachers. Children learn from each other as well as
from the teacher. Likewise, the teacher learns from students and other
teachers.

Behaviorists believe motivation to learn is extrinsic, based upon
external rewards. Constructionists believe that motivation to learn is based
upon the individual's own natural curiosity and interests, as well as the
tendency to set goals and achieve self-determined goals.

Table 2.1 (Farris 1993, p. 26) outlines the differences between the
traditional, skills-based, behaviorist approach and the nontraditional, whole
language, constructionist approach to teaching.

TABLE 2.1

■

A COMPARISON OF LANGUAGE ARTS INSTRUCTIONAL APPROACHES

TRADITIONAL (Skills)	Versus	NONTRADITIONAL (Whole Language)
1. Children are expected to be passive participants in the learning process.		1. Children are expected to be active participants in the learning process.
2. The product is the most important part of learning.		2. The process is the most important part of learning.
3. Part to whole is stressed.		3. Whole to part is stressed.
4. Learning is based on a sequence of skills.		4. Learning is based on relevant, real experiences.
5. Motivation to learn is extrinsic (material rewards such as stickers are given out).		5. Motivation to learn is intrinsic (child learns because of self-desire to learn).
6. Children are placed in groups according to ability (low, average, high).		6. Children are grouped by interests and regrouped as topics change.
7. Competition is encouraged.		7. Cooperation is encouraged.
8. The teacher makes the decisions as to what will be taught and how it will be presented to the students.		8. Children make choices as to what and how they will learn.
9. The teacher directly guides instruction, as a leader.		9. The teacher indirectly guides instruction, serving as a facilitator.
10. Textbooks serve as the materials for teaching.		10. Children's literature and children's own writing serve as materials for teaching.
11. Multiple choice, true/false, and essay tests are used for evaluation.		11. Samples of the children's own work are used for evaluation.
12. The classroom is book-centered (child must fit to the book).		12. The classroom is child-centered (the book must fit to child).

From looking at Table 2.1, it is easy to see that students are given more choices in the whole language approach than in the traditional one. In addition, they are expected to serve as active participants in their learning—making decisions, setting goals, and engaging in real and relevant learning activities.

Essential Elements of the Whole Language Approach

The whole language approach requires that the language arts (listening, speaking, reading, writing, and thinking) be integrated in instruction. This section describes the roles of listening, discussion, reading, and writing in whole language instruction.

■ Small group discussions provide for all students to contribute as
well as to ask questions.

Listening

Listening involves giving attention to others. As such it requires self-discipline. The listener must carefully consider what the other person is saying and, while doing so, think of a response. Thus, the listener must anticipate what the speaker will say and call upon previously gained knowledge to judge what the speaker is saying.

In whole language classrooms, listening is important because students are taught to value each other's contributions. Since students learn from each other, being a good listener is paramount to being a good learner. Much knowledge and understanding are gained via listening, which is in turn used in discussion, reading, and writing.

Discussion

While listening is a vital language art, it accompanies speaking in developing discussion skills. Children learn from interacting with each other. According to Eliot Wigginton (in Meek, 1990 p. 35), "Learning is basically a social enterprise, and all the great educational philosophers have reiterated that point over and over again." A discussion based on a topic of mutual interest enables children to further their knowledge and to refine their understanding regarding that topic.

FIGURE 2.1

■

Schematic diagram of the independent states that were formerly
republics of the USSR by a group of sixth-grade students.

Formerly USSR   Now independent countries

Boris Yeltsin president – INDEPENDENT STATES – Economic problems
       of Russia

Need foreign aid   Overthrow of communism

Selling nuclear weapons   Ethnic fighting

Developing discussion skills requires students to become good listeners and good speakers. They must also develop the ability to ask questions in order to probe the thoughts of others. Moreover, discussion skills
require timing, patience, and the ability to interpret what has and has not
been stated.

Reading

Reading used to be thought of as a sequence of skills that were taught in
isolation. The whole language approach has resulted in the development
of reading strategies, with skills being taught as they arise and are needed.

To become a strategic reader, the student must become familiar
with different ways to approach a topic or read textual material. For instance, if the topic is the new independent countries that formerly made
up the Soviet Union, the teacher may have students work together in
groups to develop a schematic diagram of what they already know about
these independent states (see Figure 2.1).

Thus, the students recall previously gained knowledge before
reading about the independent states. Newly gained information gleaned
through their reading will be assimilated as they continue to read about
and further discuss the topic.

Writing

Writing instruction has changed dramatically within the past 20 years.
Now reading and writing are both considered to be processes of meaning making. Writing is considered a recursive activity in that the students generate ideas and questions, gather information and organize
their ideas, draft their compositions, and revise and edit the drafts before
they share the final version of their writings (Farris, 1993; Tompkins &
Hoskisson, 1991).

The whole language approach has opened up writing instruction in that writing occurs across the curriculum. No longer are students limited to writing social studies reports; instead, new options are available, including writing in literature response journals and writing poetry, letters, plays, and so on.

Goal of the Whole Language Approach

The goal of the whole language approach is to produce lifelong learners. This is done through respecting the learner, the teacher, and the content. The learning process is stressed over product. In addition, evaluation and assessment involve a variety of methods and techniques, not just paper and pencil tests.

Teaching the Way Students Learn

Advocates of the whole language approach focus on the learner and the environment. By interacting with books, materials, and other children, students expand their own knowledge and understanding. Enjoyable learning experiences are emphasized. Children are challenged but not threatened. They are encouraged to take risks, knowing that they might fail but that in taking the risk they will have gained from the failed experience as well.

As a facilitator of learning, the teacher attempts to broaden students' interests in both breadth and depth. Refinement of interest is also supported.

Students develop a positive self-concept by being able to engage in activities of their own choosing and being decision makers. Freedom to choose, or empowerment as Goodman (1986) refers to it, results in their using leisure time to pursue their interest in a topic.

Encouraging Decision Making

In making decisions of their own choosing, students are able to pinpoint and refine topics that interest them. In so doing, they are often allowed to work with other students who share a similar interest in a topic. Such collaboration and cooperative learning activities require group decision making as questions arise and decisions must be made, just as is true in any democratic society.

Teachers can establish a variety of social studies themes as part of the social studies curriculum. Students can help determine through the decision-making process how these themes are to be covered. What materials will be read? What activities are appropriate? What kinds of projects lend themselves to a topic?

These and other questions can be addressed by the students either individually or as part of a group.

■ Collaborative projects help children develop the skills of
cooperation and become decision makers.

Creating Citizen Actors

Through democratic decision making, children learn to become "citizen
actors"; that is, they learn the role of adult citizens by taking part in classroom civics activities. They learn to express their viewpoint without criticism, the first right in the Bill of Rights being freedom of speech. They
learn the importance of casting an opinion or ballot on an issue, albeit
whether the school cafeteria should serve pizza once a week or who
should be the class postmaster for the grading period.

Young and Vardell (1993) point out the value of using Readers
Theatre with nonfiction books such as Aliki's (1986) *Feelings* or Russell
Freedman's (1992) *An Indian Winter*. Readers Theatre can help develop
empathy in children and help them understand others.

If one explores the literature that is being developed on the purposes and goals of social studies and whole language, one can find ample evidence for the logical incorporation of activities from the two to produce citizen actors. Why citizen actors?

As Linn (1990, pp. 49–50) writes:

> Social studies should be the study of how citizens in a society make personal and public decisions on issues that affect their destiny. To keep us from becoming a nation of observers instead of participants, students need to be shown early that the point of social studies is not to be found in terminology like ethnocentric, executive branch, and traditional values, but instead in one's own relationship and personal identification with these terms. One goal of social studies must be to assist youth in organizing concepts in line with their personal reality: connecting new concepts and ideas with known factors in their lives.

The role of citizen actor is a crucial one for students. Without being cast as such, they are less apt to engage fully in the rights and privileges of being a citizen in a democratic society.

The Perfect Fit: Integrating Social Studies and Whole Language Instruction

In the past, social studies instruction largely centered around the social studies textbook, with some hands-on projects added by the classroom teacher. Brophy (Bracey, 1993, p. 654) referred to elementary social studies textbooks as being "remarkably uniform, consisting of compendia of facts organized with the expanding communities curriculum structure." According to Routman (1991, p. 281),

> Typically, we have taught social studies by saying, "Take out your social studies book and open to page ———." Then there follows a whole-class, round-robin reading, with the teacher stopping occasionally to ask questions and lead the discussion. . . . [S]uch exercises are boring and fail to engage many students.

For students to develop and sustain an interest in social studies, they must have a desire to learn more about it and be motivated to do so. At that point, they become engaged learners.

As Gordon Wells (1990, p. 15) so aptly states in his reference to the necessity of whole language instruction, "Unlike many other skillful performances, literate behavior cannot be learned simply by observation and practice." The same is true of being a citizen actor. To paraphrase Wells, democratic behavior cannot be learned simply by observation and practice. Students need to engage in democratic processes in the classroom—collaborative projects, discussions, cooperative learning, problem resolution, and so on—if they are to become effective and responsible citizens as adults.

The underlying premise of whole language, which states that learning is both personal and social, is also an underlying premise of social studies. "To be fully literate is to have the disposition to engage appropriately with texts of different types in order to empower action, feeling, and thinking in the context of purposeful social activity" (Wells, 1990, p. 14).

The subject matter boundary of social studies needs to be broken down and whole language principles erected. "At the very least, school tasks can be integrated through common reading and writing processes that cross subject matter. Interdisciplinary themes that provide opportunities to grapple with interpretations, understand others' perspectives, and solve problems require the content of social studies, science, and mathematics, not just of literature" (Hiebert & Fisher, 1990, p. 63). Combining social studies with whole language serves to strengthen the tenets of the social sciences. As children listen, discuss, read, and write about social studies content, they develop a deeper understanding and appreciation of social studies and its respective social sciences. Political science and civics become more than voting in an election—they are how our government works. Supply and demand are understood through discussions and activities that demonstrate the need and demand for a product, as well as the economic impact upon a commmunity. For instance, as noted earlier, the protection of the spotted owl as an endangered species prohibited lumbering to occur in a major forestry area in the western part of the United States. This action resulted in hundreds of lumberjacks and sawmill workers being forced out of work and the price of lumber greatly increasing due to lack of supply.

Building a Whole Language/Social Studies Curriculum

In building a social studies curriculum that utilizes whole language principles, the first step is to identify which social studies concepts should be introduced to students. These should be important concepts that foster both critical and creative thinking and provide an intellectual challenge that students can achieve. The next step is to outline the type of learning experiences and skills to be taught. The types of student attitudes being developed must also be taken into consideration. Furthermore, it is imperative that the learning climate encourage both inquiry and choice (Routman, 1991).

A variety of evaluation and assessment procedures need to be used in order to gather sufficient information to determine each student's growth and development in the social studies. Checklists, anecdotal records, attitudinal surveys, lists of books read, journal entries, writing samples, and videos of plays or projects are all appropriate measures for this type of curriculum. If there are state or local testing mandates, some provision must be made so that students become used to taking paper and pencil tests under a time limitation.

■ The classroom teacher should integrate social studies throughout
the elementary curriculum.

Applying Whole Language Principles
to Classroom Activities

An excellent way to incorporate whole language principles in the social
studies curriculum is through thematic units (Pappas, Kiefer, & Levstick,
1990). A thematic unit may be based around a theme such as the Revolutionary War. The teacher may provide a variety of books for the students
to read in small groups or may select one or two books for the entire
class to read. When thematic units are used, the social studies textbook
can be used as a reference work.

Small groups of students read the same book(s) and then discuss
what they have read. In their discussion groups, they formulate questions
they want and expect to be answered in the next segment of their reading. After writing down their questions, they write down the answers as
they read the material.

Routman (1991) offers informal guidelines for planning an integrated social studies and whole language unit. She suggests that process and procedures be considered foremost in integrating a content area such as social studies with the whole language approach. Here are her specific recommendations (pp. 279–280):

1. Develop a semantic web as the class or group brainstorms the topic.
2. Have students select a subtopic by listing their first, second, and third choices of subtopics.
3. Divide the students into small groups of up to four students per subtopic.
4. Have the groups develop questions to research for their subtopic of study.
5. Have each group meet with another group to confer over the questions each group generated for their respective subtopics.
6. Have each group establish a format for using resources to discover the answers to the questions they generated about their subtopic.
7. All of the students take notes on their subtopics.
8. Students use their notes to write rough drafts.
9. Each group presents the information they gathered to the entire class. (A variety of formats may be used: quiz shows, radio shows, festivals, plays, travelogues, etc.)
10. Presentations are evaluated orally by classmates. At least two positive statements must be given by students before a suggestion for improvement can be given by a student.
11. Group interactions and content learned are evaluated. This is done by the teacher and through student self-evaluations. In addition, an essay test given by the teacher may be included at this point.

Routman's process/procedure approach allows for efficient classroom organization and structure. Little time is wasted as the students proceed through the 11 steps. All of the students contribute to each others' learning in the area of social studies. Thus, learning becomes a social activity.

Summary

The whole language approach can be integrated with social studies instruction to meet common goals. As a result, the learner, the teacher, and social studies content are respected. Students are encouraged to make choices and take risks in their learning. As citizen actors, they repeatedly engage in the democratic process in their classroom as they develop an interest in and greater understanding of social studies.

References

Aliki. (1986). *Feelings*. New York: Morrow Junior Books.

Bracey, G.W. (1993). Elementary curriculum materials: Still a long way to go. *Phi Delta Kappan 74*(8), 654, 656.

Brophy, J. (1992). Probing the subtleties of subject-matter teaching. *Educational Leadership, 49*(7), 4-8.

Freedman, R. (1992). *An indian winter*. New York: Holiday House.

Farris, P. J. (1993). *Language arts: A process approach*. Dubuque, IA: Brown & Benchmark.

Goodman, K. (1986). *What's whole in whole language?* Portsmouth, NH: Heinemann.

Hiebert, E. H., & Fisher, C. W. (1990). Whole language: Three themes for the future. *Educational Leadership, 47*(6), 62-63.

Joyce, B., & Weil, M. (1986). *Models of teaching*. Englewood Cliffs, NJ: Prentice-Hall.

Linn, J. B. (1990). Whole language in social studies. *Social Science Record, 27*(2), 49-55.

McCarty, B. J. (1991). Whole language: From philosophy to practice. *Clearing House, 65*(2), 73-76.

Meek, A. (1990). On 25 years of Foxfire: A conversation with Eliot Wigginton. *Educational Leadership, 47*(6), 30-36.

Pappas, C. C., Kiefer, B. Z., & Levstik, L. S. (1990). *An integrated language perspective in the elementary school: Theory into action*. New York: Longman.

Routman, R. (1991). *Invitations: Changing as teachers and learners K-12*. Portsmouth, NH: Heinemann.

Tompkins, G. E., & Hoskisson, K. (1991). *Language arts: Content and teaching strategies*. New York: Macmillan.

Wells, G. (1990). Creating the conditions to encourage literate thinking. *Educational Leadership, 47*(6), 13-17.

Young, T.A. & Vardell, S. (1993). Weaving Readers Theatre and nonfiction into the curriculum. *Reading Theatre, 46*(5), 396-406.

Early Childhood Social Studies: Doing the Whole Thing in Whole Language

BILLIE JOAN THOMAS
NORTHERN ILLINOIS UNIVERSITY

A child's world
is one that supports
questioning minds
by offering a variety of
"doings" designed to
satisfy and extend a child's
natural sense of wonder.

GEORGE W. MAXIM

Social Studies and
the Elementary School Child,
4th Ed.

Introduction

Integrating social studies instruction and the whole language approach enables children to be active participants in their learning. At the early childhood level, this translates into many opportunities for firsthand social studies experiences. These experiences should be accompanied by the students' language questioning to discover more information, probing ideas, making connections with previously gained knowledge, and making predictions about what to expect next.

When the methods of the whole language approach are used, then literacy and language are part of everything the teacher does in the classroom. There is no need to set aside a special time for language or literacy development. Regardless of the discipline, students will be using spoken language, listening skills, nonverbal communication, music, pictures, books, writing instruments, and field trips. This approach is successful from early childhood through postdoctoral education. Young children, in their desire to learn about the world around them, practice oral and written language skills, nonverbal communication, and print awareness that create later literacy (Seefeldt, 1989).

If equal instructional time is devoted to physical, cognitive, social, and emotional development, teachers should spend 25 percent of their instructional time on the social studies knowledge base. They cannot wait until children are in fourth grade to begin teaching social studies for the same reasons they would not wait until then to teach mathematics or literacy. Fourth grade is too late; children's basic attitudes and concepts are formed by then. Lessons in which 25 percent of the curriculum content comes from social studies will help shape the citizens of tomorrow.

Early Childhood

Early childhood is the period of development from conception to 8 years of age. It includes the unborn, infants, toddlers, and children in nursery school, kindergarten, and grades 1 through 3. This chapter focuses on methods, materials, and activities for preschool and kindergarten students, but the techniques can be applied through the early childhood age range

(Bredekamp, 1987). The traditional early childhood curriculum areas are language arts, science, mathematics, physical development, social studies, fine arts, and creativity.

Curriculum Content and Social Studies

Each curriculum area respects a body of knowledge that includes vocabulary, facts, and concepts defining the discipline. This body of knowledge is what educators call curriculum content. Information is the content of the lesson being taught about the discipline (Smith, 1982; Brown & Brown, 1985).

This chapter addresses the matter of how to teach the curriculum content for social studies in preschool through kindergarten using the whole language approach. Social studies content is taken from the knowledge base concerning human groups and how they behave. Emotional studies and social studies are often confused in classrooms. A simple way to differentiate them is to think of emotional as internal and social as external. The subject of emotional studies involves learning about what takes place within the individual. Feelings such as love, hate, fear, anxiety, hope, and so forth are part of the emotional knowledge base. Social studies, on the other hand, always involves at least two people. The social studies knowledge base thus refers to groups, whether large or small in number.

Sometimes there is confusion about the difference between the social studies knowledge base and the social process of being in groups in the classroom. Preschool teachers sometimes say, "I teach social studies during recess and lunch." However, this is incorrect because these teachers are not transmitting information from the social studies knowledge base to the child. The child is in a social situation, but we are often in social situations. This does not mean we are learning anything from a knowledge base. Being in a social group does not mean we are learning social studies; we may even be in a social group learning about another knowledge base, such as science or music (Charlesworth & Lund, 1990).

The traditional social studies curriculum at the preschool and lower grade levels focuses on content that teaches about groups of people in terms of the following: current topics, economics, geography, history, and international and global education. A brief description of each area follows with a few samples of content.

The content of *current topics* varies, depending on current topics of interest in the newspaper, on television, in the family, and in the community. Common topic content includes POLITICAL CONCEPTS, ENVIRONMENT, PEACE AND WAR, SAFETY, NEWS, and CAREER EDUCATION.

The content of *economics* in preschool and kindergarten includes information about WANTS AND NEEDS (there is a big difference between the two, as well as between supply and demand), DOING WITHOUT (to paraphrase a popular rock song, when you request something, you may

■ Having a special day for grandparents to visit the classroom can set the stage for a history discussion, particularly if the grandparents share stories of their youth.

not get what you want but you may get something you need), and MONEY, such as types of paper and coins, different countries' currency, and what money represents.

The content of *geography* in preschool and kindergarten includes information about the EARTH, such as roundness, movement, earth, sky, and water; DIRECTION, such as east, west, north, south, up, and down; LOCATION, such as poles, equator, beside, between, through, and on top of; REGIONS, such as awareness of oceans, continents, halves, and so on; MAPS as print experiences and a beginning awareness of maps representing something else in the real world.

The content of *history* in preschool and kindergarten includes information about developmentally appropriate approaches to TIME, such as yesterday, today and tomorrow; CHANGE, such as growth, beginnings, and endings; CONTINUITY OF HUMAN LIFE, such as child, parents, grandparents, great-grandparents; THE PAST, such as Daddy's pet, Daddy's baby picture, and so forth; and HOLIDAYS, such as the Fourth of July, Thanksgiving, and birthdays.

The content of *international and global education* taps a wide range of a child's previously gained knowledge. Developmentally appropriate content would include CHILDREN in different nations, FAMILIES around the world, SIMILARITIES in people (for example, all people eat and have or had mothers), CONFLICT between nations, and the INTERDEPENDENCE of people (Why does it matter to us what happens in Somalia or Kuwait?).

The child's widening awareness of the social studies environment.

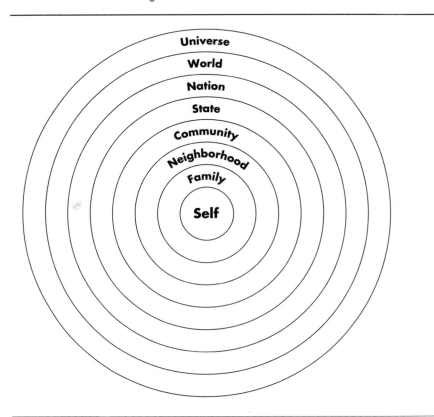

Egocentrism and Eight Circles of Awareness

In early childhood, in all five of the social studies curriculum areas, the child learns first about himself or herself. The three main areas of interest for young children are *me, myself,* and *I.* Egocentrism is the starting point for *all* curriculum areas in early childhood; then learning broadens into wider and wider circles of awareness, each directly linked to the children's *me, myself,* and *I.* The eight circles shown in figure 3.1 represent the levels of awareness about self, family, neighborhood, community, state, nation, world, and universe.

Teachers should be familiar with the eight circles of awareness because children learn the values, beliefs, and stereotypes of the community in which they live (Banks, 1992). By being introduced to the contributions of other cultures, children can learn to celebrate the diversity of humankind.

To understand how a child's awareness of the social studies environment moves from the egocentrism of self through the other seven encompassing circles, one could consider a specific topic, for instance, food preferences, means of transportation to school, or ways of celebrating certain family events. Let's take the specific topic of hair color as an example. First, the child learns about his or her own hair color, then about the hair color of family members and close friends, then about the hair color of neighbors and community acquaintances. Next, the child begins to form an impressionistic awareness of people (usually somehow related to him or her) in other states and their hair color, say, Grandpa's and Aunt Joe's; then the child begins to gain an awareness that people everywhere have hair and it has color. First, however, the child must learn about his or her hair; then the child relates further knowledge to himself or herself. The child must be exposed through whole language experiences to the vocabulary, facts, and concepts so that she or he can formulate mental ideas about hair color and acquire sufficient vocabulary to learn more.

Figure 3.1 illustrates how the child builds one concept of hair color from the inner, self dimension through the other seven levels to the universe dimension. The five areas of the social studies curriculum all build on these eight levels of awareness. Each level builds on the foundation of the previous narrower one. Figure 3.2 provides examples of activities for the self dimension for each of the five curriculum areas.

Figure 3.3 gives examples of activities for the family dimension and shows how this dimension builds around self. Figure 3.4 gives examples of how neighborhood builds around family, which has built around self.

Methods and Developmental Limitations

To be successful in early childhood classrooms, the whole language approach must operate within certain limitations that apply to all early childhood learning. Activities must be concrete, real, and relevant to the child and his or her world; they must be child directed (this implies choices). Detailed guidelines provided by the National Association for the Education of Young Children (NAEYC) appear in Bredekamp (1987).

Simply put, *concrete* means that the materials can be perceived by the senses of touch, sight, hearing, smell, and taste (Gilbert, 1989). *Real* means that the actual object should be there. For example, use a real orange rather than a plastic one or a picture of one or a story of one. Young children engage in optimal learning when they use their senses to explore something real. While doing this, they acquire vocabulary about the real thing. In the case of an orange, words such as round, soft, color, orange,

F I G U R E   3 . 2

■

Examples of concepts of self in the five social studies curriculum areas.

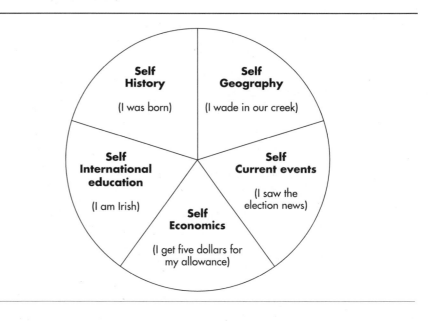

F I G U R E   3 . 3

■

Examples of family building on self in the five social studies curriculum areas.

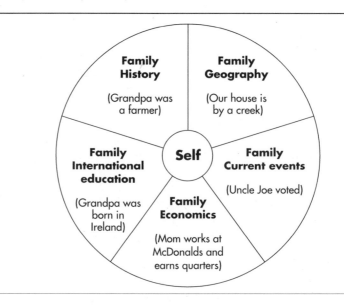

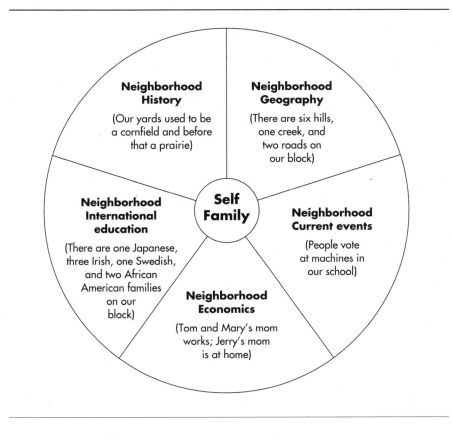

F I G U R E   3 . 4

■

Examples of neighborhood building on self and family in the five
social studies curriculum areas.

peel, sweet, and juicy might constitute acquired vocabulary. *Relevant*
means that what the child is learning about should be present in the
child's natural environment. Therefore, the child would be expected to
use this material or behavior in his or her home or community. For example, we teach young children about cars, buses, and trains (always remember the egocentrism and start with their family's main mode of
transportation, be it bicycle, bus, or car) before we teach them about rick-
shaws. We teach first about what is concrete, real, and relevant.

Returning to the orange example, we teach about oranges, ba-
nanas, and familiar fruits because we can make sure the child has them
for a class snack or eats them at home. Later, in the intermediate grades,
teachers can help children build on these early concrete, hands-on experiences and, after physical brain development is complete, relate them to
kumquats and other exotic fruits.

There are limits to the type of abstract language and abstract thinking that children under 8 years of age can engage in because of their normal but incomplete physical brain and nerve development. What concerns us here is that children in preschool and kindergarten need to choose from developmentally appropriate hands-on activities that are concrete, real, and relevant to their world (Bredekamp, 1987; Hamilton & Flemming, 1990; Hunt & Renfro, 1982).

The NAEYC defines what is developmentally appropriate in terms of age and the individual (Bredekamp, 1987, p. 2):

- *Age appropriateness.* Human development research indicates that there are universal, predictable sequences of growth and change that occur in children during the first 9 years of life. These predictable changes occur in all domains of development—physical, emotional, social, and cognitive. Knowledge of typical development of children within the age span served by the program provides a framework from which teachers prepare the learning environment and plan appropriate experiences. . . .

- *Individual appropriateness.* Each child is a unique person with an individual pattern and timing of growth, as well as individual personality, learning style, and family background. Both the curriculum and adults' interactions with children should be responsive to individual differences. Learning in young children is the result of interaction between the child's thoughts and experiences with materials, ideas, and people. These experiences should match the child's developing abilities, while also challenging the child's interest and understanding.

Techniques of the Whole Language Approach

With a knowledge of the limitations on how young children learn, teachers can use developmentally appropriate, child directed, hands-on activities with concrete, real, and relevant materials. They need to use the child's egocentism and ever-widening social perspective (Piaget, 1952), represented by the eight circles of awareness, as the foundation for their social studies curriculum plans. Building on this foundation, they are able to use the whole language approach in teaching the social studies curriculum content. Appropriate techniques include teaching vocabulary, facts, and concepts through speaking and listening vocabulary; dictated and written stories; books, magazines, and other printed materials; the child's drawn pictures and written print; nonverbal communication; field trips and print in the environment; and music.

Speaking and Listening Vocabulary

Speaking and listening vocabulary is built into everything teachers do in the classroom. The one-on-one "Good morning" greeting between teacher and child is an example of social development while language and literacy skills are also being expanded. Films and videotapes also aid vocabulary development. Other sample activities follow. The primary curriculum content area for each is given in parentheses.

- Informal small group discussion about the aquarium during free playtime (science)

- Large group discussion with a classroom visitor, such as a Puerto Rican mother with her new baby (social studies)

- Experimentation with the five types of magnets in the science corner (science)

- Listening for higher or lower (or louder or softer) sounds on the new instruments on the music table (music)

- Talking about and looking for the mile markers on a field trip to the Mathematics Museum (mathematics)

- Playing in the sociodramatic play area while dressing, talking and listening like a chosen character would (social development)

- Describing facial expressions in pictures held by the teacher, and discussing when they are appropriate and when they are not (emotional development)

- Taking down the copy of Chilton's car manual to see how many pieces the steering wheel of a car should have (mathematics) (Morgantini, 1991)

- Telephoning ill classmates from the principal's office to say the class misses them and hopes they are well soon (social development)

- Making pancakes: measuring, stirring, baking, and following the rebus-picture recipe (physical development)

In all of the foregoing activities, the main content knowledge base being taught is language or literacy. However, all the activities will directly develop skills necessary for early literacy.

Dictated and Written Stories

Along with dictated and written stories, teachers can use letters, songs, and lists across the curriculum content areas. Social studies content activities, such as the foregoing one involving the Puerto Rican mother and baby, often lend themselves to dictated written communications such as

■ Engaging in dramatic play helps children develop social skills. Through experimentation, children learn what is and is not acceptable behavior without being unduly penalized for their actions.

invitations, time schedules, maps of how to find the classroom and where to park, thank-you notes, an order for a thank-you flower, and so on. Because of their developmental level, most kindergartners and preschoolers verbally dictate these to the teacher, who then prints them for the children. The teacher should print each communication exactly as dictated, errors included, because it is the children's creation. *How to Reach Anyone Who's Anyone* by Leving (1980) lists the names and addresses of many people to whom students may want to write.

Although a rare child may write an entire message alone, this does not happen often. Most 5- and 6-year-olds will sign their name and, using invented spelling, print a few letters or words. It should be noted that it is harmful to force young children to copy words and phrases over and over.

Here are some examples of other social studies content activities that involve dictated or written material:

- Writing to the local mass transit authority for information about the system

- Writing a history of the child's life or a family history

- Writing a shopping list for purchases at the grocery store

- Writing to a kindergarten class in a foreign country

- Writing to a local politician

- Writing to the president of the United States
- Writing to someone the child has seen on the television news or in the newspaper

Books, Magazines, and Other Printed Materials

As discussed earlier, all printed materials used in the classroom should be concrete, real, and relevant to the lives of young children. This means that they should not be specially published just for education. They should exist outside of schools or home classrooms. They should be found instead in such environments as the home, workplace, grocery store, church, gas station, and so forth. Books written for young children's enjoyment, such as fairy tales, nursery rhymes and popular tales such as *The Very Hungry Caterpillar* (Carle, 1986) and *Koala Lou* (Fox, 1989) are also good choices because they were not created just to meet language or literacy goals, such as learning five new vocabulary words per day. If there had never been a formal classroom and the printed materials would still exist, they are considered real and relevant.

A well-stocked book corner is an asset to any early childhood classroom. It should include a wide variety of books, including mail order catalogs, an encyclopedia, phone books, nursery rhymes, fairy tales, big books (both commercially published and those made in class), modern books, traditional fables, poetry, children's magazines (such as *Ladybug*, *Spider* and *Our Big Outdoors*), brochures, music, and maps. A common rule of thumb is to have six books for each child in the class and to change books every three weeks. This allows the children to make choices. It is also important for teachers to allow children time on a daily basis to browse through the books.

The books and other printed materials should include content from all curriculum areas, including social studies. Examples of books that contain information from the social studies knowledge base are listed in the section "Children's Books" at the end of this chapter.

Suggestions for antibias criteria for the selection of books for young children are given in Derman-Sparks & A.B.C. Task Force (1989) and Bredekamp (1987).

Drawing Pictures and Writing Print

Drawing and writing require eye-hand coordination, visual discrimination, and fine muscle development, all of which are necessary for literacy. Regardless of what children are drawing or writing, these skills develop anyway. For example, drawing a flower is of as much benefit as printing a capital *P* over and over. If a child chooses to print the *P* over and over again, that is fine; otherwise, the skills will develop as the child uses instruments to draw or write whatever she or he wants to draw or write.

■ Children need ample opportunities to illustrate their feelings, and desires.

Drawing and writing also develop literacy skills regardless of the curriculum content area. For example, the following subjects drawn by young children all have whole language value but none have language or reading as the main knowledge base (curriculum areas are shown in parenthesis):

- My family (social studies)
- Ways we travel (social studies)
- Shoes people wore in Ancient Rome (social studies)
- Chinese paper money (social studies)
- My piano (music)
- Babies (social studies, science)
- Water (science)

Five-year-olds and younger children need large pencils, pens, and crayons because of their fine muscle developmental level. They also need paper that is at least 11 inches by 14 inches. A variety of writing instruments and kinds of paper are desirable so that children can learn about the physical limitations of each kind. While acquiring literacy skills, they also learn about the physical world (science).

Nonverbal Communication

Gestures, dress, and facial expression are types of nonverbal communication. Young children need to learn to visually discriminate similarities and differences in order to communicate verbally and read. For example someone yelling, "Stop!" with a smile on her face is communicating something very different from someone yelling, "Stop!" with a fist held up. Following are some other examples of activities involving nonverbal communication; again, curriculum content areas are given in parentheses. All these activities contribute to literacy and language development.

- The look on the bus driver's face when all 30 of us board the city bus (social development)
- A class discussion about what we and others do with our mouths when we are angry, happy, sad, and so on (social development)
- Reading a story about a girl who is afraid of flying and how her body expresses fear (emotional development)

Field Trips and Print in the Environment

Field trips and print in the environment stimulate so much spoken language and discussion, trigger so much new vocabulary, and provide so many concrete, real, and relevant materials and activities that almost everything about them contributes directly to language and literacy development. Written communication is stimulated through invitations, thank-you notes, maps, and so forth. Print is available everywhere in the environment, and children are motivated to read or pay attention to signs and then later to follow up with books and stories. Some whole language field trips with content in various curriculum areas but still developing literacy are trips to the following places:

- Science museum (science)
- Bakery (social studies)
- Grocery store (social studies, mathematics)
- Mathematics academy (mathematics)
- Music store (music)
- Circus (physical education, social studies)
- Garden (science, social studies)

Programs for young children should include as many field trips as time allows. One transported trip per month and at least two walking field trips per week are a minimum.

Field trips are useful in all areas of social studies as indicated below:

- History: visit our old park, our old school, our old classroom

- Economics: visit stores, banks, factories

- Current events: visit a newspaper office, television station

- International education: visit homes of people from other nations, ethnic museums

- Geography: visit hills, lakes, mountains, islands, whatever is in the local environment

Music

Music involves auditory communication, written communication through notes, visual memory, pattern repetition, visual discrimination, and so on. It is an important component of any whole language approach, and the skills developed through music are directly applicable to literacy and language skills. The following music activities for the social studies content area would be desirable for literacy development:

- Writing to a kindergarten class in Honduras and asking what their favorite songs are

- Playing tone bells or the xylophone by color coded musical notes (The C tone bell, xylophone C bar, and the C note on the music sheet are all red; B is blue on all; C is yellow, and so on.)

- Listening to different kinds of recorded music and identifying what country the music is from, such as jig, polka, can can

- Listening to musical selections such as a funeral dirge, "Wedding March", and Sousa marches and deciding when it is appropriate to play each and when it is not

Sample Lesson Plan Outline

Examples of general plans for vocabulary, materials, and content are shown in the following outline. The outline includes all five social studies curriculum areas for the self dimension of awareness shown in figure 3.1 and the examples of concepts of self presented in figure 3.2. Child-directed, developmentally appropriate, hands-on, concrete, real, and relevant materials and activities are used.

LESSON PLAN OUTLINE
Circle of Awareness: SELF

I. Social studies area: HISTORY

    A. Possible vocabulary

    Birth, death, generations, grandfather, grandmother, aunt, uncle, cousin, brother, sister, old, new, antique, was, is, will be, past, present, future, growth

    B. Concrete materials

        1. Photographs of the child at birth, of birthdays, of parent at birth, of parents on birthdays, of relatives

        2. Baby clothing worn by the child, by other family members; the child's old and new toys

        3. Child's old and new Valentines, birthday cards, or other greeting cards; family's cards

        4. Graphs charting child's height during the year, showing growth

        5. Puppets available in classroom showing the progression of development from birth through 6 years of age

        6. Books, films, and tapes available in the classroom that depict children in the first 6 years of life; that depict families with older, middle-aged, and young adults and teenagers, young children and infants; that depict pioneer families, Depression-era families, gay nineties families, future families, and so forth

        7. Short-lived animals (gerbils, caterpillars, and so on) in the classroom so that children have the opportunity to experience life and death

        8. A short video showing how a person walks during different ages of life

    C. Activities

        1. Have class, large group, and small group discussions about the foregoing materials and make sure each child has a concrete article to relate to, such as a photograph of himself or herself at birth, at each discussion.

        2. Have children paint or draw a picture of the historical family they liked most in the film they just saw.

        3. Have each child dictate a short letter to some older person in his or her family.

        4. Have children sing songs with you about the special occasions shown on the cards they have brought to school. Make up songs or rhymes.

        5. Have several books about families, babies, birth, and death available in the book corner for children to choose from.

      6. Take a field trip to a busy place and watch how different people walk differently at different ages.

II. Social studies area: ECONOMICS

    A. Possible vocabulary

        Money, coins, nickels, dimes, quarters, dollars, allowance, gift, presents, want, need, purchase, buy, receipt, sell, trade, honesty, cheat, greed, sharing, charity

    B. Concrete materials

      1. Nickels, dimes, quarters, dollars, sample checks

      2. Mail order catalogues

      3. Wooden puzzles about coins

      4. Paper puzzles about different paper money for each child to cut up

      5. Classroom dramatic play area set up as a grocery store or a flower store or a clothing store, and so on

      6. Examples of good chairs, cheap chairs, good shirts, cheap shirts, sturdy materials and easily broken materials, such as drinking glasses

      7. Books about money, honesty, greed, sharing, and charity available in the book corner for children to choose from

    C. Activities

      1. Have the class choose something in the room or something they will make that they would be willing to give to another class or group. Then have them dictate a letter about it, and deliver the letter and gift to the other group.

      2. Have class members draw a picture of something they would never give away.

      3. Make a large wall graph with pictures of items the children feel they must have and another with pictures of items they would like to have but could do without. They can draw them or cut them out of catalogues, or you can draw them.

      4. Discuss and show pictures of nonverbal communication. Can you tell whether someone wants to get into the movie theater but has no money? Can you tell whether someone is hungry but cannot eat? Can you tell when someone has money to spend?

      5. Sing songs about money, wishes, and hopes.

      6. Use flash cards of pictures of children being honest and dishonest. Each time a picture shows honesty, have the children play their rhythm instrument triangles. Every time a picture shows greed, have the children blow on kazoos.

III. Social studies area: GEOGRAPHY

    A. Possible vocabulary

Land, water, air, hill, mountain, rock, sand, mud, valley, sky, waterfall, cornfield, island, cliff, on, under, inside, between

B. Concrete materials

1. Sand and water table
2. Dirt and water table
3. Boxes of different kinds of rocks and dirt
4. Puppets and a box to use with prepositions such as *on, in, through,* and *above*
5. Slides, films, and tapes of mountains or other geographical features not present in the immediate locale
6. Musical recordings about the earth—for example, "This Land Is Your Land, This Land Is My Land" and "Garden Song"
7. Travel posters depicting geographical forms such as lakes and islands
8. Modeling clay to form earth features such as hills and valleys

C. Activities

1. Take a walking field trip and have a picnic. Discuss the land forms in the immediate environment.
2. Have children dictate letters to people who live in different places asking them for photographs and information about local landforms.
3. Make a collage from travel magazines of lakes, mountains, valleys, and so on.
4. Have children draw pictures with felt-tipped markers showing where they would like to live.
5. Have a picture sorting activity using magazine pictures of environmentally healthy or unhealthy mountains, islands, lakes, and so forth.
6. Have the children match calendar pictures (or other scenic outdoor pictures) to different musical compositions and explain why they matched each picture to each musical composition.

IV. Social studies area: CURRENT EVENTS

A. Possible vocabulary

Newspaper, television news, tabloid, community, state, nation, catastrophe, human interest story, weather, hurricane, accident, celebration, Hollywood, movies

B. Concrete materials

1. Newspaper articles brought by the children from home
2. Video tapes of television news programs
3. Bulletin board on which to display stories and reports
4. Weather maps

C. Activities

1. Discuss each article or picture the children bring in and put it on the bulletin board.

2. Show videotapes of television news and discuss which stories are about disasters, which are about the weather, which are about celebrations, and so on.

3. At the end of the day, have the children vote on what they would consider the "current event of the day" in the classroom.

4. Take a field trip to a local newspaper.

5. Have a local newspaper or television reporter visit the classroom.

6. Have the children forecast the weather for the next day. Make a picture record of the forecast, and check it the next day.

7. Keep a record of new art and music releases.

V. Social studies area: INTERNATIONAL AND GLOBAL EDUCATION

A. Possible vocabulary

Country, world, sharing, foreign languages, Spain, France, Third World, food, toys, homes, clothing, flag, stamps, military, war

B. Concrete materials

1. Snack foods from different countries

2. Clothing from different countries

3. Pictures of homes in different countries

4. Toys from different cultures and countries

5. Books about other countries in other languages and about war

6. Recordings of music from other countries, such as the can can, Irish jig, polka, and so on; and recordings of various national anthems

7. Recordings of the same story being read in different languages

8. Films and pictures of modes of transportation in different countries

9. A picture chart showing how children can help one another

C. Activities

1. Discuss similarities in pictures showing where people live or find shelter in different countries.

2. Show films and posters from embassies of different countries.

■ The sharing of literature with a child can help them develop empathy for other people as well as for animals and the environment.

3. Begin a resource file of children's games from around the world, and teach one game to a small group of children.

4. Have children dictate letters to children or schools in other countries asking about the similarities and differences in their schools and ours.

5. Sort pictures that depict war and those that depict peace, and make a two-part bulletin board display.

6. Have children draw pictures showing the places they would most like to visit.

7. Have the children do dances from other nations.

8. Have people from other nations visit the classroom and bring samples of baby clothes, food, toys, and music.

9. Take a field trip to homes of people who have lived in other countries.

This lesson plan outline is only one of many that could be developed for the dimension of self. Moreover, many similar lesson plans could also be developed for each of the other seven dimensions of social awareness. (Figures 3.3 and 3.4 present examples of the family and neighborhood dimensions.) The possibilities are limitless.

Summary

The whole language approach works well in teaching social studies. While mindful of the limitations on how young children learn, teachers can use child-directed, hands-on activities with concrete, real, and relevant materials. These activities should be based on the child's egocentrism and ever-widening social perspective represented by eight circles of awareness as the foundation for social studies curriculum plans. Building on this foundation, teachers can use different whole language activities (speaking and listening vocabulary; dictated and written stories; books, magazines and printed materials; the child's own drawn pictures and written print; non-verbal communication; field trips; and music) to teach the five social studies curriculum areas (history, economics, geology, international and global education, and current events).

Children's Books

Barger, T. (1980). *Special friends.* New York: Julian Messner.

> A girl tells of her rewarding and enjoyable visits with her elderly neighbor. This book reveals the differences that occur as one becomes older.

Bauer, C. (1981). *My mom travels a lot.* New York: Federic Warne.

> A little girl points out the good and bad things about a mother's job that takes her away from home a great deal.

Breinburg, P. (1973). *Shawn goes to school.* New York: Crowell.

> Shawn always wanted to go to school, but when the first day of nursery school came along, he didn't like it very much. He wouldn't play and started to cry. This book lets youngsters know that many children have a hard time when they first go to school. Pictures of an African American family and multicultural students enhance the text.

Carle, E. (1986). *The very hungry caterpillar.* New York: Philomel.

> Colorful illustrations and fluid text explain the many ways the caterpillar satisfies its hunger and grows.

Clifton, L. (1983). *Everett Anderson's goodbye.* New York: Holt, Rinehart & Winston.

> Everett Anderson comes to terms with his grief after his father dies.

Everitt, B. (1992). *Mean soup.* San Diego, CA: Harcourt Brace Jovanovich.

> Horace has a bad day. His mother boils a pot of water and then screams into it. Horace joins her, and together they make "mean soup." The book shares a way to let out emotions without hurting others.

Fisher, I. (1987). *Katie-Bo.* New York: Adama Books.

> At first Jim and his brother, Teddy, are confused and nervous when they learn their family is going to adopt a Korean baby. However, both come to agree that adoption is a very special way to have a sister, and Katie-Bo becomes a very special sister.

Fox, M. (1989). *Koala Lou* (P. Lofts, Illus.) San Diego, CA: Harcourt Brace Jovanovich.

> Koala Lou is the oldest child in a large family. Because her mother is busy with the younger children, Koala Lou believes her mother no longer loves her. But when Koala Lou finishes second in a tree climbing race, her mother gives her a big hug and tells her that she loves her, always has, and always will.

Greenspun, A. A. (1992). *Daddies.* New York: Philomel.

> The author tells how she lost her own father at an early age. She then presents a collection of pictures of fathers and their young children.

Greenfield, E. (1974). *She comes bringing me that little baby girl.* Philadelphia: Lippincott.

> A black family helps a new brother deal with a new baby sister when he really wanted a brother. This story deals with gender roles and sibling rivalry and is told in a lighthearted manner with a hint of black dialect.

Hazen, B. (1985). *Why are people different?* Racine, WI: Western.

> This story helps children understand the differences in people so that they will not be frightened of others but instead will develop relationships with children who are different.

Howe, J. (1987). *I wish I were a butterfly.* San Diego, CA: Harcourt Brace Jovanovich.

> The little cricket will not sing because he thinks he is ugly. He wants to be beautiful like a butterfly. However, the cricket finds out that everyone is special in some way, and he starts to sing. The butterfly hears him and wishes he were a cricket. This book lets each child know that he or she is special. The art work is beautiful.

Johnson, A. (1992). *The leaving morning.* (D. Soman, Illus.). New York: Orchard.

> This book describes the emotions of leaving one home and learning to love another home.

Marino, B. (1979). *Eric needs stitches.* Reading, MA: Addison-Wesley.

> Through a series of photographs Eric is shown going to the emergency room to get stitches in his knee after a bad fall. Although this story is too long for preschoolers, it does show the father as the nurturing parent.

McDermott, G. (1972). *Anansi the spider.* New York: Holt, Rinehart & Winston.

> This folktale from the Ashanti in Ghana tells the story of Anansi, an animal with human qualities who gets into trouble.

Morris, W. (1987). *The magic leaf.* New York: Atheneum.

> Long ago in China, Lee Foo, a smart man, seeks and finds the magic leaf. He also finds a lot of trouble.

Politi, L. (1973). *The nicest gift.* New York: Scribner.

> This is the story of a Mexican boy who loses his dog, Blanco, in Los Angeles. Blanco returns on Christmas Day.

Schoen, M. (1990). *Bellybuttons are navels.* Buffalo, NY: Prometheus.

As Mary and her brother, Robert, bathe together, they discover that they have similar and different body parts and learn to identify them. This book is designed to develop an acceptance of the body and to help parents and educators initiate discussion and education about the human body.

Seuss, D. (1984). *Butter battle book.* New York: Random House.

This story depicts the difficulties of battle and the possible outcomes.

Shyer, M. (1985). *Here I am, an only child.* New York: Scribner.

A little boy explains the advantages and disadvantages of being an only child.

Simon, N. (1976). *All kinds of families.* Chicago: Albert Whitman.

Exploring in words and pictures what a family is and how families vary in makeup and life-style, this book celebrates happy times but also shows that some relationships are troubled ones. Separations and sadness occur, yet the positive values of lives shared endure to provide foundations for future families.

Waxman, S. (1989). *What is a girl? What is a boy?* Culver City, CA: Peace Press.

This book describes and illustrates the anatomy of males and females. Although some people may be uncomfortable with the graphic illustrations, information is presented in a matter-of-fact manner. Sex stereotypes are addressed and often refuted.

Yolen, J. (1993). *Weather report.* (A. Gusman, Illus.). Honesdale, PA: Boyds Mill Press.

A book of poetry about the weather. Includes poems about rain, sun, wind, snow, and fog.

References

Banks, J. A. (1992). Multicultural education for freedom's sake. *Educational Leadership, 49*(4), 32–35.

Brown, C., & Brown, G., (1985). *Play interactions.* Skillman, NJ: Johnson & Johnson.

Bredekamp, S. (1987). *Developmentally appropriate practice in early childhood programs serving children from birth through eight.* Washington, DC: National Association for the Education of Young Children.

Charlesworth, R., & Lund, K. (1990). *Math and science for young children.* Delmar.

Derman-Sparks, L., & A.B.C. Task Force (1989). *Anti-bias curriculum.* Washington, DC: National Association for Education of Young Children.

Gilbert, L. (1989). *Do touch.* Mt. Rainier, MD: Gryphon House.

Hamilton, D., & Flemming, H. (1990). *Resources for creative teaching in early childhood education* (2nd ed.). Orlando, FL: Harcourt Brace Jovanovich.

Hunt, T. & Renfro, N. (1982). *Puppetry in early childhood
education.* New York: Nancy Renfro Studios.

Leving, M. (1980). *How to reach anyone who's anyone.* Los
Angeles: Price, Stern, Sloan.

Maxim, G.W. (1991). *Social studies and the elementary school
child,* 4th ed. Columbus, OH: Merrill.

Morgantini, D. (Ed.). (1991). *Chilton's car manual, 1987-91.*
Radnar, PA: Chilton.

Piaget, J. (1952). *The origins of intelligence in children.* New York:
International Universities Press.

Seefeldt, C. (1989). *Social studies for the preschool primary child.*
Columbus, OH: Merrill.

Smith, C. (1982). *Promoting the social development of young
children.* Mountain View, CA: Mayfield.

Reading, Writing, and Discussing: Communicating in Social Studies

P A M E L A   J .   F A R R I S
NORTHERN ILLINOIS UNIVERSITY

We write and read in order

   to know each other's responses,

      to connect ourselves more fully with the human world,

         and to strengthen the habit of truth-telling in our midst.

B E N J A M I N   D e M O T T
"Why We Read and Write"

Introduction

Social studies offers many opportunities for reading, writing, and discussing, skills that good citizens need to develop to their fullest. In a democratic society, it is essential that its citizenry be well educated, with each citizen able to gain information through reading and to communicate effectively through speaking and writing. As former United States Commissioner of Education Ernest L. Boyer (1990, p. 5) writes,

> While economic purposes are being vigorously pursued, civic priorities also must be affirmed. Indeed, unless we find better ways to educate ourselves as *citizens,* America runs the risk of drifting unwittingly into a new kind of dark age, a time when specialists control the decision-making process and citizens will be forced to make critical decisions not on the basis of what they know but on the basis of blind belief in so-called "experts."

The whole language philosophical tenet is based on sharing relevant material with children. Decision making is promoted as children make choices about how and what they will learn. Children are also encouraged to interact with each other as they learn.

Reading, writing, and discussing allow children the individual freedom to learn as well as maintain a social responsibility to the class to share what has been learned. As Banks (1991–1992, p. 32) states, "To create and maintain a civic community that works for the common good, education in a democratic society should help students acquire the knowledge, attitudes, and skills they will need to participate in civil action to make society more equal and just." Because students in a whole language classroom are encouraged to challenge and question both themselves and others, such a classroom is a democratic community.

A democracy is established on the belief that each citizen has worth and can offer something of value to the group. This necessitates that *trust* be gained and maintained if a democracy is to survive. In the classroom, the teacher must first establish the basic principles of democracy. In the areas of reading, writing, and discussing, this means that every child's ideas must be respected.

Support and encouragement must also pave the way if trust is to evolve in the classroom. This is not purely a one-directional matter of teacher to student but also of student to teacher, for the teacher must be willing to submit ideas that the class may openly criticize. For example, when the teacher shares a piece of his or her own writing with a class for the first time, both the teacher and the students are somewhat anxious and uncomfortable. The teacher wants the students to like what he or she has written because writing is very personal. The students feel that the situation is precarious because they are unsure of whether they should make only positive comments. That is, will the teacher consider negative comments to be ill-suited for the occasion? By opening up through sharing his or her own writing with the class, the teacher is demonstrating democratic principles: We all have different talents, we all have feelings, we all have beliefs, and we all can profit by sharing our thoughts and ideals.

According to Alfie Kohn (1991, p. 499), "If we had to pick a logical setting in which to guide children toward caring about, empathizing with, and helping other people, it would be a place where they would regularly come into contact with their peers and where some sort of learning is already taking place."

The San Ramon Valley Unified School District in San Ramon, California, fosters democratic principles by rooting its elementary curriculum in the development of social values (Schaps & Solomon, 1990). This school system relies on children's literature and cooperative learning to encourage a caring climate where learning takes place. Quality literature that depicts how values "work" is the basis for reading instruction. For instance, books with themes of fairness and kindness help students develop empathy for others; books about other cultures and circumstances represent universal issues and concerns. Cooperative learning emphasizes collaboration, extensive interaction, division of labor, use of reason and explanation, and consideration of values related to the activity in which the group is engaged (Schaps & Solomon, 1990). Cooperative learning activities in the social studies often rely on a cycle of discussing reading and writing.

Reading

Research studies in reading indicate that when children can relate their daily life experiences as well as prior knowledge to the content of a textbook, they are better able to understand and assimilate new concepts and knowledge (Alverman, Smith, & Readance, 1985). Thus, the engaging narrative style of a children's book may result in a student's discovery and retention of social studies concepts (McGowan & Guzzetti, 1991).

Reading enables children to gather information directly and to gain knowledge through vicarious experiences. For example, by reading a social studies textbook or nonfiction book, students can acquire background information about a specific social studies concept or topic, for instance *Katie's Trunk* (Turner, 1992) is a true story of a Tory family at the beginning

■ Children's literature has a powerful impact on a child.

of the American Revolution. By reading fiction, they can develop empathy for others as well as a better understanding of their own feelings and values. An award winning book in this area is *Letters from Rifka* (Hesse, 1992) which depicts a family fleeing Russia in 1919.

Children's Literature

Reading quality children's books is important for children. According to Charlotte Huck (1990, p. 3),

> Literature not only has the power to change a reader, but it
> contains the power to help children become readers.
> Traditionally, we have recognized the influence of literature on
> our thoughts and feelings, but we have been slower to discover
> the role that literature plays in *creating readers,* in actually
> helping children learn to read.

Reading quality children's literature enhances a child's understanding of social studies. According to McGowan and Guzzetti, (1991, p. 18),

> Literary works are packed with conceptual knowledge about the human condition and can supply meaningful content for skill-building experiences. . . . Perhaps more completely and certainly more intensely than with textbooks, a creative teacher can use trade books to engage students in the pursuit of such citizenship competencies as processing information, examining other points of view, separating fact from opinion, and solving problems.

The teacher must take care to provide good books. In recent years authors such as Brent Ashabranner, Jean Fritz, and Diane Stanley have written books that create vivid and accurate historical settings. Joan Lowery Nixon's (1992, 1993, 1994) Ellis Island series depicts the lives of three immigrant girls in the early 1900s—Rebeka, a Russian Jew; Kristyn, an independent Swede, and Rose, whose family was escaping famine in Ireland. Today a great number of quality children's books are appropriate for use in teaching social studies. This was not always the case, however. Consider, for instance, the area of multicultural education. As recently as the mid-1980s, there was a dearth of children's literature in this area. At that time only 1 percent of children's literature published was about African Americans, and the percentage of books about Asian Americans, Hispanics, and Native Americans was even smaller (Bishop, 1987). However, Reimer (1992) reports that there is an increase in the amount of multicultural literature being published for children.

The increased use of children's literature in social studies instruction has provided more relevant textual material for students than has the sole use of social studies textbooks. By incorporating both, the classroom teacher can capitalize on the best of both types of reading material.

The proliferation of quality children's literature with a social studies base permits the classroom teacher to enrich and expand a topic by having children read beyond the social studies textbook. For instance, Patricia MacLachlan's *Sarah, Plain and Tall* (1985) outlines a widower's search for a mail order bride to "make a difference" for his young son and daughter. Because of its rich descriptions of the Maine coastline and the Kansas prairie, the book provides an excellent opportunity for comparing and contrasting the two settings geographically in addition to discussing the differences in the plant and animal life native to each of the two regions.

Economics is the focus of *Lyddie,* a book by Katherine Paterson (1991), set in 1840. Lyddie is a young farm girl who ventures to Lowell, Massachusetts, in search of a better life. She finds work in the mills and discovers the anguish and frustrations of the dangerous mill work. The long hours, low pay, and inadequate living and working conditions are well portrayed by Paterson, providing today's students with insights as to the sacrifices made by workers and, in this case, children during the Industrial Revolution.

When I was young and in the fifth grade, Mr. Sheffield was my teacher. Mr. Sheffield was six feet, six inches tall. One day Henry broke a classroom rule. Mr. Sheffield picked Henry up and held him against the wall. I NEVER misbehaved in Mr. Sheffield's room.

Other books encourage students to reflect on their own lives. Cynthia Rylant's *When I Was Young in the Mountains* (1982) is a picture book that introduces children to the simple pleasures Rylant engaged in while growing up in the Appalachian Mountains. Rylant depicts the social and psychological aspects of life there. Ed Lane, a fifth-grade teacher, wrote his reflections about his experiences as a child in the fifth grade and shared them with his class.

After sharing what he wrote, Ed had his students write their reflections of being in the second grade. In essence, since most of the students had attended the same elementary school as second graders, they wrote not only about their own remembrances but also about the culture and history of the school itself. After writing about and editing their memories of second grade, the class went to the second-grade classroom, where each fifth-grade student was paired up with a second grader. Then the fifth graders shared their experiences with the second graders.

Concepts can be introduced by sharing a children's book with students. *How Many Days to America?* by Eve Bunting (1988) describes how a Caribbean family flees to the United States and freedom in a fishing boat. Through a dramatic and touching story, students learn the importance of freedom and the value people from other countries place upon it.

Cultural and sociological differences can also be presented through children's literature. Folktales often provide insight into a different culture. William H. Hooks' (1990) *The Ballad of Belle Dorcas* is the story of Belle Dorcas, the daughter of a slave mother and a slave master, and her love for Joshua. Because her father is white, Belle Dorcas is a freeborn slave. Thus, she is free while her mother must remain a slave. However, Joshua is a slave who is to be sold. Belle Dorcas uses a magic spell of a conjure woman to keep Joshua from being sold.

Folklore is the basis of David Wisniewski's (1991) *Rain Player*, a richly illustrated picture book based on Mayan folklore. The author provides extensive information about Mayan history and culture in a note at the end of the book.

Another example of a folktale is a very simple Chinese legend retold by Margaret Greaves (1985) in *Once There Were No Pandas*. A young girl makes a sacrifice for a white bear, which gave the first pandas their unique black markings. The author includes a pronunication key for the Chinese terms in this simple picture book. A good companion book is Laurence Yep's (1991) *Tongues of Jade*, a collection of seventeen Chinese folktales.

The use of autobiographies and diaries can be a very effective way of sharing perceptions about people and events throughout history. For instance, *All for the Union* (Rhodes, 1985) is a book that middle school students will find interesting. Containing the Civil War diary and letters of Elisha Hunt Rhodes, this book eloquently describes the Civil War through the eyes of a thoughtful soldier. Rhodes enlisted in the Rhode Island Infantry as a private at age 19 and shortly after that wrote these words as a new recruit:

> We drilled day and night and I was especially instructed by Mr. John E. Bradford, an old member of the Light Infantry Company. Standing before a long mirror, I put in many hours of weary work and soon thought myself quite a soldier. A call for recruits for the Rhode Island Regiment having come, John E. Bradford and First Sergeant James S. Hudson left our company to join the First Regiment in Washington. I was elected First Sergeant [by his fellow soldiers in his company], much to my surprise. Just what a First Sergeant's duty might be I had no idea, for I had never done duty in the militia and was ignorant of the first principles. We spent all our time in the Armory and talked of nothing but soldiering. (p. 13)

Rhodes fought in 20 battles, from the first battle of Bull Run through Appomattox. By the end of the Civil War, he had risen to the rank of lieutenant colonel and was the commander of his regiment. Rhodes's diary is featured in Ken Burns's (1990) PBS TV documentary *The Civil War.*

Informational books must be a part of social studies instruction so that children can become familiar with "what really happened." Unfortunately, many school libraries have informational books that are either outdated or present a view from only one perspective. Newly published informational books relating to social studies tend to present a variety of perspectives. For instance, *Pueblo Storyteller* by Diane Hoyt-Goldsmith (1991) depicts the contemporary life of a Cochiti Indian girl, while David Weitzman's (1982) *Windmills, Bridges, and Old Machines: Discovering Our Industrial Past,* relates how specific machines were developed and how they work. Novelist Walter Dean Myers (1991) turned his pen to nonfiction in the book *Now Is Your Time! The African American Struggle for Freedom,* which traces the civil rights movement in America by following African American slaves, soldiers, political leaders, inventors, and artists. Jerry Stanley's (1992) *Children of the Dust Bowl* is a true story of families who were lured to California by a desire for a better life during the Great Depression.

By acquainting children with literature that contains social studies themes and content, the teacher may find that student motivation is increased. In addition, for those students who find the textbook either too difficult or not very exciting, children's literature may unlock doors to historical events, light a path for geography, or explain in simple terms an economic or sociological concept.

Writing

While children enjoy reading about what interests them most, the same is true for writing. Children write best when they write about what is most familiar and interesting to them (Graves, 1983). Assigning children topics in which they have little or no interest makes it difficult for them to write because they not only lack motivation but may have little if any background in such topics.

Different forms of writing (persuasive, expository, poetic, narrative) should be used to meet different social studies goals. By using a variety of writing forms, students will maintain their interest in social studies and writing (Walley, 1991). Writing gives students the opportunity to reflect on what they have just read or discussed (Abel, Hauwiller, & Vandeventer, 1989).

Writing can also help students understand concepts and attain knowledge. For example, Langer and Applebee (1987) found that thinking is enhanced by writing. Kuhrt (1989) conducted a study with fifth graders regarding their acquisition of social studies concepts. She found that writing in learning logs or journals about what they had read in a chapter in a social studies textbook enhanced the students' knowledge of concepts.

The writing process consists of five stages typically referred to as prewriting, drafting, revising, editing, and publishing/sharing (Britton, 1978; Graves, 1983; Murray, 1984; Tompkins & Hoskisson, 1991). Figure 4.1 presents a summary of these stages.

Prewriting

In social studies the teacher may want to give the students a broad topic and allow them to write on a subtopic in which they are interested. In the prewriting stage, the teacher establishes a purpose for the writing and gives students time to think about their individual topics. Each student brainstorms to gather from within already collected ideas and thoughts about the topic. The student may brainstorm with another student to share information and to formulate questions for which they may both want to find answers.

Some teachers find *clustering,* also referred to as graphic organizing, to be a successful prewriting activity (Rico, 1983). A concept may serve as the nucleus word or words, with related words or groups of words generated by the students and each placed in a separate circle and linked in a web to the nucleus words. Students then contribute related

Effective writing is a five-stage process.

Stages of the Writing Process

Prewriting   The teacher needs to provide students with essential background experiences for writing. In addition, the assignment needs to be clearly delineated and explained. At this point the students may brainstorm to discover what they already know about the writing topic and what remains to be learned. Questions may be generated and lists made of possible sources of information. The information is then gathered and organized for the next stage.

Drafting   Drafting involves actually putting the pencil to paper. This stage focuses on content, not mechanics. In essence, it is getting the principal ideas down on paper.

Revising   In the revising stage, the writer rereads the draft and makes changes on the draft itself. Some teachers refer to this as "sloppy copy" in that words are often misspelled or crossed out and lines are drawn to indicate where sentences or paragraphs should be moved or inserted.

Editing   This stage is a polishing stage. Editing also occurs in the prewriting stage as the writer thinks about ideas, adopting some and discarding others. Likewise, editing takes place in the drafting stage as the writer makes decisions about word choice, sentence order, and so on. In the editing stage, the writer reads through the revised draft, correcting errors in both content and mechanics. The piece of writing is then recopied.

**Publishing/
Sharing**   In this stage the finished product is shared with the class. This may be done by having each child read his or her final draft, by making a class book of all the students' pieces of writing, or by placing all of the final pieces on a bulletin board. The students should discuss each other's work so that they not only learn from each other but also appreciate each other.

F I G U R E   4 . 2

■

Identifications and definitions of clusters for Women's History Month

Pioneers
Women who were first in unknown territory
Innovators

Suffragettes
Supporters of voting rights for women

Equal Rights Advocates
Supporters of same rights for women as for men

Scientists
Experts in science
Makers of new discoveries

Authors
Writers of books
Newspaper reporters
Poets

Impact On Society

Artists
Dancers
Painters
Singers
Actresses

Political Leaders
World leaders
Leaders of causes

Educators
Supporters of education

Ideas and information that they already know about the concept or topic. These ideas are also written down, either on the chalkboard in the case of class discussion or in the student's notebook in the case of an individual writing assignment. Figure 4.2 shows an example of clustering done by a sixth-grade class in reference to National Women's History Month (March).

Clustering can entail both brainstorming and discussion. For instance, the sixth-grade class brainstormed the primary theme of the cluster, women who have made an impact on society. The result was the various subclusters. These were discussed and refined until the students agreed on those shown in Figure 4.2. The class then identified

Figure 4.2 Continued.

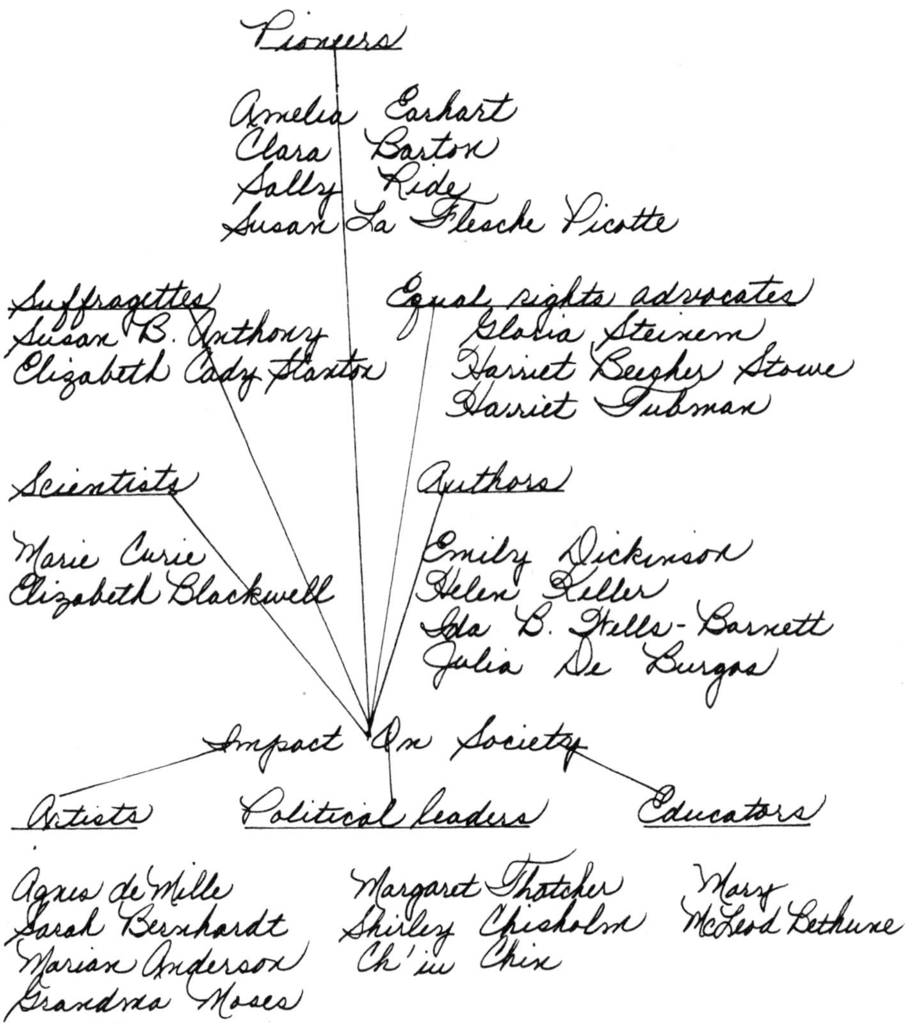

specific women for each cluster. Some library time was devoted to the project. This proved worthwhile because both known and little known names were included: Agnes de Mille, an innovator in dance choreography, who was responsible for the dances in the musical *Oklahoma!*; Ida B. Wells-Barnett, the first black investigative reporter, who led the effort against the lynching of blacks by white mobs; Julia De Burgos, a Puerto Rican poet; Ch'iu Chin, a Chinese feminist and political leader, who was beheaded for leading an uprising against the Ch'ing dynasty; and Susan La Flesche Picotte, the first Native American female physician.

The prewriting stage may also involve *interviews*. The local community can provide a wealth of individuals who are knowledgeable about specific topics. For instance, Sarah Wheeler's fifth-grade class was studying the Civil War. Living in a fairly remote rural community in Illinois, the students did not have ready access to historians and well-endowed libraries. However, several townspeople were interested in the Civil War. For example, a local minister collected songs of the Civil War period and was interviewed by members of the class.

Students may individually interview community members. First, however, they should prepare a set of questions. This may be done in pairs or small groups of students. People such as an anthropologist or economist from a local college or university, the manager of a local fast-food restaurant, a political newspaper reporter, a circuit court judge, or a state legislator can provide students with new insights. However, students should also study the particular topic prior to the interview.

Reading is part of the prewriting stage as students seek out information from various textual sources: books, newspapers, magazines, almanacs, and so forth. The students should take notes and write down sources. *Viewing* videotapes and laser discs may also be part of the prewriting stage. These are just a few of the various forms of media that can be used in this data-gathering stage.

Drafting

The actual writing of the initial draft of the paper begins when most if not all of the research has been completed. As the students write, it is best if they skip every other line so that they will have ample room for revising later. Some students may refer to the draft as "sloppy copy" or "draft" so that everyone will know that the focus is on content, not mechanics, which they will address in the next stage. In the drafting stage, the teacher should stress content and make no mention of mechanics or spelling.

Revising

The revising stage occurs when the initial draft is completed and the writer rereads what he or she has written. During this stage, the writer reads the draft, crosses out words and phrases and replaces them with other words and phrases, and circles misspelled words or those the writer believes are spelled incorrectly to be checked for accuracy later.

During the revising stage, the student tries to view the piece as a reader would. This involves asking questions: Is this clear? Is it interesting to read? Is it well organized? Are the facts accurate? Children often have difficulty realizing that not everyone has the same amount of knowledge about a topic as they possess. This in turn may cause difficulty for the reader. Therefore, it is important for the writer to consider the audience for whom the piece is written.

Editing

Editing is the stage in which the piece is polished before publishing/sharing takes place. Some teachers have the students exchange papers and edit each other's writing. Other teachers have found that having students, particularly those for whom writing is difficult, read their work out loud to themselves makes for better editing.

After making all the necessary corrections, the student recopies the paper. This ensures that it not only looks nice to the reader's eye but is also easier to read.

When students use computers for writing, spell checkers and grammar checkers are useful in their editing. Chapter 13 explains how the computer can be incorporated into social studies instruction and writing.

Publishing/Sharing

The last stage of the writing process is that of publishing/sharing. In this stage each student shares his or her writing with the class or members of the student's group. When the piece of writing is presented, each student should find something positive to say about it. This helps build trust among classmates.

It is important to note that this stage allows students to learn from each other. Thus, students should be encouraged to ask questions of the writer after the presentation. This also enhances the writer's self-esteem and self-confidence. Having written a piece, the student has expanded his or her knowledge in that particular area.

Portfolios

It is a good idea to date all pieces of writing in the area of social studies and then have each student file his or her pieces in a *portfolio* of writing samples. As Kaltsounis (1990) points out, writing in social studies is both a method of assessing students' work and a tool of learning. Titles of books the student has read should also be listed and put in the portfolio. These books will then serve as resources or motivation for the child's own writing.

Periodically, perhaps once every month or evaluation period, the teacher and the student should review the student's progress together by examining the contents of the portfolio. The student can critique the various pieces, thereby engaging in self-evaluation to determine his or her own strengths, weaknesses, likes, and dislikes. Portfolio assessment also enables the child and the teacher to establish new goals.

Types of Writing

Four types of writing are appropriate for social studies. These are narrative, poetic, expository, and persuasive writing.

Haiku

Acid Rain
Rain falls slowly now
Trees will die from the acid
Man destroys nature.
Max, eleven years old

Parallel Poetry

Freedom
Freedom is powerful.
Freedom is being able to vote
for who you want.
Freedom is being able to walk
the streets.
Freedom is sharing the
responsibility for peace.
Freedom means being on
constant guard so no one
can take it away from you.
Group of ten-year-old students

Narrative writing can be described as story writing; that is, all the elements of a story, including character, plot, and setting, are present. There is a beginning, a middle, and an end. Children between 5 and 8 years old tend to use this form of writing for social studies.

Poetic writing, which is often ignored in content areas such as social studies, should be included in social studies instruction. Some forms of poetry offer natural links to social studies. Two of these are haiku poetry, three-line poems with five, seven, and five syllables per line

Slave Auction

Here I stand on the auction block,
Waiting my turn to be sold.
I clasp my sister's hand tightly,
youth wanting together to
grow old.
Will this be the last time we'll see each
other?
A man pulls her away as she cries and leaves.
We've already lost our father, our mother.
Now we are left to face the world
Alone.

JAKE fifth grade

respectively, which depict concern for and awareness of the environment, and parallel poetry or definition poems, which examine feelings or concepts. Examples of these two kinds of poetry are shown on page 81.

The sharing of children's literature can serve as a stimulus for writing poetry. For example, the picture book *Nettie's Trip South* (Turner, 1987) is a story that was inspired by the diary of the author's great-grandmother who, as a young child, took a trip in 1859 from her home in Albany, New York, to the southern states. On her journey, she viewed a slave auction firsthand. The book is a superb choice to share with students as part of a Civil War unit. Afterward, the students may, either individually or in small groups, compose poetry that reflects their own thoughts and feelings about what Nettie saw on her trip (Farris, 1993). Above is a poem from a fifth-grade student whose teacher had read *Nettie's Trip South* to her class.

Expository writing includes the writing of informational works, such as research reports. This type of writing may be done on an individual basis or, for older students, as a collaborative effort (Tompkins, 1990). Biographies, including historical biographies, also fall into this type of writing.

Students must narrow their topic for expository writing and develop questions to be answered. Then they should use the library to research the information. After gathering the information, students must organize it, write their first draft, and then revise and edit the piece.

Tompkins and Hoskisson (1991) suggest having the students write class collaboration reports as a form of expository writing. They divide their writing approach into six steps.

1. Choose a broad topic.
   For instance, the topic might be the Middle Ages.
2. Design research questions.
   Questions such as these would be appropriate: What kinds of work did people do in the Middle Ages? What kind of political system existed?
3. Gather and organize information.
   The students work in pairs to gather the information.
4. Draft sections of the report.
   Students use their notes to write their section reports. (It is helpful if the students skip every other line so they will have space for revising and editing later.)
5. Compile the sections.
   The students put together the sections, and the class as a group under the teacher's supervision writes the introduction, conclusion, and summary.
6. Publish the report.
   The final copy is published on a word processor if the students did not use a word processor for their section reports. Each student receives a copy of the final report.

Expository writing can also be used to introduce students to the use of references and a bibliography. A simple bibliography can be introduced as early as second grade by having the students write the name of the author and the title of the book on the last page of their reports. Later, a more elaborate bibliographical style can be introduced.

Persuasive writing includes propaganda. Students in grades 4 through 6 should be encouraged to write persuasive arguments as well as to learn the various devices of propaganda. Typically, a community or school issue provides an excellent opportunity for introducing students to this form of writing as it applies to social studies.

Discussion

In teaching social studies, the teacher must give children the opportunity to discuss topics of interest to them. This may be done by allowing groups of students to find a topic of common interest and to report back to the class about that topic. More formal types of discussion include panel presentations in which the students are assigned to or elect to serve in a group of three or four students. Each group member researches a specific aspect of the topic, and all members make the final presentation to the entire class.

■ Formal discussion, either in a debate or in a panel discussion, allows children to research a specific topic of their own choosing.

A structured form of discussion for older students is the debate. This very democratic process is a formal discussion of a topic, question, or issue in which opposing sides take turns presenting arguments to the audience. A timed format is established in advance for opening statements from both sides and questions from both sides and the audience. The audience evaluates the debate and votes for the winning team. Debates require the students to research their position and to develop oral language skills.

Through discussion, students develop both listening and speaking skills. They also develop confidence in speaking before their peers, something that is an asset later in life.

Reading, Writing, and Discussing as Learning Strategies

It is important to assist children in developing and applying the appropriate strategy for different types of reading materials. For instance, in gathering factual information about the economy of the state of Arizona as compared with that of New Mexico, a student may need to read graphs. However, locating information about the capital of the state of Iowa may require that the student be able to scan through text. To find the main idea of a political speech, the student must be able to skim for information and then create a summary.

SQ3R

A study strategy introduced over 40 years ago and still in wide use is SQ3R (Robinson, 1970). Students independently work through five steps:

1. *Surveying* the material by skimming through the chapter
2. Formulating *questions* by changing the chapter's subheadings into questions
3. *Reading* to answer the questions that were generated
4. *Reciting* answers to the questions after reading the chapter
5. *Reviewing* the answers to the questions

The SQ3R approach requires self-discipline and is probably best used with average to above average students at the middle and upper grade levels.

PQRST

A variation of SQ3R is PQRST (preview, question, review, summarize, and test), which was developed by Spache and Berg (1966). This strategy may be used independently or in pairs. It, too, involves five steps:

1. *Previewing* the material to get an idea of the primary emphasis and main points of the chapter or passage
2. Developing *questions* to be answered while reading the material
3. *Reviewing* what was read
4. *Summarizing* either orally or on paper the main points of the passage
5. *Testing* to find out how familiar the student is with the material

Literature Response Journals

Literature response journals allow students the freedom to write down their thoughts about a book as they read it. To identify what passage they are reading when they write down their comments and/or reactions, students jot down the page number in the margin. Students should be instructed to leave four or five lines space so that the teacher can question or respond to what they have written.

Students may elect to write as if they were the main character of a book or choose to write as if they were the main character's good friend. Students may make any comments or illustrations they wish in such journals. The teacher responds by asking short, provocative, nonjudgmental questions.

RAFT

RAFT was designed by Santa, Havens, and Harrison (1989) as a strategy for students to use to write for a specific audience. RAFT is an acronym for *role* of the writer, *audience* to whom the writing is directed, *format* of the writing, and *topic* of the piece itself.

The student identifies a theme about which to write, such as the Revolutionary War, identifies the audience, and then selects a format. Possible formats include advice columns, editorials, advertisements, horoscopes, invitations, diaries, journals, songs, obituaries, and poetry. Thus, a RAFT outline about the Revolutionary War might look like this:

R: Members of the Sons of Liberty
A: King George III
F: A rap song
T: Why people living in the New England colonies should support the separation of the colonies from England

At this point, the students create their own rap song to share with the class.

RESPONSE: An Interactive Approach to Study Skills

RESPONSE is yet another study strategy. Developed by Jacobson (1989), RESPONSE was designed with the purpose of creating interaction between the student and teacher.

The teacher assigns a passage or chapter to be read by the student. As the student reads the text, he or she uses a RESPONSE form to make notations, write down questions, and jot down unfamiliar concepts or names (see Figure 4.3).

Upon receiving the student's RESPONSE sheet, the teacher reviews it, responding to questions or unfamiliar terms that the student has marked with an asterisk (*). In addition, the teacher clarifies any errant statements or misunderstandings the student may have shown. For instance, in Figure 4.3, Kenny had written under "New Words/Concepts/Terms" "Patrick Henry" followed by "The Great Compromiser." However, Henry Clay was known as the "Great Compromiser," so Kenny had confused the two men. His teacher clarified the differences between Clay and Henry so that Kenny could better clarify the contributions of each of these leaders.

By combining all of the students' questions and unknown terms, the teacher gets a picture of what the students understand and what is unclear to them. Rather than trusting one's instincts as a teacher, RESPONSE serves as a more precise measure of what direction the class discussion should take.

By writing notes in the margins of the RESPONSE sheet, the teacher can give positive feedback to a student as well as offer guidance in finding information. In doing this, it is important to personalize the comments by using the student's first name. For instance, Carol Fuhler, Kenny's teacher, wrote this as her final comment to Kenny: "Very complete, Ken—nice job!"

FIGURE 4.5

■

Name: Kenny Maxwell   Date: Oct. 27, 1994

Chapter: Nine, Section 2

IMPORTANT POINTS: As you read, write down important information and the page on which you found the information.

p. 174 Patrick Henry and Samuel Adams thought that making the government more powerful would harm the freedoms won in the Revolutionary War

p. 174 The delegates decided to write a new constitution and give more power to the central government.

p. 174 They were called the Founding Fathers and the meeting was known as the Constitutional Convention. They met in 1787

p. 174 Each State had different concerns.

p. 177 Problems were settled by compromises

p. 177 Congress would have two houses—Senate and House of Representatives—both needed to agree on a law— The Great Compromise

p. 177 Three-Fifths Compromise— of every five slaves only three would be counted for tax.

p. 177 National government divided into three parts. Legislative made up of two houses of congress. They made the laws. Executive headed by the president. See that the laws of Congress were carried out. Communicated with foreign governments. Judicial the federal courts.

QUESTIONS: As you read, write down any questions that you may have along with the page number. Some questions will be for our class discussion. If you want an answer to a question, place an asterisk (*) by it.

p. 177 How could one part of the government make certain other part followed the law?

NEW WORDS/CONCEPTS/VOCABULARY/NAMES: Write the word or phrase along with the page number on which you found it. Place an asterisk (*) by those you would like to have defined or explained.

p. 174 Patrick Henry, "The Great Compromiser"

* p. 174 Three-Fifths Compromise

RESPONSE can be used as a group activity, with each student completing a RESPONSE sheet and then sharing the information with the other members of the group. The group then discusses each of the important points, questions, and words/concepts and creates a RESPONSE form that summarizes what the group believes is significant. The students hand in their individual forms and the group form to the teacher. Used in this manner, RESPONSE becomes a cooperative learning activity.

Cooperative Learning

While whole class instruction tends to be the predominate method of instruction, cooperative learning has proved to be an effective, noncompetitive instructional approach that allows for student interaction. According to Gunter, Estes, and Schwab (1990, p. 169) "Working *cooperatively* . . . may be the most critical social skill that students learn, when one considers the importance of cooperation in the workplace, in the family, and in leisure activities." Reading, writing, and discussing are essential elements of cooperative learning because each student must contribute to the group's overall success. The basic premise of cooperative learning is that each student must contribute in order for the goal of the group to be accomplished.

Calkins and Harwayne (1991) assert the need for children to be allowed to work cooperatively, in particular, to be given ample opportunities to interact and discuss with each other matters of substance. They point out that "If we were designing schools from start to finish, clearly we'd build in hours and hours of interactive learning. Youngsters need to talk about books, molecules, the Civil War, and current events" (p. 100).

Studies of children who have engaged in cooperative learning activities on a regular basis found that the students gained in self-esteem and were more accepting of cultural and individual differences (Slavin, 1983). Augustine, Gruber, and Hanson (1989–1990) are three elementary teachers who have used cooperative learning for several years in their classrooms (grades 3, 4, and 6). They believe that cooperative learning promotes higher achievement, develops social skills, and places the responsibility for learning on the student. According to Augustine, Gruber, and Hanson (p. 7), "If other educators believe as we do that higher achievement, increased acceptance of differences, improved attitudes toward school, and enhanced self-esteem are valuable goals for all children, then we all need to promote the continued use of cooperative learning."

Johnson and Johnson (1985), two of the leading proponents of cooperative learning, have found that cooperative learning can promote higher thinking skills as students are forced to clarify their own thinking as they explain issues to others.

Johnson and Johnson (1993) outlined five elements of cooperative learning. Each element is essential if cooperative learning is to be successfully established as an instructional strategy in a classroom. The elements particularly foster civics education. Here are the five elements:

1. Positive interdependence must be developed. The students must care about each other's learning and understand that "they are responsible for and benefit from one another's learning" (p. 44).
2. Students need lots of opportunities and time to interact with each other in discussions. They need to disclose, delineate, argue, expand, elaborate, bolster, and compromise on issues.
3. Individual accountability must be present in any cooperative learning activity. Students need to realize they are each responsible for their own learning. No free rides are available.
4. Social skills need to be taught in order for cooperative learning to be successful. Students need to understand how to communicate, serve as an effective group leader, build trust, compromise, and resolve differences.
5. Group processing, or group assessment needs to occur on a regular basis so that the group can determine its strengths and weaknesses and can determine how to perform better in the future.

A cooperative learning activity that can be used as part of a social studies unit is roulette writing (Farris, 1988). Students in groups of four or five each write about the same topic. After writing for approximately 3 minutes, each student hands his or her piece of writing to the student at the left. Upon receiving a new writing piece, the student reads what has been written and then continues the piece until the teacher indicates that it is time to pass the paper to the next writer. Each successive writer receives additional time to read what has already been written and to think about how to continue the work. The object of the activity is to continue the same theme and content the first writer in the group used. The last student who writes on the piece writes the conclusion. This is an excellent cooperative learning activity because a student need only contribute one sentence to be a part of a successful activity.

Figure 4.4 shows an example of roulette writing based on a pioneer unit in a fifth-grade class. This group's topic was "The Day Our School Burned Down." Different handwriting indicates where one student stopped writing and the next began.

Group investigation is another cooperative learning strategy that is effective in social studies instruction and relies on the use of reading, writing, and discussion skills. Sharan and Sharan (1989–1990) believe that group investigation focuses on children's individual interests and gives them control over their learning. Children are grouped by common interests, and then they plan what they will study and how. All members of the group plan and discuss what they will research, or investigate. The

FIGURE 4.4

■

An example of roulette writing.

The Day Our School Burned Down

The year was 1870. It was hot, and we found it difficult to pay attention to the teacher in the stuffy class room. The building was all made of wood.

Laura Ingalls was our teacher. She tried disparately to make the day a good one but it was no use, it was just too hot. She dismissed us earlier than usual. We all ran across the lane to the creek.

While playing in the creeks, we noticed a grey cloud of smoke rising above the trees. We followed the smoke to see where it came from. It was our school! Our school was on fire! Miss Ingalls ran to the saw mill down the road to get Pa Ingalls. We and the other mill workers began bringing water down to put out the fire.

But it was too late. The school was gone and so too was the church. Where would we learn and pray? The children cried.

The adults cried. Then Pa Ingalls prayed for divine guidance. Right then we decided to rebuild. The debris would be cleaed tomorrow and the next day everyone would come and help build a new school. The children could do the running, the women the cooking, and the men the building. Yes we would have a bigger and better schoolhouse than before. We'd even have new desks, slates and books. It'd be hard work, but together we could do it.

group then divides the work, giving each member a task to carry out as part of the overall investigation. The entire group reviews, synthesizes, and condenses into a summary the information gathered through individual research and then presents the summary to the entire class.

In group investigation, the teacher initially presents a broad, multi-faceted topic to the class for discussion. Groups are formed as subtopics emerge and students indicate their interests. The groups then plan how they will investigate their particular subtopic and then carry out their research investigations. Next, the groups reconvene to review and discuss all of the information gathered as well as to synthesize, analyze, and summarize the information in their final report. Then all groups present the final reports (Sharan & Sharan, 1989–1990).

Timely issues are especially good for group investigation because students tend to have a high degree of interest in current events. Jodie Williams, a sixth-grade teacher, uses group investigation as an effective research strategy for her students. During the Persian Gulf War (Operation Desert Storm), Jodie's students became actively involved in following the events of the war. Jodie gave her class the broad topic of how the events in the Middle East affect our lives and those of people in other nations of the world. The students came up with several subtopics: United States dependence on foreign oil, the role of the United Nations Security Council, religious differences, the role of neutral nations (Israel and Jordan) in the

Persian Gulf War, the wealth of oil sheiks and how it is used, and whether all the allied nations should send military assistance or whether providing financial assistance was sufficient.

The students divided into groups on the basis of their own interests. Each group then narrowed the group's topic, brainstormed for more refined subtopics, and developed a set of questions. Each group then discussed the work and allocated it to individual group members. Members divided the questions among themselves to help guide each person's inquiry.

Jodie served as a facilitator for the class by bringing in atlases and reference books about the Middle East. Since she was unfamiliar with the region, she scurried to research information to add to her own knowledge base and understanding as well. Students brought in daily newspapers and weekly newsmagazines. They videotaped television news from CNN and brought the tapes to class not only for the use of members of their own group but other groups as well.

As part of the thematic unit, Jodie enlisted the assistance of her school's media specialist to find historical fiction, biographies, and contemporary fiction relating to the nations of the Middle East for the students to read. The students were allowed to select one book to read from among the books Jodie and the media specialist had gathered. The students then shared the information they found with their respective groups.

Jodie moved around the classroom and media center observing the students as they diligently gathered and read the information and took notes of what they thought they needed to share with their respective groups. Jodie, too, was armed with paper and pencil as she noted each student's work.

Upon reconvening the groups a few days later, Jodie noted how each student contributed to the group's overall goal and topic. The groups were allowed to sign up for specific time slots for their presentations to the class as a whole.

Since many of the students had relatives or friends who were serving in the Persian Gulf region, Jodie knew the broad topic would be of great interest to the students. The final reports proved her correct. The students were highly informed as to the commonalities and differences between the Middle Eastern countries and those of the allied forces. A major discussion ensued on the ethics of war, who should and should not participate, and to what degree. The quick and successful ending of the war resulted in the class holding a welcome home party for some of the relatives and friends who had taken part in Operation Desert Storm.

Summary

Reading, writing, and discussion skills are important in social studies instruction. Recently published children's literature offers students new perspectives and insights into the social studies. This literature can not only be used to stimulate reading and discussion but to suggest ideas for writing as well.

The writing process is composed of five stages: prewriting, drafting, revising, editing, and publishing/sharing. Through these stages, the students reflect on what they want to convey to their audience of readers and how their message will be interpreted. Among the different types of writing are narrative, poetic, persuasive, and expository writing.

Along with the process approach in writing, a similar approach should be introduced in reading. Students need to learn to use a variety of reading strategies for different types of text.

In developing communication skills, it is important to foster group interaction. Cooperative learning is one way to encourage the interdependence of students when conducting small group activities or projects.

Reading, writing, and discussing are essential in the development and refinement of thinking skills. By encouraging the development of these skills, the classroom teacher can assist students in some very fundamental aspects of being a good citizen. Without these skills, it is questionable whether a democracy can exist.

Children's Books

Bunting, E. (1988). *How many days to America?* (B. Peck, Illus.). Boston: Clarion Books.

Boat people from the Carribean flee to America.

Greaves, M. (1985). *Once there were no pandas.* New York: Dutton.

A Chinese folktale about the origin of panda bears.

Hesse, K. (1992). *Letters from Rifka.* New York: Henry Holt.

A journal is kept by a young girl as her family flees the Russian Revolution in 1919.

Hooks, W. H. (1990). *The ballad of Belle Dorcas.* New York: Knopf.

A Southern folktale about a magical woman who wants a husband.

Hoyt-Goldsmith, D. (1991). *Pueblo storyteller.* (L. Migdale, Photog.). New York: Holiday House.

A young Pueblo Indian girl, the tribal storyteller, tells the old tales of her tribe.

MacLachlan, P. (1985). *Sarah, plain and tall.* New York: Harper & Row.

Sarah is a mail order bride who leaves her home in Maine to travel to the plains of Nebraska.

Myers, W. D. (1991). *Now is your time! The African American struggle for freedom.* New York: Harper Collins.

A nonfiction historical account of African Americans in America.

Nixon J. L. (1992). *Land of hope.* New York: Bantam Starfire.

A young Jewish girl escapes Russia in the early 1900s and yearns for an education.

Nixon J. L. (1993). *Land of promise.* New York: Bantam Starfire.

Kristyn, a very independent girl, leaves Sweden for a life on a Minnesota farm in the early 1900s.

Nixon J. L. (1994). *Land of dreams.* New York: Bantam Starfire.

Rose, an Irish Catholic, comes to America to live with her family in Chicago early in the 20th century.

Paterson, K. (1991). *Lyddie.* New York: Dutton/Lodestar.

Lyddie works in the cotton mills of Massachusetts during the Industrial Revolution. Child labor and working conditions are examined in this book.

Rhodes, E. H. (1985). *All for the Union.* New York: Orion.

The actual diary of a Union soldier during the Civil War.

Rylant, C. (1982). *When I was young and in the mountains.* (D. Goode, Illus.). New York: Dutton.

This book portrays life in the Appalachian Mountains.

Stanley, J. (1992). *Children of the Dust Bowl: The true story of the school at Weedpatch Camp.* New York: Crown.

True stories of Oklahoma families who lived in Weedpatch Camp in California during the Great Depression.

Turner, A. (1987). *Nettie's trip south.* (R. Himler, Illus.). New York: Macmillan.

The author depicts life in the South before the Civil War as her great-great grandmother wrote about it in a diary.

Turner, A. (1992). *Katie's trunk* (R. Himler, Illus.). New York: Macmillan.

The actual experiences of a Tory family at the beginning of the American Revolution.

Weitzman, D. (1982). *Windmills, bridges, and old machines: Discovering our industrial past.* New York: Macmillan.

A nonfiction book that relates inventions to industrial efficiency.

Wisniewski, D. (1991). *Rain player.* New York: Clarion Books.

A Mayan Indian legend about a young boy who challenges the rain god to a ball game.

Yep, L. (1991). *Tongues of jade* (D. Wiesner, Illus.). New York: Harpercollins.

Seventeen Chinese folktales are shared in this book.

References

Abel, F., Hauwiller, J., & Vandeventer, N. (1989). Using writing to teach social studies. *Social Studies, 80*(1), 17-20.

Alvermann, D., Smith, L. C., & Readance, J. E. (1985). Prior knowledge activation and the comprehension of compatible and incompatible text. *Reading Research Quarterly, 20*(4), 420-36.

Augustine, D. K., Gruber, K. D. & Hanson, L. R. (1989-1990). Cooperation works! *Educational Leadership, 47*(4), 4-7.

Banks, J. A. (1991-1992). Multicultural education for freedom's sake. *Educational Leadership, 49*(4), 32-35.

Bishop, R. S. (1987). Extending multicultural understanding through children's books. In B. Cullinan (Ed.), *Children's literature in the reading program* (pp. 60-67). Newark, DE: International Reading Association.

Boyer, E. L. (1990). Civic education for responsible citizens. *Educational Leadership, 48*(3), 4-7.

Britton, J. (1978). The composing process and the functions of writing. In C. R. Cooper & L. O'Dell (Eds.), *Research on composing: Points of departure.* Urbana, IL: National Council of Teachers of English.

Burns, K. (1990). *The Civil War.* Public Broadcasting System.

Calkins, L. M., & Harwayne, S. (1991). *Living between the lines.* Portsmouth, NH: Heinemann.

DeMott, B. (1990). Why we read and write. *Educational Leadership, 47*(6), 6.

Farris, P. J. (1988). Roulette writing. *Reading Teacher 42*(1), 91.

Farris, P. J. (1993). *Language arts: A process approach.* Dubuque, IA: Brown & Benchmark.

Graves, D. H. (1983). *Writing: Teachers and children at work.* Portsmouth, NH: Heinemann.

Gunter, M. A., Estes, T. H., & Schwab, J. H. (1990). *Instruction: A models approach.* Boston: Allyn & Bacon.

Huck, C. S. (1990). The power of children's literature in the classroom. In K. Short & K. Piece (Eds.), *Talking about books (pp. 3-16).* Portsmouth, NH: Heinemann.

Jacobson, J. M. (1989). RESPONSE: An interactive study technique. *Reading Horizons, 29*(2), 85-92.

Johnson, D. W., & Johnson, R. T. (1993). What to say to advocates for the gifted. *Educational Leadership 50*(2), 44-47.

Johnson, R. T., & Johnson, D. W. (1985). Student-student interaction, ignored but powerful. *Journal of Teacher Education, 36*(6), 22-26.

Kaltsounis, T. (1990). Interrelationships between social studies and other curriculum areas: A review. *Social Studies, 81*(6), 283-286.

Kohn, A. (1991). Caring kids: The role of the schools. *Phi Delta Kappan, 72*(7), 496-506.

Kuhrt, B. L. (1989). The effects of expressive writing on the composing and learning processes of sixth-grade students in social studies. DeKalb, IL: Northern Illinois University.

Langer, J., & Applebee, A. (1987). *How writing shapes thinking: A study of teaching and learning* (NCTE Research Report No. 22). Urbana, IL: National Council of Teachers of English.

McGowan, T., & Guzzetti, B. (1991). Promoting social studies understanding through literature-based instruction. *Social Studies, 33*(4), 16-21.

Murray, D. (1984). *Write to learn.* New York: Holt, Rinehart & Winston.

Reimer, K. M. (1992). Multiethnic literature: Holding fast to dreams. *Language Arts, 69*(1), 14-21.

Rico, G. L. (1983). *Writing the natural way.* Los Angeles: Tarcher.

Robinson, F. P. (1970). *Effective study.* New York: Harper & Row.

Santa, C., Havens, L., & Harrison, S. (1989). Teaching secondary science through reading, writing, studying, and problem solving. In D. Lapp, J. Flood, & N. Farnan (Eds.), *Content area reading and learning* (pp. 137-151). Englewood Cliffs, NJ: Prentice-Hall.

Schaps, E., & Solomon, D. (1990). Schools and classrooms as caring communities. *Educational Leadership, 48*(3), 38-42.

Sharan, Y., & Sharan, S. (1989-1990). Group investigation expands cooperative learning. *Educational Leadership, 47*(4), 17-21.

Slavin, R. (1983). *Cooperative learning.* New York: Longman.

Spache, G. D., & Berg, P. C. (1966). *The art of efficient learning.* New York: Macmillan.

Tompkins, G. E. (1990). *Teaching writing.* Columbus, OH: Merrill.

Tompkins, G. E., & Hoskisson, K. (1991). *Language arts: Content and teaching strategies* (2nd ed.) Columbus, OH: Merrill.

Walley, C. (1991). Diaries, logs, and journals in the elementary classroom. *Childhood Education, 67*(3), 149-154.

Another Time, Another Place: Bringing Social Studies to Life Through Literature

MARJORIE R. HANCOCK
KANSAS STATE UNIVERSITY

"The thread of people's lives weaves through the past,

the present, and into the future. . . .

Through the pages of historical fiction,

the past becomes alive."

DONNA E. NORTON

Through the Eyes of a Child, 3rd Ed.

[*Chapter Five*]
■

Introduction

Just as literature brings life to the philosophy of whole language, so too does literature breathe life into an elementary social studies program. The wealth of literature linked to social studies spans all literary genre and provides a complement, indeed a possible alternative, to the factualized textbook that has long been the mainstay of the traditional social studies curriculum. Levstik (1990, p. 850) quotes a fifth grader who preferred reading historical novels about the Revolutionary War rather than her social studies textbook. According to this student, the textbook "just says that Americans were right, but it doesn't tell you exactly why they were right or why the British fought."

The trend toward whole language instruction and its dependence on literature has obviously influenced an explosive increase in quality children's trade books, many of which are linked to the teaching of social studies. This new bounty of literature is embellished with rich, realistic detail and historical characters with whom the reader may easily identify; it also provides an unprecedented way to make social studies interesting and meaningful to the elementary reader. Literature has the power to transport readers to another place and allow them to become a part of it. Literature provides the opportunity to transport readers to another time and allow them to become a part of history. Literature possesses the magic to bring social studies to life and, at the same time, to bring deeper understanding and meaning to students of social studies.

What child, for example, could resist the detailed research, captivating titles, and lively biographies of Jean Fritz, including *Bully for You, Teddy Roosevelt* (1991) and *The Great Little Madison* (1989)? What child's imagination would not be aroused by the vivid geographic descriptions of Diane Siebert's (1990) *Sierra*? What child's empathy for the trials of our westward pioneers would not be enhanced by living through the realistic drama and bitter tragedy of Pam Conrad's *Prairie Songs* (1985) or *My Daniel* (1989) or Ann Turner's *Grasshopper Summer* (1989)? What child would not like to be invited to compare his or her own classroom to those in *Going to School in 1876* (Loeper, 1984)? What child could not develop an understanding of the Great Depression while reading *As Far as*

Mill Springs by Patricia Pendergraft (1991)? What child could not be touched by the power of a memorial as described in Brent Ashabranner's (1992) *A Memorial for Mr. Lincoln*?

Whole language advocates have strongly encouraged teachers to expand the use of literature in their classrooms to enhance reading and writing (Cullinan, 1987). Now the literature connection is also being extended to the realm of social studies as a means of personalizing and making the social sciences more relevant to the lives and needs of students (Ammon & Weigard, 1993; Ceprano & English, 1990; Sanacore, 1990). Quality children's literature linked to the social studies curriculum encompasses both geographic and historical concepts. It also encompasses a variety of literary genre (picture books, folklore, poetry, historical fiction, biography, informational books) that have been found to provide effective links to the curriculum (Johnson & Ebert, 1992; Moir, 1992).

The purpose of this chapter is to provide the classroom teacher with a supply of ideas for incorporating literature into a whole language social studies program. Practical reading and writing applications supported by recent research and built around the literary genre of picture books, historical fiction, and biography will be suggested. The whole language ideal of thematic units will be addressed through sample concept-based units. These whole language applications of literature to an elementary social studies program provide only a beginning for classroom teachers as they start to bring social studies to life through the use of literature. Their personal perspectives, knowledge of literature, and related activities can provide even further impetus for implementing a whole language perspective of elementary social studies.

From Sea to Shining Sea: Across the U.S.A. with Picture Books

Picture books have been found to be an excellent means of conveying an understanding of both geography and history to elementary level students (Dowd, 1990; Pritchard, 1989; Sisson, 1990). Once considered the realm of the primary grades, picture books now provide a means of adding a lively dimension to social studies teaching, whatever the age or grade of the student. Quality picture books can capture student interest in the places associated with characters. Picture books with geographic features motivate student interest in maps and geographic information (Levstik, 1985). As Louie (1993, p. 17) writes: "Whereas textbooks present factual information and explanation, literature can make geographic concepts come alive for children. When teachers use literature as a medium to teach location, they also extend children's love of stories to geographic concepts.

A challenging means of combining a geography and history trip across the nation is through an exploration of children's picture books with settings from throughout the United States. The integration of social studies, reading, and writing is effectively accomplished through a classroom journey in which a combination of picture books transports students to another time and another place and also provides regional information about the United States today.

A large outline map of the United States is required for this journey. Throughout the unit (or even throughout the school year), names and symbols of books will be added to this map, until it finally becomes a class mural.

A whole class activity built around *Alphabet Annie Announces an All-American Alphabet Book* (Purviance & O'Shell, 1988) can serve as an introduction to the entire United States. This alphabet book is composed of a series of alliterative sentences that include the names of American cities and the characteristic traits of each (for example, "Susie Strauss skis, sings, and strums on the slopes of Sun Valley"). Each city can be located on the classroom map.

The opportunity for research and writing is encouraged later as students create their own book, using states instead of cities. Each group of students chooses a region of the country, and each group member chooses one or more states within that region about which to write an alliterative sentence. Resource books on the 50 states, encyclopedias, and atlases will help students locate appropriate words. For example, "Melissa Missoula masterfully managed the mountains and mines of Montana." These alliterative sentences are then compiled in an illustrated class book, and each state sentence is inscribed on the class map.

Students' initial exposure to the entire United States can be further enhanced by an oral reading and discussion of *Anno's U.S.A.* (Anno, 1983). This horseback journey from west to east through the cities and the countryside combines a view of the culture and history of America. Attention to detail will reveal visual discoveries about our country. Anno's journey across the nation may even be traced with a colored line on the map.

In a similar manner, Vera and Jennifer Williams's (1988) *Stringbean's Trip to the Shining Sea* (1988) can be shared orally. In this book, Stringbean and his brother take a trip in a truck from Kansas to the Pacific Ocean. The book is composed of a series of picture postcards, written messages, and snapshots taken en route. Stringbean's journey can also be traced with a colored line on the map, and students can draw or bring in postcards to enhance the map.

A sampling of picture books dealing with the various regions and states of the United States are briefly described in the rest of this section.

The Northeast

Let's journey to Maine where Peter Parnell's *Winter Barn* (1986) provides the tranquil setting for the activities of creatures who inhabit a memorable barn during the long, cold New England winter. Moving to Vermont, the reader experiences the family tradition of gathering sap for boiling into maple syrup in *Sugaring Time* (Lasky, 1982). A good companion book is *Farmboy's Year* (McPhail, 1992) which evokes a boy's life on a New

■ By reading picture books about different areas across the United States, children learn about the geography and history of the various regions of our country.

England farm in the 1800's. The work, dress, leisure, and education of today's Pennsylvania Amish are shown in informative black and white photographs of a peaceful and meaningful way of life in *Where Time Stands Still* (Foster, 1987). *The Inside-Outside Book of Washington, D.C.* (Munro, 1986) captures the spirit of the nation's capital as the interiors and exteriors of 12 sites are presented in detailed illustrations. Young readers of *In Coal Country* (Hendershot, 1987) are transported back in time to a small Ohio coalmining town of the 1930s. The author's roots in a family of coal miners and the illustrator's experience of growing up during the Great Depression combine to capture the pride of a vanishing way of American life.

The Southeast

On Grandaddy's Farm (Allen, 1989) offers a nostalgic visit to Tennessee in the 1930s. The serene, rustic setting and simple pleasures of times gone by evoke a vivid sense of America's past. Although the chores and responsibilities were demanding, there was plenty of time for having fun and making memories for the hard working farm family depicted in this book.

■ Picture books offer rich illustrations that add to a child's vision of what life is like in another part of our country.

The folk traditions of Appalachia are captured in a fanciful collection of rhymes, riddles, and verse aptly titled *Granny Will Your Dog Bite? And Other Mountain Rhymes* (Milnes, 1990). These humorous portrayals can be tempered with Cynthia Rylant's (1991) serious recollections of the land where she grew up, in *Appalachia: The Voices of Sleeping Birds.* Several of Rylant's books reveal her memories of growing up in the Appalachian Mountains.

North Central States

The agricultural belt of the Midwest and Great Plains is the next stop on our literary journey. *Heartland* (Siebert, 1989) portrays the seasons and places of America's heartland in lyrical verse and color paintings that reveal the essence of farm and small-town life. Westward migration through the rugged north central region is described in *Cassie's*

Journey: Going West in the 1860s (Harvey, 1988). The daily rigors of the wagon train, the reality of flood and drought, the tragedy of buffalo stampedes and death are realistically retold from true accounts kept by women on their journey west. As for those who ventured no farther, *Dakota Dugout* (Turner, 1985) describes the hardships and joys of a sodbuster. *Klara's New World* (Winter, 1992) describes 19th century immigrants from Sweden to rural America. Likewise, *Going West* (Van Leeuwen, 1992) provides insights into pioneer life on the prairie—the joy of moving into a newly built cabin and the delight of having a new neighbor.

In *My Prairie Year* (1986), Brett Harvey has taken the words of her homesteading grandmother and shared her experiences on the vast prairie of the Dakotas. The raging tornadoes and the unending blizzards of winter were but two of the realities pioneer families faced.

The Southwest

Turning southward, the literary road leads to Texas and *The Best Town in the World* (Baylor, 1983). Life in this small country town in the Texas hills around the turn of the century seems little different from that of many American towns of that era. However, its residents take special pride in it. While in Texas, share Tomie de Paola's Comanche tale, *The Legend of the Bluebonnet: An Old Tale of Texas* (1983). The beautiful state flower results from the selflessness of an Indian girl who sacrifices her dearest possession to bring rain to save her people. Stephen Kellogg's tall tale *Pecos Bill* (1986) describes how the title character is raised by a pack of coyotes and grows up to become a legendary Texas cowboy.

The many faces of the desert area of the Southwest are portrayed in the lyrical poem *Mohave* (Siebert, 1988), which captures the Mohave's lonely beauty.

The Far West

The character of the Northwest is often linked to its ties to westward expansion. Our literary journey westward leads us to *Long Ago in Oregon* (Lewis, 1987), a series of poetic vignettes set in an Oregon town in 1917. The daily lives of the townspeople in this book reveal their strong character and determination, traits necessary for the settling of this seemingly remote part of the country.

Western folklore and legends abound. *The Cremation of Sam McGee* (Service, 1987) details the adventures of a Yukon prospector during the Alaskan gold rush. Among the legends of the huge expanse of remote western mountains and valleys is *The Legend of the Indian Paintbrush* (de Paola, 1988), the story of a beautiful western flower. Paul Goble's (1985) *The Great Race of the Birds and Animals* recounts a Cheyenne myth of the Indians' close relationship with nature.

Linking the Regions Together

As teachers read a wide selection of books to their students and students read even more books independently, the mural map will come alive with literary memories of the regions of the United States. Students might record the author, title, location, and time period of each book on a slip of paper and attach it in the proper place on the map. They might also draw a picture or symbol of each story on the map to create a permanent memory of each book read. Lila Perl's (1992) *It Happened in America* is a superb book to share with a class as it contains stories from pre-colonial times to present day, with stories from all fifty states.

Discovering our country's geography and history through picture books can be a unit lasting a few weeks. It can also be expanded to cover the entire school year. What is created on the classroom wall map is a collage of literature experiences ranging in time from the founding of our country to the present and ranging in location "from sea to shining sea."

Meeting Famous People Face-to-Face Through Biography

Biography has provided a natural literature link to social studies for decades. The serial biographies of the past provided dry, factual information about famous people. Current authors, however, have begun to present authentic, flesh-and-blood individuals to elementary grade readers by relating interesting historical information in a realistic and entertaining manner. Authors such as Jean Fritz, Charles Freedman, and Diane Stanley have introduced students to the multidimensional characteristics of famous people and their public and private lives.

Children in the intermediate grades seem to be almost magnetically drawn to the achievements of those who have overcome obstacles on their journey toward personal success. According to Levstik (1993), older elementary students link themselves closely with biographical characters. Biographies enable readers to experience real life vicariously by tapping the experiences of achievers while providing a historical context for understanding such people's lives. Biographies are written about people who have had a positive impact on society and therefore leave the reader with an optimistic view of his or her potential as an individual in our society (Zarnowski, 1990).

Perhaps Jean Fritz's explanation of the appeal of biography over time and generations best explains why biographical accounts should be included in the social studies curriculum.

> We all seek insight into the human condition, and it is helpful to
> find familiar threads running through the lives of others,
> however famous. We need to know more people in all

circumstances and times so we can pursue our private, never-to-be-fulfilled quest to find out what life is all about. (Quoted in Commire, 1982, p. 84)

Extending biography beyond famous individuals in American history to those renowned throughout the world can increase student awareness of the traits that characterize past and present global leaders. Two activities can be used to bring children face-to-face with historical figures. The first involves exposing students to picture book biographies and then having the students write biographical poems (bio-poems) describing traits of these famous individuals. The second activity, geared more toward intermediate level students, involves making biographical comparisons to better understand the researching and writing of biographies of famous figures. An author study and comparative biographical readings focus on the process of biography and can eventually lead students to biographical composition efforts.

From Simple Biographies to Bio-Poems

A plentiful supply of simple biographies that combine a picture book format with historical data on a famous person are available for third- through fifth-grade students. Reading these biographies, learning the historical background surrounding a famous person, and incorporating a related writing activity are an efficient way to use a whole language approach to social studies. Picture book biographies by David Adler, such as *A Picture Book of Martin Luther King, Jr.* (1989) and *A Picture Book of Benjamin Franklin* (1990), are brief but accurate accounts of the lives of famous Americans. Similarly, Diane Stanley's (1986) *Peter the Great* and Aliki's (1989) *The King's Day: Louis XIV of France* introduce the young reader to famous world leaders.

A related writing activity emerging naturally from a study of historical figures involves composing a nine-line "bio-poem" (Danielson, 1989) about the individuals portrayed in picture book biographies. Here is the format of the nine-line bio-poem:

Line 1: First name of biographical subject
Line 2: Four adjectives describing the subject
Line 3: Husband/wife/sibling, etc., of . . .
Line 4: Lover of . . . (three people, places, things)
Line 5: Who feels . . . (three things)
Line 6: Who fears . . . (three things)
Line 7: Who would like to see . . . (three things)
Line 8: Resident of . . . (city, state, country)
Line 9: Last name of biographical subject

Following the reading of *Good Queen Bess* (Stanley and Venneman, 1990), Sarah, a sixth-grade student, composed a biopoem highlighting the personality and achievement of Queen Elizabeth I of England. (See figure 5.1.)

F I G U R E   5 . 1

■

By writing and sharing biographical poetry about famous leaders, students gain greater insights into historical figures.

(handwritten poem)

Elizabeth I
Well-educated, intelligent, cautious, loyal
Daughter of Henry VIII and Anne Boleyn
Lover of England, Robert Dudley, and her loyal subjects
Who feels more powerful than most men, capable of ruling her homeland, and proud to serve her people
Who fears her imprisonment in the Tower, leaving no heir to the throne, and the treasonous Mary Queen of Scots
Who would like to see the defeat of the Spanish Armada, the flowering of the Elizabethan Age, and herself remembered as a great monarch
Resident of London
Queen of England 1558-1603.

A collection of such bio-poems may be displayed on a "Who's Who" bulletin board. A class discussion often elicits common traits, goals, and accomplishments of famous people. The bio-poem provides an encapsulated view of these people.

Becoming an Expert on Biographers and Their Subjects

Becoming a "biography buff" (Zarnowski, 1990) involves not only learning about famous historical figures but also learning about the literary genre of biography in the process. Students can become biography buffs by reading (1) biographies of different subjects written by the same author and (2) biographies about the same subject written by different authors. Some specific examples and suggestions should help further this use of biography in the social studies curriculum.

Several children's authors have become known for their special treatment of historical figures in their well-written, award-winning biographies. Ingri and Edgar d'Aulaire, Jean Fritz, Milton Meltzer, F. N. Monjo, and Diane Stanley have each written a number of high-quality biographies of historical figures.

An interesting whole language idea is to study not only the historical characters biographers portray in their works but to become an expert on the biographers themselves. Students can do this by reading several biographies by the same author. For example, Jean Fritz is known for her motivating titles of books about Revolutionary War heroes, including *And Then What Happened, Paul Revere?* (1973), *Can't You Make them Behave, King George?* (1982), *Where Was Patrick Henry on the 29th of May?* (1975), *Why Don't You Get a Horse, Sam Adams?* (1974), and *Will You Sign Here, John Hancock?* (1976). Students not only learn from and enjoy the unique portrayals of these historical subjects but may come to understand the significance and style of biography itself. An analysis of Fritz's books for writing style, sense of humor, historical accuracy and documentation, characterization, and theme can provide students with some general insights into Fritz's process of writing her biographies.

Ideas gleaned from a similar analysis of several works by the same author may inspire a young writer of biography to research and construct a biographical sketch of a favorite historical personality. Other authors to study include F. N. Monjo, who often tells his stories from an outsider's point of view as in *Poor Richard in France* (1973) and *King George's Head Is Made of Lead* (1974), which are each told from a statue's point of view. Milton Meltzer is another biographer famous for his use of authentic voices and words from the past, as in *Voices from the Civil War* (1989), with excerpts from documents, diaries, interviews, and speeches. Russell Freedman's photobiographic essays, including *Indian Chiefs* (1987a), *Lincoln: A Photobiography* (1987b), and *Franklin Delano Roosevelt* (1990), provide another means of sharing biography. The varied techniques of these biographers introduce exemplary styles and models for young biographers in the elementary classroom.

Another way to become a biography buff is to become an expert on one historical figure by reading several biographies of the same person. A comparison and contrast chart can be used to determine each author's portrayal of the subject's strengths and weaknesses, use of authentic materials for conveying the story (maps, documents, photographs, and so on), style of writing (point of view/tone), documentation, and type of biography (complete/partial). Such comparisons and contrasts may reveal a variety of information, even conflicting information, on the subject. As a culminating activity students might write a biographical sketch of the character, gleaning information, style, and means of presentation from the assorted biographies read.

For example, through the years, many authors have attempted to capture the life of Abraham Lincoln in their own special styles. The d'Aulaires' (1957) classic, illustrated portrayal of the life of Lincoln is a good place to begin. In contrast, Russell Freedman won a Newbery Medal for *Lincoln: A Photobiography* (1987b). Other authors have presented portions of Lincoln's life, including Carl Sandburg (1985) in *Abe Lincoln Grows Up* and Richard Kigel (1986) in *The Frontier Years of Abe Lincoln*. These titles serve only as a beginning for developing expertise on this great statesman. Students' comparisons and contrasts will begin to clarify their own preference for biographical portrayal and lead them toward the development of their own written portrayal of Lincoln or another figure.

On the other hand, students might focus on biographies that have won the Newbery Medal or explore series biographies for characteristic traits of chosen subjects. A theme, such as explorers, also invites students to compare and contrast the subjects of biography.

The possibilities seem unlimited as whole language brings social studies and the genre of biography together in a meaningful reading and writing interaction. Whole language's emphasis on process supports the use of author studies and comparative studies to assist young writers in developing their own writing style. The integration of reading and writing through the use of biography epitomizes the philosophy of the whole language approach.

Sharing Personal Responses to Historical Fiction Through Journals

Historical fiction has long-held literary ties to the social studies curriculum. The benefits of using historical fiction to enhance social studies instruction have been enumerated (Cianciolo, 1981; Gallo & Barksdale, 1983; Odland, 1980). Historical fiction can help children "experience the past—to encounter into the conflicts, the suffering, and the despair of those who lived before us. . . . Well-written historical fiction offers young people the vicarious experience of participating in the life of the past" (Huck, Hepler, & Hickman, 1993, p. 600). The case for historical fiction has been convincing indeed. Teachers have traditionally responded by reading historical fiction aloud to their classes and by assigning book reports on historical fiction.

Recently, however, a response-based view of the role of children's literature in the elementary classroom has been brought to the attention of researchers and teachers (Galda, 1988); that is, children are encouraged to respond to literature by writing as they read. Research informs us that written language captures ideas concretely and may even influence the development of reading (Langer & Applebee, 1987).

The need for encouraging personal responses to literature has been supported by Louise Rosenblatt (1976, 1978), whose transactional theory of reader response articulates the essential reciprocal relationship

■ Literature response journals allow for the aesthetic to be part of the social studies curriculum.

between the reader and the literary text. Likewise, children as readers have their own story to tell as they interact with the pages of a book. The reader response theory further suggests that readers be active participants in making meaning from the literature they encounter (Probst, 1984).

Too often, when teachers assign historical fiction "book reports," students choose a book from a list and summarize the content after they have read the book. But what about the informative thoughts they experienced *while* reading the book? What about these connections students have made with the historical facts that have become part of their reading schema? How can those connections be captured so that teachers and students alike can experience the link between historical fiction and historical fact?

Responding to historical fiction by writing in a variety of journal formats is an effective way of capturing this personal interaction of the reader with a part of history brought alive through quality children's literature. While the textbook may be essential for presenting the facts of a historical period, the catalyst that can bring those facts to life may be books of historical fiction that place "real" characters in "authentic" periods of history allowing the reader to "live through" the life and times portrayed.

The insightful interaction of the reader with historical fiction may be lost if thoughts, emotions, and responses are not permanently captured throughout the reading of the book. The solution, therefore, is to capture the internal connections between historical fact and historical fiction by writing in a response journal. A historical response journal and/or a character journal aids students in connecting fact and fiction by vicariously experiencing an unfolding piece of history as they read historical fiction.

Historical Fiction Response Journals

A response journal is a place for students to express their thoughts, insights, feelings, reactions, questions, connections, and opinions while reading a book (Hancock, 1991). According to Hancock (1993), "Written response to literature is a powerful means of preserving those special transactions with books that make reading a rewarding, personal journey" (p. 467). The teacher might give brief talks on a variety of historical fiction books geared to a particular period of American or world history. After the students have personally chosen one of these books, the teacher should encourage them to record their individual thoughts while they are reading the book. Students must be assured that the journals will not be graded and that spelling and punctuation will not be corrected. Emphasis should be on the free expression of ideas as the students interact with literature.

The resultant journal entries may indicate a transfer of the reader to another time and place in history. Readers tend to bring life to fictional characters, and the students may talk to, advise, and judge the actions of a character within the context of history in their journal entries. The students may also make mention of historical facts and names that are part of the background for reading and discuss the historical setting. In reading journal entries, the teacher may discover the personal connection with history as a student assumes the guise of a fictional character. Identification with a character can transport the reader to a historical period that is brought alive through reading.

Some teachers find it difficult to turn students loose with an assignment as free as the foregoing. They prefer giving students a list of response prompts that focus their responses more on the historical aspects of the books they are reading. Here are a few sample response prompts:

> What historical facts are mentioned in the book that you already knew from our study of this historical period?
>
> What new and interesting historical facts were presented?
>
> How does the life of the main character fit into the historic period (education, dress, social expectations)?
>
> How do the actions of the main character fit into the standards of the historical period?
>
> What impression of life during this historical period is projected?

If teachers prefer prompts to free expression and impressions, it is still essential to capture responses to these prompts *while* the students are reading the book rather than retrospectively after they have completed it. Growth of understanding of the historical period can only be indicated through the unfolding reactions of the reader during the reading process.

Character Journals

Another interesting way of extending response to historical fiction while assuring the reader's vicarious interaction with history is to have the students write in a character journal. The character journal encourages the reader to "become" the main character. Entries in the journal are written as if the reader/writer were that character. Entries are usually written down at the end of each chapter in diary form.

An excellent book that models a character journal is *A Gathering of Days: A New England Girl's Journal, 1830–32* (Blos, 1979). Written in a first-person narrative style, the story is presented as a series of diary entries written by 13-year-old Catherine Cabot Hall. In these entries Catherine records her impressions of what life is like on a New England farm. Over the two-year span of her entries, she shares what it is like for her widowed father to remarry, to have a new mother and brother, and to experience the death of a best friend. *The True Confessions of Charlotte Doyle* (Avi, 1990) also represents a narrative sharing of a personal incident that took place during the late 1800s, when a proper young lady is transformed into a ship's crewman while on a mutinous journey home to America. The type of historical fiction that lends itself best to character journals must have a strong main character with whom the reader can identify. The character and plot must be closely linked, and a strong sense of the historical period should be evident.

Suggested Readings for Both Types of Journals

The following list of American historical fiction would work well for both literature response journals and character journals. The social studies teacher should investigate these meaningful possibilities for connecting historical fact, fiction, and personal response.

> *Caddie Woodlawn* (Brink, 1936)
> *I'm Deborah Sampson: A Soldier in the War of the Revolution* (Clapp, 1977)
> *Wildflower Girl* (Conlon-McKenna, 1991)
> *Prairie Songs* (Conrad, 1985)
> *The Courage of Sarah Noble* (Dagleish, 1954)
> *The Slave Dancer* (Fox, 1973)
> *Jenny of the Tetons* (Gregory, 1989)
> *Sweetgrass* (Hudson, 1989)
> *A Circle Unbroken* (Hotze, 1988)
> *Across Five Aprils* (Hunt, 1964)

The Witch of Blackbird Pond (Speare, 1958)
The Purple Heart (Talbert, 1992)

Interacting with historical fiction through response and character journals is an almost certain means of fostering personal involvement in and understanding of a particular period in history. As the students become a living part of history by keeping a journal, reflective thinking compels them to place the historical period in the context of the character's life, resulting in a deeper understanding of both history and human nature.

Putting It All Together: Thematic Social Studies Units

Because the whole language approach advocates the teaching of the whole rather than isolated pieces of information, the thematic unit becomes an essential component of a whole language classroom. The selection and elaboration of a social studies theme or concept through literature, reading, and writing symbolize the synthesis of the whole language philosophy. A similar concept-based interdisciplinary approach to teaching social studies with literature has been introduced by James and Zarrillo (1989). Thematic units built around a central theme can lead students beyond facts and dates to a deeper understanding of a concept.

Two thematic social studies units are described below. The first, "Change," is appropriate for students in the middle grades. The second, "In Quest of Freedom," is suited for students in the intermediate grades. Although these units focus on social studies concepts, the literature, reading, and writing activities incorporate a true whole language perspective.

Thematic Unit: Change

The world is changing constantly. The Soviet Union no longer exists; the two German states have been reunited. In the United States suburbs creep into farmlands, local roads become interstate highways, and small towns grow into booming cities. For some people, change signals progress. For others, including children, change can be stressful and disappointing. The more personal aspects of our daily lives also change. New jobs, moves to a new location, and the fluid structure of the family unit can be unsettling changes for ourselves and the students we teach.

Reading about the changes in familiar ways of life can help children put change in a proper perspective. Books can help them understand the loss of something special while coming to understand that places and people are always evolving. Literature about change in towns, communities, and cities can lead to insightful discussions and activities that may help young children cope with the unsettling changes that take place

■ Urban sprawl continues to change the life-styles of many individuals who happen to lie in its path.

around them. A thematic unit built on quality literature enhanced by writing and discussion activities can awaken students to this broad concept that will sweepingly affect their future.

Children's literature reflects change from both an urban and a rural perspective. These two focal points become the first layer of this thematic unit. Reading books aloud sparks thought and discussion on change, while generating questions about people and places in one's own community.

City changes, although expected, can seem overwhelming over time. *New Providence: A Changing Cityscape* (Von Tscharner & Fleming, 1987) looks at the development of a downtown area in a fictitious city between 1910 and 1987. The town is viewed historically through changing architecture, vehicles, and storefronts. One building, for example, changes from a dry goods store to a pharmacy to a computer outlet during its 77-year history. This book provides a natural extension for gathering photographs, maps, and newspapers from your own city or town to discover how history has been reflected over the years in its development. Economic and sociological changes as well as political influences over time might also be examined.

Alice and Martin Provensen's (1987) *Shaker Lane* follows the evolution of a community from farmland to growing rural area to sprawling suburb on the shores of a new reservoir. While the community changes, some people, like Old Man Van Sloop, stay and adjust to the changes. To complement this book, the class might invite a long-time resident of the community to share an oral history of change. Some students might be encouraged to interview several long-time residents and record their perspectives in a permanent written record of community reflections.

The classic *The Little House* by Virginia Lee Burton (1942) can serve as a transitional book from an urban to a rural perspective of change. The encroachment of the city on the country is portrayed through the house that stood on the hill and watched day and night as the seasons passed. Gradually, a road is built, traffic increases, and a city surrounds the little house. A happy ending is assured as the house is relocated by the great-great-granddaughter of the man who built it. This simple, yet sensitive story can foster a discussion on change and its personal effect on people. Although the house is inanimate, its imaginary emotions parallel those of some residents of a changing community.

The rural perspective of change is also well represented in children's literature. *Toddlecreek Post Office* (Shulevitz, 1990) takes the reader to a small town whose small post office serves as the activity center for townspeople and dogs. While the kindly postmaster, Vernon Stamps, has spent years listening to people's joys and woes on their daily visits, his mail dispersal becomes inefficient. The locals lose their gathering place, and the building is eventually torn down. This portrait of vanishing small-town America possibly reflects a deeper vanishing American way of life. Related activities might include a debate on changes in one's own community and whether they are beneficial or not.

A personal connection to change may be made by reading *One-Room School at Squabble Hollow* (Hausherr, 1988). The text depicts the success of a one-room school, while the afterword reveals that the school was closed shortly after the book was written. Children might want to research the history of their own school, when it was built, what was on the site before; where earlier schools were located; and why their school might have to be closed, torn down, expanded, or moved in the future. The interaction of facts and speculation can provide an exciting outlet for exploring change. Journal entries on reactions to this book can be insightful.

The family farm is becoming endangered in the United States. In the book *Family Farm,* Locker (1988) offers a fictional account of a family who face the possibility of losing their farm. At the same time the children face the trauma of their school closing because so many families have moved away. The struggles, arguments, and sacrifices of each family member are shared, but a hopeful ending finds the family trying new crops to reach a wider market. The detailed close-ups of family members are filled with emotion. A follow-up writing activity might be to chose a character from this story and relate the trauma of change as revealed from that character's perspective.

Although cast in a farm setting, *Time to Go* (Fiday & Fiday, 1990) captures a child's emotions about moving and giving up a special place. This story of the loss of a family farm describes a child's feelings as he recalls a happy past on the day that it is time to go and accept change. While our nation becomes increasingly mobile, children need to know they are not alone in their feelings of loss. A written, chronological reflection of change in a child's life can provide personal insights to the classroom teacher. Voluntary sharing of such reflections can help children cope when it is "time to go."

The foregoing books and suggested extension activities provide a simple beginning for a thematic unit on change. Although limited to personal and historical perspectives on change, these resources provide a model of how whole language teaching and learning transcends the traditional textbook. The unit could last a week or be expanded to include additional perspectives over a period of several weeks. The concept of change will be better understood because the students' own lives and community will have become an integrated part of the study. Reading, writing, researching, reflecting, and discussion activities that augment quality literature will give students a multidimensional perspective on change in the community and in one's own life.

An Investigative Thematic Unit: In Quest of Freedom

A journey through history provides a multitude of views on the struggle for the attainment of freedom. A thematic unit based on the general concept of freedom can provide a thought-provoking perspective for studying the efforts of people striving to achieve independence, emancipation, civil liberty, or autonomy that ultimately leads to self-respect and self-determination. Throughout history, the quest for freedom has spanned the globe and the ages. Exploring personal stories of difficult struggles to achieve freedom provides an exciting vehicle from which to study this broad historical topic. Although this thematic unit will be limited, it can be covered in from three to nine weeks, depending on teacher augmentation and student motivation.

This particular unit is designed to be used with three groups of students within a classroom. Each group should investigate one type of freedom from a specific historical perspective: political freedom (based on the Revolutionary Period, 1773–1785), personal freedom (based on the struggle of African-Americans for equality), and freedom from persecution (based on the Holocaust of World War II).

Researching

Each group begins the unit by defining its type of freedom, discussing what group members already know about it, and deciding what they would like to learn from their research and reading. Although the initial

■ An investigative theme unit allows children to research a topic of
common interest. The group define the topic, discuss what they
already know about it, and decide what they want to learn about it.

work involves research from textbooks and encyclopedias, findings should
be geared toward answering the following questions from a variety of
literature:

What were the causes of this quest for freedom?

What effects did lack of freedom impose on the individuals
involved?

What steps did those involved directly take to move toward
freedom?

What individuals emerged as catalysts in supporting the quest for
freedom?

What outcomes prevailed as a result of this quest?

Does this quest for freedom continue today? If so, how? If not,
why not?

The three groups come together at the end of their investigation
and share the information they have discovered, citing the literature that
led them to their discoveries. All groups compare and contrast their answers to the foregoing guideline questions. Commonalties and generalities
often emerge as students engage in higher-level reasoning and thinking.

Reading

Along with informational books and encyclopedias, a wealth of literature of all genre can assist students in achieving a fuller understanding of the quest for each type of freedom. The following lists suggest a variety of literary genre that can be used in this investigative unit.

POLITICAL FREEDOM FOR A NATION

Anticaglia, *Heroines of '76* (biography)

Avi, *The Fighting Ground* (historical fiction)

Collier & Collier, *My Brother Sam Is Dead* (historical fiction)

Collier & Collier, *War Comes to Willy Freeman* (historical fiction)

Fritz, *Shh! We're Writing the Constitution.* (informational)

Longfellow, *The Midnight Ride of Paul Revere* (picture book/poetry)

Marrin, *The War for Independence: The Story of the American Revolution* (informational)

Meltzer, *The American Revolutionaries: A History in Their Own Words, 1750–1800* (diaries/documents)

Spier, *We the People: The Constitution of the United States of America* (picture book)

PERSONAL FREEDOM AND INDIVIDUAL EQUALITY

Hamilton, *Anthony Burns: The Defeat and Triumph of a Fugitive Slave* (biography)

Hamilton, *The People Could Fly: American Black Folktales* (folklore)

Hansen, *Which Way Freedom?* (historical fiction)

Hansen, *Out from This Place* (historical fiction)

Lester, *To Be a Slave* (firsthand accounts)

Lester, *Long Journey Home: Stories from Black History* (historical fiction)

Meltzer, *The Black Americans: A History in Their Own Words* (letters, speeches, diaries, documents)

Turner, *Take a Walk in Their Shoes* (collective biography)

Winter, *Follow the Drinking Gourd* (picture book/poetry)

FREEDOM FROM PERSECUTION—THE HOLOCAUST

Abells, *The Children We Remember* (picture book)

Adler, *We Remember the Holocaust* (informational)

Bunting, *Terrible Things: An Allegory of the Holocaust* (picture book)

Hurwitz, *Anne Frank: Life in Hiding* (biography)

Lowry, *Number the Stars* (historical fiction)

Meltzer, *Never to Forget: The Jews of the Holocaust* (quotes/journal entries)

Meltzer, *Rescue: The Story of How Gentiles Saved Jews in the Holocaust* (informational)

Neimark, *One Man's Valor: Leo Baeck and the Holocaust* (biography)

Yolen, *The Devil's Arithmetic* (historical fiction/time travel)

Writing

Each of the three groups of students incorporates the information compiled from the various types of literature into a newspaper explaining the struggle for freedom. Group members cooperatively choose an appropriate name for their newspaper. Each student then writes a feature or column on information gleaned from a particular book that was read or shared. The newspaper may be a mixture of fact and fiction, but it must stay within the historical context of the quest for freedom. Diary entries, personal vignettes, and ancedotes can be written to capture the human spirit of individuals struggling toward freedom.

The use of word processing and/or software programs in newspaper format is highly desirable. Duplication of each newspaper for each member of the class will provide a means to share and compare written information from each group. The cooperative group effort required during this unit not only provides a wealth of information on the topic of freedom and the spirit of those who fought for it but may also increase each student's desire to further explore an aspect of freedom surveyed by other members of the class.

The development of thematic units is limited only by the desire of the teacher to integrate reading, writing, and social studies in the curriculum. A whole language approach empowers the classroom teacher to tear down traditional curricular boundaries while providing meaningful integration through unit teaching.

Summary

The whole language philosophy of instruction has provided classroom teachers with a justification to introduce quality literature across the curriculum. The realm of social studies has always been associated with biography and historical fiction, but whole language instruction has provided integration of these genre with related writing and discussion activities. In addition, the world of picture books provides an extension of literature into both geographic and historical concepts.

Literature linked to social studies widens a child's world by providing the opportunity to participate in new experiences, visit new places, and be a genuine part of the past. The rich resource of literature available for use in whole language instruction brings social studies to life through literary journeys that offer meaningful links to the child's own life and world.

Children's Books

Abells, C. (1986). *The children we remember.* New York: Greenwillow.

> The story of Jewish children before, during, and after the Holocaust told through black and white photographs.

Adler, D. (1989a). *A picture book of Martin Luther King, Jr.* (J.C. Walner, Illus.). New York: Holiday House.

> Illustrated biography of the Baptist minister and civil rights leader who helped blacks win many battles for equal rights.

Adler, D. (1989b). *We remember the Holocaust.* (J.C. Walner, Illus.). New York: Holt, Rinehart & Winston.

> Personal accounts of the Holocaust from survivors who reveal their experiences of persecution and death camps.

Adler, D. (1990). *A picture book of Benjamin Franklin.* New York: Holiday House.

> Survey of the life of Benjamin Franklin, highlighting his work as an inventor and statesman.

Aliki (1989). *The king's day: Louis XIV of France.* New York: Crowell.

> The daily ceremonial rituals in the life of King Louis XIV at Versailles.

Allen, T. B. (1989). *On grandaddy's farm.* New York: Knopf.

> Events from the 1930s, when the author and his cousins spent summers on their grandparents' farm in the hills of Tennessee.

Anno, M. (1983). *Anno's U.S.A.* New York: Philomel.

> The author journeys from West to East on horseback through the countryside and cities of the United States, and his detailed illustrations enhance our understanding of history and culture.

Anticaglia, E. (1975). *Heroines of '76.* New York: Walker.

> A chronicle of the involvement of 14 outstanding women in the Revolutionary War.

Ashabranner, B. (1992). *A memorial for Mr. Lincoln* (J. Ashabranner, Photographer). New York: Putnam.

> The search for the location and design for the memorial are vividly outlined.

Avi (1984). *The fighting ground.* Philadelphia: Lippincott.

> Thirteen-year-old Jonathan goes off to fight in the Revolutionary War and discovers the real war is being fought within himself.

Avi (1990). *The true confessions of Charlotte Doyle.* New York: Orchard Books.

> As the lone young woman on a transatlantic voyage in 1832, Charlotte learns of a murderous captain and a rebellious crew.

Baylor, B. (1983). *The best town in the world* (R. Himler, Illus.).
New York: Scribner.

> Life in a small country town in the Texas hills around the turn of the century
> poetically reveals the "best" of everything.

Blos, J. W. (1979). *A gathering of days: A New England girl's
journal, 1830–32.* New York: Scribner.

> The journal of a 14-year-old girl reveals daily events in her small New
> Hampshire town, her father's remarriage, her encounter with a runaway slave,
> and the death of her best friend.

Brink, C. (1936). *Caddie Woodlawn.* New York: Macmillan.

> A self-willed independent tomboy grows up in the Wisconsin backwoods in the
> 1860s.

Bunting, E. (1989). *Terrible things: An allegory of the Holocaust*
(S. Gammell, Illus.). New York: Jewish Publication Society.

> An allegorical tale in which animals disappear from the forest while others look
> away. Little Rabbit survives to share the horror.

Burton, V. L. (1942). *The little house.* Boston: Houghton Mifflin.

> A country house is unhappy when the city, with all its buildings and traffic,
> grows up around it.

Clapp, P. (1977). *I'm Deborah Sampson: A soldier in the war of
the revolution.* New York: Lothrop.

> Real-life adventure of a New England woman who, posing as a man, served
> for more than a year in the Continental Army.

Collier, J., & Collier, C. (1983). *War comes to Willy Freeman.* New
York: Delacorte.

> The wartime problems of blacks in the northern colonies touch the life of a
> young black woman who futilely hopes for liberty and equality under the new
> government.

Collier, J., & Collier, C. (1985). *My brother Sam is dead.* New
York: Four Winds.

> A family is divided by the Revolutionary War as the protagonist is caught
> between his loyalist father and his rebel brother.

Conlon-McKenna, M. (1991). *Wildflower girl.* New York: Holiday
House.

> In 1850, a 13-year-old girl leaves Ireland to make a better life for herself in
> Boston.

Conrad, P. (1985). *Prairie songs.* New York: Harper & Row.

> Louisa's life in a loving pioneer family on the Nebraska prairie is altered by
> the arrival of a new doctor and his beautiful, tragically frail wife.

Conrad, P. (1989). *My Daniel.* New York: Harper Collins.

> A woman recalls her love for her brother and their home on the prairie.

Dagleish, A. (1954). *The courage of Sarah Noble* (L. Weisgard, Illus.). New York: Scribner.

> A courageous 8-year-old girl finds courage to go alone with her father to build a new home in the Connecticut wilderness and then stay alone with the Indians while her father goes back to get the rest of the family.

d'Aurlaire, I., & d'Aulaire, E. P. (1957). *Abraham Lincoln* (Rev. ed.). New York: Doubleday.

> Classic children's biography of Lincoln from his birth through the Civil War by a famed author-illustrator team.

de Paola, T. (1983). *The legend of the bluebonnet: An old tale of Texas.* New York: Putnam.

> A retelling of the Comanche Indian lesson of how a little girl's sacrifice brought the bluebonnet flower to Texas.

de Paola, T. (1988). *The legend of the Indian paintbrush.* New York: Putnam.

> Little Gopher becomes an artist for his people and brings the colors of the sunset down to earth as his paintbrushes are transformed into the brilliantly colored western flower.

Fiday, B., & Fiday, D. (1990). *Time to go* (T.B. Allen, Illus.). San Diego, CA: Gulliver.

> As a child and his family prepare to leave, he takes one last look at the family farm.

Foster, S. (1987). *Where time stands still.* New York: Dodd.

> The work, dress, leisure, and education of the Pennsylvania Amish are highlighted in informational black and white photographs.

Fox, P. (1973). *The slave dancer.* New York: Bradbury.

> Thirteen-year-old Jessie is forced to join the crew of a slave ship and experiences degradation and human suffering on a journey from Africa to New Orleans.

Freedman, R. (1987a). *Indian chiefs.* New York: Holiday House.

> Biographies of six western Indian chiefs who led their people in historic moments of crisis when pioneers encroached on their lands.

Freedman, R. (1987b). *Lincoln: A photobiography.* New York: Clarion.

> An absorbing look into Lincoln's career shown through numerous photographs, prints, and reprints of original documents. The 1988 Newbery Medal winner.

Freedman, R. (1990). *Franklin Delano Roosevelt.* New York: Clarion.

> Presents FDR, the longest-serving president of the United States, in a series of photographs.

Fritz, J. (1973). *And then what happened, Paul Revere?* (M. Tomes, Illus.). New York: Coward, McCann.

> Description of the well-known and lesser-known details of Paul Revere's life and exciting ride.

Fritz, J. (1974). *Why don't you get a horse, Sam Adams?*
(M. Tomes, Illus.). New York: Coward, McCann.

> The blatant defiance of British authority is exemplified by the behavior of this noble statesman.

Fritz, J. (1975). *Where was Patrick Henry on the 29th of May?*
(M. Tomes, Illus.). New York: Coward, McCann.

> A brief biography of Patrick Henry that traces his progress from planter to statesman.

Fritz, J. (1976). *Will you sign here, John Hancock?* (T. S. Hyman,
Illus.). New York: Coward, McCann.

> John Hancock's vanity and penchant for flourishes is captured in this brief biography.

Fritz, J. (1982). *Can't you make them behave, King George?*
(T. de Paola, Illus.). New York: Coward, McCann.

> Unpopular English monarch George III is viewed through a humorous, yet historical perspective.

Fritz, J. (1986). *Shh! We're writing the Constitution.* New York:
Putnam.

> A beginner's history of how the Constitution came to be written and ratified. Includes the full text of the document produced by the Constitutional Convention in 1787 as well as historical notes.

Fritz, J. (1989). *The great little Madison.* New York: Putnam.

> The life and contributions of the sickly child with the small voice who grew up to become the fourth president of the United States.

Fritz, J. (1991). *Bully for you, Teddy Roosevelt.* New York: Putnam.

> The life of the dynamic, 26th president is revealed through his conservation work, hunting expeditions, and political career.

Goble, P. (1985). *The great race of the birds and animals.* New
York: Bradbury.

> A retelling of the Cheyenne Sioux myth about the Great Race, a contest called by the Creator, to settle the question of whether man or buffalo should have supremacy as the guardian of Creation.

Gregory, K. (1989). *Jenny of the Tetons.* San Diego, CA: Gulliver.

> Orphaned by an Indian raid on a wagon train, 15-year-old Carrie Hill is befriended by a trapper and taken to live with his Indian wife and their six children.

Hamilton, V. (1985). *The people could fly: American black
folktales* (L. & D. Dillon, Illus.). New York: Knopf.

> Retold African-American folktales of animals, fantasy, the supernatural, and the desire of slaves for freedom.

Hamilton, V. (1988). *Anthony Burns: The defeat and triumph of a
fugitive slave.* New York: Knopf.

A biography of the slave who escaped to Boston in 1854, was arrested at the instigation of his owner, and whose trial caused a furor between abolitionists and supporters of the Fugitive Slave Act.

Hansen, J. (1986). *Which way freedom?* New York: Walker.

Obi escapes from slavery during the Civil War, joins a black Union regiment, and becomes involved in the fighting at Fort Pillow, Tennessee.

Hansen, J. (1988). *Out from this place.* New York: Walker.

Following the emancipation, a 14-year-old black girl tries to find a fellow ex-slave who had joined the Union Army during the Civil War. A sequel to *Which way freedom?*

Harvey, B. (1986). *My prairie years: Based on the diary of Elenore Plaisted.* New York: Holiday House.

Nine-year-old Elenore describes her experiences living with her family in the Dakota Territory in the late 1800s.

Harvey, B. (1988). *Cassie's journey: Going west in the 1860s* (D. K. Ray, Illus.). New York: Holiday House.

Revelation of the hardships and dangers of a family traveling in a covered wagon from Illinois to California during the 1860s.

Hausherr, R. (1988). *One-room school at Squabble Hollow.* New York: Four Winds.

A one-room school in northern Vermont (Caledonia county), which has been functioning for over 100 years, is brought to life through text and pictures.

Hendershot, J. (1987). *In coal country* (T.B. Allen, Illus.). New York: Knopf.

A child growing up in a coal mining community finds both excitement and hard work in a life deeply affected by the local industry.

Hotze, S. (1988). *A circle unbroken.* New York: Clarion.

Captured by the Sioux Indians and raised as the chief's daughter, Rachel is found by her white family. Her adjustment is difficult as she longs to return to the tribe.

Hudson, J. (1989). *Sweetgrass.* New York: Philomel.

A 15-year-old Blackfoot Indian girl in western Canada saves her family from a small pox epidemic and proves her maturity to her father.

Hunt, I. (1964). *Across five Aprils.* Chicago: Follett.

Nine-year-old Jethro Creighton takes responsibility for his family's Illinois farm when his brothers and cousins go off to fight in the Civil War. Divided loyalties teach Jethro the realities of war.

Hurwitz, J. (1988). *Anne Frank: Life in hiding.* New York: Jewish Publications Society.

A moving telling of Anne Frank's years in hiding in Amsterdam during World War II highlighted by the publication of Anne's celebrated diary.

Kellogg, S. (1986). *Pecos Bill.* New York: Morrow.

Incidents from the life of the legendary cowboy from his life among the coyotes to his unusual wedding day.

Kigel, R. (1986). *The frontier years of Abe Lincoln; In the words of his friends and family.* New York: Walker.

The years of Lincoln's childhood and young adulthood are viewed from the point of view of those who knew him best.

Lasky, K. (1983). *Sugaring time* (C. G. Knight, Illus.). New York: Macmillan.

The record of how a Vermont family carries on the tradition of gathering sap for boiling into maple syrup is enhanced by black and white photographs.

Lester, J. (1968). *To be a slave.* New York: Dial.

The verbatim testimony of former slaves is combined with the author's own commentary on the conditions and inequality of slavery.

Lester, J. (1972). *Long journey home: Stories from black history.* New York: Dial.

Six short pieces, ranging from slave days to the 1920s, tell of common folk as they search for freedom and dignity.

Lewis, C. (1987). *Long ago in Oregon* (J. Fontaine, Illus.). New York: Harper & Row.

A collection of poetic vignettes describe a year in the life of a young girl living with her family in a small Oregon town in 1917.

Locker, T. (1988). *Family farm.* New York: Dial.

A family nearly lose their farm until they begin to raise and sell pumpkins and flowers to supplement their corn and milk sales.

Loeper, J. (1984). *Going to school in 1876.* New York: Atheneum.

A depiction of the life of school children in 1876—their dress, teachers, books, lessons, discipline, and pastimes.

Longfellow, H. W. (1990). *The midnight ride of Paul Revere.* (T. Rand, Illus.). New York: Dutton.

Illustrated version of the narrative poem recreating the famous event of 1775 in which Revere warned the people of the Boston countryside that the British were coming.

Lowry, L. (1989). *Number the stars.* Boston: Houghton Mifflin.

In 1943 during the German occupation of Denmark, 10–year-old Annemarie learns courage and bravery when she helps shelter her Jewish friend from the Nazis.

Marrin, A. (1988). *The war for independence: The story of the American Revolution.* New York: Atheneum.

A detailed account of the Revolutionary War beginning with its origins in the French and Indian War.

McPhail, D. (1992). *Farmboy's Year.* New York: Atheneum.

Illustrations of farm life, month by month throughout the year, give vivid images of New England farm life.

Meltzer, M. (1976). *Never to forget: The Jews of the Holocaust.* New York: Harper & Row.

> A history of the atrocities committed against the courageous Jews documented by historical sources.

Meltzer, M. (1984). *The black Americans: A history in their own words, 1619-1983.* New York: Crowell.

> A history of African Americans in the United States told through authentic documents and eyewitness accounts.

Meltzer, M. (1987). *The American revolutionaries: A history of their own words, 1750-1800.* New York: Crowell.

> Letters, diaries, memoirs, interviews, ballads, newspaper articles, and speeches depict life and events in the colonies before, during, and after the American Revolution.

Meltzer, M. (1989a). *Rescue: The story of how Gentiles saved Jews in the Holocaust.* New York: Harper & Row.

> A recounting drawn from historical sources of the many acts of heroism performed to thwart the extermination of the Jews during the Holocaust.

Meltzer, M. (1989b). *Voices from the Civil War: A documentary history of the great American conflict.* New York: Crowell.

> Authentic source materials document the life and events of the 4 years of the Civil War.

Milnes, G. (1990). *Granny will your dog bite? And other mountain rhymes* (K. Root, Illus.). New York: Knopf.

> A collection of rhymes and songs about various aspects of life in the Appalachians.

Monjo. F. N. (1973). *Poor Richard in France* (B. Turkle, Illus.). New York: Holt, Rinehart & Winston.

> Benjamin Franklin's trip to France is revealed from the point of view of his 7-year-old grandson.

Monjo, F. N. (1974). *King George's head is made of lead.* New York: Coward, McCann.

> The statue of George III, erected in Battery Park after the repeal of the Stamp Act, tells his version of the events leading to the American Revolution.

Munro, R. (1987). *The inside-outside book of Washington D.C.* New York: Dutton.

> The interiors and exteriors of twelve landmarks of the nation's capital are viewed in detail; color illustrations.

Neimark, A. (1986). *One man's valor: Leo Baeck and the Holocaust.* New York: Lodestar.

> Biography of Leo Baeck, the rabbi of Berlin, who aided escapees from Germany during the Holocaust and miraculously survived his own ordeal in a concentration camp.

Parnell, P. (1986). *Winter barn.* New York: Macmillan.

> A dilapidated old barn shelters a wide variety of animals during the subzero temperatures of a Maine winter.

Pendergraft, P. (1991). *As far as Mill Springs.* New York: Philomel.

In the 1930s two depression-weary children search for their mother in California.

Perl, L. (1992). *It Happened in America: True Stories from the Fifty States* (I. Ohlsson, Illus.). New York: Holt.

The fifty states are briefly introduced along with stories about each.

Provensen, A., & Provensen, M. (1987). *Shaker Lane.* New York: Viking.

When the town decides to build a reservoir on its land, the residents of Shaker Lane decide to move away rather than fight to keep their homes.

Purviance, S., & O'Shell, M. (1988). *Alphabet Annie announces an all-American alphabet book.* Boston: Houghton Mifflin.

An alphabetical tour of characters performing various activities in American cities makes for an interesting array of alliterative rhymes.

Rylant, C. (1991). *Appalachia: The voices of sleeping birds.* San Diego, CA: Harcourt Brace Jovanovich.

Poetic recollections of the author growing up in Appalachia are enhanced by evocative, full-color portraits of the region.

Sandburg, C. (1985). *Abe Lincoln grows up* (J. Daugherty, Illus.). San Diego, CA: Harcourt Brace Jovanovich.

Reprinted from Sandberg's *Abraham Lincoln: The prairie years.*

Service, R. (1987). *The cremation of Sam McGee.* New York: Greenwillow.

An illustrated version of a well-known poem that captures the mystery and romance of the Alaska gold rush and tells the tale of an interesting Yukon prospector.

Shulevitz, U. (1990). *Toddlecreek post office.* New York: Farrar, Straus & Giroux.

Vanishing small-town America is portrayed as the local post office, the center of town activity, is closed down and a town faces a lost identity.

Siebert, D. (1988). *Mohave* (W. Minor, Illus.). New York: Crowell.

The vast expanse of western desert comes alive through vivid text and illustrations.

Siebert, D. (1989). *Heartland* (W. Minor, Illus.). New York: Crowell.

Poetic text and powerful illustrations evoke the land, animals, and people of the Middle West.

Siebert, D. (1990). *Sierra* (W. Minor, Illus.). New York: Harper/Collins.

One of the Sierra mountains speaks of the beauty and timelessness of herself and her sister peaks.

Speare, E. G. (1958). *The witch of Blackbird Pond.* Boston: Houghton Mifflin.

> Classic tale of a young girl who comes to Puritan New England from Barbados and finds herself caught by the repressive forces of a small village and a trial for witchcraft.

Spier, P. (1987). *We the people: The Constitution of the United States of America.* New York: Doubleday.

> An appealing array of illustrations from American life accompany each phrase of the Preamble to the Constitution.

Stanley, D. (1986). *Peter the Great.* New York: Four Winds.

> A biography of the czar who began the transformation of Russia into a modern state in the late 17th and early 18th centuries.

Stanley, D., & Venneman, P. (1990). *Good Queen Bess.* New York: Four Winds.

> The life of the strong-willed queen of England during the time of Shakespeare and the defeat of the Spanish Armada is presented through beautiful illustrations and text.

Turner, A. (1985). *Dakota dugout* (R. Himler, Illus.). New York: Macmillan.

> A pioneer woman describes her experiences living with her husband in a sod house on the Dakota prairie.

Turner, A. (1989). *Grasshopper summer.* New York: Macmillan.

> In 1874, 11-year-old Sam and his family move from Kentucky to the Dakota Territory, where harsh conditions and a plague of hungry grasshoppers threaten their chances for survival.

Turner, G. T. (1989). *Take a walk in their shoes.* New York: Cobblehill.

> Biographical sketches of 14 notable blacks, including Martin Luther King, Jr., Rosa Parks, and Satchel Paige. The text is accompanied by brief skits in which readers can act out imagined scenes from their lives.

Van Leeuwen, J. (1992). *Going west* (T. B. Allen, Illus.). New York: Dial.

> Details the hardships of travel on the prairie and the joy of having a new neighbor.

Von Tscharner, R., & Fleming R. (1987). *New Providence: A changing cityscape.* San Diego, CA: Harcourt Brace Jovanovich.

> A visual treatment of the emerging urban environment as an imaginary town moves through economic, political, and architectural changes from 1910 to 1987.

Williams, V. B., & Williams, J. (1988). *Stringbean's trip to the shining sea.* New York: Greenwillow.

> A summer vacation to the West Coast is described through a series of postcards.

Winter, J. (1988). *Follow the drinking gourd.* New York: Knopf.

> By following the directions in a song, "The Drinking Gourd," runaway slaves journey north along the Underground Railroad to freedom in Canada.

Winter, J. (1992). *Klara's New World.* New York: Knopf.

> Klara's family leaves Sweden in the 19th century to immigrate to America.

Yolen, J. (1988). *The devil's arithmetic.* New York: Viking.

> Hannah resents the traditions of her Jewish heritage until time travel places her in the middle of a small Jewish village in Nazi-occupied Poland.

References

Ammon, R., & Weigard, J. (1993). A look at other trade book topics and genres. In M. O. Tunnell & R. Ammon (Eds.), *The story of ourselves.* Portsmouth, NH: Heinemann.

Ceprano, M., & English, E. B. (1990). Fact and fiction: Personalizing social studies through the tradebook-textbook connection. *Reading Horizons, 30,* 66–77.

Cianciolo, P. (1981). Yesterday comes alive for readers of historical fiction. *Language Arts, 58,* 452–461.

Commire, A. (Ed.). (1982). *Something about the author, 29,* 79–83. Detroit, MI: Gale Research.

Cullinan, B. E. (1987). *Children's literature in the reading program.* Newark, DE: International Reading Association.

Danielson, K. E. (1989). Helping history comes alive with literature. *Social Studies, 80,* 65–68.

Dowd, F. (1990). Geography is children's literature, math, science, art and a whole world of activities. *Journal of Geography, 89,* 68–73.

Galda, L. (1988). Readers, texts, and contexts: A response-based view of literature in the classroom. *New Advocate, 1,* 92–102.

Gallo, D. R., & Barksdale, E. (1983). Using fiction in American history. *Social Education, 47,* 286–289.

Hancock, M. R. (1991). *A case study investigation of the process and content of literature response journals.* Doctoral dissertation, Northern Illinois University, DeKalb.

Hancock, M. R. (1993). Exploring and extending personal response through literature response journals. *Reading Teacher, 46* (6), 466-474.

Huck, C. S., Hepler, S., & Hickman, J. (1993). *Children's literature in the elementary school* (5th ed.). New York: Holt, Rinehart & Winston.

James, M., & Zarrillo, J. (1989). Teaching history with childen's literature: A concept-based, interdisciplinary approach. *Social Studies, 80,* 153–158.

Johnson, N. M., & Ebert, M. J. (1992). Time travel is possible: Historical fiction and biography—Passport to the past. *Reading Journal, 45,* 488–495.

Langer, J., & Applebee, A. (1987). *How writing shapes thinking: A study of learning and teaching.* Urbana, IL: National Council of Teachers of English.

Levstik, L. (1985). Literary geography and mapping. *Social Education, 77,* 38–43.

Levstik, L. S. (1990). Research directions: Mediating content through literary texts. *Language Arts, 67,* 848–853.

Levstik, L. S. (1993). "I wanted to be there": The impact of narrative on children's thinking. In M. O. Tunnell & R. Ammon (Eds.), *The story of ourselves.* Portsmouth, NH: Heinemann.

Louie, B. Y. (1993). Using literature to teach location. *Social Studies and the Young Learner, 5,* 17–18, 22.

Moir, H. (Ed.). (1992). *Collected perspectives: Choosing and using books for the classroom.* Boston: Christopher Gordon.

Norton, D. E. (1991). *Through the eyes of a child* (3rd ed.). Columbus, OH: Merrill.

Odland, N. (1980). American history in fact and fiction: Literature for young readers. *Social Education, 44,* 474–481.

Pritchard, S. F. (1989). Using picture books to teach geography in the primary grades. *Journal of Geography, 88,* 126–127, 137.

Probst, R. E. (1984). *Adolescent literature: Response and analysis.* Columbus, OH: Merrill.

Rosenblatt, L. (1976). *Literature as exploration.* New York: Appleton-Century-Crofts.

Rosenblatt, L. (1978). *The reader, the text, the poem.* Carbondale, IL: Southern Illinois University Press.

Sanacore, J. (1990). Creating the lifetime reading habit in social studies. *Journal of Reading, 33,* 414–418.

Sisson, J. (1990). Read your way across the U.S.A. *Journal of Geography, 89,* 175–177.

Zarnowski, M. (1990). *Learning about biographies: A reading-and-writing approach for children.* Urbana, IL: National Council of Teachers of English.

Facilitating Learning: Strategic Instruction in Social Studies

BONNIE L. KUHRT
CARL SANDBURG JUNIOR HIGH, ROLLING MEADOWS, IL

PAMELA J. FARRIS
NORTHERN ILLINOIS UNIVERSITY

Highlighting the Issues

Point: *Above all, textbooks must try to lay bare the fundamental structures of history, geography, health, and science—and in a manner that permits children and youth to grasp the structure.*

RICHARD ANDERSON ET AL.
Becoming a Nation of Readers

Counterpoint: *The report ignores the role of the student as a constructive participant in learning and places the teacher in the role of a giver of information whose task it is to follow the organization of a well-written textbook.*

BONNIE C. WILKERSON
"A Principal's Perspective"

Introduction

Children need to develop learning strategies that they can apply effectively in social studies as they read, write, and discuss. This results in student control, or empowerment. The instructional questions that therefore arise are these: Should social studies teachers use textbooks? Do textbooks enable students to be active learners or limit them to being passive recipients of information?

Currently, educators are faced with social studies textbooks that lack integration of concepts and contain superficial treatment of topics, which according to Osburn, Jones, and Stein (1985), impede attempts to unlock the structure and meaning of the text. Avoidance of poorly written social studies textbook materials in the lower grades has resulted in reduced content knowledge; however, dependence on the social studies text in the upper grades, in particular, has resulted in the depressed levels of knowledge due to the poor quality of the materials. Further complicating matters, *The Educational Products Information Exchange Institute Report* (Fancett & Hawke, 1980), indicates that 90 percent of classroom time is used for commercially prepared materials. Given these facts, does the student have the opportunity to become an active participant in the learning process?

With continued use of expository text on evaluation measures designed at the state and national levels, avoidance is not a valid alternative. Students are expected to read and write descriptive, explanatory, and persuasive text, the three kinds of expository text. Students, along with their teachers, remain accountable for the information presented in the expository passages. Rather than wait for the reorganization of social studies textbooks, the teacher must draw up instructional plans that focus on strategies that empower students to control their own learning. Yet as Resnick and Klopfer (1982, pp. 206–207) suggest, "Knowledge is acquired not from the information communicated and memorized but from the information that students elaborate, question, and use." The question becomes: How can the reasoning activities necessary for acquiring content knowledge be activated to give students control over their learning in social studies?

Because many schools either lack the quality children's literature selections needed for a whole language social studies program or want to use both children's literature and a social studies textbook for instructional purposes, this chapter examines strategies for helping students gather, organize, relate, and retain knowledge in social studies. The chapter examines strategies that activate learning (such as K-W-L) and describes the characteristics of graphic organizers. Thus, a basic framework for strategic instruction as well as the integration of reading, writing, and reasoning in social studies emerges.

Strategies to Activate Learning

Through the process of relating new information to prior knowledge (Jones, Palincsar, Ogle, & Carr, 1987), a comparison takes place between the students' knowledge of a subject and the new information contained in the text. Defined as complex knowledge structures that help students process information effectively, the schemata are classified as three distinct types: (1) content and organizational patterns, (2) processes, and (3) conditions. By familiarizing students with the expository text structures, recognition of the content and organizational patterns can help the students acquire the information in the text. The process of the schemata involves the following phases: (1) activating prior knowledge, (2) monitoring comprehension, and (3) evaluating the meaning and inconsistencies with regard to prior knowledge. As students develop the "when" and "why" for the application of these phases, the conditions for the transfer of these strategies to a new context emerges.

Finally, the interplay between the process of prediction and verification that takes place during reading, suggests strategies to activate prior knowledge and to analyze text material.

K-W-L

One strategy to help students take an active role in reading social studies text is K-W-L (Ogle, 1986, 1989), which stands for *k*now, *w*ant to know, and *l*earned. This strategy is a three-step approach to assist students as they prepare to read, engage in reading, and come to understand informational text such as social studies material. The teacher and each student begin with a chart containing three columns: (1) *K*now, (2) *W*ant to Know, and (3) *L*earned. Then the teacher and students proceed through the following steps:

1. *Prereading Activity.* Before reading, the teacher asks the students to brainstorm what they already know about a topic. The pooled information is then recorded on the class chart under "*K*now." As students contribute more and more information, some conflicts and disputes arise. Such information is then turned into questions and listed under the "*W*ant to Know" column.

   By brainstorming information for the "*K*now" column, students activate their prior knowledge. Formulating questions for the "*W*ant to Know" column, students discover their purposes for reading the text.

■ All children should be encouraged to be active participants in the learning process.

At this point, the teacher and the students look for ways to categorize both the information they brainstormed and the information they expect to find as they read. For example, for the topic "France" being studied by a fourth-grade class for an international unit, the teacher chose the social sciences of economics, geography, history, and political science.

2. *During-Reading Activity.* Students look for both new information and the answers to the questions in the "*Want* to Know" column. Depending on the difficulty of the text and its length, the students may read the entire selection or sections designated by the teacher. Students may either take notes as they read or recall information upon finishing their reading of the text.

3. *Postreading Activity.* In a class discussion, students reflect on what they have learned. During this time, the final column, "*Learned*," is completed on the class chart. Each student then completes the "*Learned*" column of his or her individual chart.

FIGURE 6.1

■

An example of K-W-L by a fourth-grade class.

Topic: France

Know	Want to Know	Learned
Country	What products are	Cars, pottery, wine
In Europe	manufactured?	Cattle, grain
Mountains	What kinds of farming	Citrus fruits,
Produces wine	& agriculture?	vegetables, grapes
Produces perfume	What kind of govern-	Parliamentary
France is the	ment?	Tennis, soccer,
money	What are popular	snow skiing
French is the	sports?	French words: broil,
language		saute, pâté, etc.
		A banking center for
		the world
		Member of Common
		Market

Figure 6.1 provides an example of a K-W-L chart.

Using specific reasoning strategies along with prior knowledge helps students comprehend the ideas contained in the text. Through this active engagement, readers are able to link new information with their personal knowledge of the subject. By learning to monitor and control such reasoning strategies, students develop an understanding of how they learn. This metacognitive awareness allows them to control the learning process.

Graphic Organizers

Graphic organizers help activate student learning when used with social studies textbooks. According to Indrisano and Paratore (1992), graphic organizers are also very appropriate for use with nonfiction informational books: "These descriptive or main idea/supporting detail maps help readers focus attention on, organize, and recall their reading of expository text" (p. 146). The teacher should explain that when students are reading material that contains a large amount of information, a visual display can help them remember what they have read.

To demonstrate the use of graphic organizers, the teacher may elect to read aloud five or six pages from the social studies textbook or an informational children's literature book. Then in pairs, students can reread the passage the teacher read aloud and begin to map the information,

Scandinavia, terrorism, driving on the left side of the road, Cliffs of Dover, cooperating with their slaves, trying to trade together, Alps & valleys, an underwater tunnel between France & England, the Berlin Wall is coming down, Germany reunited, borders change in Europe, France, Netherlands, Spain, countries are small like some of our smaller states, the countries are close but the cultures are different, Austria, Scotland, & Ireland, densely populated, that's why they came here, England used up all its resources, steel is made in some countries that have iron & coal, you can go on trains all over Europe, landforms protect some of the countries, plains & swamps may be all the landforms, not deserts

much like the clustering described in Chapter 4. Each piece of information the students identify as key information is classified under a heading and then related to the nucleus word or words that identify the primary topic.

Designed to reflect many of the reasoning patterns in the structure of the schemata, these visual representations of information make the organizational patterns more explicit for the learner. However, distinctive differences exist between the graphic organizer and reasoning. While the graphic organizer can activate the reasoning strategies, learning takes place during the interaction between the learner's prior knowledge and the demands of the visual representation along with the information contained in the textbook. Therefore, differences in the visual representations created from text material appear because of the learner's prior knowledge as well as the reasoning strategies applied.

The graphic organizer aids comprehension of the social studies text by making the patterns clear. Designed as a means of organizing text material in relationship patterns, the graphic organizer centers attention on the key information contained in the text. This manipulation of the text material promotes the relationship between concepts and main ideas. By helping students control and process large amounts of information, the graphic organizer helps students better comprehend the text. The book *Faithful Elephants* (Tsuchiya, 1988), has as its setting Tokyo just before the end of World War II. The Japanese are losing the war, and leaders fear massive bombings of cities, such as occurred in Germany. Zoo keepers are ordered to kill many of the larger animals because if the zoo were to be bombed directly, the animals could escape and threaten the lives of people in the city. The only way to kill the trustful, beloved elephants is to starve them to death.

In examining the impact of the graphic organizer on meaningful learning, Armbruster (1985) identifies three stages: (1) selection of information from the text, (2) organization into a coherent structure, and (3) integration of the new information. Armbruster applies this model to three basic structural patterns used in social studies texts: (1) description,

F I G U R E   6 . 2

■

Sample graphic organizers.

Feudal Society Groups

Clergy	Nobles	Peasants
- teach religion	- govern	- farm land
- help poor and sick	- enforce laws	- provide services
- have more rights	- protect people	- work for clergy
	- have more rights	and nobles
		- largest group

Believed God wanted it that way → few tried to make improvements or change way of life

→ remained in group they were born into

a

(2) comparison/contrast, and (3) explanation. Parts *a, b,* and *c* of figure 6.2 show examples of graphic organizers. These represent three different approaches to feudal societal groups generated by sixth-grade students.

In a later publication, Armbruster, Anderson, and Ostertag (1989) expanded the list by dividing the explanation pattern into (3) sequence, (4) cause and effect, and (5) problem solution. Regardless of the labels, these patterns organize the majority of social studies text materials. Graphic organizers, designed as visual representations of these patterns, help focus the learner on the important information within the text and clarify the purpose in reading.

F I G U R E   6 . 2

■

Continued

Ties of Loyalty		Duties
Lord	-protected vassals from enemy attack -if he failed to do this, vassal owed no loyalty	-gave vassal a fief -gave symbol of trust -gave right to govern
Vassel	-less powerful noble -fief vassals for life -upon death, passed to son -did not lose respect for seeking protection -gave loyalty to lord -some supported the one likely to win	-helped lord in battle -supplied knights -owed 40 days of battle a year -paid lord when sons became knights and daughters married -paid ransom for lord's release -supplied food and entertainment -decided cases

b

By setting the focus for learning, a graphic organizer gives the student control over the text and aids his or her comprehension. The value of such visual models lies in ordering the integration of reading, writing, and group work toward a specific learning outcome. Rather than examining these patterns in isolation, the rest of this chapter describes the means of sequencing the activities in a sixth-grade geography lesson.

Strategic Sequencing

Activating the learner's prior knowledge is central to his or her comprehension of the text material. With regard to social studies text materials, direct instruction of the organizational patterns within the text helps students identify the text structure. This facilitates their comprehension. Following the phases of learning, the sequencing of strategies will involve (1) participation in pre-reading activities to activate prior knowledge, (2) the use of a graphic organizer to monitor comprehension, and (3) the evaluation of inconsistencies between new information and prior knowledge.

Residence

Type	Time period	Description

Manor   9-11th centuries — wooden buildings high wooden fences
- 1 room, high ceiling and straw floor
- all activities
- fire for cooking and heating

Castle   12th century — stone fortress
- lookout tower and arches
- moat -- soft muddy bottom
- drawbridge -- heavy door
- portcullis -- heavy gate/iron gate
- keep -- tall tower with all, many rooms and dungeon

---

c

Phase One: Activating Prior Knowledge

Before students read social studies text, learning theory suggests that they engage in activities that activate their prior knowledge of the topic. Davidson (1982) suggests a strategy that involves the whole class in the use of mapping strategies as a means of assessing the class's level of prior knowledge. The students first list random associations and classifications of this information. Using an overhead transparency to record student predictions for the geographic region under study, the teacher creates a visual representation of the current interconnections identified by the students. Following this procedure gives students a model of the predictive process.

Because of the descriptive pattern used in social studies books, particularly when describing geography, such text provides an opportunity to classify specific characteristics of a geographic region. During the initial introduction to a region, students access their prior knowledge. This strategy follows the same logic involved in the K-W-L instructional model (Ogle, 1986). Visual maps of the text can help students determine what they know, predict what will be discussed, and assess what was finally learned. As students progress through various geographic regions, familiarity with the pattern organization establishes their future expectations.

Repetition of the classification pattern enables the students to develop sensitivity to the text structure and cues. For example, seventh-grade students predict categories for the "prompt" Western Europe. Through the process of generating information in a learning log, each student activates his or her prior knowledge. Fulwiler (1978) defines this kind of writing as a means of connecting the personal and the academic functions of writing. While a daily journal entry focuses on self-discovery and a class notebook concentrates on academic learning, the learning log allows for the rehearsal of ideas and the discovery of position prior to the interaction with others. By initially recording prior knowledge in the learning log, the student takes an active role in generating the information base necessary for learning the new material. Following a time span of 3 to 5 minutes, the teacher records the student associations of Western Europe on an overhead transparency (see figure 6.3). All student associations are recorded regardless of their accuracy. Associations can only be removed from the prereading list when they are disproved or are not validated in the textbook. No attempt at classification occurs during this stage. Associations are recorded in the random order in which students present them.

After listing their associations, students classify the information on the overhead transparency into categories. In following this process, students examine the class list to determine whether any words could be grouped together. For the topic Western Europe, the category of countries presents the most obvious classification. By circling each of the countries

F I G U R E   6 . 3

■

Listing random Western Europe associations.

Scandinavia, terrorism, driving on the left side of the road, Cliffs of Dover, cooperating with their money, trying to trade together, Alps & valleys, an underwater tunnel between France & England, the Berlin Wall is coming down, Germany reunited, borders change in Europe, France, Netherlands, Spain, countries are small like some of our smaller states, the countries are close but the cultures are different, Austria, Scotland, & Ireland, densely populated, that's why they came here, England used up all its resources, steel is made in some countries that have iron & coal, you can go on trains all over Europe, landforms protect some of the countries, plains & swamps may be all the landforms, not deserts

and listing the category and symbol at the top of the transparency, the teacher models the process for the students. Students continue the process by classifying the information in their learning log. As the classification of the information in the logs begins to slow down, students record the reasons for their various classifications. This encourages awareness of one's thinking process. Finally, the teacher records the categories the students identified on the transparency (see figure 6.4) and clearly identifies similar categories and those that overlap. Depending on the students' familiarity with this type of text, categories based on geography concepts may emerge.

Following this predictive activity, the students move to the next phase and preview the passage. Evaluating the classification of associations and predicted structure will help them examine the effectiveness of class predictions.

FIGURE 6.4

∎

Classifying associations.

Western Europe

Countries
Austria
Sweden
England
Netherlands
Spain
Scotland
Ireland
France
Germany

Landforms
mountains (Alps)
valleys
Cliffs of Dover
swamps
plains
all types except desert
can protect countries

Natural
Resources
coal
farms
iron ore
steel

Economics
economic community
cooperate with money
trade together

Transportation
drive on left side in England
trains all over
underwater tunnel
between France & England

Problems
terrorism
Berlin Wall coming down
small like U.S. states
England used up resources
densely populated
close but different cultures
borders change

Phase Two: Monitoring Comprehension

By previewing the information in the text, students begin to evaluate the predictions made earlier. They begin monitoring their comprehension by previewing the text for concepts missed in their classification of associations. Following this preview, the teacher identifies the cues that reveal the text organization by modeling the process of previewing the text material. Next, the teacher generates questions to predict the information presented in the text. Finally, students read the text to find the information to answering the questions. This strategy combines the thought processes involved in the K-W-L strategy and the explicit framework of the graphic organizer.

The teacher has students revise their predictions by focusing on the subtopics identified in the text. Were any categories excluded? Is there a need to extend the categories?

Through the process of examining the pictures, maps, graphs, and subheadings, students begin to revise their original predictions. Examining the descriptive map of the region helps them identify the countries, whereas bar graphs and crop and land-use maps suggest information about the agriculture of the region. Following this skimming process, the students construct concept maps in their learning log.

Initially, students depend on the subheadings to suggest the concepts presented in the text structure. Another helpful strategy is to use the introduction; however, examination of the first sentence of each paragraph helps in the identification of the central concepts in case the material lacks other cues.

To activate students' schemata of the expository text structure, questions focused on the signals used in the text are applicable at this point.

1. What major concepts are suggested by the subheadings used in this text?
2. What information is contained in the introductory paragraph that signals the organization of the information that follows?
3. After examining the maps and visuals contained in the text, what categories should be added or deleted from the predicted categories?

Next, through group discussion, the teacher constructs the basic structure of the chapter overview as students share predictions drawn from their notes in the learning log. (See figure 6.5.)

After the teacher constructs the text overview, students formulate questions that predict the information the text will answer. The use of these questions guides the students' identification of important information in the text passage.

Taking one subtopic at a time, the teacher constructs the concept map on the overhead transparency as students draw relevant information from their learning log. Comparing the association map representing prior knowledge and the concept map drawn from the text helps students clarify the organizational structure of the text. In addition, this process helps students reformulate their preconceptions concerning the structure of the text, which facilitates the transfer of this predictive process to the study of the following unit.

F I G U R E   6 . 5

■

Predicted structure of previewed text.

Western Europe

Countries
Which countries
are part of the
region?

Agriculture
What is the
agriculture like?

*Mineral & Fuel
Resources*
What types does
the region have?

Landforms
What types are
in this area?

Grains & Dairy
What types of
grains are raised?
Why is the region
good for dairy
farming?

*Industrialization
of Ruhr Valley*
What industries
developed in this
region?

Seasons
What is the
weather like
in this region?

Common Market
What is the Common
Market?

Contrasts
What things are
being compared?

*Farming Hills
& Mountains*
How is this done?

*Protecting the
Environment*
Why is this
a problem?

Phase Three: Evaluating Inconsistencies and Written Extensions

The teacher moves students to the evaluative level during the final phase of instruction, beginning with an analysis of the classification of associations and the descriptive map of the text (see figure 6.6). Comparing these refines the strategies, allowing for transfer to the next text chapter and extension activities for interconnections of information across chapters.

By placing the classification of associations (see figure 6.4) on the overhead transparency and having students refer to the descriptive map they created while reading the text, the teacher ensures that students can evaluate the effectiveness of their predictions. The focus of this analysis should center on students becoming more effective in making future predictions. Through an awareness of concepts covered in the first chapter, expectations for future chapters are changed.

Examination of the descriptive maps suggests that many of the countries originally classified as part of the region were correct. However, the classification contained too many countries, and the two incorrect countries in the original prediction will appear in other regions. Since no consideration was given to the categories of agriculture and climate in the initial classification of associations, these categories need to be added to the future predictions. In this chapter, the concept of transportation appears under the category of industrialization. The problems cited in the chapter are more environmental and general than those in the news. Using this critique as a basis, the predictive process is repeated for the following chapter.

Through the predictive process, students identify the organizational pattern to refine the process for more effective future predictions. This involves only the preliminary phases of the investigation because the descriptive mapping strategies can extend into group discussion, research, and writing. Using the maps generated for chapters on Northern and Western Europe, students experience more rehearsal of the material through manipulating the information while writing a paper comparing and contrasting the two regions.

A sensitivity to the structure required in expository writing becomes evident as the maps generated from the expository text serve to structure the points of comparison. Signal words cue readers to the structure of the written product as students make transitions from the material on one descriptive map to that on the other (see figure 6.7).

Clues for Teaching Further Thinking Skills

By examining the influence of descriptive mapping activity on the expository writing, one can see how the mapping process gives students control over aspects of focus and organization. By using the descriptive maps, the reader learns to identify points of comparison in the text. This establishes the focus and organization of the paper while moving the reader into the body of the paper. Following the series of topics established in the introductory paragraph, each point of comparison can be isolated and examined for similarities and differences.

FIGURE 6.6

■

Student-generated concept map by Shannan.

Western Europe

Countries
Ireland
France
Germany
Austria
Switzerland
Belgium
United Kingdom
Netherlands
Monaco
Leichinstein
Luxenberg.

Agriculture
Yield highest
in the world
Large farms
Migrant workers
rotate with crops
Have fertile crops
because of chemical
advanced machinery
Cooperate farms
(W World)
Average 30 acres

Mineral/Fuel Resources
Rich mineral resources
Well developed trans-
portation
Mining manufacture
Iron ore
Coal

Economics
Common Market
Share economic
opportunity
Free trade
No Tariffs
between common
Market countries
(7 from Western
Europe, 3 aren't)

Landforms
plains
plateaus
hills
mountains

Grains/Dairy
Because of plains
there's large crops
of grain
Wheat, livestock
40% of land is
reclaimed by sea.

Industrialization
Coal deposits
produce steel
from Iron
Transportation
(railroads and
canals) brought
in products from
other countries
Countries are
interdependent
exchange resources

Climate
Seasonal
changes are not
extreme
Precipitation
is moderate and
cool and damp

Farming Hills
Special crops
Good income
Poor soil, cool
climate
Grapes and fruit
Dairy products
Meat products

Protecting the Environment
Dwindling coal supply
Researchers trying
to develop ways
to tap other energy sources
Pollution

Patterns of Living
Country life (rural)
cathedral, castles
Cities industrialized
Variety of jobs
Education, science
Modern architecture

FIGURE 6.7

■

An example of expository writing.

Northern and Western Europe
by Shannon

Have you ever visited Europe?
Examination of Northern and Western
Europe shows that many similarities
and differences can be seen in many
areas. By refering to agriculture, resources,
climate, contries, and land, you can see just
how alike and different they really are.

When comparing Northern European
agriculture to Western European agriculture,
it becomes clear that there are many
similarties and differences.
Western Europe proves to be more of an
agriculture region, unlike Northern
Europe in many ways. Farming in Western
Europe is more basic since boulders and
rocks soil don't interfere with the
flurishing plains and basins. Western
Europe produces a large variety of grain,
wheat, and livestock, similar to its
neighbor, Northern Europe. Northern Europe
although it has swamps and marshes, and
rocky soil yields more than Western
Europe. Northern Europe produces large
quantities of daily, grains, and livestock.
Such examples are exported cheese,
butter, oats, wheat, rye, barley, and livestock
products like meat and hide. This conclusion
is drawn from the hard workers and the
various farming techniques. Northern
Europe and Western Europe are similar

FIGURE 6.7

■

since they both use cooperative farms to help keep costs down. Unlike most Western farmers, in Northern Europe, farmers often share their equipment and profits. Western Europe benefits by having migrant workers rotate with their crops. Also, crops are more fertile because of chemical advanced machinery.

Resources play a great deal of importance in Northern and Western Europe. While Northern Europe is famous for its fish and forests, Western Europe has rich mineral resources. Both areas produce steel and iron or, although Western Europe also has coal deposits. In order to trasport the products, Western Europe has many railroads and canals which have their transporion well developed. In comparison, Western Europe produces more natural resources while Northern Europe stays less industrialized.

Through climate, simalarties and differences became clear in Western and Northern Europe. Northern Europe has a moderate climate, as well as Western Europe, until you reach areas north of the Artic Circle. This area includes long winters and short growing seasons. Western Europe doesn't appear to have extreme seasonal changes and precipitation is moderate. Over all, most of this area is cool and damp.

F I G U R E   6 . 7

■

Continued

Such countries within Western Europe are Ireland, France, West Germany, Austria, Switzerland, Belgium, United Kingdom, Netherlands, Monaco, Liechtenstein, and Luxenburg, Countries located in Northern Europe are Iceland, Norway, Sweden, Finland, and Denmark. These countries make up all the similarities and differences contained in this article.

A distinctive difference between northern and western Europe is the land type. In northern Europe glaciers remain, while marshes and swamps are present. This land permits limited farming because of its infertile soil with boulders and gravel. On the Other hand, western Europe has large farms and fertile crops, the average being thirty acres. Landfarms there include plains, plateaus, hills, and mountains.

As concluded from information gathered, many similarities and differences have arisen between the two countries. While western Europe proves more as an agriculture region, northern Europe is big in the fishing industry. Through examination of agriculture, resources, climate, countries, and land a better understanding can be reached about these two famous countries.

The students then make appropriate transitions between the information contained in each of the chapters in order to establish these comparisons. As a result, the information drawn from each of the chapters does not remain as isolated facts but emerges as part of an interrelated information bank. This process of creating connections between the information in different chapters encourages rehearsal of the information and facilitates long-term retention of the material. Based on this assumption, drawn from the results of a 3-year study funded by the National Institute for Learning, the research of Langer and Applebee (1987) supports the positive impact of this type of manipulation and integration of material. Moreover, the research of Armbruster, Anderson, and Ostertag (1989) concludes that instruction on text structure has a positive impact on reading and writing expository text. This finding is based on their research on the problem-solution structure with a fifth-grade population. Since this is one of the most difficult text structures, the researchers suggest that there is a strong basis for the assumption that this type of instruction could be beneficial in learning content area material and have a positive impact on writing as well.

Finally, through the use of the learning log, students have the opportunity to think about how they process the information and evaluate the structure of the information presented in the chapters, in other words, the opportunity to develop a metacognitive awareness. The student comments shown in figure 6.8 on text structure echo many of the same complaints adults make. This student's identification of the lack of uniformity in the organizational pattern and sections that are choppy and difficult to understand shows how effectively a student can critique materials when expectations are established. The comments suggest that the student is actively engaged in manipulating the information to create classifications across the chapters. This suggests that the student is transferring the strategies across units and establishing connections between the material in different chapters. Her criticism that the lack of uniformity in the text hinders her ability to learn the material suggests that this student has developed an awareness of her needs for learning and feels that the text has not met them. This also creates a sensitivity necessary in her own writing when she considers the needs of her audience.

Table 6.1 summarizes the three phases of strategic sequencing.

FIGURE 6.8

∎

An example of expository writing by Kim.

Comparison of two chapters in this text book—Northern and Western Europe, lack uniformity. While headings and titles are given, the information isn't gathered under appropriate columns. Such columns include agriculture and resources.

Under agriculture many topics aren't in correct positions. In Northern Europe, climate is visible in the agriculture section whereas it should be placed in a separate subsection for students to find it easy to use. Text books should be arranged in a proper, easy-to-use manner to assist students in learning, they should not be arranged in a boring pattern that loses your audiences attention. Throughout these two chapters many items are displaced, especially in agriculture. Land types, methods of farming, and crops are scattered throughout the paragraphs, not organized in form. These poor sources of organization under agriculture, hinder the achievement ability of the student.

FIGURE 6.8

■

Continued.

Many of the same problems of the organizational form also occur under resources in Western and Northern Europe. For instance, while the abundant fishing resources are discussed in a separate section, fishing is also partly discussed under agriculture.

Unlike the agriculture sections, each resource is divided into a column. The variation of the format in these text books are choppy and not understandable. In western Europe; though, all of the resources are placed under only one heading. Students can not possibly find an organized form that is continued throughout the text to help studying and test taking.

From the information gathered in these two chapters, concludes that this book is incapable of teaching students geography. A lack of uniformity misleads students to unimportant, unorganized details. This hinders the students learning ability, and increases time of studying little details. This text book should be reorganized and republished to serve as a proper learning tool.

TABLE 6.1

■

STRATEGIES FOR READING AND WRITING

Phase One: Activating Prior Knowledge

Record concept response in the learning log
Brainstorm class associations and put them on the overhead transparency
Model classification of prior knowledge "think aloud" technique
Continue classification in the learning log
Record possible categories suggested by the class

Phase Two: Monitoring Comprehension

Preview text and expository signals
Predict topics in the learning log
Construct class concept map on the overhead transparency
Record questions the text may answer
Read text and complete map in the learning log

Phase Three: Evaluating Inconsistencies and Written Extensions

Compare classification of associations and descriptive map in learning log
Discuss similarities and differences in class

Encouraging Transfer

Predict text structure for the next chapter
Repeat the instructional pattern for the next unit

Written Extensions

Use chapter maps to identify points of comparison
Review transition words for comparison and contrast
Draft introductory paragraph identifying points of comparison
Draft paper following the organizational pattern established in the introductory text
Get peer response to the draft for focus and organization
Conference

Evaluating Structure

Use the learning log to record characteristics of the text that helped or hindered learning
Record thinking strategies used with this type of writing

Summary

While the inadequacy of content area textbooks has been documented and the need for change established, teachers do not have the luxury of waiting for the problem to be resolved. According to Lipson, Valencia, Wixson, and Peters (1993, p. 254), "Students who cannot see meaningful connections across content or skills are . . . unlikely to be able to use their knowledge and skills to solve problems or make decisions about issues raised in the curriculum."

Students and teachers are held accountable for student performance in social studies as well as for reading and writing in the expository mode. Awareness of the active nature of the learner in constructing the meaning of the text suggests direction in addressing this issue. Combining selections from children's literature with the social studies textbook and applying learning strategies may be the most efficient way to help students understand and relate concepts.

With strategic sequencing of instruction and the use of graphic organizers to focus comprehension, students can acquire the necessary awareness of text structure to increase their comprehension. The use of descriptive maps developed while reading the text helps students compare and contrast the information in the brainstorming of ideas, as well as link the concepts they are learning. This procedure of generating writing from graphic representations enhances the production of expository writing by centering attention on the focus and organization, primary targets on most writing assessment measures. Finally, through the use of the learning log in this process, students develop the metacognitive awareness necessary in taking control of their own learning. Through the application of this kind of prototype, attention to student learning in the social studies can have the added benefits of facilitating reading comprehension and improving the focus and organization of the students' own writing.

References

Anderson, R. C., Hiebert, E. H., Scott, J. A., & Wilkinson, I. A. G. (1984). *Becoming a nation of readers: The report of the commission on reading.* Washington, DC: National Institute of Education.

Armbruster, B. B. (1985). Using graphic organizers in social studies. *Ginn Occasional Papers, 22.*

Armbruster, B. B., Anderson, T. H., & Ostertag, J. (1989). Teaching text structure to improve reading and writing. *Reading Teacher, 43,* 130–137.

Clarke, J. (1991). Using visual organizers to focus on thinking. *Journal of Reading, 34,* 526–534.

Davidson, J. L. (1982). The group mapping activity for instruction in reading and thinking. *Journal of Reading, 26,* 52–56.

Fancett, V., & Hawke, S. (1980). Instructional practices. In I. Morrissett (Ed.), *Social studies in the 1980s* (pp. 61–78). Alexandria, VA: Association for Supervision and Curriculum Development.

Fulwiler, T. (1978). *Journal writing across the curriculum* (Report No. CS 204 467). Denver, CO: Conference on College Composition and Communication. (ERIC Document Reproduction Service No. ED 161 073)

Indrisano, R., & Paratore, J. R. (1992). Using literature with readers at risk. In B. Cullinan (Ed.), *Invitation to read: More children's literature in the reading program* (pp. 138–149). Newark, DE: International Reading Association.

Jones, B. J., Palincsar, A. S., Ogle, D. S., & Carr, E. G. (1987). *Strategic teaching and learning: Cognitive instruction in the content areas.* Alexandria, VA: Association for Supervision and Curriculum Development.

Kuhrt, B. L. (1989). *The effects of expressive writing on the composing and learning processes of sixth-grade students in social studies.* Unpublished doctoral dissertation, Northern Illinois University, DeKalb.

Langer, J., & Applebee, A. (1987). *How writing shapes thinking.* Urbana, IL: National Council of Teachers of English.

Lipson, M. Y., Valencia, S. W., Wixson, K. K., & Peters, C. W. (1993). Integration and thematic teaching: Integration to improve teaching and learning. *Language Arts, 70* (4), 252–263.

Ogle, D. M. (1986). K-W-L: A teaching model that develops active reading of expository text. *Reading Teacher, 39,* 564–570.

Ogle, D. M. (1989). The know, want to know, learn strategy. In K. D. Muth (Ed.), *Children's comprehension of text: Research into practice* (pp. 205–223). Newark, DE: International Reading Association.

Osburn, J. H., Jones, B. B., & Stein, M. (1985). The case of improved textbooks. *Educational Leadership, 42,* 9–16.

Resnick, L. B., & Klopfer, L. E. (1989). Toward rethinking the curriculum. In L. B. Resnick and L. E. Kolpfer (Eds.), *Toward rethinking the curriculum.* Arlington, VA: Association for Supervision & Curriculum Development.

Tsuchiya, Y. (1988). *Faithful elephants* (T. Lewin, Illus.). Boston: Houghton Mifflin.

Wilkerson, B. (1988). A principal's perspective. In J. Davidson (Ed.), *Counterpoint and beyond* (pp. 79–85). Urbana, IL: National Council of Teachers of English.

Drama in the Social Studies: Gateway to the Past, Pathway to the Future

PAMELA A. NELSON
ROSARY COLLEGE, RIVER FOREST, IL

The wise teacher capitalizes

on children's natural urge to imitate adult life

by making creative dramatics an integral part

of social studies instruction.

GEORGE W. MAXIM,
Social Studies and the Elementary School Child, 4th Ed.

Chapter Seven

Introduction

Tim was small of stature, and at age 13 his face still bore more resemblance to a child than an adult. He wore T-shirts emblazoned with the insignias of heavy metal rock groups and carried an enormous black, lizard-grained, three-ring binder to class. According to a student teacher, this was a bit puzzling to the regular teachers because though the binder was 3 inches thick, it was always empty. Tim did not complete assignments and only rarely arrived at the classroom with required materials and supplies. In general, Tim did not do well on examinations, and his participation in class discussion was minimal.

Although Tim consistently lost points for not completing daily assignments, his involvement in a program associated with the study of the period prior to the Civil War was complete and positive. For that program the class traveled from the classroom to a local museum village. There the class met with museum staff members to work with primary source materials that indicated the views of local families on issues of slavery and the Union. The students then proceeded to homes or businesses staffed by volunteers who portrayed three homemakers of the 1850s. They met the wife of a new attorney and supporter of the Compromise of 1850; the wife of a blacksmith, who was an ardent abolitionist; and the wife of the editor of the newspaper, who strove to remain neutral on the political and religious issues of the day.

During their visits with each of the women, the students assumed the role of children in 1856 and engaged in tasks that were common to children of that time. They helped prepare for the visit of a famous Illinois senator, Stephen A. Douglas. They mended clothing for fugitives who were being hidden by conductors on the Underground Railroad. They sorted type as apprentices at the newspaper. When they gathered at the schoolhouse to rehearse the choral reading for Douglas's visit, they encountered a fugitive slave and heard the story of his escape and journey to freedom in Canada. In the closing portions of the program, the students were faced with their duty in regard to the Fugitive Slave Law. That law stated that it was illegal to aid fugitives from labor in their flight and that those who knew of such fugitives were legally bound to make their presence known to appropriate law enforcement agents.

A woman who enacted the role of one of the wives was also involved in volunteer work at Tim's school. Upon her return to the classroom,

■ Local museums can provide invaluable opportunities for students to
become involved in living history programs as the children take a
giant step back in time.

she was greeted by a number of student comments on the program. None
was more surprising than Tim's. He approached the volunteer and said, "I
didn't know. I didn't know. I didn't know all that was going on. All that
just livin' and decidin'. It was really hard."

Unfortunately, Tim's initial response to social studies is not that
uncommon. Sewall (1988) found that students at all grade levels considered social studies to be their most boring subject, largely blaming dull
social studies textbooks as the primary reason. According to Goodlad
(1984), junior and senior high students view social studies as the least
useful subject in relation to their present and future needs. He also reports that elementary school students perceive social studies to be the
most difficult and least liked subject in their curriculum. After stating
these findings, Goodlad puzzles over the responses because he believes
that the topics covered in social studies seem intrinsically associated with
great human interest and drama. He charges that "something happens to
them on the way to the classroom" (p. 212).

The National Council for the Social Studies has responded to concerns such as this through a variety of task forces that have reported their
findings in the council's journal, *Social Education* (National Council for the
Social Studies, 1984, 1989a, 1989b). Two regular and respected contributors
to that journal, Levstik (1990) and Thornton (1990), have suggested that the
focus on the potential of outside curriculum reform to effect a change in the
quality of social studies/history instruction may be misplaced. They believe, instead, that resources should be devoted to encouraging and

161

*Drama in the Social Studies:
Gateway to the Past,
Pathway to the Future*

supporting classroom teachers and students as agents of change by identifying vital content and selecting, creating, and evaluating resources and methodologies in the teaching of social studies.

This chapter describes how classroom teachers can use drama as a medium through which students may confront social studies content. First, the chapter clarifies the meaning of drama as it is used in the whole language/social studies classroom. Second, it offers theoretical rationales for the use of drama in meeting currently proposed objectives. Third, it offers practical suggestions on how drama can be used to explore topics, themes, and issues and provides examples of various techniques and planning formats for using drama to teach social studies concepts and generalizations.

What Is Drama as It Is Used in Education?

Over the years drama has been defined in many ways and included in the curriculum in the hope of promoting growth toward a variety of goals. According to Bolton (1985), early emphasis on drama in the schools was on producing a polished performance. The dramas that resulted were not only an important form of entertainment in the local community, but also a means of exhibiting students' levels of accomplishment and expertise to the community at large. Teachers worked with students on elocution, declaration, and choral reading with the goal of producing articulate citizens. Not until the 1950s and 1960s did teachers who worked with students in drama focus their attention on self-expression, introspection, and the interpretation of inner states.

In the late 1960s and through the 1970s, new aspects of drama began to emerge as Moffett (1968), in *Teaching the Universe of Discourse,* directed attention to the relationship of drama to language and cognitive development. For Moffett (1968, p. 61), drama is defined as "What is happening." The type of drama he advocated closely resembles the imaginative play of children or the improvisational drama and comedy that have become popular in both the professional theater and on television. This is the means through which events from the past, present, or future can be brought to the classroom so that students can experience them as participants.

Putnam (1991) supports Moffet's view and identifies drama as a viable alternative to direct experience for building background knowledge—schemata, representations, or scripts—of how particular things work or worked in a given culture and what particular terms and concepts mean. According to Putnam (p. 464),

> What nonfiction dramatizations accomplish, in my view, is a kind
> of transformation of factual information into events scripts.
> These scripts . . . provide a meaningful frame in which the
> significant actions, facts, vocabulary, and concepts presented in

■ By actually doing the same task as that of a pioneer, children transform factual information into meaningful schemata.

expository text can be incorporated. Acting out this information generates a rich context of extra linguistic associations which children can easily relate to and recall. Important information is lifted off the page, in effect, and experienced as a complex, dynamic, and holistic event.

Dorothy Heathcote (Heathcote & Herbert, 1985) is generally credited with the new focus on drama as a teaching tool or method that can be used in content areas in the pursuit of knowledge and understanding of key concepts. She views drama as a way of making meaning from the data of events and issues on which social scientists and historians base their interpretations and generalizations. According to Huck, Hepler, and Hickman (1993, p. 791), "The child broadens living and learning experiences by playing the roles of people in the past, in other places, and in different situations." Teachers who involve students in this type of drama are not as concerned with dramatic elements or performance as they are in providing an environment in which and a means through which students can gain an understanding of the complexity of social situations and problems and a desire to explore and reflect on particular themes and topics more deeply.

Current views on drama in the classroom can best be characterized by the work of Heathcote's followers. As a result of the work of O'Neill (1985), O'Neill and Lambert (1987), and Fines and Verrior (1974), teachers have moved closer to viewing drama as an educative medium than was the case earlier. While the decisions of the students engaging in

163

*Drama in the Social Studies:
Gateway to the Past,
Pathway to the Future*

a drama are still of highest priority in determining the course of action and the manner in which characters are interpreted, considerable emphasis is currently placed on reflection about those interpretations and on supporting interpretations through the inquiry methods of the social sciences (Philboin & Myers, 1991).

Fines and Verrior (1974) provide a classic example of drama as both an inquiry and an educative medium. Their students were asked to assume the roles of various members of an archaeological team. The assignment was based on a real excavation on a nobleman's estate in the early 19th century.

> The children had worked away well in role, and right up to the discovery of the antiquities we found no problems at all.
> On digging up the case full of silver the laborers decided that they must show it to his lordship and plodded up to the big house. They came into the study and plunked their burden down on the desk and said, "We found that. Now give us a reward. We want more pay." And it was not gently spoken, either! The class was as worried about this as were the teachers, so we stopped at that point to discuss whether the tenantry would have addressed his lordship in such a fashion in those days, and most of us felt fairly sure they would not. (Fines & Verrior, 1974, p. 43)

At that point the children and their teachers began a brief inquiry into the concepts of authority held by people who lived in the particular area during the 19th century. The children pursued the topic through written sources, both fiction and nonfiction, and through the teachers' descriptions of the daily lives of the nobility and of the working class during the period. Students also engaged in dramatic play in which they explored some of their personal conceptions of authority before returning to the topic at hand with a better understanding of the social system and culture in which the workers and landowners lived.

Drama cannot be said to enable students to access the attitudes and feelings that people of former times had about certain events (Shand, May, & Linnell, 1990). It may, as in the foregoing example, however, make it possible for students to generate feelings and meanings that relate to those former times or other situations. Drama enables students to construct and approach the multiple realities that are believed to have existed at different times and in different cultures and to do so in very concrete and tangible ways.

This most recent use (or goal) of drama may hold the most promise in the social studies classroom when one considers the current emphasis on content and accountability in the reports of the Bradley Commission on History in Schools (1988) and the curriculum task force of the National Commission on Social Studies in the Schools (1989), and in the work of individuals such as Ravitch and Finn (1987) and Egan (1986).

Theoretical Underpinnings for the Use of Drama in Meeting the Goals of Social Studies Education

In the stated goals that appear in reports of and responses to the National Council for the Social Studies curriculum task forces, there seems to be agreement that social studies is supposed to provide students with the opportunity to acquire the knowledge, skills, attitudes, and values that will enable them to participate fully as citizens of a democracy in an increasingly interdependent world. The following section will provide support for the use of drama as it relates to the preparation of students for participatory citizenship as problems solvers and decision makers who can consider events or issues from multiple perspectives.

In addition, the following section will provide support for drama's three major contributions: (1) drama provides a nurturing environment for the development and acquisition of the attitudes and values that stimulate individuals to participate as citizens, (2) drama provides an environment that permits and encourages individuals to represent and respond to experience in a variety of ways, and (3) drama provides an environment in which students must work together and make decisions that will truly affect the course of the dramatic action.

Drama and Attitudes, Values, and Perspective Taking

In considering the acquisition of knowledge or information, according to Gagne (1984), it is critical that information be presented to students in organized and meaningful contexts. While organization and context are central to presenting information verbally, Gagne goes on to assert that if skills are being taught, there is a critical need for the opportunity to practice the skills with varying degrees of supervision and feedback.

When we turn to the development of attitudes, however, we enter a unique domain. Kohlberg (1976), Selman (1971), and Taba (1955) have provided the theoretical and research support for methods that facilitate the development of attitudes, values, and the ability to consider issues from a variety of perspectives. Their findings indicate that in promoting the development of attitudes and the ability to consider different perspectives, it is helpful to present students with dilemmas—in story form—that involve characters to whom the students can in some way relate. Students then need opportunities to discuss the dilemmas and consider choices made and options available from their perspectives as observers and also from the perspectives of the participants in the dilemma situations. Opportunities to draw conclusions, to propose possible solutions, and then to reflect on and discuss what has been proposed are essential.

Putnam (1991) relates her observations of a kindergarten dramatization of the concept of civil rights based on the true story of Rosa Parks. Over a 3-day period, the children heard the story of the seamstress who

165

Drama in the Social Studies:
Gateway to the Past,
Pathway to the Future

■ Drama affords students the opportunity to develop empathy for others. In this case, students are in a one-room school house on the prairie.

was arrested for her refusal to move to the back of a city bus. They also learned of subsequent events that served as the beginning of the civil rights movement of the 1960s. The students then assumed and enacted the roles of Parks, Martin Luther King, Jr., and the police chief and members of the community of Montgomery, Alabama—both African American and white. As the students reenacted the drama and changed roles, they had repeated opportunities to vicariously experience the event from different perspectives.

Knight (1989) and Lee (1983) provide additional support for the significance of perspective taking and empathy in the development of historical and social understanding. Lee, in particular, believes that while mature historians and social scientists must merely be willing to entertain different beliefs and value systems, it may be necessary for children who are studying the same events or issues to first share the point of view of the individuals involved if they are later to move to the more mature position. If children are not encouraged to develop the skill of empathizing early in life, Lee fears that they will find it difficult if not impossible to develop a mature sense of empathy or perspective taking.

Drama affords students not only the opportunity to consider choices and options that were or are available to "characters" but also the opportunity to "try out" the options and "live through" the consequences of those choices in a protected environment.

Drama and Response to Social Studies Content

Jerome Bruner (1966) identifies three systems through which human beings represent their experiences for consideration, storage, retrieval, and application. He calls these systems or forms the inactive, the iconic, and the symbolic. In the inactive form, knowledge is translated into action because it is difficult to express in words. Humans represent experience in this form when it is easier to demonstrate, show, or act out what they know. In the iconic form, knowledge or understanding is translated into visual or other sensory organizational systems. Drawings, charts, and diagrams are examples of iconic representations of experience. The third form of representation, the symbolic, is the most sophisticated of the three systems and is the last to develop. It is best represented by both written and spoken language. Written records, oral histories, and stories are examples of experience that is preserved through symbolic representation. It is in this form that children come into contact with history and the social studies most often in school and in society.

Bruner (1977), is quick to point out, however, that while adults have command of all three forms, the first two are the most developed in children. He encourages those who work with and for children to recognize the importance of accepting all three forms as valid and appropriate ways of representing experience. Vass (1992) also cautions against the tendency of adults to rely only on a child's ability to frame responses in the symbolic form of written or oral answers as the "true" test of the child's understanding of concepts or processes. Vass notes that understanding as well as the restatement of facts must be considered in assessment programs.

According to Bruner (1977, p. 13),

> It is only when . . . basic ideas are put in formalized terms as equations or elaborated verbal concepts that they are out of reach of the young child, if he has not first understood them intuitively and had a chance to try them out on his own. The early teaching of science, mathematics, social studies, and literature should be designed to teach these subjects with scrupulous intellectual honesty, but with an emphasis upon the intuitive grasp of ideas and upon the use of these basic ideas . . . [children] can grasp the idea of tragedy and the basic human plights represented in myth. But they cannot put these ideas into formal language or manipulate them as grown-ups can.

Drama permits students to make use of all three forms of representation as they express their ideas and understanding. Drama allows them to show others what they mean.

Drama as a Basis for Interaction with Others

Because of the corporate nature of drama, students must truly engage with each other when drama is used in the classroom, thereby avoiding being what Stahl (1992, p. 8) refers to as "academic loners." Participation in drama allows students to work as creators, directors, and decision makers and to respond to the work and suggestions of others in functional, meaningful, and relevant contexts (Lehr, 1983). Students also have the opportunity to share and celebrate the work of others and to better reflect on their own (Heathcote & Herbert, 1985; O'Neill, 1985). In improvisational

167

Drama in the Social Studies:
Gateway to the Past,
Pathway to the Future

dialogues, students become attuned to seeking meaning in such interactions and in the activities of life. They can also become more involved with an author's thoughts or those of a character and better reflect on their own point of view, according to Booth (1985).

Drama also allows children of different ethnic and economic backgrounds and achievement levels to work together in small groups. This finding was noted by Johnson (1983) and Ritchie (1991) in regard to cross-cultural understanding. Gimmestad and DeChiara (1982) found that participation in ethnic drama decreases children's verbalizations of prejudice. Most important was their finding that "when small heterogeneous groups of children are asked to work together on learning tasks where some success is guaranteed, they tend to develop positive attitudes toward each other" (p. 49).

Drama participation gives students the opportunity to use language for purposes and in ways that may not be available to them in everyday life. In assuming different roles, students speak, act, and think as their characters would regardless of how unlike themselves those characters may be. Students also find themselves in circumstances that they may never have had the opportunity or misfortune to encounter in real life.

During periods provided for planning and reflection when students are out of role, they use language to convey their thoughts to others and to learn of the thoughts of others. Students have opportunities to use language to let others know what they need, to control others, to establish relationships, to express pride, to question, to convey information, to negotiate rules and regulations, to record what has happened, to imagine and to make jokes. Dramatizing gives students the opportunity to use the various functions of language in cooperative groups as they negotiate with classmates. Johnson and Johnson (1992) and Slavin (1983) have found that such opportunities produced greater feelings of self-efficacy and involvement among students as well as increased mastery of content.

When we consider these findings, we see a basis of support for using drama in the social studies classroom. As Johnson and O'Neill (1985, p. 90) state:

> Dramatizing makes it possible to isolate an event or to compare one event with another, to look at events that have happened to other people in other places and times perhaps, or to look at one's own experiences after the event, within the safety of knowing that just at this moment it is not really happening. We can, however, feel that it is happening because drama uses the same rules we find in life. People exist in their environment, living a moment at a time and taking those decisions which seem reasonable in light of their present knowledge about the current state of affairs. The difference is that in life we have many things to consider at the same time and often cannot revise a decision taken, except in the long term. So drama can be a kind of playing at or practice of living, tuning up those areas of feeling-capacity and expression-capacity as well as social-capacity.

Drama can provide opportunities for students to explore the attitudes, values, and perspective that others hold and also to consider their own. Drama allows students to interpret and respond to experience intuitively through movement, construction, and words. It also provides the opportunity for students to use language and problem-solving skills for real purposes as they work with peers in their classrooms.

Initiating Drama with Children

In preparing to use drama in the social studies classroom, it is helpful to precede through three planning phases and then plunge in, returning to the same three phases again and again. First, teachers need to engage in a preparation period of reflection on the needs of their students and on their own personal strengths and weaknesses. Second, teachers need to investigate possible topics and resources related to selected and required topics. Third, teachers need to become familiar with new planning formats that will guide them in their work with students in the classroom.

Preparatory Reflection

Dorothy Heathcote (Johnson & O'Neill, 1985) outlined three teacher attitudes toward students that facilitate work in drama in the classroom. First, she identified the need for respect for the children and what they bring to each situation and experience. Second, she highlighted the need for a willingness to accept and use students as the choreographers of the drama once it begins. Finally, Heathcote indicated,

> Teachers need to identify themselves as members of a team who have the responsibility to keep the team together, to work them to capacity, to forward projects efficiently, to encourage group members in using their strengths and helping them know and overcome their weaknesses, to stretch their potential, and to keep their sights on the task at hand. (Johnson & O'Neill, 1985, p. 44).

In addition to reflecting on what students bring to a situation, Heathcote stressed that the classroom teacher must also develop an attitude of respect for the unique perspectives, talents, and abilities that he or she brings to the classroom. However, before perspectives, talents, and abilities can be respected, they must be identified. Keeping a journal helps many teachers at this stage. Reflection is often aided by asking and writing about what seem to be very basic questions. Teachers must ask themselves what life experiences, course work, and networks throughout the community, nation, and world they bring to the classroom? What readily available objects or artifacts from home, the community, or the school might be springboards to drama? What former travels or occupations might yield new insights and understandings about people and the regions and cultures in which they live? What topics are of particular interest? Which issues

169

*Drama in the Social Studies:
Gateway to the Past,
Pathway to the Future*

■ Journals offer children an opportunity to reflect before they become involved in a drama.

seem to be of greatest concern to students today and for the future? Teachers should identify the areas in which they might be able to offer unique perspectives, as well as identify their greatest strengths and weaknesses. The process of reflection through journal writing generally suggests additional areas for consideration and may be returned to throughout the course of a teacher's work with drama in the classroom. This process also helps the teachers clearly identify areas in which development is needed and effectively plan for development in those areas.

The second step in this preparatory stage involves using what has been identified. Insights that were gained should be considered from the perspective of how they may be used in introducing drama into *one* social studies unit. Which topics are most associated with high interest and ready resources—human, media, artifacts, and time? Which topics from the curriculum have been especially appealing to the students? How much time would it take to add drama to one unit? Which goals and objectives of the current curriculum are essential, and which are of lower priority? Which of those goals and objectives might better be met through work in drama?

Finally, teachers need to identify with others as members of a community or team of learners. The dissemination, acceptance, and application of whole language philosophy and practices (however diversely the term *whole language* may be defined) have come about largely because of the emphasis on a bottom-up rather than a top-down approach to change. They have depended on personal decision making, commitment, and willingness to risk in order to grow. Those who have made changes have stressed the need for teachers to form support groups in the process. It is important that teachers find at least one other individual in their building, district, college classes, or community to work with as they add drama to the social studies curriculum. Such support groups offer ideas and encouragement as well as a sounding board to teachers interested in incorporating drama in their social studies classes. Atwell (1987, 1990), Graves (1983), and Routman (1991) among others emphasize this point and outline the benefits of such support systems for teachers.

At the end of this planning phase, classroom teachers should have additional insights about their students and themselves, have identified a topic or theme to investigate, and have made contact with others who are engaged in the same process.

Investigating Resources

Egan (1986, p. 47) has said, "The educational achievement is not to make the strange seem familiar, but to make the familiar seem strange. It is seeing the wonderful that lies hidden in what we take for granted that matters educationally." Teachers must be willing to look at a topic or concept through a variety of lenses so that the wonder of the ordinary can be appreciated and brought from the textbook into personal focus.

Some of the resources to be examined and gathered in the investigation phase will be of the traditional kind. Teachers and students need background information. This is most often provided by secondary sources—textbooks, nonfiction—that give overviews of topics or events. In working with drama, however, teachers must also locate resources that give an individual perspective and a sense of drama to the topic. These often come from fiction and personal narrative, or primary source material. Literature for children or young adults that deals with social studies topics is plentiful and of high quality (see Suggested Thematic Units in the appendix). The April/May issue of *Social Education,* the journal of the National Council for the Social Studies, provides listings and reviews of outstanding children's books for the social studies published during the preceding year. Examples of primary sources include letters, diaries, court transcripts, and oral histories. Many of these—for example, the narratives of former slaves that were collected by WPA writers during the 1930s—are excellent sources. If excerpts are carefully chosen and organized, many are readable and accessible to upper-elementary students.

Teachers need to talk about topics with colleagues, asking them about the materials and approaches they use. Talking with others provides teachers with information on what has already been done and where gaps occur. Such discussion with colleagues provides a base from which to begin.

Teachers should also turn to librarians and other specialists for help. Teachers may begin with the learning center specialist or the children's librarian at the local library. In addition, librarians in the "adult

171

*Drama in the Social Studies:
Gateway to the Past,
Pathway to the Future*

department" of the local library, such as reference librarians and those in charge of government documents, interlibrary loan, and microforms, are often willing to share their considerable expertise. Once these individuals have an idea of what was initially interesting and compelling about a topic and an idea of the objectives of the unit, they can be a great asset to planning.

Nearly all communities have a number of resource people who may also be of help. Teachers find that resources from the community often come serendipitously, so they need to be prepared and to prepare others to seize opportunities when they arise. For example, an important resource for a museum program was a bill-of-sale for two slave children. The community resident who owned this document lent it to the class because he had read an article about the forthcoming program in the local newspaper.

One teacher, doing the initial planning for a drama involving students in considering the implications of technology, spent time leafing through books that told stories of inventors and their inventions. While reading *Mothers of Invention* (Vare & Ptacek, 1988), the teacher came across the story of the woman who had done the pioneering work on the operation that was to save the lives of babies born with a heart defect that gave them a bluish cast. If these "blue babies" lived, they usually suffered from impaired physical and mental development because their heart could not supply needed oxygen. The teacher's husband had been a blue baby and had had an operation called the Blalock-Taussig shunt. To the teacher's amazement, she learned that the first successful blue baby operation was performed in 1944. Her husband had been born in 1944! As it turned out, his operation was either the eighth or the thirteenth performed in the country. He was a wonderful resource in terms of talking about his parents' stories of their decision to allow him to have the experimental surgery and the drama of his recovery. The effects of technology on human lives are no longer an abstraction when students are allowed to interview or read the personal recollections of those who have been affected by it—both positively and negatively.

The following list of suggested sources of information provides a starting point from which to develop a resource network.

Community resources

Libraries (census reports, microfilms of daily and special-interest newspapers, published diaries, cookbooks, art books, maps, files of community organizations and resource people)

Historical societies (photographs, maps, diaries and letters, artifacts, resource materials on the use of objects and primary sources with children)

Courthouses (transcripts of trials, records of political figures, health records of disease control and dates of major epidemics in the area)

Churches (parish lists of births and deaths, sacramental records, descriptions of services, statements of positions on local and national issues, cookbooks with household tips produced at different times, artifacts associated with various time periods)

Flea markets and charity resale shops (artifacts, articles of clothing, old books, pictures)

Professional organizations (Association of Newspaper Publishers, chamber of commerce, service organizations, the American Bar Association, the American Medical Association)

University libraries
Microfilm and microfiche (area and national newspapers, special collections of documents and publications associated with local and national movements)

Government documents and publications (congressional records, presidential papers, contemporary biographies and photographs of political figures, National Park Service travel brochures, current national and international maps prepared by the CIA, transcripts, diaries, posters, indexes for material available from various departments of the federal government)

Special collections (rare books, displays, oversized books, recordings, private papers of individuals associated with the institution)

National resources
National Archives, Education Branch
Office of Public Programs
Washington, DC 20408

Earth Science Information Centers
U.S. Geological Survey
507 National Center
Reston, VA 22092

National Public Radio Audience Services
2025 M Street Northwest
Washington, DC 20036

Commissioner of Patents and Trademarks
United States Patent and Trademark Office
Washington, DC 20231

Fines and Verrier (1974) and Morgan and Saxton (1987) stress the need for the teacher to commit time to becoming familiar with the most current and valid information and resources on selected topics so that students can be guided toward sources that represent and accurately portray a variety of perspectives. Levstik (1986) also cautions that the emotional loading of narratives used in studying particular issues may lead students to identify with the main characters of narratives to the exclusion of other views. Levstik maintains that the teacher's ability to present students with alternative views and the rationales for those views will help them move beyond a myopic approach to issues and topics. Print, other media, and artifacts that provide insights into the many facets of an issue should be available for students who are using drama as a learning tool.

173

Drama in the Social Studies:
Gateway to the Past,
Pathway to the Future

Developing and Utilizing Specialized Planning Approaches

The planning formats with which teachers are most familiar (Ausubel, 1960; Gagne, Briggs, & Wager, 1988) were designed to enhance the learning, retention, and retrieval of large amounts of verbal material and skills in relatively short periods of time. They may not be the most effective planning guides when working with drama in the classroom. Egan (1986) offers an alternative planning model, the "story form model," that may be a more effective planning tool for experiences with drama. Egan suggests that selected topics be considered as stories to be told rather than as information to be disseminated.

The most compelling stories, he notes, involve powerful and universal life themes that attract students. In using Egan's model, the teacher's first task is to identify life themes or big ideas that may be involved in required or supplementary content. In the case of the program on the Underground Railroad, mentioned earlier, which was closely coordinated with the textbook, the theme revolved around questions of what course of action one should take in a democracy when the laws of the state conflict with what are considered by some to be higher laws.

Second, stories have a rhythm: a beginning, in which the topic or theme is introduced; a middle, in which something happens to complicate things; a climax, in which some sort of resolution or action takes place; and a conclusion, which brings a degree of closure. Attention must be given to planning and generating options for events that will make use of story rhythm. The following questions provide guidelines for the teacher in this process.

> What exact words and stimuli will I use to introduce the drama to the students?
> What object or artifact might I use to draw students in?
> What will compel this particular group of students to participate?
> What areas of the classroom, building, or grounds will be used?
> How will I arrange space, light, or furniture in the area or areas?
> Where will supplies, resources, pictures, and objects to which students may turn in developing understanding of characters or the situation be located?
> What role or roles should I assume?
> How can I help students through the initial phases of the drama?
> How can I move the drama along if it gets stuck?
> How can I help students bring the drama to a conclusion?

Finally, the teacher must plan for reflection on the drama—on what has occurred. Students should be given the opportunity to reflect on their experiences. Manna and Lawson (1992, p. 231) emphasize conscious reflection when they say,

> By encouraging students to step back from a dramatic event which they have been instrumental in developing, the teacher gives them an opportunity to examine such things as the issues

that surfaced, the understandings and insights they gained, and the discoveries they made about the power of drama itself to reflect and distill human experience.

How will this period of reflection be structured and guided? Where will it take place? What options for response to the drama will be available to students? Will students talk, write, or draw about their experiences? How much time will be allotted to individual response and to group response? Will students share their impressions with those who participated in the drama or with other significant individuals in the school or community who were not present? The teacher must plan this period carefully, for it is during the period of reflection that the power of the drama and the insights gained may be fully realized and extended by participants and spectators alike.

Swartz (1988) emphasizes that after initial planning, drama should be gradually introduced so that experiences can be as positive as possible for both teachers and students. The next section provides suggestions and resources for such beginnings.

Resources and Ideas for Drama

The suggestions that follow are not meant to be complete units in themselves, though they may be developed more fully to form units. They are meant to function as a part of a unit of study and highlight "big ideas" or key concepts and generalizations that often appear in social studies units (Banks & Clegg, 1985). They are suggested ways of introducing a variety of dramatic techniques and rely on the use of literature and the familiar and reassuring activity of shared book experience as the stimulus in each case. These suggestions are followed by two in-depth plans that are based on the formats of two well-known drama teachers. The first format, that of Larry Swartz (1988), is particularly appropriate for use with primary and intermediate students. The second format comes from the work of Cecily O'Neill and Alan Lambert (1987) and is particularly appropriate for use with older students in considering more controversial social issues and concepts.

Discipline- and Concept-Related Drama

SOCIAL SCIENCE DISCIPLINE: ECONOMICS

KEY CONCEPT: Scarcity

GENERALIZATION: A conflict between unlimited wants and limited resources created the need for decision making.

LITERATURE STIMULUS: Levinson, R. (1985). *Watch the stars come out.* New York: Dutton.

DRAMATIC ROLES: The story tells of the journey of a brother and sister to join their parents who immigrated to America at an earlier date. The parents had gone ahead to find jobs, establish a home, and raise the money to bring the children to America.

175

*Drama in the Social Studies:
Gateway to the Past,
Pathway to the Future*

■ A drama may evolve from a portion of a children's literature book such as the spinning of wool from *Ox-Cart Man*.

After reading the book, have the students assume various roles—the parents, the children, the relatives with whom the children were left, and so on. Have them improvise a scene that might have occurred before the story began. This drama might explain how and why the parents made the decision to leave the children in the care of relatives and come to the United States ahead of them. It might involve the parents telling the children that they are leaving but will send for them. It might be an improvisation of the parents joining others on the ship and saying good-bye. It might take another turn and be an improvisation based on what happened after the children arrived in the United States.

SOCIAL SCIENCE DISCIPLINE: HISTORY

KEY CONCEPT: Exploration

GENERALIZATION: Explorations that people made into what were to them strange territories resulted in tremendous cultural exchange as well as conflicts between cultural and ethnic groups. In general, more technologically advanced cultures have assimilated or destroyed cultures that were less technologically developed.

LITERATURE STIMULUS: Blumberg, R. (1985). *Commodore Perry in the land of the Shogun.* New York: Lothrop, Lee and Shepard.

DRAMATIC ROLES: After reading the book, which tells of the visit of Commodore Perry to Japan, which was closed to other nations until the mid-19th century, have the students assume the roles of Japanese who were present at the initial meeting with the American representatives and the exchange of gifts. The teacher may assume the role of emperor or a senior adviser. The improvisation should be conducted with the aim of determining a course of action toward the outsiders. The question might be whether to continue to work to develop a strong relationship between Japan and the United States or to imprison the foreign intruders.

SOCIAL SCIENCE DISCIPLINE: POLITICAL SCIENCE

KEY CONCEPT: Authority

GENERALIZATION: When authorities feel that the ideology and/or general well-being of their political system is threatened, they sometimes take extreme action against individuals and groups, denying them the basic rights guaranteed under the law of the state.

LITERATURE STIMULUS: Hamanaka, S. (1990). *The journey: Japanese Americans, racism and renewal.* New York: Orchard Books.

DRAMATIC ROLES: This book deals with the treatment of the Japanese in the United States. It covers the period of World War II and the internment camps.

Have 5 to 10 students assume the roles of government officials. Have at least 10 other students assume the roles of spectators and reporters. Have the remaining students assume the roles of Japanese who were interned at one of the camps during World War II and who are being asked to tell of their experiences.

SOCIAL SCIENCE DISCIPLINE: POLITICAL SCIENCE

KEY CONCEPT: Political participation

GENERALIZATION: Private citizens act by voting, lobbying, campaigning, attending political meetings, preparing petitions, and running for office.

177

Drama in the Social Studies:
Gateway to the Past,
Pathway to the Future

LITERATURE STIMULUS: Provensen, A., & Provensen, M. (1987). *Shaker Lane*. New York: Viking Kestrel.

DRAMATIC ROLES: The story tells of the life-styles of the residents of Shaker Lane, who are notified that they are to be relocated because of the construction of a new reservoir. Have students assume the roles of residents of Shaker Lane or residents of Foster Hollow. When they have assumed their roles, have them write letters, diary entries, petitions, and so forth expressing their views, fears, hopes, and demands. Have them share what they have written at a town meeting.

SOCIAL SCIENCE DISCIPLINE: GEOGRAPHY

KEY CONCEPT: Spatial interaction

GENERALIZATION: A variety of relationships exist between the sections of a city and the smaller towns surrounding it. The relationships are based on ethnic, racial, and social views and the exchange of trade, services, and ideas. They are altered by technological change.

LITERATURE STIMULUS: Von Tscharner, R., Fleming, R., & the Townscape Institute. (1987). *New Providence: A changing cityscape*. San Diego, CA: Harcourt Brace Jovanovich.

DRAMATIC ROLES: The story traces the growth, decline, and restoration of New Providence from 1910 to 1987. Have students create frozen pictures (tableaux) using their bodies to depict scenes from the story. These can be done individually or in groups to demonstrate changes in occupations or modes of travel, the social and economic characteristics of the times that altered activities, and so on.

SOCIAL SCIENCE DISCIPLINE: SOCIOLOGY

KEY CONCEPT: Social groups

GENERALIZATION: People live in social groups of two or more individuals. These groups help them satisfy their needs.

LITERATURE STIMULUS: Fox, M. (1985). *Wilfrid Gordon McDonald Partridge* (J. Vivas, Illus.). New York: Kane/Miller.

DRAMATIC ROLES: The story tells of a group of nursing home residents who are concerned with Miss Nancy Alison Delacourt Cooper's loss of memory. A young child gathers objects that help Miss Nancy recall incidents in her life and regain her memory. Have one student assume the role of Wilfrid Gordon McDonald Partridge, the child who gathers a set of objects and then listens to the monologue of the student who assumes the role of Miss Nancy, who is 80 years old. The amount of research conducted on events that the elderly resident would recall will depend on the age of the students. Students might then reverse the roles. The teacher might assume the role of the nursing home director.

SOCIAL SCIENCE DISCIPLINE: ANTHROPOLOGY

KEY CONCEPT: Culture

GENERALIZATION: Every society consists of a diverse, human-made system of artifacts, beliefs, and behavior patterns that enable individuals within it to meet common human needs according to their physical and social environment.

LITERATURE STIMULUS: Goor, R., & Goor, N. (1986). *Pompeii: Exploring a Roman ghost town.* New York: Crowell.

DRAMATIC ROLES: Following the sharing of the book, have students interview each other. Ask one child to assume the role of a reporter from the local newspaper. Have the other assume the role of one of the archaeologists, who has recently returned to persuade a foundation to extend funding because of the important discoveries the archaeologists have made. The teacher might assume the role of editor in chief of the newspaper that will publish the stories of the archaeological team's new discoveries.

Drama Unit Using the Format of Larry Swartz

The following unit would be appropriate, with modifications, at both the primary and intermediate levels and is an example of how the format proposed by Larry Swartz (1988) can be used to develop ideas around a theme.

Swartz places special emphasis on the use of literature as a springboard for curriculum- and theme-related drama. His book *Drama Themes: A Practical Guide for Classroom Teachers* is especially helpful to teachers who are working with students who have not been involved with drama before. The format provides warm-up activities that enable students to become more comfortable in working as part of a group and that stimulate flexibility of thought in regard to a theme or topic. His inclusion of pantomime and tableaux is also helpful for those just beginning to explore drama as a learning tool. Finally, his models make provisions for periods of reflection during the following dramas.

THEME: Relocation

FOCUS: Geography, sociology, economics

Technological and economic changes, in both the workplace and the family have increased the likelihood of frequent moves for large numbers of people. Children who move frequently, even those who adjust well and enjoy the opportunities that moves offer, often encounter problems with the losses created by the moves and separations from family members and friends. The decision-making processes related to moving, to maintaining connections with absent loved ones, and to becoming established in a new area are the focus of this unit. A related focus is that of how one might find out about a new area. This includes consideration of what things are important to know about an area. The literature selections found in the "Extended Improvisations" section establish the time period for the drama. One provides a contemporary setting, and the other places the setting in the 1930s or the Depression era. Interviews with various individuals or discussions with family members who are familiar with current economic concerns or those that existed during the Great Depression provide additional information from which the context of the drama can be built.

GOALS: To use literature as a stimulus for role playing and improvisation

To provide a context in which students face issues associated with relocation

Warm-Up Games

Packing a Trunk. Play a familiar circle game that involves packing a trunk for a journey, including the necessities from A to Z. This is also a memory game that requires each person to repeat all of the previously named items before adding another one. For example, the first player begins, "I'm going on a journey, and I'm going to take my adding machine. The second player then says, "I'm going on a journey, and I'm going to take my adding machine and my bathrobe." The third player says, "I'm going on a journey, and I'm going to take my adding machine, my bathrobe, and my cartoon book."

Geography. The first player in this game gives the name of a state (country or city). The next player must think of the name of a state (country or city) that begins with the last letter of the previous player's choice. For example, the first player says, "Ohio." The second player might then say, "Oregon." The third player must give the name of a state that begins with an N.

Dramatic Activity

Pantomime Packing. Have each student choose a location for a 3-day trip. Ask each to share with a partner information about the place he or she has chosen. Where do the pair plan to stay? Have them locate the destination on a map or globe. How do they plan to get there? Have them make a list of all of the items they will need for this 3-day trip. Have the partners return to their seats, and ask volunteers to share their ideas. Have students omitted any items they will need in their particular location? If so, what are they?

Give the students the dimensions of the suitcase or backpack they are to take on their trip. Have them each "locate that space" in some visual way. Ask them to tell their partner about the suitcase or backpack they have selected. What color is it? How would they describe it to an official if it were lost? What special outside markings does it have? What is it like on the inside when it is empty?

Inform the students that they must fit everything they are taking on their 3-day trip in one bag. What will they leave behind? How will they get things that they cannot take with them? Have them share this information with their partner and then begin to pantomime the folding of items and packing of the suitcase or backpack.

Short Improvisation

Harness, C. (1992). *Three young pilgrims.* New York: Bradbury.

After reading the book, have each student recall or imagine a voyage or adventure. Have students work in pairs. One student assumes the role of the person who has been on the trip. The other assumes the role of a neighbor or relative who stayed at home. Have the student who has assumed the role of the traveler tell the other about what occurred on the trip. Then have the students reverse roles. When everyone has had a chance to share, gather the students into a large group. Have each student indicate the location of the trip his or her partner described on the map or globe and tell the group about the most interesting part of the trip.

Extended Improvisation

Contemporary setting:
Siebert, D. (1989). *Heartland* (W. Minor, Illus.). *New York: Crowell.*

Fiday, D., & Fiday, B. (1990). *Time to go.* New York: Gulliver/Harcourt Brace Jovanovich.

Depression-era setting: Gates, D. (1972). *Blue willow.* New York: Viking.

Hunt, I. (1970). *No promises in the wind.* New York: Tempo Books.

Day One. Read the books listed above in the order given. Ask the students to respond to the pictures they have just seen or the stories they have just read or heard. Do they think each area is like the region of the country in which they live? How is it like theirs? How is it different? What geographic features make the land good for the types of use to which it was put? Have the students describe the smells associated with the settings in the stories. What are their reactions to the various smells? Have them touch the soil with their bare feet or hands. How does it feel? What similarities or differences exist between the time periods? Have the students continue to develop their experience of the books by using all of their senses.

Day Two. Divide the class into smaller family groups, and have each group sit together. Have the groups decide on the role each member will play. Have them make a "family album" by drawing pictures of their characters and have each family member tell the others about the character he or she is playing. Then tell the students to imagine that the head of each family has been fired or has lost the family business. Everything will be auctioned off to pay their creditors. They will be allowed to keep a vehicle and to gather the things they would like to keep as essential items before the auction begins.

They then must decide what they will need and what they most want to take with them. Have them use pantomime and engage in dialogues

181

*Drama in the Social Studies:
Gateway to the Past,
Pathway to the Future*

and monologues to describe what they are taking. They should be able to use their visualizing skills from the packing drama to help them decide on how much space they have. You can act as the auctioneer who is ready to begin as soon as the characters have made their selections and so keep the pace moving. After the students have described their selections, have them discuss their decisions.

Ask half the students to assume their roles again, and have the others assume the roles of those who will say good-bye. After they have begun this process, assume the auctioneer's role and tell them they are short $500 and they must raise the $500 in some way. They must then decide which of the items they had planned to keep they must now sell to raise the $500.

Day Three. Have the students reassemble into their family groups. The auction is over and they have traveled a short way from their old community. Have each family group gather information about possible new locations and make notes on large sheets of paper. In what state or country is each possibility located? What is it bordered by on the north, east, south, and west? What is its capital or major city? What are the important industries in the area? Will families members who are old enough be able to get jobs in those industries? What are the geographic features of the area? What modes of transportation are used by most people in each location, and how does one get to each location? What kinds of trees, ground cover, plants and wildlife are there in each location? What are areas of recreation and interest in each location? What products are produced in each area?

Have all the students hand in their notes, and then display them prominently on a bulletin board or wall. Instruct the students to remain in their family roles and discuss the merits and feasibility of making the move to each of the locations. Finally, have the members of each family choose one location for the rest of the sessions.

Day Four. The students should assume the roles of members of the new community to which their family is moving. As each arrives at the regularly scheduled town meeting, he or she must tell those seated near him or her what task, job, or activity he or she was engaged in prior to coming to the meeting.

In the gossiping that takes place before the meeting begins, it is evident that each member of the community has heard something different about the new family that is coming to the area. Assuming the role of the mayor, police chief, banker, or real estate broker, draw information concerning the family from community members. This should include physical descriptions, background information on personal interests, their supposed reasons for selecting the particular community, benefits and disadvantages of having them as neighbors, things the current members could do to help the new residents *or* things they could subtly do to prevent them from feeling at home.

Day Five. Have students return to their family groups for this session. Remind them of their family's choice of location. Tell them that they have arrived at that location and each family member has gone off to

■ By comparing different periods in history, students can examine similarities and differences. In these two pictures, children's games and toys from two different time periods are inspected.

explore a different section of the area. Help each student visualize the area by asking the following questions: What is right in front of you? What is immediately beneath your feet? What are the three most important features of the room or location in which you are standing? What other people are with you? What are they doing? Where are you in relation to them? How did you get into the group or how do you plan to make yourself known to them? What do you feel, hear, smell, or taste in this situation? What are the objects in the scene? Do you know how to use them? If not, how will you find out?

183

*Drama in the Social Studies:
Gateway to the Past,
Pathway to the Future*

Have the family members gather for a midday or an evening meal and share what has happened during the day in this new place. Have them discuss whether or not to make this place their permanent home.

Beyond the Drama

Picture Postcard. Design a postcard similar to those included in *Stringbean's Trip to the Shining Sea* (Williams, V., & Williams, J., 1988) that illustrates a particular feature of the new location in which the members of each family group have found themselves. Have students assume their roles and write notes on the postcards. Their notes should indicate whether or not they have decided to stay in the new location. The notes should also describe similarities or differences between the old community and the new community. How will those similarities or differences make it easier or harder for the family members to become a part of the new area?

Newspaper Ad. All members of the family who are able to work must get a job. Have them assume their roles and write a "position-wanted ad" for the local newspaper.

Drama Unit Using the Format of Cecily O'Neill and Alan Lambert

O'Neill and Lambert (1987) advocate the use of dramas that lend themselves to investigative work by upper level students. Their suggestions are particularly appropriate for middle school, junior high, and senior high school programs with an emphasis on the acquisition of content knowledge and on inquiry methods. In *Drama Structures: A Practical Handbook for Teachers,* O'Neill and Lambert (1987) offer suggestions for dramas that relate to specific areas of the social studies and provide complete drama projects that involve student investigations of themes. Excerpts from primary source documents, especially trial transcripts, oral histories, newspaper articles, and case study interviews, serve as excellent springboards for this type of drama.

Title: Inventions, Inventions

Introduction: Our daily lives are touched in both positive and negative
ways by the technology that surrounds us. For students
who will soon enter a new century, the ability to
carefully consider the consequences of technology and
its distribution is critical.

Source material:
Caney, S. (1985). *Invention book.* New York: Workman.

Clarke, D. (1978). *The how it works encyclopedia of great inventors and discoveries.* London: Marshall Cavendish.

Vare, E., & Ptacek, G. (1988). *Mothers of invention: From the bra to the bomb: Forgotten women and their unforgettable ideas.* New York: Morrow.

Yankee Magazine. (1989). *The inventive yankee: From rockets to roller skates, 200 years of yankee inventors and inventions.* Dublin, NH: Yankee Books.

Time frame: Each lesson is planned for a 55-minute time period, excluding research.

Introductory Lesson

Before introducing this unit, select stories of inventors and those affected by their inventions or technology from the resources you have gathered. Have the students read or examine those resources and discuss discoveries. Then have the students interview parents, grandparents, senior citizens, or neighbors about inventions that dramatically affected their families when they were children. The following questions might serve as guides. How were their lives changed? How were other lives or other products changed as a result? How did the invention(s) make life easier or more interesting? What negatives did the interviewees or others see or perceive about the invention(s)?

Follow-Up and Discussion

The next day have students assume the roles of the individuals whom they interviewed. Have each one tell the group about his or her individual's view of the groundbreaking invention or technology and the changes it brought to the home or the workplace. Encourage questions and discussion between the student who is telling about the invention and members of the audience. Particularly encourage dialogues between those whose interviews concerned the same invention or technology.

Bring the talks to a close and discuss the issues raised by the inventions and technologies that the relatives and friends who were interviewed remembered.

Ask for suggestions of related themes that could be pursued through drama and inquiry as follow-ups to this lesson. Consider building on some of the suggestions below.

Further Development

1. Have some students use information from the Patent and Trademark Office to produce an invention and apply for a patent on it. Have other students assume the roles of Patent and Trademark Office officials and decide whether or not to grant a patent.

2. Have students gather information on an invention that has been patented. (One can order any patents by writing to the Patent and Trademark Office and requesting the documents by number. Public libraries have listings of patent numbers, such as those for household items, surgical instruments, and business equipment.) Then have students assume the roles of marketing and advertising people who are going to promote particular inventions to consumers: individuals, corporations, government agencies, or foreign countries.

185

*Drama in the Social Studies:
Gateway to the Past,
Pathway to the Future*

3. Have students use current periodicals and pamphlets produced by various consumer groups to investigate the effects of technology on individuals and communities. They may trace one or several cases. Develop a case that is similar to but not exactly the same as the ones in which they role played earlier. Have some students assume the roles of individuals who are to testify before a Senate committee and share their views. Have other students assume the roles of the investigators. Still other members of the class should assume the roles of spectators or members of the press who will later attempt to discuss the proceedings with the individuals who testified and with members of the committee.
4. Have students read at least one of the following books: Collier, J., & Collier, C. (1992). *The clock.* New York: Delacorte. Paterson, K. (1991). *Lyddie.* New York: Lodestar Books.

Assume the role of a mill employee who has been sent out to recruit new employees. Have students assume the roles of young people in the community, older business owners and landowners in the community, and parents and other relatives. During the drama, students should make their decisions about the use of child labor and poor working conditions. Then, still in their roles, the students should tell others of their decisions.

Summary

Using drama in the social studies classroom can contribute significantly to the development of attitudes, values, and group skills that promote healthy interrelationships and cooperation among those in families, schools, communities, the nation, and the world. Used in conjunction with literature and other resources, drama can illuminate the human characteristics and concerns—the faces—that textbooks and expository teaching methods sometimes strip from the content of the social studies.

When Louise Rosenblatt (1982, 1985) refers to the process of evoking meaning from text, she speaks of two types of stances that a person reading or listening to text can assume. One stance involves the individual in a meaning-making process in which the goal is "carrying away" needed information. The other stance involves the individual in "living through" the experience described. Rosenblatt (1983) believes that the transactional view of the meaning-making process offers much to the development of citizens because it acknowledges and values the importance of both stances. She goes on to say,

> Of all the elements which enter into the educational
> process—except, of course, the actual personal relationships and
> activities which make up the community life of the
> school—literature possesses the greatest potentialities for . . .
> direct assimilation of ideas and attitudes. For literature offers the
> closest approach to the experiences of actual life. It enables the

youth to "live through" much that in abstract terms would be meaningful to him. He comes to know intimately, more intimately perhaps than would be possible in actual life, many personalities. He shares vicariously their struggles and perplexities and achievements. He becomes a part of strange environments, or he sees with new emotions the conditions and the lives about him. And these vicarious experiences have at least something of the warmth and color and emotion that life itself possesses. . . . [L]iterature can be an important means of bringing about the linkage between intellectual perception and emotional drive that we have agreed to be essential to any vital learning process. (pp. 214-215)

In the social studies, whether we deal with written or spoken words, we have been most focused on those aspects that enable students to "carry away" information. We should value as highly the stance that permits and encourages students to live through experiences described in text. Engaging in those experiences will stimulate the interest of students and provide the development of perspective abilities that are so critical to citizens in a democracy.

Drama also makes the "living through" of content possible for students who may not have experienced it as they read or prepare daily assignments. Drama was the stepping-stone for the student described at the beginning of this chapter. That young man engaged in a decision-making process as did the three 19th-century homemakers in the museum village. He came to know a fugitive slave who had made the decision to flee toward an uncertain future rather than retain the security of what was well know to him. Tim, the student, then had to struggle with the dilemma of whether his obligation as a citizen was to *obey* or *oppose* laws that he believed to be unjust, knowing that those very laws protected his right to protest them. Drama helped Tim view the past, his present, and possibly his future in new ways.

References

Atwell, N. (1987). *In the middle: Writing, reading, and learning with adolescents.* Portsmouth, NH: Heinemann.

Atwell, N. (1990). *Coming to know: Writing to learn in the intermediate grades.* Portsmouth, NH: Heinemann.

Ausubel, D. P. (1960). The uses of advanced organizers in the learning and retention of meaningful verbal material. *Journal of Educational Psychology, 51,* 267-272.

Banks, J., & Clegg, A. (1985). *Teaching strategies for the social studies: Inquiry, valuing, and decision making.* New York: Longman.

Blumberg, R. (1985). *Commodore Perry—in the land of the Shogun,* New York: Lothrop, Lee, and Shepard.

Bolton, G. (1985). Changes in thinking about drama in education. *Theory into Practice, 24,* 151-157.

Drama in the Social Studies:
Gateway to the Past,
Pathway to the Future

Booth, D. (1985). Imaginary gardens with real toads. *Theory into Practice, 24,* 193–198.

Bradley Commission on History in Schools & Gagnon, P. (1989). *Historical literacy: The case for history in American education.* New York: Macmillan.

Bruner, J. (1966). *Toward a theory of instruction.* Cambridge, MA: Harvard University Press.

Bruner, J. (1977). *The process of education.* Cambridge, MA: Harvard University Press.

Caney, S. (1985). *Invention book.* New York: Workman.

Clarke, D. (1978). *The how it works encyclopedia of great inventors and discoveries.* London: Marshall Cavendish.

Collier, V., & Collier, C. (1992). *The clock.* New York: DelaCorte.

Egan, K. (1986). *Teaching as story telling: An alternative approach to teaching and curriculum in the elementary school.* Chicago: University of Chicago Press.

Fiday, D., & Fiday, B. (1990). *Time to go.* New York: Gulliver/Harcourt Brace Jovanovich.

Fines, J., & Verrior, R. (1974). *The drama of history: An experiment in cooperative teaching.* Aberdeen, AK: Central Press.

Fox, M. (1985). *Wilfred Gordon McDonald Partridge* (J. Vivas, Illus.). New York: Kane/Miller.

Gagne, R. (1984). Learning outcomes and their effects: Useful categories of human performance. *American Psychologist, 39,* 377–385.

Gagne, R., Briggs, L. J., & Wager, W. W. (1988). *Principles of instructional design.* New York: Holt, Rinehart & Winston.

Gates, D. (1972). *Blue willow.* New York: Viking.

Gimmestad, B., & DeChiara, E. (1982). Dramatic plays: A vehicle for prejudice reduction in the elementary school. *Journal of Educational Research, 76,* 45–49.

Goodlad, J. (1984). *A place called school: Prospects for the future.* New York: McGraw-Hill.

Goor, R., & Goor, N. (1986). *Pompeii: Exploring a Roman ghost town.* New York: Crowell.

Graves, D. (1983). *Writing: Teachers and children at work.* London: Heinemann.

Hamanaka, S. (1990). *The journey: Japanese Americans, racism and renewal.* New York: Orchard.

Heathcote, D., & Herbert P. (1985). A drama of learning: Mantle of the expert. *Theory into Practice, 24,* 173-180.

Huck, C. S., Hepler, S., & Hickman, J. (1993). Children's literature in the elementary school. Orlando, FL: Harcourt Brace Jovanovich.

Johnson, D. (1983). Natural language learning by design: A classroom experiment in social interaction and secondary language acquisition. *TESOL Quarterly, 17,* 55-68.

Johnson, D. W., & Johnson, R. T. (1992). Approaches to implementing cooperative learning in the social studies classroom. In R. J. Stahl & R. L. Van Sickle (Eds.), *Cooperative learning in the social studies classroom,* (pp.44-51). Washington, D.C.: National Council of Social Studies.

Johnson, L., & O'Neill, C. (Eds.). (1985). *Dorothy Heathcote: Collected writings on education and drama.* London: Hutchinson.

Knight, P. (1989). A study of children's understanding of people in the past. *Educational Review, 4,* 207-219.

Kohlberg, L. (1976). Moral stages and moralization. In T. Lickona (Ed.), *Moral development and behavior.* New York: Holt, Rinehart & Winston.

Lee, P. J. (1983). History teaching and philosophy of history. *History and Theory, 22,* 19-49.

Lehr, F. (1983). Developing language and thought through creative drama. *Language Arts, 60,* 385-388.

Levinson, R. (1985). *Watch the stars come out.* New York: Dutton.

Levstik, L. S. (1986). The relationship between historical responses and narrative in a sixth-grade classroom. *Theory and Research in Social Education, 14,* 1-19.

Levstik, L. S. (1990). The research base for curriculum choice: A response. *Social Education, 54,* 442-444.

Manna, A., & Lawson, A. (1992). Making drama with literature. In K. Wood & A. Moss (Eds.), *Exploring literature in the classroom: Content and Methods.* Norwood, MA: Christopher-Gordon.

Maxim, G. W. (1991). *Social studies and the elementary school child.* Columbus, OH: Merrill.

Moffett, J. (1968). *Teaching the universe of discourse.* Boston: Houghton Mifflin.

Morgan, N., & Saxton, J. (1987). *Teaching drama: A mind of many wonders . . .* Portsmouth, NH: Heinemann.

National Commission on Social Studies in the Schools. (1989). *Charting a course: Social studies for the 21st century: A report of*

189

*Drama in the Social Studies:
Gateway to the Past,
Pathway to the Future*

the curriculum task force of the National Commission on Social Studies in the Schools. Washington, DC: National Commission on Social Studies in the Schools.

National Council for the Social Studies. (1984). In search of a scope and sequence for social studies: Report of the National Council for the Social Studies Task Force on Scope and Sequence, November 1, 1983: Preliminary position statement of the board of directors. *Social Education, 48,* 249–262.

National Council for the Social Studies. (1989a). In search of a scope and sequence for social studies: Report of the National Council for the Social Studies Task Force on Scope and Sequence, July 1, 1989. *Social Education, 53,* 375–387.

National Council for the Social Studies. (1989b). Social studies for early childhood and elementary school children preparing for the 21st century: A report from NCSS task force on early childhood/elementary social studies. *Social Education, 53,* 14–23.

O'Neill, C. (1985). Imagined worlds in theatre and drama. *Theory into Practice, 24,* 158–165.

O'Neill, C., & Lambert, A. (1987). *Drama structures: A practical handbook for teachers.* London: Hutchinson.

Paterson, K. (1991). *Lyddie.* New York: Lodestar.

Philboin, M., & Myers, J. (1991). Classroom drama: Discourse as a mode of inquiry in elementary school social studies. *Social Studies, 82,* 179–182.

Provensen, A., & Provensen, M. (1987). *Shaker lane.* New York: Viking Kestrel.

Putnam, L. (1991). Dramatizing non-fiction with emerging readers. *Language Arts, 68,* 463–469.

Ravitch, D., & Finn, C. (1987). *What do our 17-year-olds know? A report on the first national assessment of history and literature.* New York: Harper & Row.

Ritchie, G. (1991). How to use drama for cross cultural understanding. *Guidance Counselor, 7,* 33–35.

Rosenblatt, L. (1982). The literary transaction: Evocation and response. *Theory into Practice, 21,* 268–277.

Rosenblatt, L. (1983). *Literature as exploration.* New York: Modern Language Association of America.

Rosenblatt, L. (1985). Viewpoints: Transaction versus interaction—A terminological rescue operation. *Research in the Teaching of English, 19,* 96–107.

Routman, R. (1991). *Invitations: Changing as teachers and learners K-1.* Portsmouth, NH: Heinemann.

Siebert, D. (1989). *Heartland* (W. Minor, Illus.). New York: Crowell.

Selman, R. (1971). The relation of role taking to the development of moral judgment in children. *Child Development, 45,* 803–806.

Sewall, G. T. (1988). American history textbooks: Where do we go from here? *Phi Delta Kappan, 69,* 553–558.

Shand, G., May, D., & Linnell, R. (1990). History as ethnography: A psychological evaluation of a theatre in education project. *Teaching History, 65,* 27–32.

Slavin, R. (1983). *Cooperative learning.* New York: Longman.

Stahl, R. J. (1992). From "academic strangers" to successful members of a cooperative learning group: An inside-the-learner perspective. In R. J. Stahl & R. L. Van Sickle (Eds.), *Cooperative learning in the social studies classroom.*(pp. 8-15). Washington, D.C.: National Council for the Social Studies.

Swartz, L. (1988). *Drama themes: A practical guide for classroom teachers.* Portsmouth, NH: Heinemann.

Taba, H. (1955). *With perspective on human relations: A study of peer group dynamics in an eighth grade.* Washington, DC: American Council on Education.

Thornton, S. (1990). Should we be teaching more history? *Theory and Research in Social Education, 18,* 53–60.

Vare, E., & Ptacek, G. (1988). *Mothers of invention: From the bra to the bomb: Forgotten women and their unforgettable ideas.* New York: Morrow.

Vass, P. (1992). Overwhelming evidence: Written sources and primary history. *Teaching History, 66,* 21–26.

Yankee Magazine. (1989). The inventive yankee: From rockets to roller skates, 200 years of yankee inventors and inventions. Dublin, NH: Yankee Books.

Williams, V., & Williams, J. (1988). *Stringbean's trip to the shining sea.* New York: Greenwillow.

Civic Education: Building Participation Skills in a Democratic Society

PHYLLIS MAXEY FERNLUND

CALIFORNIA STATE UNIVERSITY, SAN BERNARDINO

Democracy is not simply a system whereby people elect those who govern them, but a system in which every member of the community participates in self-governance.

WALTER C. PARKER
"Participatory Citizenship: Civics in the Strong Sense"

The primary purpose of social studies is to help young people develop the ability to make informed and reasoned decisions for the public good . . . .

NATIONAL COUNCIL
FOR THE SOCIAL
STUDIES

Introduction

Teaching social studies at the elementary level involves several content areas as well as interpersonal and intrapersonal skill building. Civics is a content area in which students can be active participants. The teacher in a whole language classroom acts as a model and guide to lead students in experiences that allow them to interact in a democratic society. They can create this democratic society in their own classroom community. Active, hands-on learning is facilitated by the students' ability to create their own democratic environment through daily civics experiences.

This chapter describes how students can learn about people in the past and the present who have influenced and/or continue to influence our government and the Constitution. Examples of ways that students can experience the democratic process and construct new environments for themselves are included.

The Importance of Civic Education

"We the people" is the opening phrase of the preamble to the U.S. Constitution. Participation in self-governance is only possible if people develop the values, beliefs, and skills needed in a democratic society. School districts throughout the United States have mission statements that pledge to educate children and youth to participate in a democratic society. Teachers have the important task of providing the education that will enable students to assume responsible roles in the workplace, neighborhood, nation, and international community. Supreme Court Justice Sandra Day O'Connor (1987, p. 33) states:

> Our Constitution was not intended solely, or even primarily, for judges. The strength of our system of government and of our freedoms depends on how firmly they stand in the hearts of our citizens. . . . Without an educational structure which fosters and encourages each successive group of students to learn about the structure of our government and the history of its development, we would soon see young hearts barren of those sentiments and understandings out of which our nation came into existence.

"We the people" give and take away the authority for elected officials to make decisions on our behalf. A democratic nation needs citizens who can participate in the important decisions of its society. People who expect differences in viewpoints and who have the skills to work toward acceptable solutions are crucial to the survival of democracies. Citizenship skills, knowledge, and attitudes are quite different for citizens of an authoritarian regime, in which all decisions are made at the top levels of government. Citizens who are passive, trusting of a leader's choices, and uninvolved in decision making are valuable to such a society. Dictators decide on the individual and collective welfare of their citizens. There are no meaningful votes, no debates, no choices.

When we look at American classrooms, do we see education for a democratic or an authoritarian society? Do students have an opportunity to make decisions, or does the teacher decide? Are students encouraged to raise questions and contribute to a discussion, or is the questioning always initiated by the teacher who is looking for the right answers? Do all students participate or only a few? Does the teacher have a supportive classroom climate or one characterized by fear, sarcasm, and intimidation? Is history presented from multiple perspectives and many sources or from one text as "the truth"—the only way it could have happened?

As teachers set up a classroom, they make choices that have important consequences for their students. The school and community expect teachers to participate in the task of socializating the young, presenting students with the existing traditions of our society, including knowledge, values, behavior, and rules. Socialization can mean indoctrination, using fear and repression to create passive and loyal citizens. A democratic society places certain limits on the methods that one can use to socialize the young because there is a strong belief in individual freedom and justice as well as a concern for an orderly society. Before looking at civic education in the classroom, it is important to clarify what the word *democracy* means.

Democratic Ideals: Core Values

A fundamental value in a democratic society is respect for human dignity. The individual is seen as a person with rights by virtue of being human, not according to family name, wealth, or power. Rights of life, liberty, and the pursuit of happiness are called inalienable rights in the Declaration of Independence. They cannot be taken away from an individual without due process of law. All humans are equal with respect to their common humanity. As Mortimer Adler (1987, p.43) has said, "Human equality consists of the fact that no human being is more or less human than another." Equality extends to making the rules of the game equal, so that defeat of one's candidate or oneself in an election can be accepted with the knowledge that one can compete again.

■ Teachers need to set aside time at the beginning of the school year for students to discuss and establish class rules.

Another important democratic value is that of popular sovereignty, government by consent of the governed. The individual is seen as someone capable of making decisions that affect the entire society. In some cases this influence is reflected in public opinion polls or letters to the editor in newspapers. In other cases it is reflected in voting for public officials or ballot propositions. Every individual is entitled to be represented in the political system. Abraham Lincoln's phrase "government of the people, by the people, and for the people" is an expression of the supreme role for citizens in choosing the temporary administrators of their government.

A basic tenet of American democracy is a belief in individual freedom, the right of the individual to be independent of the group, to have a society where government does not dominate all of life, to have a private sector where individuals are free to make choices. Freedom to make choices is not limited to elections but extends to choices about spending one's income, choosing a school and a career, and living where one wants to live. Freedom of the press, freedom of religion, and freedom of assembly are basic rights that serve to limit the power of government over the individual. The Constitution and Bill of Rights enumerate a variety of rights that protect the individual from the abuses of government power.

Democratic governments come in many forms among the world's nations. Anderson (1988) has divided the countries of the world into two groups: (1) those countries in which all elements of individual rights are specified by law and extended to all people without restriction and (2) those countries in which legal rights are not extended uniformly to some minorities or recent immigrants. The United States and several other heterogeneous Western nations are placed in the second group because of their histories of discrimination against racial and ethnic minorities. Older students can learn to identify the critical attributes of a democracy and apply those criteria to our nation as well as others (Fernlund, 1990). In discussing the democratic changes in Eastern Europe and the former Soviet Union, Becker (1992, pp. 83–84) reminds us of the global context of American democratic citizenship:

> As citizens living in a large, influential, multicultural, democratic society, our actions have an impact on others as well as on the physical and social environment. . . . Citizen power seems to be on the rise [in the world]. Are we preparing our citizens for a new world order?

Skills for a Democratic Society

Given the basic values of democracy, what skills will citizens of the twenty-first century need? In a pluralistic society such as ours, there are many diverse viewpoints on almost every given issue. Although freedom of speech is a basic value in American society, the debate on public issues and resulting dissent can be upsetting to people. The various arguments are hard to analyze, and right action may be difficult to determine. People need to be able to work together, to question the meaning of what they hear, and to make decisions about responsible action.

Figures 8.1, 8.2, and 8.3 present three different lists of skills essential for a democratic citizen. The California *History/Social Science Framework* (California State Board of Education, 1987) divides the skills into three areas: basic information acquisition skills, critical thinking skills, and participation skills. Similarly, the National Council for the Social Studies (1984) lists among its essential skills these three: (1) skills related to acquiring information, (2) intellectual skills, and (3) skills related to interpersonal relationships and social participation. Engle and Ochoa (1988) are specifically concerned with decision-making skills and the ability to take action in the political system as they elaborate on necessary intellectual and participatory skills.

There is a strong relationship between knowledge acquisition, information processing, and social participation skills. Sunal and Haas (1993) refer to this as "political socialization." They believe that political socialization is a "developmental process during which three distinct types of political identification processes are experienced: affiliation, knowledge, and participation" (p. 340). According to Figures 8.1 and 8.2, it is only with the participatory skills that the emotional context for learning seems to be included. The relationship between knowledge, emotion, and action is integrated in the skills listed in Figure 8.3. It provides the motivation for children to become engaged in learning. As Hunt and Metcalf (1968, p. 78) point out,

F I G U R E   8 . 1

■

Skills Goals of California History/Social Science Framework,
California State Board of Education (1987).

Basic Study Skills

1. Acquire information by listening, observing, using community resources, and reading various forms of literature and primary and secondary source materials.

2. Locate, select, and organize information from written sources.

3. Retrieve and analyze information by using computers and other electronic media.

4. Read and interpret maps, globes, models, diagrams, graphs, charts, tables, pictures, and political cartoons.

5. Understand the specialized language used in historical research and social science disciplines.

6. Organize and express ideas clearly in writing and in speaking.

Critical Thinking Skills

1. Define and clarify problems.

2. Judge information related to a problem.

3. Solve problems and draw conclusions.

Participation Skills

1. Develop personal skills: sensitivity to others, ability to express personal convictions, recognition of personal biases and prejudices, and the ability to adjust one's behavior to work effectively with others.

2. Develop group interaction skills: willingness to listen to differing views of others, ability to participate in making decisions, leadership skills and the willingness to follow, skills of persuading, compromising, debating, negotiating, and resolving conflicts, ability to confront controversial issues in ways that work toward reasoned solutions free of aggressions that destroy group relations.

3. Develop social and political participation skills: ability to identify issues that require social action, commitment to accept social responsibilities associated with citizenship, willingness to work to influence those in power, willingness to assume leadership roles in clarifying goals and mobilizing groups for political action, willingness to accept the consequences of one's own actions.

FIGURE 8.2

■

Social Participation Skills National Council for the Social Studies (1984).

Personal Skills

- Express personal convictions.

- Communicate own beliefs, feelings and convictions.

- Adjust own behavior to fit dynamics of various groups and situations.

- Recognize the mutual relationship between human beings in satisfying each other's needs.

Group Interaction Skills

- Contribute to the development of a supportive climate in groups.

- Participate in making rules and guidelines for group life.

- Serve as a leader or follower.

- Assist in setting goals for the group.

- Participate in delegating duties, organizing planning, making decisions, and taking action in a group setting.

- Participate in persuading, compromising, debating, and negotiating in the resolution of conflicts and differences.

Social and Political Participation Skills

- Keep informed on issues that affect society.

- Identify situations in which social action is required.

- Work individually or with others to decide on an appropriate course of action.

- Work to influence those in positions of social power to strive for extensions of freedom, social justice, and human rights.

The fact that students have read a chapter entitled, The Farm Problem, does not mean that they have a problem, unless it is a problem of understanding what the chapter says—or, what is more likely the case, the problem of figuring out what the teacher wants them to note as important in the chapter. A problem as we define it is felt by someone. It belongs to someone.

As the following activities illustrate, this integration of the cognitive and affective dimensions of learning is vital to building participation skills.

F I G U R E   8 . 3

■

Intellectual skills (Engle and Ochoa, 1988).

1. Being able to size up a problem and identify the real point of conflict or the real issue, including the underlying values that are at stake.
2. Being able to select information which is relevant to the problem and relate it logically to proposed solutions; being able to judge the reliability of various sources of information, including firsthand experience as well as research-based information.
3. Being able to see a problem in its broadest possible context, including the value considerations involved.
4. Being able to build a scenario of likely consequences regarding any proposed solution to a problem.
5. Being able to make reasoned judgments where the evidence is conflicting or where there is conflict between desired values.
6. Being able to empathize with people whose points of view with respect to the problem differ from yours.
7. Being able to choose a solution that, though less than ideal, is politically viable and makes progress toward resolving an impasse possible.
8. Being able to exercise political influence toward implementing justifiable decisions; being able to organize others and to work in organizations to achieve justifiable political goals.

Democracy in Action: Creating a Democratic Classroom

If students are to have experiences that enable them to participate actively in a democratic society, the teacher is the key person in planning those experiences. When the students first arrive to begin a new school year, classroom rules and procedures have to be explained to them. Although the routines and procedures are probably best established by the teacher, rules for getting along with each other can be developed with the students. Creating a classroom constitution is a wonderful way to help children understand the reasons for rules as well as participate in a rule-making process.

Begin the discussion of class rules by reviewing with the students the reasons why children go to school. Then develop a list of rules that they think will help them reach these goals. You might want to group rules into different categories, such as rules that help people get along, rules that protect property, rules that protect individual freedoms, and rules that create a safe environment.

Introduce the concept of a constitution. Simply defined, a constitution is a set of important rules that people have discussed and agreed to live by. You may want to limit your list to about 10 rules. Introduce the

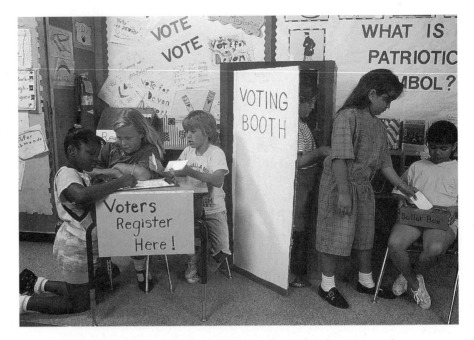

■ Children need to see democracy in action and to learn how to be citizen actors. For instance, children wonder what occurs when people vote in an election. Arranging for them to vote in an actual voting booth the day before an election will be a highlight they will long remember.

idea of majority rule—a simple majority of 50% plus 1 or a stricter requirement such as a two-thirds or three-fourths majority. After the students have voted, put the rules that received majority approval in the classroom constitution. Instruct students to write the new list on a large piece of paper, and have all members of the classroom—students, teacher, and aides—sign it to show their agreement.

The preamble to the classroom constitution should state the reasons for the document: "We the teacher and students in Room 10, in order to learn and grow together, have agreed to follow these rules." You may want to establish an amendment procedure, so that if the constitution needs to be changed or a new rule added, the students have a process for doing that. Some teachers have found that important rules that could not be agreed upon at first were eventually added later in the year as students saw the need for such rules. Amendments should be attached to the constitution, with a new round of signatures for each one. For very young children, the amendment process may be too complicated. A simple constitution such as that shown in Figure 8.4 will give them experience in rule making. Older students who have studied the U.S. Constitution may include a preamble, articles, and an amendment procedure in their classroom constitution, as shown in Figure 8.5.

F I G U R E   8 . 4

■

Room 3's constitution.

Room 3's Constitution

We, the members of this class, have decided that we will work, learn, play, and grow together this year. We will try to be "Super Citizen." We feel these rules will help us do this.

1. Cooperate with everyone and work together.
2. Be kind, polite, and good in school.
3. Take your own turn and be fair.
4. Raise your hand to speak.
5. Pay attention and follow all directions.
6. Listen to the adults and your classmates.
7. Work quietly in the classroom—whisper.
8. Use the chair the right way.
9. Always walk quietly in school.
10. Take care of all property

The members of this class, the children and the teacher, shall have the responsibility to make sure these rules are followed. The teacher shall make the final decision as to whether the rules have been obeyed.

If we need to change these rules, or add to them as the year goes on, we will talk about it, and do what is necessary.

Signed:

Scott   Rydell
Ericka   Gary
Michael   Nicole
Sean
Towanda   Billy
Teko
Nathan
Katherine   Ms. Stein
Jamie   Gina
MoniqueAli   Andrew
Jonathan   Lena
Timmy
Crystal
Reid
Rodney

October 1, 1985

FIGURE 8.5

■

The constitution of Room 301.

. . .IN ORDER TO FORM A BETTER CLASSROOM. . .

Joan Gunther, eighth grade teacher at Chicago's Belding Elementary School, tells how two of her classes wrote classroom constitutions and used them to discipline themselves this year.

THE CONSTITUTION OF ROOM 301

We, the students of room 301, in order to form a better classroom, hereby create this Constitution to establish the freedoms and laws for the equal justice of the student.

Article 1. Every student has the freedom of choice where choices are available. Every student has to respect others' opinions and ideas and cannot make fun of them.

Article 2. Every student has the freedom of speech. The students have the right to express their feelings to the class and the teacher in a proper manner.

Article 3. The president, two senators, and the two representatives will be elected every semester.

Article 4. The Supreme Court will consist of two elected student judges and the teacher. Once elected, the seats are permanent. If the students feel that any one of the judges is unfair, they can call for another election by a petition signed by 3/4 of the class.

Article 5. No student can invade anyone's desk without a search warrant.

Article 6. Any student can petition a judge for a trial if he/she states, in writing, the causes for same. The date of the trial will be decided by the three judges. If any of the student judges are somehow involved in the case, a jury of 5 students will be called upon.

Article 7. The Constitution can be amended by a petition signed by 3/4 of the class or by the legislature and president submitting an amendment, to which they agree, to the class for ratification. Ratification will be accomplished by 3/4 of the class in agreement.

This Constitution was ratified by the class of 301 on the 23rd day of October, 1990. Signed and attested to by the elected delegates:

Gizelle Crosby   Brian Lindgren   Januario Natanauan   Taylor Williams

F I G U R E   8 . 6

■

The case study method.

Step 1   Review the facts of the case.

       What happened in this story?
       Who is involved?
       What facts are important?
       Is there any information missing that would be helpful?
       Why did the people act the way they did?

Step 2   State the issue in the form of a question.
       This step raises the level of abstraction.
       (The teacher may need to frame the issue.)

       Is it a legal, ethical, or policy issue?

Step 3   Discuss the arguments.

       What are the arguments for and against each side?
       What alternative courses of action are there?
       What would be the consequences for each alternative?

Step 4   Make a decision.

       What is your decision in this case?
       What is your stand on the issue we posed?
       What are your reasons for taking this position?

Teaching with Case Studies

Meaningful language is functional, social, informative, and aesthetic (Klesius, 1988). The case study method draws on all of these aspects of language in reading, listening, discussing, and writing an opinion on a case. A case study is a problem situation that involves some conflict among the parties in a dispute. A case may be drawn from a story, a newspaper article, a school conflict, or a court case. The power of the case study method comes from the interest generated by the emotion inherent in a situation. Critical thinking skills are used to analyze that situation and reach a decision. Students confront the particulars of a case study by using their natural abilities to search for patterns and meaning. See Figure 8.6.

    Let's take the case of the Little Red Hen. After reading the story, review the facts of the case. The Little Red Hen did all the work involved in making bread. She asked for help, but no one helped her. Duck, Pig, and Cat chose to play rather than work. Everyone wanted the freshly baked bread, but the Little Red Hen ate the bread herself and did not share it with her friends.

The next step in the case study method is to frame the issue. This is an important step because it keeps the focus on one issue. Let's say that in this case the issue is: Should friends who don't help with a task benefit from the rewards when the task is completed? After you have written the issue on the board, give the students an opportunity to respond individually in writing.

Discussion is the third step. What are the arguments in favor of the Little Red Hen's point of view? What are the arguments against it? Which are more convincing? One of the points that students in the primary grades often raise is that their parents provide food for them even when they fail to clean their room or do other chores. To help students work through the arguments, you may want to identify different actions that the Little Red Hen could have taken and the consequences of each. What would have happened if the Little Red Hen had chosen to feed her lazy friends? What happened because she refused? Consequences can be listed as positive or negative, and then the results can be evaluated.

The final step in the case study method is to reach a decision. Students need to answer the original question individually and as a group: Should friends who don't help with a task benefit from the rewards when the task is completed? The values underlying the decision can be examined, and other cases can be chosen to test those values in another context, another situation.

If a particular theme is the focus of a unit, a variety of cases that touch on different elements related to that central theme can be discussed. For example, Corbin (1991) used historical novels—*Across Five Aprils* by Irene Hunt (1987), *Turn Homeward, Hannalee,* by Patricia Beatty (1990), and *The Two Hundred Ninety* by Scott O'Dell (1976)—to teach fifth-grade students about three different perspectives on the Civil War: those of the North, the South, and other countries (England and France). In comparing the unit based on literature and diverse perspectives to the text, she found that the students were reluctant to return to the textbook:

> Before when we were in the textbook, I didn't feel any emotions and nobody was getting hurt, so I just thought it was something we had to learn.

> It felt like you were more in the action and you knew what you were doing . . . not like in the textbook. It just says who won the war. It doesn't say the man's thoughts. (p. 25)

Literature is a rich resource for civic education. By integrating the cognitive and affective, students have the opportunity to understand another's perspective in the narrative.

Using Role Plays and Simulations

Although students need to practice participation skills, there may be limited real world opportunities for them to vote, debate, take leadership roles, or make important decisions that affect others. Moreover, society is extremely complex, and its institutions are remote from children's lives. Role play and simulation are strategies that reduce such complexity and at the same time encourage the practice of certain essential skills.

An example of a simulation that involves children as well as community resource people is Police Patrol (Clark, 1981). In this simulation, children play the roles of police officers, suspects, and observers. The teacher divides the class into several small groups, and each group picks two police officers, one or more observers, and citizens who will have encounters with the police. Cards contain police calls requesting officers to investigate a suspected drunken driver, two people fighting in a home, a shoplifter, and so on. For each situation, the role plays are carried out by all groups simultaneously. Then the roles change, and each group selects two new students to be police officers and respond to a new call. By the end of the simulation, students have had to put themselves in the shoes of suspects as well as police officers facing a wide variety of situations. Debriefing questions raise issues regarding the training police officers need, the qualities that make good police officers, and the impact of laws on police procedures. An excellent addition to this simulation is to invite police officers to observe the simulation, comment on the role plays, and share with students some of their training for responding to such calls. Students often develop empathy for the suspect and the police through their role play. In the follow-up discussion, they expand their understanding of the role of the police in a democratic society.

Many simulations place students in city council hearings debating a budget, an environmental issue, or the location of a halfway house. Others are historical simulations set during the time of the Salem witch trials, the Constitutional Convention, or the Civil War. Although simulations take time, they offer wonderful opportunities for building language skills, as well as empathy, leadership, group cooperation, and decision-making skills.

In recreating the Philadelphia Convention of 1787, students can investigate the lives of the delegates and write a journal from a particular person's point of view. Books by Jean Fritz (1987) such as *Shh! We're Writing the Constitution!,* offer insights into different times and people. Students might predict how their delegate would vote on a particular subject and prepare arguments for a constitutional debate. An interesting approach to this topic for middle school students is a computer simulation, *Our Constitution Then and Now.* This program uses AppleWorks© word processing and data base software to assist students with their research, writing, and debate.

Law-related educational organizations at the local, state, and national levels have produced role plays and simulations concerned with the legal system. A particular type of simulation is the mock trial. In its simplest form, a mock trial has a script and different students read the parts of judge, witnesses, defendant, and attorneys. Children's fairy tales have been rewritten into mock trial scripts, such as *State v. Gold E. Locks* (Yeaton & Braeckel, 1986). In more complex mock trials, the students are given the case, but they must further develop the statements by the witnesses, defendant, and attorneys. Other roles include judge, bailiff, court reporter, and jury members. A complex mock trial may take a week of class time. Mock trial experiences introduce students to decision making in an adversary system. They can see both sides of an argument and struggle to sort out the facts and interpret the law as it applies to a particular case. If the case has actually been argued in a court, the teacher may want to present the court's decision and reasoning after the students have completed their trial. If the case has moved from a trial court to an appellate court, there may be differing views at the different levels. In Supreme Court cases there is a majority opinion as well as dissenting opinions. Some of these have been rewritten so that children can understand the most important arguments. See, for example, *Great Cases of the Supreme Court* (Ratcliffe, Gordon, & Gallagher, 1989) and *Great Trials in American History* (Arbetman & Roe, 1985).

Complex Instruction

Complex instruction is a type of cooperative learning that focuses on status differences in the classroom. Research studies have shown that low-status children receive less teacher attention and participate far less than do high-status students. Status may be based on socioeconomic background, academic achievement, or popularity. Cooperative learning groups that always reward the able readers and writers may exacerbate these status differences. The goal of complex instruction is to increase participation of low-status children, thus raising their achievement level. Research at Stanford University (Cohen & Lotan, 1990; Cohen, Lotan, & Catanzarite, 1990) has demonstrated achievement gains for all children, but particularly low-status children, when the following factors are present in the classroom:

Small group work with multiple roles
Learning tasks requiring multiple abilities
Teacher intervention for low-status children
Concept immersion and simultaneous groups

Let's use an example from a unit on responsibility for fourth graders (Fernlund & Crowell, 1990). The children have just been told the story of the little match girl. Orphaned at a young age, she went to live with some relatives who were very poor. She was sent to sell matches in the cold, and feeling very sad, she lay down in the snow. In the original version of this story, the girl dies from the cold. Other versions have happier endings.

In complex instruction, the teacher's first task is to immerse students in the concept. The focus of all the literature and social studies in this unit is on the concept of responsibility. In connection with this story, the teacher creates three immersion activities to give students different experiences with the concept and the story. One experience is a role-playing task in which students first write an ending or, if they have been told the ending, make up a new ending. They then dramatize the story with their ending. Another experience is the creation of decision trees, painted on large pieces of newsprint. The children depict the choices the girl faces and the consequences of each choice. The third experience is an individual reflective writing assignment, followed by small group discussion. The writing task is presented as follows:

> In the story of the little match girl, we find her sad, cold, and lonely. Who do you think should have taken responsibility for her? Was it the girl herself, her parents, her relatives, people passing by? Decide by yourself, and write your thoughts down before you discuss them with your group.

Members of each small group then discuss their opinions. Students are assigned the roles of recorder, discussion leader, facilitator (who makes sure that each person has a chance to speak), reporter of the majority opinion, and reporter of the minority opinion.

Each student in the class participates in the three experiences. The teacher divides the class into six groups and after an introduction, the groups begin their work. Two of the groups will be doing the same task. (If time permitted, the teacher could create six experiences with each group working on one of the six and then rotating.) The experiences are not only designed to immerse the students in the concept of responsibility but to highlight different abilities: acting, writing, discussing, drawing, and speaking. The tasks are open-ended, and students are encouraged to rely on their group rather than the teacher for direction.

The purpose of the teacher's status intervention is to help the group appreciate the skills of the low-status students. For example, if a student with limited English is the artist drawing a decision tree, the teacher can praise that contribution to a group composed primarily of English speakers. Children who struggle with reading may be quite adept at role playing or creating new endings for stories. A limited teacher intervention is used to recognize the skills of these children and build their self-esteem and recognition from their peers.

Complex instruction lessons have been developed for science and social studies. This approach is valuable for building students' participation skills and for creating a classroom climate that celebrates diversity and the talents of all students.

The Teacher as Role Model

A teacher's actions have a profound influence on the behavior and attitudes of students. If the teacher models democratic practices, the students will absorb powerful lessons. The teacher who shows respect for students when they are expressing their ideas is communicating the importance of each individual's contribution. The teacher who regularly includes alternative points of view in the curriculum is preparing students to live with diversity and to question the truth of just one source of information. In looking at the teacher as a role model, two past presidents of the National Council for the Social Studies, Shirley Engle and Anna Ochoa (1988, pp. 24–25), ask:

> Is the teacher a concerned, thoughtful citizen? Is the teacher interested in public issues? Is he or she well read and informed on significant issues? Does the teacher become involved in public causes? These questions reflect our belief that teachers will be more effective if they serve as models of concerned and involved citizenship to their students.

Research has shown the significant impact of the teacher as a model of democratic practices. In a famous study originally conducted in the 1930s by Lewin, Lippett, and White (1939), three different leadership styles were investigated: democratic, autocratic, and laissez-faire. When fifth graders were exposed to three different types of leaders, their behavior changed. The autocratic leader made all the decisions and gave detailed directions on work assignments. The students' response was to be submissive and to work in the presence of the leader, but when the leader left the room, work slowed down. The students experienced hostility and tension, some of which was directed at a single student. The laissez-faire leader gave the children a great deal of freedom. The leader was aloof, giving minimal direction, no work assistance, and no praise or criticism. The students became aggressive, frustrated, and uncooperative, and the group task was never accomplished. The democratic leader provided guidance by suggesting alternatives, but decisions were left to the group. The leader supplied information when students requested it, encouraged self-direction, and reminded students of their goals. The students showed greater participation and cooperation with the democratic leader than with the other leaders and were more effective in accomplishing their task. The democratic climate was less stressful and more efficient. Figure 8.7 summarizes the goals of a democratic classroom.

Other researchers have looked at the classroom in terms of an open or closed climate (Hahn, Tocci, & Angell, 1988; Hepburn, 1991). An open climate is characterized by teachers who encourage student questions and opinions and who help students explore controversial issues by allowing a variety of views to be represented and expressed. A closed climate is characterized by little controversy, with the teacher frequently expressing opinions but the students feeling reluctant to share their opinions.

F I G U R E   8 . 7

■

Goals of a democratic classroom.

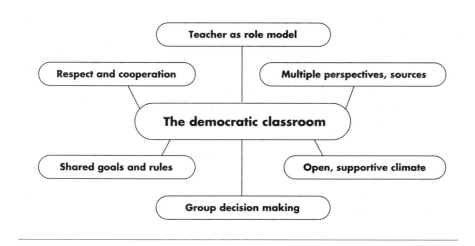

In Glenn's (1972) study of children in grades 3, 5, and 6, the classrooms with an open climate fostered a sense of political efficacy in the children. They felt that they could have an influence on government to make things better.

A second-grade "open-climate" teacher in Michigan created a classroom community called Betterburg, which included law enforcement, a bank, a library, and a variety of community activities (Gilstrap, 1991). Students wrote letters every night to mail at their post office. Some were letters to their friends, and others were to people in the real town in which they lived. Their letter-writing skills resulted in civic action: the installation of traffic lights, planter boxes, and sidewalks and clean-up efforts. This represented a powerful combination of whole language and civic education.

The classroom teacher has a significant role to play in the education of children for active participation in their society. When this goal is reinforced on a schoolwide basis, the impact is even stronger. Some schools require students to take a training course on how to be a mediator. On the playground, the mediators help their peers find solutions to conflicts. In other schools, students plan community action projects to solve neighborhood problems and make their surroundings cleaner and safer. In one elementary school, the student council has been transformed into a true problem-solving representative body (Shaheen, 1989). Through their own modeling of such skills, teachers provide daily examples of democratic processes in action. If the curriculum includes repeated experiences that help children build citizenship skills, they will have the opportunity to enhance the contribution they make to a democratic society.

Summary

In a whole language classroom, the teacher is the key person in orchestrating experiences that will build students' interest, knowledge, and skills to participate in a democratic society. Of course, it is far easier for the teacher to use a basal reader or standardized textbook, follow a preset curriculum, and assess students by using the publisher's tests. The result of this, however, is to produce "believers rather than thinkers" (Resnick, 1991), passive recipients of other people's knowledge rather than students who are actively involved in their own learning. Participatory experiences in the classroom, such as making rules, analyzing case studies, role playing, and cooperative learning, provide children with a rich context for meaningful writing, listening, and speaking. Such learning experiences also build the citizenship skills needed in a democratic society and allow students to be contributing members of their learning community.

References

Adler, M. (1987). *We hold these truths: Understanding the ideas and ideals of the Constitution.* New York: Collier Books.

Anderson, T. D. (1988). Civil and political liberties in the world: A geographical analysis. In J. Norwine and A. Gonzalez, *The Third World.* Boston: Unwin Hyman. p.143–151.

Angell, A. (1991). Democratic climates in elementary school classrooms: A review of theory and research. *Theory and Research in Social Education, 19(3), 241–266.*

Arbetman, L., & Roe, R. (1985). *Great trials in American history.* St. Paul, MN: West.

Beatty, P. (1990). *Turn homeward, Hannalee.* Mahwah, NJ: Troll Associates.

Becker, J. (1992). A new world order, *Educational Leadership, 49*(5), 83–84.

California State Board of Education. (1987). *History/social science framework.* Sacramento: California State Board of Education.

Clark, T. (1981). *Police patrol.* Culver City, CA: Zenger Productions.

Cohen, E., and Lotan, R. (1990). Teacher as supervisor of complex technology. *Theory into Practice, 29*(1), 78–84.

Cohen, E., Lotan, R., & Catanzarite, L. (1990). Treating status problems in the cooperative classroom. In S. Sharan, (ed.) *Cooperative Learning: Theory and Research, p.203–229. New York: Praeger.*

Corbin, D. (1991). Bringing social studies to life through children's fiction. *Social Studies Review, 31*(1), 22-25.

Engle, S., & Ochoa, A. (1988). *Education for democratic citizenship.* New York: Teachers College Press. p.25.

Fernlund, P. (1990). What is a democracy? *Update on Law-Related Education, 14*(3), 16-19.

Fernlund, P., & Crowell, S. (1990, November 18). *Complex instruction in elementary social studies.* Paper presented at the meeting of the National Council for the Social Studies, Anaheim, CA.

Fritz, J. (1987). *Shh! We're writing the Constitution* (T. De Paola, Illus.). New York: Putnam.

Gilstrap, R. L. (1991). Can writing be used to improve learning and thinking? *Social Studies Review, 31*(1), 26-32.

Glenn, A. D. (1972). Elementary school children's attitudes toward politics. In B. Massialas (Ed.), *Political youth, traditional schools: National and international perspectives, p.51-63. Englewood Cliffs, NJ: Prentice-Hall.*

Hahn, C., Tocci, C., & Angell, A. (1988, June). *Five nation study of civic attitudes and controversial issues discussions.* Paper presented at the International Conference on the Social Studies, Vancouver, BC.

Hepburn, M. (1991). School climate: Research insights for the education of social studies teachers. In C. Anderson and D. T. Naylor (Eds.), *Law-related education and the preservice teacher* (pp. 41-48). Chicago: American Bar Association.

Hunt, I. (1987). *Across five Aprils.* New York: Berkley.

Hunt, M., & Metcalf, L. (1968). *Teaching high school social studies.* New York: Harper & Row.

Klesius, J. (1988, December). What is whole language? *Florida Reading Quarterly, 20,* 17-23.

Lewin, K., Lippett, R., & White, R. (1939). Patterns of aggressive behavior in experimentally created social climates. *Journal of Social Psychology, 10,* 271-299.

National Council for the Social Studies. (1984, April). Essential skills for social studies. *Social Education,* pp. 260-261.

National Council for the Social Studies. (1992). *Mission Statement.* Washington, D.C.

O'Connor, S. (1987, August 2). Justices on the Constitution: What children should know. *New York Times,* Education Life Section, p. 33.

O'Dell, S. (1976). *The two hundred ninety.* Boston: Houghton Mifflin.

Parker, W. C. (1989). Participatory citizenship: Civics in the strong sense. *Social Education, 53,* 353–354.

Ratcliffe, R., Gordon, I., & Gallagher, A. (1989). *Great cases of the Supreme Court.* Boston: Houghton Mifflin.

Resnick, D. (1991, August). As quoted in D. Gursky. After the reign of Dick and Jane. *Teacher Magazine,* p. 28.

Shaheen, J. (1989). Participating citizenship in elementary grades. *Social Education, 53*(6), 361–363.

Sunal, C. S., & Hass, M. E. (1993). *Social studies and the elementary/middle school student.* Orlando, FL: Harcourt Brace Jovanovich.

Yeaton, C., & Braeckel, K. (1986). *A salute to our Constitution and the Bill of Rights,* Grades 1–3. Indianapolis, IN: Indianapolis Star, pp. 66–68.

Moving Beyond Indoor Classrooms: Outdoor Education and the Social Studies

CLIFFORD E. KNAPP
NORTHERN ILLINOIS UNIVERSITY

The teacher should become intimately acquainted with the conditions of the local community, physical, historical, economic, occupational, etc., in order to utilize them as educational resources.

JOHN DEWEY

Experience and Education

What we must realize is that the walls of those buildings we imprison kids in now must come crashing down, and the world must be their classroom, the classroom a reflection of their world. The two must work as one.

ELIOT WIGGINTON

Foxfire 2

Socializing most effectively happens simply by living in societies day by day, and schools are generally rather ineffective socializing institutions when they try to teach what is best learned from out-of-school experience.

KIERAN EGAN

Teaching As Story Telling

Introduction

The foregoing observations by Dewey, Wigginton, and Egan over a span of almost 50 years chart the course for this chapter. Simply stated, outdoor education programs can provide students with meaningful ways to reach the goals of the social studies through the whole language approach. This chapter explores the theory and practice behind this thesis. The interconnecting links between outdoor education, social studies, and whole language are first examined descriptively and then through examples of instructional activities and models.

Christopher T. Cross (1990, p. 1), assistant secretary of the U.S. Department of Education, pinpoints the lack of student motivation as one of our most pressing problems:

> All the changes we hope to see in our schools will matter little
> unless we also motivate America's students to want to learn.
> Unfortunately, research shows far too many students are
> disengaged and bored, seeing little connection between school
> performance and life.

If low student motivation is a prime factor in the currently poor image of American education, then educators should examine the ideas in this chapter. The authors cited here firmly believe that students do become excited about learning when the teacher artfully combines a teaching style with particular out-of-classroom sites. Let's explore how teachers can integrate outdoor education, social studies goals and objectives, and the whole language approach.

Outdoor Education

Outdoor education is defined as the use of resources outside the formal school classroom to meet educational goals and objectives. These resources are studied as directly as possible through student involvement rather than vicariously through books, films, television, computers, or other means. However, when appropriate instructional technology can support or stimulate learning outside the classroom, it is freely used. Outdoor

■ To respect the environment, children need to interact with nature.

education involves more than merely selecting a setting outside the school, although that is an important first step. Practitioners espouse particular educational philosophies that incorporate firsthand experience and direct contact with reality—urban, suburban, or rural. Because of the constraints of finances, travel time, leadership expertise, and other logistical and philosophical factors, not all learning can be implemented in this way. The basic rationale for selecting outdoor educational experiences is to teach those topics outside the classroom that can best be taught there. This is a decision that most teachers are well qualified to make, although they can always improve their ability to make it. One purpose of this chapter is to expand teacher's visions so that the educational potential of the world outside the school will be more fully realized. Outdoor educators firmly believe that the educational setting and the instructional methodology used there are two keys to meaningful learning.

Outdoor education is multidisciplinary because if a topic is studied in the proper context, many of the traditional subjects are involved. Educators originally divided experiences into separate subjects in order to make them easier to learn. However, one result was that students had difficulty seeing the relationship of each subject to the whole and to life outside the classroom. Many outdoor educators support small group problem-solving approaches to learning and therefore use subject matter as tools to uncover meanings rather than as structures that govern activity selection. The success of schooling must be evaluated in terms of what students can do with and how they feel about what they learn.

Although many educators believe that outdoor education simply provides the optimal setting and methodology for implementing existing curricular goals and objectives, others believe that it expands the present curriculum and leads to an increased appreciation of natural and cultural communities and links the school more closely to the surrounding area and the world.

Outdoor education can be traced back 300 years or more. In fact, before schools were constructed, all learning took place in the context of life situations in which people met their basic needs. John Amos Comenius advocated direct experience as a way to achieve lifelong learning. He wrote, "Instruction must begin with actual inspection, not with verbal description of things. . . . The object must be a real, useful thing, capable of making an impression upon the senses" (Minton, 1980, p. 28). Other early educators and philosophers such as Rousseau, Pestalozzi, Froebel, and Dewey supported the basic tenets of outdoor education through the years.

George Counts (1932, p. 275) characterized the key commitments of those who considered themselves progressive educators this way:

> They have focused attention squarely upon the child; they have recognized the fundamental importance of the interest of the learner; they have defended the thesis that activity lies at the root of all true education; they have conceived learning in terms of life situations and growth of character; they have championed the rights of the child as a free personality.

"Dewey rejected the traditional notion of thinking as the mind acting independent of the body. Rather, he construed thinking as an operation involving the total organism's interaction with the environment" (Lauderdale, 1981, p. 15).

Outdoor educators today still hold many of the commitments of earlier thoughtful progressive educators. They react negatively to students sitting in chairs, dutifully memorizing assigned information discovered by someone else in a distant place long ago, and seeing no relevance to their lives except to get a passing grade. There are many good reasons to leave the classroom to learn about the world. Here is a beginning list:

1. A change of setting and pace is often useful for motivation.
2. There is usually more physical space outdoors to do certain activities.
3. Direct experience often expands our understanding of words and language.
4. We can better examine objects and events found in context and understand how they are interrelated and related to the whole.

5. Some students can learn better outside by using their senses and whole body in the process (kinesthetic learners).

6. Teachers can get to know their students in different ways because some students respond differently to outdoor learning.

7. Teachers can expand their awareness and knowledge of the environment outside the school and may become more motivated to teach.

8. Students have opportunities to practice skills they have mastered and apply what they know to meaningful and new situations.

9. Students can better understand how their community and region are connected to what is taught and learned in school.

10. Students can gain new outdoor skills and attitudes that may be applied during their leisure time.

11. Students can learn to identify and investigate community and regional problems and consider ways to solve them.

12. Teachers can create different types of challenges and problems for students to overcome and solve.

13. There are many more teaching/learning aides outside the classroom than inside the classroom.

Social Studies

The umbrella term *social studies* provides us with a variety of people-related opportunities beyond the classroom walls. "Social studies began in the 1930s as an effort to make the subject more 'relevant'" (Alter & Denworth, 1990, pp. 31–32). Although not everyone agrees on the topics that comprise the social studies, the following categories are often included: sociology (families, neighborhoods, communities, and broader cultures), history (local, state, national, and international), geography (the earth's surface), and political science or civics (citizen involvement and government) (Knapp, Swan, Vogl, & Vogl, 1986, p. 1). In addition, the areas of anthropology, economics, psychology, and environmental studies are also included at some grade levels.

Early in 1990, the National Assessment of Educational Progress (NAEP) revealed grades 4, 8, and 12. The NAEP is a congressionally mandated project directed by the National Center for Education Statistics and often referred to as our nation's report card. Here are just a few of the results in the social studies, as reported in *ETS Developments* (Educational Testing Service, 1990):

HISTORY: "Students show little in-depth understanding of the circumstances that led to major historical events" (p. 5).

"Only one-third of the eighth graders recognized the opening statement in the Declaration of Independence" (p. 6).

"Fourth graders reported they spent most of their time studying American Indians, pilgrims, New World explorers, and inventors" (p. 6).

CIVICS: "Students attending schools in advantaged urban communities displayed higher civics proficiency than those attending schools in disadvantaged urban communities" (p. 6).

"At all three grade levels (4th, 8th, 12th), students reported that reading from a textbook was the instructional method most often used by their civics teachers" (p. 6).

GEOGRAPHY: "Most high school seniors did not perform as well when asked to identify cities or physical land features" (p. 7).

"Seniors had trouble interpreting all the information given on a single map or integrating information presented on more than one map" (p. 7).

"Most seniors displayed little in-depth understanding of environmental issues frequently addressed in the news" (p. 7).

"Students in the U.S. are poorly equipped to deal with the skills, concepts, and basic knowledge of geography" (p. 7).

How would these limited NAEP findings be different if the students who had taken the tests had studied these topics outside the classroom? That is hard to say, but we could imagine that if students had visited the site of a historical event, they might have better understood what actions led up to it. If they had done more than read from the textbook, they might have had a better grasp of some civics concepts. Or if they had taken a map and used it to find polluted areas in their community, they might have been better able to interpret the map and understand the environmental issues in greater depth.

According to Ernest Boyer (1990), president of the Carnegie Foundation for the Advancement of Teaching, one of the goals of social studies education is to help students become responsible citizens. Therefore, he proposes (pp. 6–7) that programs must have several important characteristics:

1. A focus on communication skills (town meetings, city councils, study groups, and other opportunities to think critically, listen carefully, and communicate through verbal and written means)
2. A core of basic knowledge about social issues and institutions and their role in the democratic process
3. Learning activities that go well beyond textbook reading assignments (Theories of government must be tested in experiences.)

4. Discussion of value differences—even the most controversial issues of our time

5. The school and surrounding community must become laboratories for learning about civic education. (Most citizenship lessons come from students observing how teachers and administrators manage classes and schools.)

6. Student assistance in connecting their lessons with their life outside the school (Boyer is promoting a new Carnegie unit based on service in the community. He advocates that every student become involved in volunteering service in retirement villages, day care centers, youth camps, and outdoor centers. If implemented, it is hoped that some of this service learning will occur during regular school hours.)

Social studies, as an academic area of focus, is one of the most exciting subjects to explore outside the confines of the school because it holds such varied potential for providing meaningful student experiences.

Relating Whole Language Philosophy to Social Studies Outside the Classroom

Canadian Judith Newman (1985, p. 1) calls whole language a "shorthand way of referring to a set a beliefs about curriculum." This definition also fits the terms, *outdoor education* and *social studies*.

According to Smith (1992, p. 440), whole language instruction "is without doubt the most vital movement in education today, and its political and social influence has been enormous." Smith urges that teachers respect learners and provide meaningful and productive activities for them, not pointless drills and rote memorization. He suggests (p. 432) that if teachers hold an informal view of learning—that learning is social, continuous, spontaneous, and effortless and requires no particular attention, conscious motivation, or specific reinforcement—the whole language approach will be more compatible with their philosophy.

To summarize the major points made thus far, learning language processes (listening, speaking, reading, and writing) can be successful if teachers venture beyond the classroom walls to study how people think and respond individually and in groups.

The whole language approach involves students actively in solving meaningful problems—sometimes those they choose themselves. They explore objects and events on the school grounds and in the community and beyond to learn about the connections between the outside and the inside classroom. They construct meaning from experience in the same ways they learned the language when they were younger. They are encouraged to take risks and not be afraid of failure.

■ These children walked the same forest that the famous Sauk Indian Chief Blackhawk (depicted in the sculpture in the background) did decades prior to their birth.

Teachers using this approach, capitalize on student interests in the world outside the classroom. They encourage students to keep in touch with important events and ask questions about them. They offer students an array of hands-on/minds-on learning opportunities with just enough structure to keep them motivated. They try to extend as much trust to the students as possible because they know trust can be rewarded by creative learning and increased risk taking.

It is easier to read about how to do all of this than to actually do it. Teachers need to be patient and gentle with themselves, knowing that personal change is often one of the slowest and hardest endeavors in life. "Where there is a will, there is a way," states an old adage. Do you have the will to give some of the following activities a try?

Activities that Blend Outdoor Education with the Social Studies

The remaining sections of this chapter provide some concrete teaching suggestions and models, problems to investigate, and lesson and unit ideas that illustrate how teachers can implement the theory outlined previously.

Essence Cards: An Innovative Approach to Urban Studies

In the early 1970s the American Geological Institute sponsored and the National Science Foundation funded the Environmental Studies for Urban Youth Project. The instructional materials took the form of cards packaged in two kits, *Essence I* (American Geological Institute [AGI], 1970, 1971) and *Essence II* (AGI, 1975). Each card invites learners to investigate a problem, "the action." For example, "Go outside and find a million of something and prove it." The action is purposely ambiguous because the developers believe that ambiguity encourages student decision making. Built into each investigation are elements of awareness of environmental conditions, adventure and choice, and acceptance for differing opinions and values in solving the problem. Following each main action are related extensions labeled "more." Although *Essence I* and *Essence II* are now out of print, some libraries and instructional material centers may still have them on their shelves. For those who have difficulty in locating these materials, the following actions from *Essence II* (Community Activity Cards) will help you get the idea and assist you in exploring a community.

1. "Go outside and observe economic movements in your community. Map these movements."
2. "Go outside and examine the physical and social characteristics of a community. Record your observations."
3. "Visit a community and learn about housing practices."
4. "Go into the community and try to gather enough stuff to feed you one meal a day . . . two meals . . . all meals."
5. "Go outside and map the friendly centers of your community."
6. "Go outside and find *public* facilities. Then find public facilities that are private . . . and private facilities that are public."
7. "Go to the best lookout spot available in your community. Investigate how much can be seen from it . . . both quantitatively and qualitatively."
8. "Find out where 10 things come from that you find in your supermarket."
9. "Observe as many media as you can. Identify causes and effects of humor employed in these media."
10. "Go outside and observe your community. Then make it a tree . . . identifying its soil, nutrients, root structure, etc."

11. "Go outside and find shopping centers. Find out what makes them be."
12. "Find some ideas you'd like to plant in your community. Plant them. See what happens."
13. "Identify political activities in a community that seem to have positive and beneficial results. Look for those political activities that seem to have negative results."
14. "Go outside and find people willing to communicate things they know and like in new ways. Do something with what you find."
15. "Go outside and see if you can find some place where nothing seems to be happening. Make something you want to happen . . . happen!"
16. "Go outside and look at your community. Figure out who lives in the community, why they live there, and what they do. Then do something unpredictable with what you find out."

These are just a small sample of the type of "actions" that invite awareness and adventure through ambiguity. A total of 249 cards were published in both sets. They can be used by individual students or in teams. Teachers can structure the assignments more, although the advantage of keeping them open-ended is that students are encouraged to make decisions about how and what to learn. When students and teachers understand and become enthusiastic about this approach, they can construct their own essence card actions and extensions.

The Foxfire Approach to Community Investigation

Perhaps the most successful and sustained effort in cultural journalism at the high school level has been that of Eliot Wigginton. A high school English teacher who always seems to be searching for a better way to teach, Wigginton is still perfecting his skills. His approach is alive and well in Rabun County, Georgia, and in many other areas around the world.

In an effort to involve more of his students and excite them about learning, Wigginton started with a classroom-produced magazine titled *Foxfire.* It contained an assortment of student writing, mostly about the life and ways of the local people. Armed with tape recorder and notebooks, teams of students conducted interviews with the people in their community. They asked them about making soap or wagon wheels, finding medicinal plants, building log cabins, and anything else that was part of their life-style. Later, these transcribed interviews and articles were

■ Children have different strengths. The child who is not the highest academic achiever may be the highest achiever in the environmental awareness.

developed into *The Foxfire Book* (Wigginton, 1972). Eight other books followed over the years, and the series became a national best-seller. Somewhat surprised at the success of his idea, Wigginton (1986, p. 126) concludes:

> The only new wrinkle I had added to that process [collecting folklore and oral history] was to have such collecting done by the grandchildren—not by professionals—and to add those findings to the contents of our own literary magazine. Was it that unusual to ask high school students to talk to their elders and write down what they had learned?

Wigginton always analyzes what he does and experiments to find better ways to teach. In his autobiography, *Sometimes a Shining Moment* (1986), he challenges educators to make a list of memorable, positive experiences they had in school. When he examined his own list, he grouped the experiences into broad categories:

1. "Times when there were visitors to our class from the world outside the classroom" (p. 37)
2. "Times when, as students, we left the classroom on assignments or field trips" (p. 37)
3. "Times when things we did, as students, had an audience beyond the teacher" (p. 38)
4. "Times where we, as students, were given responsibility of an adult nature, and were trusted to fulfill it" (p. 39)

5. "Times when we, as students, took on major independent research projects that went far beyond simply copying something out of an encyclopedia, or involved ourselves in periods of intense personal creativity and action" (p. 41)

In his early years as a teacher, Wigginton did not provide his students with enough of these meaningful experiences that he thought were positive and memorable. This realization helped him change his methods slowly over the years and take more risks. Although Wigginton is still experimenting, he has developed a list of overarching truths or principles that he thinks make the difference between effective and ineffective teachers. Here are some conclusions from his autobiography.

1. "Fine teachers see their subject matter whole" (p. 199).
2. "They know how learning takes place" (p. 201).
3. "They know their students and their environments" (p. 216).
4. "They are careful about the assumptions they make" (p. 223).
5. "They understand the role of self-esteem" (p. 233).

The Foxfire approach pushes the classroom walls into the community. The subject matter springs from the culture of the area and the interests of the students.

> The inescapable linkages between that subject matter, their communities, their students, and the globe come so automatically that for them to teach otherwise—to teach a course in isolation from the world outside the school facility—would be literally impossible. The two are seen as inextricably married. (Wigginton, 1986, p. 208)

The curriculum often grows from students' questions about their surroundings. For example:

> Why do those spring flowers have color and fragrance?
> How do they acquire it?
> Of what is it made?
> What is the connection between flowers and bees?
> How do bees work?
> How do they build?
> Why are the cells in their combs hexagonal?
> Are there relationships between their architecture and Buckminster Fuller's domes?
> What is the mathematics involved? (Wigginton, 1986, pp. 200–201)

These investigations are multidisciplinary because that is the way life's problems are solved. Although Wigginton was assigned to teach English, he rarely let the traditional disciplinary boundaries limit student learning. He believes the best teachers are led to say,

If my course has no direct application to, or utility within, other courses being taught in this school as well as the world outside these walls, and I can find no way to help my students make those linkages and relate them to their own lives, then I can only conclude that the course should not be offered at all. (1986, p. 201)

Today, after almost 30 years of teaching, Wigginton and the foundation he started, support a teacher outreach program that is affiliated with colleges, universities, and staff development agencies. They offer workshops and graduate courses in Foxfire's approach to instruction; grants for teachers who develop hands-on, community-based, academically sound units of instruction; regional networks of teachers; and a quarterly journal. One of Foxfire's core practices is this: "Connections between the classroom work and surrounding communities and the real world outside the classroom are clear" (*The Brain Based Education Networker*, 1990, p. 6).

Other Ways to Investigate a Community

Diane Cantrell (1990), who works for the Ohio Department of National Resources, describes an in-service teacher institute designed to improve teacher skills in investigating a community. She evaluated the effectiveness of the institute in achieving the project goals, which included having teachers implement a community study with their students back at school. The institute used several resources to assist the teachers. One was a lesson plan developed by the U.S. Forest Service (1978, pp. HC-1–18) titled, "Investigating the Human Community." This material presents a 10-step process for identifying parts of a community, looking for land use patterns, constructing a plan to investigate one part of the community, analyzing the data collected, and developing alternative solutions and a plan to implement them. Other helpful references were written by Hungerford, Litherland, Peyton, Ramsey, and Volk (1988); Roth and Lockwood (1979); and the National Wildlife Federation (1982). During the institute the teacher participants investigated a pioneer farm at the Great Smoky Mountain National Park. A seventh-grade teacher commented in an interview:

When we started doing the community study I felt like this is really an imposition on people who are busy. Think when I go home I would have continued to feel that way had I not actively done it myself and gotten the response that we got from the people. That made me feel totally different. (Cantrell, 1990, p. 6)

Cantrell recognizes that full implementation of all the steps involved in a community study is difficult. She cites barriers such as limited planning time, an overcrowded curriculum with state accountability testing, and difficulties organizing field trips (no money for buses, scheduling problems for departmentalized classes, and restrictive district field trip policies). "In spite of these issues, almost two-thirds of the teachers indicated they would increase the level of community involvement the next

FIGURE 9.1

■

Continuum of community involvment. Typically, students enjoy
engaging in community activities. However, most teachers choose to
assign classroom activities and projects that require little or no
community involvement.

High involvement of students in community

Action project — Implement community activities
Conduct community study

Outside of school — Conduct survey/interview
Attend public hearing
Go on a field trip

Action project — Implement school-oriented activities
Do class activities reaching beyond the school
Involve parents

Inside school — Conduct survey/interview
Listen to guest speaker
Write to agency
Read and/or watch local media

Activities/projects — Do classroom activities

**Low involvement
of students in community**

year'' (Cantrell, 1990, p. 16). To determine the extent to which the teachers became involved in investigating issues in the community, Cantrell devised three criteria: (1) how near or far away the activity occurred in location, relative to the classroom; (2) the amount of interaction students had with people in the community; and (3) the extent to which students were involved on the awareness level (passively) or the action level. Specific ''community involvement'' activities were categorized and placed along a composite continuum ranging from ''low involvement'' to ''high involvement,'' as shown in Figure 9.1 (Cantrell, 1990, p. 14).

The purpose of this continuum is to provide a way of thinking about the involvement rather than to categorize and place activities definitively. It illustrates the range of activities in which the teachers and students engaged. The majority were classroom activities and projects, at the "low involvement" end of the continuum. This category includes making murals and replicas of animals, writing a play, participating in essay contests and laboratory and hands-on activities, watching videos, reading textbooks or children's literature, and singing. Many of these activities are general in nature but can be connected to the community through discussion or example.

Another example of blending outdoor education, social studies, and whole language is described in an article by Stephen Tchudi (1992). In a two-week graduate course, Teaching Whole Language, Tchudi and his wife team taught 23 school and college teachers on Martha's Vineyard, an island 6 miles off the coast of Cape Cod. To focus the learning outcomes, the instructors chose the immediate environment, the sea, as the central theme. The main course goal was "to help participants learn about the sea through hands-on (or 'feet wet') experiences" (Tchudi, 1992 p. 31). Another goal was for the teachers to return home with practical ideas for using the whole language approach in their teaching. The course assignments included keeping daily journals, developing scrapbooks or portfolios of artifacts from the sea, and exploring the sea from several multidisciplinary perspectives. The teachers were required to participate in a variety of experiences related to living on the island and to interact with each other and the people of Martha's Vineyard.

Tchudi describes his and his wife's whole language approach with the acronym SCOPE (pp. 31–32). The letters represent the following five elements:

1. *S*urvey (find out what participants know from prior experiences and reading and discover the learning resources available on the island)
2. *C*ollect ("gather" experiences such as interviewing the residents, visiting libraries, bookstores, and art galleries, attending history lectures and nature walks, collecting shells, seaweed and other artifacts, and making simulated scrimshaw carvings)
3. *O*rganize (create a meaningful whole from the various experiences)
4. *P*resent (share knowledge and skills creatively through a variety of formats, including slide shows, demonstrations, and writings)
5. *E*valuate (assess what and how participants learned and what questions still remain unanswered)

The SCOPE approach incorporates Kathleen Strickland's definition of whole language: "an umbrella term for a number of concepts, including the process approach to writing, interdisciplinarity, holistic learning, student centeredness and choice, the use of multi-age and multicultural literature, and the natural integration of the disciplines" (Tchudi, 1990, p. 33).

When students of any age become immersed in a living/learning setting for a period of time, traditional subject-matter divisions often disappear and learning becomes a natural function of relating to the surrounding nonhuman environment as well as to people. The process of communicating the meanings of these living/learning experiences to others becomes one way to assess the acquisition of meaningful knowledge and skills.

Outdoor Activities for Social Studies

The outdoors provides unique learning experiences as children discover nature in their immediate community or at a park or field site. Years later, as adolescents and adults, they recall such living/learning experiences because of their extraordinary magnitude. A square foot of dirt, for instance, is a microcosm of the universe just as the corner grocery store is a microcosm of the world's economy. Such living laboratories offer priceless learning opportunities.

The following suggested activities incorporate social studies and whole language principles in outdoor or community settings. Each activity specifically details what is to be learned and how the teacher can serve as a facilitator or collaborative learner.

Society in Action

PROBLEM: What are some of the essential elements involved in establishing a new society?

OBJECTIVE: To solve cooperatively some of the problems related to establishing a new society.

INTRODUCTION: This activity has been used successfully with groups of intermediate and junior high school students to increase understanding and appreciation of cultures other than their own. It also provides them with the opportunity to work cooperatively in solving problems.

The activity can take place in a park or other natural area. Students are divided into groups of 10 to 12; each group has an adult observer or responsible student leader.

Each group is provided with a set of general instructions (see page 230) and a second sheet of instructions for a specific situation (see example that follows). All groups receive the same *required* tasks. *Group and individual or pair* tasks vary according to the situation provided.

The observer evaluates the group according to a score sheet that is provided. After about 2 hours, the groups gather together and report their accomplishments.

PROCEDURES AND ACTIVITIES

1. Go over the instruction sheet for the lesson Society in Action.

2. Find a territory (location) for your society.

   a. Perform at least two of the group tasks.

   b. Do as many of the individual/pair tasks as possible.

You will be rated on a combined point scale according to how much you do and how well you do your tasks.

3. After completing the tasks, return your territory to as natural a state as possible.

4. Return to the main assembly area.

   a. Bring all of the portable articles you have produced.

   b. Be prepared to participate in an evaluation of the success of your society.

Note. Adapted from Knapp et al., 1986, pp. 25–27.

Your Situation: You Are a Group of Homesteaders Settling in the Area

Task Instructions		Max. Points	Points
1.	Large groups		
	a. Give your community a name.	5	_____
	b. Establish a system of government, select leader(s), and delegate responsibilities.	10	_____
	c. Determine the rules and responsibilities of your community leader(s).	10	_____
	d. Create a banner or flag for your community.	5	_____
2.	Small groups (No more than four members each)		
	a. Make a map of your campsite.	10	_____
	b. Build a fire.	15	_____
	c. Explore the area to become familiar with the plants, animals, and terrain.	10	_____
	d. Prepare some applesauce.	10	_____
	e. Make a rope.	10	_____
3.	Individuals or pairs		
	a. Make a weapon.	10	_____

b.	Make or find a container for water.	10	____
c.	Weave a mat or basket.	5	____
d.	Make some jewelry.	5	____
e.	Dig a 3′ × 3′ pit, 2′ deep to store apples.	5	____
f.	Create some art that you can sell or trade to another community.	5	____
g.	Build an animal trap.	10	____
h.	Make something else that would be useful to the community.	10	____

Evaluation

1. Which tasks were most difficult? Why?
2. What problems did you encounter when working in a group or pair or as an individual?
3. In general, would you rather work as an individual or as part of a pair or group?
4. What tasks do you think early societies found most difficult to accomplish? Why?
5. If you were to begin this activity again, what would you do differently?

An Environmental Study of a Town

■ *Investigating Oregon, Illinois*

Directions: Investigate a natural or cultural resource in Oregon and create a proposal for how it should be developed, managed, or left alone. Possible areas for investigation:

Mix Park   West Bank of the Rock River
Local history   Main (Washington) Street buildings
Traffic patterns   Courthouse Square
Coliseum

Your report should include answers to the following questions:

1. What have you identified as a local resource?
2. What are the problems and opportunities associated with the resource?
3. Do the residents value it? Explain.
4. What should be done to change it, if anything?
5. What is the estimated cost (in dollars) if changes are made?
6. What are costs to the environment if changes are made?

7. What are the benefits to the people and the environment if changes are made?
8. What are some other interesting facts you learned about the resource?

Note: You are to submit a report of your findings at the town meeting to be held Monday evening at 7:00 P.M. at the Yellow Bird Center. At the meeting, reports will be given by five of the following six task forces:

1. Rock River Development
2. Vacation/Recreation Utilization and Development
3. Industrial/Commercial Development
4. Downtown Preservation/Restoration and Development
5. Community Center Development
6. Area Historical Preservation/Restoration

Using a Story as a Springboard

■ *Tell-What-Your-Favorite-Thing-Is Game*

Directions: Listen to the story *Guess Who My Favorite Person Is* by Baylor (1977). When choosing your favorite things in nature, try to find examples so you can share them with others later on. If you are not able to find something or decide not to bring it back, you can describe it with words, pictures, or in any other way. You may even want to take the group to the place where the object is. Use your judgment about whether to pick a living thing or leave it alone. Spend as much time with each object as you wish and don't be concerned about finding all the items on the list. Really get to know each of your favorite things.

What is your favorite?

1. Insect
2. Color
3. Thing to touch (Be sure to touch it.)
4. Sound
5. Place to be (Spend several minutes in that place.)
6. Thing to see moving
7. Thing to taste (Don't really taste it unless you are absolutely sure it is safe. You can still share your idea with the group.)
8. Smell (What does it smell like?)
9. Shape
10. Time of day (Explain why you chose this time.)
11. What other items would you like to add to the list? Add at least five new items before you go searching for your favorite.

Note. Idea from Baylor, 1977.

■ *Creating a Celebration for Today*

Directions: Listen to the story *I'm in Charge of Celebrations* (Baylor, 1986). Do you believe you can be the one in charge of celebrations? Why don't you try to create a celebration for this day? In the spaces below, write your name and today's date and then go off alone or with a small group and invent a celebration that you might like to remember for the rest of your life. After describing your celebration, write the name of the celebration day in the space provided.

Name of person in charge: _____

Date: _____

Description of the Celebration: _____

Name of Celebration Day:_____

■ *Ten Suggestions for Learning the Other Way to Listen*

Directions: Listen to the story *The Other Way to Listen* (Baylor & Parnall, 1978).

In it, the authors teach us about another way to listen by suggesting the following:

1. "It takes a lot of practice."
2. Stay "there long enough to understand the quiet. You can't be in a hurry."
3. Ask hard questions such as, "I wonder how that lizard feels about the rock it's sitting on and how the rock feels about the lizard."
4. "Sometimes everything being right makes a kind of a sound"—like a good feeling coming from a rock.
5. The hills, ants, lizards, weeds, and things like that do the teaching. "Don't be ashamed to learn from bugs or sand or anything."
6. "Go get to know one thing as well as you can. It should be something small, like a seed pod, dry weed, handful of dirt, sandy wash, or tree."
7. "You have to respect that tree or hill or whatever it is you're with."
8. If you go alone, "you can always stop and listen at the right time."
9. If nature doesn't sing to you, you can sing to nature.
10. It helps to think "Here I am" and "listen."

If you follow these directions carefully, you too may discover the other way to listen. Remember, once you learn, it will seem to be a natural thing to do.

Now go off alone without talking and be prepared to discuss what you heard when you return in 20 minutes. Have fun but listen hard!

Cooperative Learning in the Out-of-Doors

Outdoor education involves the use of learning resources outside the classroom to meet educational goals and objectives. Some goals and objectives in science, social studies, language arts, art, music, mathematics, and physical education can be met more effectively outdoors than in. The following cooperative learning tasks can be completed within a relatively short time period with minimal instructional equipment.

1. Go outside and select one object or event to focus upon. Each member of the group is to view the same object or event from a different angle or perspective (e.g., from above, from ground level, sideways, upside down, squinting, jumping up and down, and so on). Each person is to create a phrase or sentence that describes the object or event. Combine the phrases or sentences into a free-form poem.

2. Go outside and write a short poem with a selected form or structure (e.g., haiku, tanka, cinquain, limerick, and so on). Then share this type of poem with the other members of your group. Make sure everyone in the group understands the poetry form or structure you taught them.

3. Go outside and select an area in which to construct a short nature trail. Each group member should select a location along that trail and write a paragraph that gives interesting information or raises questions that expand awareness of the natural objects there. Then walk the trail together and help each other learn about the area.

4. Go outside and select something that is found in abundance. As a group, develop a plan that will enable you to count a million (or 500,000 or 250,000) of these objects in the shortest time possible. Then use that strategy to count them.

5. Go outside and select a limited area to investigate. Each group member is to role play a particular type of scientist: ornithologist (birds), agronomist (soils), herpetologist (snakes), botanist (plants), meteorologist (weather), and so forth. After studying the area for a period of time, each "scientist" is to share his or her research findings.

6. Go outside and select an area in which you can safely build a fire. Gather materials (use only natural fuels) for the fire together. Everyone in the group should assist in the process. Select the person with the *least* fire-building experience to light the fire. If that person needs advice and directions, provide assistance.

7. Go outside and, as a group, select a location to set up camp for the night. Indicate where you would set up the tents, build the fire, put waste water, dig a latrine, store food, cut firewood, eat meals, and perform the other functions of living together. Reach a consensus on these decisions.

8. Go outside and with the other members of your group, form a line (arm's length apart) and systematically walk over an area to collect litter. Before you begin, reach a consensus on your definition of litter. If any questions arise about what to pick up and include, stop and discuss the definition again. Make a general statement about the type of people who litter the area.

9. Go outside and draw a map of an area. Decide on how to accomplish this task so that each member of the group has an important role to play in the process.

10. Go outside and invent a game that promotes cooperation skills and uses some of the natural features of the area. After inventing the game, play it with the members of your group.

11. Go outside and construct a list of 20 "things to find and bring back" for a scavenger hunt. Be sure that the list reflects an environmental ethic so that the area will not be diminished or radically changed. Design the scavenger hunt so that it can be done in pairs or trios.

12. Go outside and mix some soil by using the types of materials that make up rich, fertile soil. Compare the product to a sample of the best soil you can find in the area.

13. Go outside and select a type of material that is found in abundance, such as leaves, rocks, or sticks. As a group, use the material to build the highest structure possible within a 5-minute time period. Everyone must contribute equally to the project. If the structure falls or is lowered in height, it must be dismantled and the group must begin again. If at any time a member wants to stop the construction process, he or she may say, "Stop" and the building will end.

14. Go outside and use a large piece of paper to make a group drawing of a scene. Do this without speaking to each other.

15. Form pairs within your group and take turns leading your partner around the area. The person being led is to keep his or her eyes closed until the "leader" presses gently on the "blind" person's shoulder. After a few moments of looking, the "blind" person closes his or her eyes again and is led to another object. After a few minutes, switch roles with your partner. The purpose of this activity is to share pleasant experiences with each other.

School Site Questions to Explore the Social Studies

1. What natural resources are available for jobs in the community? (e.g., trees for a lumber business)
2. How could the Woodland Indians live on the school grounds? How would you place or arrange their village? Defend your answer.
3. How could the school site be used for something other than a school?
4. Who uses the school site other than schoolchildren? (e.g., adults, animals) What evidence can you find to prove your answers?
5. What natural resources are found on our school site?
6. What effects have people had upon the land that constitutes our school site?
7. What is the main topographical feature of the area?

Note. From members of CIOE 592 Special Topics in Outdoor Education: Using School Sites, Hanover Park, Illinois, Fall 1986.

8. What benefits to settlers does the brook provide?
9. What trees are indigenous to the area, and which have been introduced by people?
10. What direction does each exit of the school building face? (Compass study)
11. Is this area good for crop raising?
12. What would be the best way to transport your crop to market?
13. Would irrigation be needed to raise crops in this area?
14. Demonstrate how our ancestors told time without clocks. (e.g., by sun and shadows)
15. From what you find on the school site, how do you think the Indians colored their drawings on their tepees and the pioneers their clothing?
16. What different things in nature would have helped the Indians survive when living in this area? (e.g., shelter, clothing material, food)
17. What kind of soil is found in this area and how is it important to people?
18. How would you use the environment outside the school as a shelter in each of the four seasons?
19. How long could you survive in each season on what the land has to offer for food?
20. What human-caused changes do you see in the area?
21. What materials are necessary for people to live?
22. What materials are necessary for animals and plants to survive?
23. Do humans need as many materials from the environment as they think they do?
24. Do people live, work, play, or shop around here?
25. What are communities? How are they arranged? What are their basic needs?
26. Can you map out an area where birds tend to feed more frequently?
27. Are there any signs that this area was used as farmland?
28. Can we make a topographical map of our area?

Summary

This chapter shows how theory and practice come together in three areas of curriculum and instruction: social studies, whole language, and outdoor education. Many educators clearly recognize the importance of participating in groups in the teaching/learning process and acknowledge the social studies as a critical topic for investigation. Many educators have enthusiastically endorsed the whole language approach and have identified it as an attitude or philosophy grounded in modern views of how we learn best. Many educators have long recognized the value of leading students beyond the confines of the school building and into the community and surrounding areas to learn. Outdoor education, like the whole language approach, is a way of viewing students as active builders of meaning drawn from their experiences. Outdoor educators have been attempting to reform classroom-based programs and instructional methods since the 1930s.

This chapter illustrates how to mesh these three broad areas and, in the process, change education. The primary aims for doing this have been to transform student involvement from passive to active, isolated to group, irrelevant to meaningful, vicarious to direct, and detached to empowered. The blueprints for action are here for teachers to interpret and set into motion. Educators are the keys to implementation or stagnation.

References

Alter, J., & Denworth, L. (1990, September). A (vague) sense of history. *Newsweek,* pp. 31–32.

American Geological Institute, Environmental Studies for Urban Youth Project. (1970, rev. 1971). *Essence I* Reading, MA: Addison-Wesley.

American Geological Institute, Environmental Studies for Urban Youth Project. (1975). *Essence II.* Reading, MA: Addison-Wesley.

Baylor, B. (1977). *Guess who my favorite person is.* New York: Aladdin Books.

Baylor, B. (1986). *I'm in charge of celebrations.* New York: Scribner's.

Baylor, B., & Parnall, P. (1978). *The other way to listen.* New York: Scribner's.

Boyer, E. (1990). Civic education for responsible citizens. *Educational Leadership, 48*(3), 4–7.

Cantrell, D. C. (1990, July). *Final Evaluation Report for the Southern Highlands Environmental Project.* Unpublished report, Ohio State University at Newark.

Counts, G. (1932). Dare the school build a new social order? In R. L. Vassar (Ed.), *Social History of American Education, 2,* pp. 274–288. Chicago: Rand McNally, 1965.

Cross, C. (1990, Fall/Winter). Motivating students. *Office of Education Research and Improvement Bulletin,* pp. 19–27.

Dewey, J. (1938). *Experience and education.* New York: Collier Books.

Educational Testing Service. (1990, Summer). *ETS Developments,* pp. 1–8. Princeton, NJ: Author.

Egan, K. (1986). *Teaching as story telling.* Chicago: University of Chicago Press.

Hungerford, H. R., Litherland, R. A., Peyton, R. B., Ramsey, J. M., & Volk, T. L. (1988). *Investigating and evaluating environmental issues and actions: Skill development modules.* Champaign, IL: Stipes.

Knapp, C. E., Swan, M., Vogl, S., & Vogl, R. (1986). *Using the outdoors to teach social studies: Grades 3–10.* Charleston, WV: Appalachia Educational Laboratory. (ERIC Clearinghouse Rural Education and Small Schools, P. O. Box 1348, Charleston, WV 25325)

Lauderdale, W. B. (1981). *Progressive education: Lessons from three schools.* Bloomington, IN: Phi Delta Kappa Educational Foundation.

Minton, T. G. (1980). *The history of the nature-study movement and its role in the development of environmental education.* Unpublished doctoral dissertation, Indiana University, Bloomington.

National Wildlife Federation (1982). *The CLASS project.* Washington, DC: Author.

Newman, J. M. (Ed.). (1985). *Whole language: Theory in use.* Portsmouth, NH: Heinemann.

Roth, C. E., & Lockwood, L. G. (1979). *Strategies and activities for using local communities as environmental education sites.* Columbus, OH: ERIC Clearinghouse for Science, Math and Environmental Education.

Smith, F. (1992). Learning to read: The never-ending debate. *Phi Delta Kappan, 73*(6), 432–441.

Tchudi, S. (1992). The interdisciplinary island. *Holistic Education Review, 5*(1), 30–36.

U.S. Forest Service. (1978, October). *Investigating your environment: Teaching materials for environmental education.* Washington, DC: United States Department of Agriculture.

Wigginton, E. (1972). *The Foxfire book.* New York: Anchor Books.

Wigginton, E. (1973). *Foxfire 2.* New York: Anchor Books.

Wigginton, E. (1986). *Sometimes a shining moment: The Foxfire experience.* New York: Anchor Books.

It All Depends on Your Point of View: Multicultural Education in the Social Studies

CARLA COOPER SHAW
NORTHERN ILLINOIS UNIVERSITY

One of the most significant and visible features of the contemporary United States is its multiethnic and culturally pluralistic character.

■

NATIONAL COUNCIL FOR THE SOCIAL STUDIES,
"The Columbia Quincentenary Position Statement"

"Daddy, why did the Indians attack the settlers?"
"Because they were a wild and savage people."
"Who—the Indians or the settlers?"
"The Indians, of course. The settlers were just like you and me."

Introduction

Children are not born prejudiced, but by the time they enter kindergarten, they may possess misconceptions and negative attitudes about cultural groups different from their own (Byrnes, 1988; Banks & Banks, 1989). Among the causes of prejudice in children are two natural tendencies: to evaluate and categorize people and to adopt the attitudes of respected adults and other children. The relationship between personal identity and the need for group membership also plays a role in the formation of prejudice. In their quest for belonging, children may express group loyalty by denigrating people belonging to cultures unlike their own (Byrnes, 1988).

Regardless of the causes of prejudice, its pernicious effects are legend. World history and current events, as they affect whole nations and races of people, are replete with the harmful results of prejudice. On a more individual level, prejudice limits the opportunities of both those who are prejudiced and their victims, who often internalize society's negative stereotypes, leading to weakened self-esteem and ability to achieve. In a prejudiced society, the potential for various cultural groups to live together peacefully and to work together productively is greatly diminished.

This last effect assumes special significance in light of the large-scale demographic changes underway in the United States. If current trends continue, it is projected that by the year 2000, approximately one out of every three schoolchildren will be nonwhite (Banks & Banks, 1989); and by 2020, that figure will have increased to almost one out of two (Pallas, Natriello, & McDill, 1989). Diversity is rapidly becoming a fact of everyday life. If it is to be a cause for celebration rather than a cause of contention, the prevention and reduction of prejudice are imperative.

A major goal of multicultural education is to help all students— regardless of their culture affiliations—develop more positive attitudes toward different cultural, racial, and ethnic groups (Banks & Banks, 1989). "Being an active participant in American society requires individuals to assume many different roles and often requires the ability to interact with people from diverse backgrounds" (Sunal & Haas, 1993, p. 346). Our task is no simple matter. As Sleeter and Grant (1988, p. 208) note, "People tend to live in small, rather insulated worlds with others who share their advantages or disadvantages." For children, this insulation is heightened. It

■ Once children begin to feel empathy for others, they are on their way toward respecting diverse points of view.

would seem that learning about different ethnic groups, perhaps by researching and preparing reports on the contributions of diverse cultural groups, would lead to positive attitudes. But such is not necessarily the case, for knowledge or cognition alone does not lead to enlightenment. Prejudice is a complex phenomenon consisting of at least three related components—the cognitive, the affective, and the behavioral—and so it demands a multidimensional attack (Pate, 1988).

Children who are low in prejudice show "more sensitivity and openness to other points of view" (Byrnes, 1988, p. 269) and are able to think critically. Among the attitudes necessary for the growth of critical thinking are open-mindedness, flexibility, and respect for other viewpoints (Walsh, 1988). Research suggests that activities and materials with a strong affective component that invite children to enter vicariously into the lives of people of different ethnic groups are effective in the development of this flexibility of perspective (Byrnes, 1988). Once students begin to feel empathy, they are well on their way toward respecting diverse points of view and thus becoming less prejudiced.

The overarching goal of this chapter is to outline an instructional unit that represents the meshing of an important affective goal of multicultural education with social studies content. The goal is the development of the ability to understand perspectives different from one's own, and the content is knowledge of diverse cultural groups. Beginning in phase one with student participation in a variety of ethnic experiences, the unit proceeds to help students focus on a particular cultural group in phase two and to develop an understanding of point of view and empathy in phase three. The unit culminates in phase four with students creating characters from different cultural groups, writing from their characters' points of view, and sharing their products. An optional extension provides students with an opportunity to envision a multicultural community.

The unit engages students in most of the elements of the whole language approach as outlined by Robbins (1990). It uses children's books that invite vicarious experience with characters from a variety of cultural groups. These books, when taken together, represent a multicultural perspective. Research suggests that reading such multiethnic literature can lead to increased awareness and decreased negative stereotyping of people from other cultures (Walker-Dalhouse, 1992). Following the unit is a bibliography of pertinent children's literature categorized by cultural group.

The unit's first three phases serve as rehearsal for subsequent stages of the writing process—revision, editing, and sharing—contained in the final phase. As the unit progresses through the stages of the whole language approach, it also guides students through important aspects of the creative process: sensory stimulation, focusing, and incubation.

Phase One: Bombardment of Experiences

In phase one, students participate in a variety of ethnic experiences, both print and nonprint. The emphasis here is on exposure to diversity, on immersion without discrimination in the lives of people from a wide variety of cultural backgrounds. The teacher begins the unit by reading aloud a number of books that focus on the lives of children from various American cultures. The bombardment of experiences continues with whatever resources are available: guest speakers from the community; field trips to ethnic neighborhoods, restaurants, and museums with relevant exhibits; events for children such as might occur during Black History Month; recordings of ethnic music, such as salsa, African American spirituals, rap, and reggae; videotapes and films.

It is important in this phase for both print and nonprint experiences to be as primary and authentic as possible. That is, speakers should relate their own personal experiences in the spirit of storytelling rather than provide histories of their cultural groups. In selecting stories to read aloud, the teacher should try to choose those that reflect accurate patterns of language use, such as folktales and stories with realistic dialogue. In reading aloud, the teacher should remain true to those patterns and inflections to the best of his or her dramatic ability. Films and videos should be stories of lifelike, sympathetic characters rather than documentaries. When visiting ethnic neighborhoods, children should be encouraged to interact with residents and shopkeepers instead of communicating through the teacher or an interpreter.

The keys to continuity throughout this initial bombardment of experiences are quiet times, occurring at regular intervals, in which the teacher reads stories selected with an eye toward reinforcing and clarifying experiences students have recently had or whetting their appetites for

■ When reading multicultural folktales and stories aloud, the teacher should attempt to use his or her best dramatic skills.

experiences yet to come. Younger students may benefit from the shared book experience as created by Holdaway (1979). Through a series of seven steps, the entire class becomes involved in reading a single book. Typically, a "big book" is shared because the illustrations and print are large enough for children to see as they sit on the floor, gathered together around the teacher. The seven steps outlined by Holdaway (1979) are these:

1. The teacher selects a book and briefly introduces it to the students.
2. The teacher asks the students to make predictions about what they think will happen in the story.
3. The teacher reads aloud to the class, pointing to the words as they are read.
4. At preselected points, the teacher asks student to validate or invalidate their predictions and to make new ones.
5. The book is reread, with the students joining in the oral reading with the teacher.
6. Students, singly or in pairs, volunteer to read the book or portions of it to the class.
7. The book is read either by the teacher or students to the entire class every day of the week.

Later, both students and teacher engage in sustained silent reading.

Primary level students can engage in choral speaking or the reading of simple poetry. They can select a scene from a picture or a chapter from a book and act it out. They can make overhead transparencies to illustrate a story they have written about a specific culture and share them with the class.

Within the body of materials set aside for this phase of the unit, students should be encouraged to read whatever appeals to their interests of the moment. Time might be provided for students to respond actively and creatively to their reading. Hoyt (1992) suggests that students give expression to their reading by dramatizing and illustrating stories and interpreting them through readers' theater. Students might also translate poetry into song and dance and write rap lyrics and perform them.

Phase Two: Focusing Through Guided and Individualized Reading

After their immersion in a potpourri of diversity, students will probably be interested in particular cultural groups. Once students have decided which group they would like to focus on for further study, the teacher divides the students into learning teams according to their stated preferences and assigns one or two books to each team. Each student reads silently and individually and engages in periodic conferences with the teacher or aide for the purpose of monitoring comprehension.

When a team finishes a book, the teacher conducts reading conferences with that team. Discussions are shaped by a sequence of questions designed to move students gradually from viewing the character from the outside in to viewing the world from the inside out—or getting inside the character's skin to achieve empathy. In the first stage, *viewing the character from the outside,* the teacher asks students to describe the character in terms of such characteristics as physical attributes, home and home life, family, school, food, feelings, beliefs, and religion. In the second stage, *comparing oneself to the character,* the teacher prompts students to select the most important aspects of the character's life. To facilitate comparison, he or she lists these aspects on a chart and instructs students to do the same. Students individually complete their charts, and the ensuing discussion focuses on comparing themselves with the character.

Still using the charts, in the third stage, *identifying with the character,* students discuss the ways in which their lives are similar to the character's life. Finally, in the fourth stage, *developing empathy,* the teacher asks students to predict their own and the character's responses to hypothetical situations.

The following is a sequence of questions that might be used with "You Rap, I'll Reap," one of eleven poignant short stories about African Americans in *Guests in the Promised Land* by Kristin Hunter (1973), which is appropriate for upper elementary students. "You Rap, I'll Reap" is a story about Gloria, who lives in an urban housing project where the residents on one's floor function as an extended family, and money, possessions, and living space are freely shared.

Stage One: Viewing the Character from the Outside

- Gloria says her skin is like "Yuban Coffee in the jar." What color is coffee?

- Gloria says Sheilah's skin is like Gulden's Spicy Brown Mustard. What color is that?

- Who has darker skin—Gloria or Sheilah?

- In what sort of a home does Gloria live—a house or an apartment building? How do you know?

- Some children live in families with a mother and a father and sisters and brothers. Some children live in a family with just a mother. Sometimes the people in a neighborhood are like a family. What kind of family does Gloria have?

- How old do you think Gloria and her friend Lola are? What makes you think that?

- How far does Gloria live from school?

- What is Gloria's job?

- Gloria says of Mrs. Stevens, the woman for whom she works: "There's a lot she *don't* know, because she's white, and I ain't about to tell her." What do you think Mrs. Stevens doesn't know? Why isn't Gloria going to tell her these things? Why do you think Gloria doesn't tell Mrs. Stevens about lending clothes to Sheilah and money to Mrs. Dawkins?

- Why can't both Gloria and Lola have roast beef sandwiches for lunch?

- What does Gloria like to do in her free time alone? What does she like to do with her friends?

Stage Two: Comparing Oneself to the Character

In small groups with the teacher's help, students develop charts, such as the one shown in Figure 10.1, with the first two columns completed, while the third and fourth columns vary from individual to individual. The questions in this stage might be used with a predominantly white class in a middle-class suburban school.

- How is your family different from Gloria's?

- How is your home different from Gloria's?

- Gloria and her family and friends are poor. How is her life different from yours?

FIGURE 10.1

■

Sample comparison chart.

Aspect	Gloria	Me	Same/Different?
Family	everyone on her floor		
Home	project - a very large apartment building		
Mother	strict - "won't let me leave the house unless I'm neat and clean"		
Economic background	poor		
Attitude toward possessions	sharing		
Free time alone	reading, watching TV		

- How do you get to school? How far away is your school from your house? Why didn't Gloria's mother drive her to school?

- How do you feel about your possessions and money? Do you share them the way Gloria shared hers? Why do you think Gloria has such a sharing attitude? Gloria bought lunch for Sheilah even though she works for her money and Sheilah doesn't. Do you think you would have done the same thing?

- How is the way Gloria talks different from the way you talk?

- Gloria says of Mrs. Stevens: "And now she really pulls her whiteness on me." What do you think she means?

- When Sheilah talks about the brothers and sisters, who is she talking about? When you talk about brothers and sisters, who are you talking about? Why do you think Sheilah refers to other African Americans as brothers and sisters?

Stage Three: Identifying with the Character

- Think about your grandparents and aunts and uncles and cousins. How is your family like Gloria's?

- How is Gloria's mother like your mother?

- What TV show do you think you and Gloria would both like?

- What are some of Gloria's special words, and what do they mean? (Students might construct a chart with Gloria's words in the left column and students' corresponding words in the right—e.g., *rap-talk.*) What are some of your special words, and what do they mean? Do you think that all children and teenagers have their own slang?

- Think of all the ways that you and Gloria are alike.

Stage Four: Developing Empathy

- Suppose you spent a Saturday in the project with Gloria. What would you see and hear and smell? What would you and Gloria do?

- What would you like about living in Gloria's project? What would you dislike?

- How would you feel if you transferred to Gloria's school?

- How would Gloria feel if she joined our class?

- What would you and Gloria do if you had her over to your house to spend the night?

- Suppose you had to go without lunch because you didn't have enough money. How would you feel? How would you feel during the afternoon at school? Would you do well in your schoolwork? Do you think Gloria ever had to go without lunch?

- Do your sisters or brothers or friends ever borrow things from you and forget to return them? What do you do when that happens? If you were Gloria and your friend borrowed a Nintendo game and didn't return it, what would you do?

- Suppose you are Gloria and you really want Madame James down the hall to tell your fortune with her cards. She charges $3, but you have only $1. What would happen?

- Gloria is returning home after spending the night with you. How would she describe you and your home and your family to her friend Lola?

Sequence Flexibility

The progression suggested by this questioning sequence leads students in a gradual manner from viewing the character from an external, observer point of view to developing empathy, or viewing the world from the character's perspective. However, if students appear to be ready to empathize upon completing their books, this sequence need not be followed in a lockstep manner. Depending on students' states of readiness, stages of the sequence might be omitted; the boundaries between the stages should remain flexible.

Similarly, at the conclusion of this phase of the unit, students should have a strong intuitive grasp of the concept "point of view" and may be ready to move immediately into the fourth phase of the unit, that of creating a character through language experience. However, the teacher may wish to use some or all of the activities in the third phase to provide students with additional practice in empathizing.

Phase Three: Point of View

The purpose of the third phase of the unit is to facilitate a deeper understanding of point of view and to discuss the concept with students in an explicit manner. Like the sequence of questions in the previous phase, the sequence of activities here moves students in a gradual progression—this time from their own physical points of view regarding an object to viewing life from the perspectives of people different from themselves.

Activity 1. The teacher places a globe in the center of the room, positions students around it in various locations, and asks them to draw it. The teacher then guides the students in comparing their finished pictures with questions such as these:

- You have all drawn the same thing. Why are all the pictures different?

- Tiffany and Jonathan were in almost the same place, but their pictures are still different. Why?

- Is one point of view right and the others wrong? Why or why not?

■ Small group interaction builds self-confidence and citizenship skills.

Activity 2. The teacher states that the students have learned that everyone has his or her own point of view or own way of seeing things and that no two points of view are ever exactly the same. Now the teacher asks the students to think about the globe's point of view with such questions as the following:

- If the globe had eyes, how do you think our room would look to it? What is the globe's point of view on our room?

- Is the globe a male or a female? Why?

- How does the globe feel being looked at by us? Do you think it feels popular? Or do you think it would like a little privacy?

- How does the globe feel when we spin it around?

Activity 3. As a variation on activities described by Walsh (1988) and Joyce and Weil (1986), the teacher asks students to take pennies from their pockets and *become* those pennies:

- How do you feel jangling around in somebody's pocket with lots of other coins that are worth more than you?

- How does a human's hand feel to you?

- How do you feel when someone sees you on the sidewalk and doesn't bother to pick you up?

- Suppose someone sees you and says, "Aha! I've found a penny. Now I'll have good luck!" How do you feel?

- Describe a day in your life as a penny.

Activity 4. Students simulate the experience of being blind or deaf by wearing blindfolds or earplugs. Once they are sighted and hearing again, the teacher encourages them to discuss their experiences.

BLIND

- How did you get around? Which senses did you use?
- Did you depend on other people to help you get around? How did you feel about having to depend on other people?
- Since you couldn't see the faces of people talking to you, how could you tell what they were feeling?
- Describe our classroom from your point of view as a person who is blind.

DEAF

- How did you communicate? How did you know whether you were talking loudly enough? Which senses did you use to understand other people?
- How did it feel to see people playing and talking and having a good time and not being able to hear them?
- Since you couldn't hear people's voices when they were talking to you, how did you know what they were feeling?
- Describe our classroom from your point of view as a person who is deaf.

Up until Activity 2, when the teacher provides the meaning of point of view, the class has been "sneaking up" on a definition. When the teacher is sure that students grasp the meaning of the concept, she or he should reinforce it at every opportunity by relating point of view back to the characters in the books read in the second phase of the unit. For example, after asking students to describe a day in the life of a penny, the teacher might ask them to do the same for a particular character. For "You Rap, I'll Reap," the teacher might ask, "What would Gloria's point of view be on our classroom?"

Phase Four: Creating a Character Through Language Experience

At this point, students have been steeped in a salad bowl of ethnic experiences, and they have delved deeply and vicariously into the lives of one or more characters belonging to the cultural group in which they are the most interested. Students also possess a firm cognitive and affective understanding of point of view. They are now ready to create characters and write their own stories.

The fourth phase of the unit begins with a questioning sequence designed to help students imagine characters of their own creation, visualize settings for these characters, and as professional fiction writers do, view the world from the characters' perspectives. After informing students of the purpose of the upcoming activity, the teacher asks students individually to imagine people from the cultural groups they have explored in depth. The teacher leads them through the process with questions, separated by pauses for reflection, such as the following:

- Is your person male or female?

- Is he or she a child or an adult?

- Is your person fat or thin or in between?

- What are the colors of your person's skin, hair, and eyes?

- What language does he or she speak?

- How does your person's voice sound? Is it soft or harsh, high or low?

- What is his or her name?

- Where does your person live? Does he or she live in the country with trees and rivers? Or in the desert? Or in the ice and snow? Does he or she live in the city?

- In what sort of dwelling does your person live—a house, an apartment, a tent, a cabin, or something else?

- What makes your person happy and sad?

The teacher then asks students to add flesh and bones to their characters by compiling portfolios consisting of completed character data sheets, such as the one shown in Figure 10.2, and drawings of the character, his or her family, home, and other important aspects of his or her life. To help students get started, the teacher may wish to model the process with the character she or he has created. However, it is crucial that students begin work on their own portfolios as soon as possible before images fade.

When the portfolios are complete, students convene in teams representing their characters' cultural groups and are instructed to introduce each of their characters in such a way that all team members can "see each one in their mind's eye" and imagine each as a living person. After each introduction, students should be encouraged to ask each other questions similar to the fourth-stage questions in phase two. For example:

- How would your character feel in our classroom?

- What is your character's point of view on McDonald's? Would it seem like a strange place to him or her?

- If your character had a whole free day, what would he or she do?

F I G U R E   1 0 . 2

■

A CHARACTER DATA SHEET such as this one is designed to help
students flesh out their story characters.

Character Data Sheet

Name _____ Age _____

Birthday _____ Ethnic group _____

Height_____ Weight _____ Hair color _____ Eye color _____

Address _____

_____

Place of birth _____

Describe your family_____

_____

_____

_____

What do you do during the day? _____

_____

What do you do for fun? _____

_____

If you go to school, what is you favorite subject?_____

What do people like most about you? _____

_____

In answering these and similar questions, students round out aspects and visualize details of their characters that had not previously occurred to them. Before concluding this stage of character development,
the teacher informs students that soon they will write stories from their
characters' points of view.

Students engage in language experience as they dictate their
stories. When the written versions are ready, students enter the writing
pro-cess, as outlined by Robbins (1990), at the revision stage and proceed
on to editing, either individually or in cooperative groups. The teacher
works on her or his own story while not working with students.

■ Field trips require much preplanning and preparation by the teacher
and students as well. The knowledge gained and aesthetic
appreciation from such experience often lasts into adulthood.

Finally, students share their stories with the rest of the class and
compile them in final form into a book. Students decide how they would
like to present their creative efforts to parents and other students and
teachers—perhaps via a program in which they dramatize their stories or
read them in fireside storytelling sessions.

Extension: The Multicultural Community

This unit began with a wide-angle, multicultural view as students were
immersed in a plethora of ethnic experiences. Starting with phase two,
the focus narrowed, with students selecting particular cultural groups they
wished to explore further. The focus narrowed even more as students ar-
ticulated their visions of single characters. As the unit progressed, its
focus became still finer and more specific.

If student interest remains strong, the teacher may consider widening the focus again to help students develop a fresh multicultural perspective. Implementing this extension, in which students create
multiethnic communities and write stories about them, will bring the unit
full cycle.

As a whole group, students decide which characters might live in
the same community, with the only stipulation being that a variety of cultural groups must be represented. Arranged in community groups, students engage in discussions with a purpose similar to that of the previous
character-creation questioning sequence. They travel together on a collective imaginative journey, hitchhiking off each other's ideas, to visualize a

community: its physical setting, its name, the characters' relationships to one another, and the ways they interact. Materials in the group portfolio might include such items as maps of the community and class rosters.

Keeping in mind the physical and interactive communities they have created, students engage in group language experiences as they discuss possible story lines, with their ideas being recorded. Students review these ideas and select the ones to be included in the story. Each group dictates its story, perhaps in "chain" fashion. When the initial version of the story is complete, students begin revising and editing, both of which promise to be more involved and time-consuming than they were earlier because students are now working cooperatively. Finally, students decide on the means for sharing their work and receiving feedback.

To reinforce the theme of this unit's extension, the teacher should conduct debriefing sessions both in groups and with the whole class. Questions conducive to reflection on living together in multicultural communities include the following:

- As you were thinking of your story, did it matter that your characters came from different cultural groups? Why or why not?

- Were some people more powerful and important than others? Why or why not?

- You probably did not write down any rules or laws your community had for living together. If you had, what would these rules and laws be?

- How did the people in your community deal with conflicts?

- Do you think people in your community live together the way people *should* live together? Is your community a good model for us to follow in the real world?

- Let's think about our own country as a great big community with many, many different cultural groups. How should we treat each other if we are going to live and go to school and work together peacefully?

This extension takes an inductive approach as students derive codes of conduct from the ways their individual characters interact in a multicultural setting. To place special emphasis from the beginning upon the means by which people live together in diverse communities, the teacher may wish to take an opposite, deductive approach in which students first formulate rules and laws for peaceful coexistence and the resolution of conflicts. Story lines then unfold in accordance with these predetermined codes of conduct. The ensuing debriefing explores with students the extent to which their characters abided by the community's rules and whether these rules should be modified.

Summary

The goal of the unit described in this chapter is to facilitate the development of the ability to view life from cultural perspectives different from one's own. After immersing students in a variety of ethnic experiences in phase one, the unit's scope is progressively refined. In phase two, students focus on particular cultural groups for further exploration; in phase three, they develop an understanding of point of view; and finally, in phase four, students become creative writers as they write from the points of view of characters of their own creation. At the beginning of the unit, students view ethnic groups through their own cultural lenses. By the unit's conclusion, students add new cultural lenses to their repertoire of perspectives. In short, they achieve a flexibility of perspective.

Moreover, implementation of the unit's extension leads to the development of a fresh multicultural perspective in two ways. Students create a diverse community and in the process, they engage in the same kinds of cooperative interactions as their characters. Further, if students in the learning groups are themselves from different cultural groups, prejudice will probably diminish in the process of working together toward a common goal (Slavin, 1989–1990).

In addition to aiding both the reduction of prejudice and the growth of critical thinking in all subject areas, the skill of perspective taking, together with the knowledge gained about diverse cultural groups, provides students with an intuitive grasp of a number of issues related to living in a multicultural society. This deep understanding, which is at once cognitive and affective, can serve as a foundation for dealing with these issues in more complex ways later in life.

Multicultural Literature for Children

AFRICAN AMERICAN

Adoff, A. (1973). *Black is brown is tan.* New York: Harper & Row.

Adoff, A. (1973). *The poetry of black America: Anthology of the 20th century.* New York: Harper & Row.

Arkhurst, J. C. (1964). *The adventures of spider: West African folktales.* Boston: Little, Brown.

Arkhurst, J. C. (1986). *Lion and the ostrich chicks.* New York: Atheneum.

Bryan, A. (1991). *All night, all day: A child's first book of African-American spirituals.* New York: Macmillan/Atheneum.

Collier, J., & Collier, C. (1981). *Jump ship to freedom.* New York: Delacorte.

Note. From *Language Arts: A Process Approach* (pp. 358–361) by P. J. Farris, 1993, Dubuque, Iowa: Brown & Benchmark. Reprinted by permission.

Hamilton, V. (1974). *Paul Robeson: The life and times of a free black man.* New York: Harper & Row.

Hamilton, V. (1985). *The people could fly: American black folktales.* (L. Dillon & D. Dillon, Illus.). New York: Knopf.

Hamilton, V. (1991). *The all Jahdu storybook* (B. Moser, Illus.). Orlando, FL: Harcourt Brace Jovanovich.

Hansen, J. (1986). *Which way freedom?* New York: Walker.

Harris, J. C. (1986). *Jump! The adventures of Brer Rabbit.* Orlando, FL: Harcourt Brace Jovanovich.

Haskins, J. (1977). *The life and death of Martin Luther King, Jr.* New York: Lothrop, Lee, & Shephard.

Hurmence, B. (1982). *A girl called boy.* New York: Houghton Mifflin.

Isadora, R. (1991). *At the crossroads.* New York: Greenwillow.

Kimmel, E. A. (1988). *Anansi and the moss-covered rock.* (J. Stevens, Illus.). New York: Holiday House.

Knutson, B. (1990). *How the Guinea fowl got her spots: A Swahili tale of friendship.* New York: Carolrhoda.

McKillack, P. (1986). *Jesse Jackson.* New York: Scholastic.

Meltzer, M. (1984). *Black Americans: A history in their own words.* New York: Harper/Collins.

Myers, W. D. (1991). *Now is your time: The African-American struggle for freedom.* New York: Harper Collins.

Myers, W. D. (1988). *Scorpions.* New York: Harper & Row.

Petry, A. (1955). *Harriet Tubman: Conductor on the underground railroad.* New York: Crowell.

Ringgold, F. (1991). *Tar beach.* New York: Crown.

Yates, E. (1950). *Amos Fortune, free man.* New York: Dutton.

ASIAN AMERICAN

Clark, A. N. (1978). *To stand against the wind.* New York: Viking.

Compton, P. A. (1991). *The terrible eek.* (S. Hamanaka, Illus.). New York: Simon and Schuster.

Conger, D. (1987). *Many lands, many stories: Asian folktales for children.* New York: Tuttle.

Dunn, M., & Ardath, M. (1983). *The absolutely perfect horse.* New York: Harper & Row.

Hamanaka, S. (1990). *The journey: Japanese Americans, racism and renewal.* New York: Orchard.

Hong, L. T. (1991). *How the ox star fell from heaven.* New York: Albert Whitman.

Nhuong, H. Q. (1982). *The land I lost: Adventures of a boy in Vietnam.* New York: Harper & Row.

Say, A. (1990). *El chino.* Boston: Houghton Mifflin.

Siberell, A. (1990). *A journey to Paradise.* New York: Holt.

Surat, M. M. (1983). *Angel child, dragon child.* Racine, WI: Carnival/Raintree.

Wallace, I. (1984). *Chin Chiang and the dragon's dance.* New York: Atheneum.

Yee, P. (1990). *Tales from gold mountain: Stories of the Chinese in the new world* (S. Ng, Illus.). New York: Harper & Row.

Yee, P. (1991). *Roses sing on new snow.* (H. Chan, Illus.). New York: Macmillan.

Yep, L. (1989). *The rainbow people.* (D. Wiesner, Illus.). New York: Harper/Collins.

HISPANIC

Bunting, E. (1990). *The wall* (R. Himler, Illus.). New York: Clarion.

Clark, A. N. (1980). *Secret of the Andes.* New York: Viking.

De Gerez, T. (1981). *My song is a piece of jade: Poems of ancient Mexico in English and Spanish.* Boston: Little, Brown.

De Paola, T. (1980). *The lady of Guadalupe.* New York: Holiday House.

Ets, M. H., & Labastide, A. (1959). *Nine days to Christmas: A story of Mexico.* New York: Viking.

O'Dell, S. (1981). *Carlota.* Boston: Houghton Mifflin.

Soto, G. (1990). *Baseball in April and other stories.* Orlando, FL: Harcourt Brace Jovanovich.

NATIVE AMERICAN

Baylor, B. (1975). *A god on every mountain top: Stories of southwest Indian mountains.* New York: Scribner's.

Baylor, B. (1978). *The other way to listen.* New York: Scribner's.

Bierhorst, J. (1979). *A cry from the earth: Music of the North American Indians.* New York: Four Winds.

Bierhorst, J. (1983). *The sacred path: Spells, prayers, and power songs of the American Indians.* New York: Four Winds.

Carey, V. S. (1990). *Quail song: A Pueblo Indian tale.* (I. Barnett, Illus.). New York: Putnam.

Cherry, L. (1991). *A river ran wild.* Orlando: Harcourt, Brace, Jovanovich.

Cohen, C. L. (1988). *The mud pony: A traditional Skidi Pawnee tale* (S. Begay, Illus.). New York: Scholastic.

De Felice, C. (1990). *Weasel.* New York: Macmillan.

Ekoomiak, N. (1990). *Arctic memories.* New York: Holt, Rinehart & Winston.

Freedman, R. (1988). *Buffalo bunt.* New York: Holiday House.

Fritz, J. (1983). *The double life of Pocahontas.* New York: Putnam.

George, J. C. (1983). *The talking earth.* New York: Harper & Row.

Goble, P. (1988). *Iktomi and the boulder: A plains Indian story.* New York: Orchard.

Goble, P. (1990). *Dream wolf.* New York: Bradbury.

Gregory, K. (1990). *The legend of Jimmy Spoon.* Orlando, FL: Harcourt Brace Jovanovich.

Grossman, V. (1991). *Ten little rabbits.* (S. Long, Illus.). San Francisco: Chronicle Books.

Hoyt-Goldsmith, D. (1991). *Pueblo storyteller.* (L. Migdale, Photog.). New York: Holiday House.

Jassem, K. (1979). *Sacajawea, wilderness guide.* New York: Troll.

Kesey, K. (1991). *The sea lion.* (N. Waldman, Illus.). New York: Viking.

Marrin, A. (1984). *War clouds in the west: Indians and calvarymen,* 1860–1890. New York: Atheneum.

Moore, R. (1990). *Maggie among the Seneca.* New York: Harper/Collins.

O'Dell, S. (1988). *Black star, bright dawn.* Boston: Houghton Mifflin.

Paulsen, G. (1988). *Dogsong.* New York: Bradbury.

Rodanas, K. (1992). *Dragonfly's tale.* New York: Clarion.

Sewall, M. (1990). *People of the breaking day.* New York: Atheneum.

Sneve, V. (1989). *Dancing teepees: Poems of American Indian youth.* New York: Holiday House.

Speare, E. G. (1983). *The sign of the beaver.* Boston: Houghton Mifflin.

White deer of Autumn. (1983). *Ceremony—In the circle of life.* Racine, WI: Raintree.

Wisniewski, D. (1991). *Rain player.* New York: Clarion.

OTHER MULTICULTURAL

Ashabranner, B. (1991). *An ancient heritage: The Arab-American minority.* (P. S. Conklin, Photog.). New York: Harper/Collins.

Hamilton, V. (1988). *In the beginning: Creation stories from around the world.* Orlando, FL: Harcourt Brace Jovanovich.

Haviland, V. (1979). *North American Legends.* New York: Philomel.

Heide, F. P., & Gilliland, J. H. (1990). *The day of Ahmed's secret.* (T. Lewin, Illus.). New York: Lothrop, Lee, & Shepard.

Langton, J. (1985). *The hedgehog boy: A Latvian folktale.* (I. Plume, Illus.). New York: Harper/Collins.

Philip, N. (1991). *Fairy tales of Eastern Europe.* (L. Wilkes, Illus.). New York: Clarion.

References

Banks, J. A., & Banks, C. A. M. (1989). *Multicultural Education: Issues and Perspectives.* Boston: Allyn and Bacon.

Byrnes, D. A. (1988). Children and prejudice. *Social Education, 52,* 267–271.

Holdaway, D. (1979). *The foundations of literacy.* Urbana, IL: National Council of Teachers of English.

Hoyt, L. (1992). Many ways of knowing: Using drama, oral interactions, and the visual arts to enhance reading comprehension. *Reading Teacher, 45,* 580–584.

Hunter, K. (1973). *Guests in the promised land.* New York: Scribner's.

Joyce, B., & Weil, M. (1986). *Models of Teaching* (3rd ed.). Englewood Cliffs, NJ: Prentice-Hall.

National Council for the Social Studies. (1992). The Columbia Quincentenary Position Statement. *Social Studies and the Young Learner, 4,* n.p.

Pallas, A. M., Natriello, G., & McDill, E. L. (1989). The changing nature of the disadvantaged population: Current dimensions and future trends. *Educational Researcher, 18* (5), 16-22.

Pate, G. S. (1988). Research on reducing prejudice. *Social Education, 52,* 287-289.

Robbins, P. A. (1990). Implementing whole language: Bridging children and books. *Educational Leadership, 47*(6), 50-54.

Slavin, R. E. (1989-1990). Research on cooperative learning: Consensus and controversy. *Educational Leadership, 47*(4), 52-54.

Sleeter, C. E., & Grant, C. A. (1988). *Making choices for multicultural education: Five approaches to race, class and gender.* Columbus, OH: Merrill.

Sunal, C. S., & Haas, M. E. (1993). *Social studies and the elementary/middle school student.* Orlando, FL: Harcourt Brace Jovanovich.

Walker-Dalhouse, D. (1993). Using African-American literature to increase ethnic understanding. *Reading Teacher, 45,* 416-422.

Walsh, D. (1988). Critical thinking to reduce prejudice. *Social Education, 52,* 280-282.

Social Studies, Bilingualism, Respect, and Understanding: Making the Connections

MARY LOUISE GINEJKO
JR./SR. HIGH HISPANIC DROP OUT PREVENTION PROGRAM TEACHER, AND CHAPTER I TEACHER
SAMUEL GOMPERS JUNIOR HIGH, JOLIET, IL

Scholars describe the United States as one of history's first universal or world nations—its people are a microcosm of humanity with biological, cultural, and social ties to all other parts of the earth.

NATIONAL
COUNCIL FOR THE
SOCIAL STUDIES

*"The Columbian Quincentenary
Position Statement"*

Chapter Eleven

Introduction

While there is an increasing awareness of the diversity of students, there is also great controversy over the placement of bilingual students. Rosalie Pedalino Porter (1990) has questioned whether placement decisions are based on the children's needs or on the needs of politicians and bureaucrats. She condemns transitional bilingual education (TBE), which demands native-language instruction. She purports that this is an unjust form of segregation, thereby sending a message that these students are remedial or less than acceptable in general education classes. The editors of *When They Don't All Speak English,* Pat Rigg and Virginia G. Allen (1989, p. ix) agree: "[S]econd-language students need to be with first-language students. If they are isolated from active-English-speaking students, they cannot learn English from them, nor can they share any of the riches they have to offer." According to Lim and Watson (1993, p. 393),

> Combining authentic and natural language experiences with content-rich classroom practices leads to optimal language learning and optimal subject matter learning. When the instructional focus moves away from language as an object and away from content as facts to a content-rich, usable language, second-language learners will gain confidence in themselves, and their knowledge of both language and content will flourish. Effective language learning, either native or second language, depends not on the direct teaching of identified skills, but rather on a sound philosophy of learning and teaching, underlying a meaning-filled curriculum.

Many educators disagree with this argument.

One of the boldest conclusions Porter offers is a rejection of the concept that first language and cognitive abilities must be learned in the native language before these skills can be transferred into the second language. Much research to the contrary indicates that it takes more than 5 years for ESL (English as a second language) students to become proficient enough to compete with their general education peers (Cummins, 1981, 1984). Although this is worthy of detailed examination, the focus of this chapter is on the challenges of the general education classroom teacher.

This chapter addresses the concerns of the general education teacher, who is becoming increasingly aware of the large number of students in the classroom who speak English only as a second language. According to the 1990 census figures 31.8 million people in the United States communicate in 329 different foreign languages. Spanish is the most common foreign language. It is spoken by over 17 million people of whom 54% do not speak English at home (Vsdansky, 1993). Many of these are Mexican American students. They are part of a group referred to as people of color. Membership in this group is exclusively reserved for nonwhite minority individuals. James A. Banks (1991, p. xix) defines *people of color* as follows:

> In most instances, the phrase *people of color* rather than *ethnic minority* is used to refer to groups such as Mexican Americans, African Americans, Puerto Ricans, and Native Americans. *People of color* is used to reflect new demographic realities: These groups are majorities rather than minorities in a growing number of schools and school districts.

Of the three major Hispanic groups, Mexican Americans are increasing in the United States population at a much faster rate than Puerto Ricans and Cubans. In 1988, Mexican Americans accounted for approximately 62% of all Hispanics in this country.

When considering statistics, one should keep in mind that the population figures given by the U.S. Bureau of the Census are invalid in terms of the Mexican American population in the United States because a substantial number of undocumented Mexican aliens are continually entering the United States. Moreover, the birthrate in the Hispanic communities is high.

Because of this unknown number of illegal aliens and the large number of legal immigrants coming from Mexico to the United States, teachers in this country have more Hispanic students to teach each year. Yet few general education teachers have had any specialized training in ESL. However, this has not prevented teachers from encountering each student with predisposed expectations about the student and themselves. Although xenophobia (fear of foreigners) is still an intricate part of American society, teachers must be sensitive to the needs of all children. General education teachers can gain confidence in themselves and their professional abilities by becoming more knowledgeable about Mexican American culture and by examining teaching strategies that promote rather than impede learning in both first-language and second-language classrooms. The next section offers insights into respect and understanding of culture. Educators have the responsibility to assist their students in reconceptualizing American society.

Cultural Awareness

Cultural awareness means more than the designated multicultural month of February celebrated in most American schools. It means more than speeches, reports, bulletin boards, displays, and school assemblies to acknowledge that—at least for one month of the year—everyone has a culture. Cultural awareness does not mean presenting the contributions of each culture in isolation. It does mean understanding the interaction of the contributions of various cultures. It means making cultural connections.

Cultural awareness means understanding that each of us has a culture that is part of our very being. Together, we all make up the tapestry called America. We each bring threads of cultural values, historical pride, experiences, and aspirations to this fabric. Understanding and respecting cultural differences and similarities perpetuate an environment conducive to an appreciation of life.

In the 19th and 20th centuries, our society viewed the perfect solution to cultural differences as a melting pot. It expected each person to begin the process of acculturation, acquiring the culture from a geographic area rather than maintaining and nourishing his or her own unique language and customs, in essence, his or her own consciousness. This ideological assumption fostered a nation where people of diverse backgrounds would blend into one. Ethnic groups would assimilate to form one culture identity. It resulted in no identification of individual culture appreciation, no existence of ethnicity. If all the cultures in the United States could be melted together, they would only produce a tasteless homogenized pretense of humanity.

After society recognized the folly of the melting pot idea, the metaphor of a stew or salad began appearing to capture society's view of its cultural self. However, this allowed individuals to dictate which culture qualities should or should not be chosen to be part of an America stew or salad. Such elitism promotes the destruction of cultural pride and esteem, encouraging discrimination and prejudice. It does not recognize the need for society's pluralism or the individual's need of enculturation, the process of absorbing one's own culture. The variations in culture patterns are the strength of a multigroup society with an emphasis on diversity.

The image of a national fabric or tapestry precludes a respect and acceptance of all humankind's diversities. It makes all of us a part of this nation and allows for the appreciation and interaction of cultures. No social intimidation threatens the loss of any individual culture. While allowing for cultural assimilation, it does not rob the individual of his or her culture. The following abbreviations used by educators recognize the diversity of our population in the area of language.

ESL	English as a second language
LEA	Language experience approach
LEP	Limited English proficiency
LEPS	Limited English proficiency speakers
LPL	Language proficiency level
PEP	Potential English proficiency (new term now being used to replace LEP)
REAL	Readers and writers of English and another language
TBE	Transitional bilingual education
TESOL	Teachers of English to speakers of other languages
TPR	Total physical response

■ Variations in culture patterns are the strength of a multigroup society.

Personal Observation of the Mexican American Community

The Mexican American enters the U.S. educational system with a rich literary, political, economic, and historical background. Acuña (1988), Kanellos (1990), and Keefe and Padilla (1987) provide an extensive account of the Mexican American experience in the United States. For our purposes, we will briefly examine the cultural values of Mexican Americans and how they influence teaching styles.

While recognizing the diversity within the Mexican American culture, one can make the following observations about the traditional Mexican American value system. This culture promotes a strong emotion of identity with its loyalty to family, community, and ethnic group. Achievement for children means achievement of the family, not necessarily individual achievement as is encouraged in many Anglo-American children. It is important to the education of Mexican American students to include parent involvement as part of the educational process. Parents provide a positive support system. Every possible attempt should therefore be made to keep parents informed of their child's progress. Sending work home or accepting items from the home for display strengthens the necessary home-school relationship.

Competition in school can be confusing when one's culture dictates cooperation for mutual rewards. Mexican American students function better in cooperative learning situations. Motivation is found in the group activity rather than in the personal gain of achievement or grade.

Another strong value to be considered is sensitivity to the needs and feelings of other people. Relationships become personalized and interpersonal. Teachers should encourage children to help each other. Mexican American children are attuned to verbal and nonverbal calls for help. They are also the recipients of such help in their culture. This may in part explain their reluctance to ask the teacher a question; their request for help may be nonverbal.

The Mexican American humanistic orientation extends beyond the immediate family into the community. Extended families include: *primos* (cousins), those with the same last name but no blood relation; *tocayos* (namesakes), those with the same first name; *concuños* (brothers-in-law), two or more men married into the same family; *cuñadas* (sisters-in-law); and very important *padrinos* (godparents), *ahijados* (godchildren), and *compadres,* natural parents to godparents and vice versa. Children acquire two godparents at baptism, one godparent when they receive the Sacrament of the Eucharist, and one godparent when they make their confirmation in the Catholic church. Female children may also choose to have a *quinceñiera* when they become 15 years old. It is possible at this ceremony for a girl to receive an additional 10 to 15 godparents. *Damas* (bridesmaids) and *chamberlan* (grooms) also become participants. In this ceremony, as throughout their life, the *abuelos* (blood grandparents) play a major role.

Mexican American children learn security through interpersonal relationships rather than institutional assistance. In school, students also expect a close and personalized relationship with the teacher. They view their teacher as a mother or father in a classroom environment. They expect to see personal family pictures or even visits from the teacher's family members. Mexican American students function better in a humanized curriculum. Traditionally, a more personalized curriculum offers more meaning. Their culture is child-centered rather than task-centered.

In such an extended family, the status and role of the individual is precisely defined. These are usually dictated by sex and age. Older children have more responsibilities than younger children. This should be a consideration when assigning homework. Mexican American parents may find it difficult to understand why teachers feel that schoolwork is more important than home responsibilities. Parents may feel that staying home for a family commitment is as important as going to school for the day. Respect for parents is expected of all individuals regardless of age. Sexual roles are clearly defined. Females are responsible for the condition of the

■ Mexican American families tend to be child centered rather than task centered.

home, preparation of food, health care, child rearing, and religious obligations. Males have a higher status. They are the wage earners. Teachers should be aware of this when assigning duties.

A powerful factor in the lives of Mexican Americans is their identification with Mexican Catholic ideology. This forceful power reinforces their value system. Lack of respect for parents or customs is sinful. Any interpretation of failure to meet family responsibilities is a serious infraction. Guilt becomes a serious consequence. A cycle of failure begins. This is evident in the psychological and physical school drop-out rate. Teachers must intervene by making students aware of the educational continuum and long-range goals rather than let them become discouraged by immediate setbacks.

Cultural Sensitivity Through Whole Language Teaching Strategies

Being sensitive to the educational needs of Mexican American children means applying whole language principles in the classroom. It means listening to all cultural voices and promoting the skills necessary to become a successful member of society. Whole language instruction provides a reason to learn a language. Students become active learners.

Bilingual students experience specific academic difficulties that teachers should consider. This section suggests ways in which teachers can use whole language strategies to promote the language development of these students.

Initially, bilingual students are placed in a bilingual or an ESL classroom. In a bilingual classroom the students usually receive ESL instruction for part of the day and instruction in their native language during the rest of the day. This is justified by the premise that it is more important not to interrupt the learning process than it is to teach English. The ESL program differs. Students attend ESL classes for part of the day and are mainstreamed into general education classes for the remaining portion of the day. Exit from either program is accomplished by passing an LPL (language proficiency level) test.

Bilingual students entering general education classrooms emphasize the fact that there is a difference between the skills needed to communicate in English and the skills necessary to comprehend content material.

It may take from 5 to 7 years for students with limited English-speaking abilities to acquire the command of English they need in order to perform successfully in academic areas (Cummins, 1984). Barriers to their effective communication, comprehension, and understanding exist, especially in tasks that involve reading and writing. Sometimes such barriers are disguised by the students' relatively quicker acquisition of conversational language and mastery of decoding skills in reading. Thus those students who appear to have command of English may in actuality be struggling to communicate and discover meaning when they are faced with academic settings and tasks that are decontextualized and cognitively demanding (Sutton, 1989).

This problem can be compounded by the age of the student. Academic content is much more difficult at the middle or high school level, where students may be more inclined to drop out of the school system completely. If they have been isolated from content subjects because of time spent learning English, there will be gaps of knowledge in their schema. Teachers must consider this fact when establishing a foundation of prior knowledge before assigning an activity.

Vocabulary development also becomes an essential part of a bilingual student's learning development. Strategies to elicit meaning from words must be taught. Vocabulary development is essential in language learning, language processing, communication, reading comprehension, and understanding concepts that are content specific. Teachers should be aware that vocabulary is learned most successfully through personal experiences, interaction with the environment. Using this knowledge, teachers can provide an environment rich in language experiences. They can emphasize a hands-on environment where a love for learning is nurtured through concrete experiences.

Journal writing provides a vehicle for a real communicative situation, while allowing the teacher to become more aware of a student's development. A journal kept by a bilingual student, explaining strategies used to elicit meaning from content material, can provide the teacher with valuable insights into the student and the learning process. Such insights can then be used as a basis for future instruction to aid other students. An excellent example of this is provided by the RESPONSE method, mentioned earlier in this book, as conceived by Jacobson (1989) and further tested by Farris, Fuhler, and Ginejko (1991).

Journals allow the teacher to learn what students already know (prior knowledge), how well they understood the concepts that have been discussed, and what misconceptions they may hold. Through journals the teacher learns what students view as teaching approach strengths and weaknesses that they believe affected their learning, how aware students are of themselves as learners, and whether they perceive any problems with the material. Journals provide a personal glimpse of each student's feelings and emotions and are a window to each student's progress.

Because learning is a social process, cooperative learning is a viable strategy to foster the development of pragmatic skills. The whole language learner interacts with people of diverse backgrounds, and a sharing of ideas and self results in better understanding.

Whole language means interaction with the printed word, with people, and with learning. It allows the development of skills necessary to lead a fulfilling life. It is REAL (readers and writers of English as another language). It includes an exposure to language through model reading, book sharing, LEA (language experience approach), SSR (sustained silent reading), and all the culturally sensitive strategies listed thus far in this chapter.

Social Studies for Bilingual Students

This section provides examples of activities designed to encourage language and content learning. The activities are instructionally organized into a thematic unit. The purpose of including such a large number of activities is twofold. First, they offer variety to students and teachers; whole language incorporates choice. Second, even though not all the activities presented here could be used in any one thematic unit, they may, with minor changes, be applied to other thematic units.

The thematic unit selected is entitled "Pioneers." An extensive variety of published teacher-directed materials provide a wealth of ideas. A thematic unit on Mexican Americans was not selected because "culturally sensitive" does not mean one thematic unit a year per culture. Each thematic unit should contain opportunities for students to be proud of their own culture while respecting other cultures.

A. *Prereading Activities/Cooperative Groups/Discussion*

1. Make a *T* chart. In column 1 list all the items that are necessary for your life in this country. In column 2 list reasons why each item is necessary. A *T* chart can be made by drawing one vertical line down the middle of a sheet of paper and one horizontal line across the top, leaving room above this for column headings only.

2. Make a *T* chart. In column 1 list all the items you would take with you if you moved to another country. In column 2 list reasons why you would take each item. First list 12 items. Then eliminate 2 items. Now eliminate 5 items. Finally, choose the one item you would most want to take with you.

3. Make a *T* chart. In column 1 list all the dangers you encounter in a day. In column 2 list the solution to each danger. Make another *T* chart. In column 1 again list all the dangers you encounter in a day in this country. In column 2 list all the dangers you might encounter in a day in another country. Highlight dangers that are the same in both countries.

4. Make a *T* chart. In column 1 list all the forms of entertainment you enjoy. In column 2 list all the forms of entertainment your grandparents enjoyed at your age. Make another *T* chart. In column 1 again list all the forms of entertainment you enjoy in this country. In column 2 list all the forms of entertainment you might enjoy in another country. Highlight items that are the same in both columns.

5. Using a map of your choice, make a matrix of the regions (desert, mountains, plains, seacoast) to compare and contrast their geographic elements. Write a paragraph for each comparison or contrast point, explaining what life would be like in each region.

6. Using an appropriate map, locate where you live and a place you have visited or would like to visit. Make a *T* chart comparing and contrasting the two locations.

7. Create a K-W-L chart (what you know, what you want to know, what you learned) entitled "Pioneer Life on the Prairie." Cite the sources of your information. A K-W-L chart is made by dividing a sheet of paper into thirds by drawing two vertical lines and then drawing one horizontal line across the top of the paper, leaving room only for the column headings (*K*, *W*, and *L*).

8. Create a K-W-L chart for Native Americans or Mexicans in southwestern regions before those regions became part of the United States. Cite the sources of your information.

9. Create a semantic map or web entitled "Types of Pioneers" (for example, in space, in medicine, in westward movement, immigrants).

10. Create a semantic map about pioneers' schools, clothing, food, travel, homes, dangers, hardships.

11. Show an artifact such as a hand tool or piece of harness to the class. Identify the item. Explain its use. Has the item been replaced? If so, what has replaced it?

12. Read "Western Wagons," a poem by Rosemary and Stephen Benét. As a class, give a choral reading of the poem.

13. Listen to *Where the Buffaloes Begin,* an award-winning picture book by Olaf Baker (1981). Then write about the book in your literature response journal or draw a picture about the book.

14. Search for evidence to validate or invalidate the right of Native Americans to receive compensation for the land that was taken from them. Debate the issue. (After the research is completed, students should draw slips from a hat to determine which side of the issue they are to defend. Emphasis should be placed on the difference between facts and opinions. The teacher may find it beneficial to videotape the debate and show the video at the end of the unit.)

15. Listen to a recording of "Polly-Wolly-Doodle" or a Native American musical recording. Do a square dance. Compare the types of instruments originally used to play these selections with instruments commonly used today.

16. After explaining historical fiction, the teacher writes down a class list of historical fiction titles that students have read.

17. Write what you think life was like for an American Indian before the United States became a country.

18. Write what you think life was like for a pioneer on the prairie.

19. The teacher presents a book talk, introducing each literature book of the unit and including information about the author. Then the teacher asks students to predict how the cover or title might relate to the book.

20. Form small groups and with other members of your group, choose a book to read for the unit.

B. *Postreading Activities/Discussion*

1. Choose a pioneer (Daniel Boone, Davy Crockett, Buffalo Bill Cody, Jim Beckwourth, Kit Carson, or someone else of your choice). Research and then trace the route of the pioneer on a map with yarn or cut out covered wagons.

2. Research and write articles about why some cities grew more rapidly than others.

3. Write an essay comparing frontier prairie life to your own life. What aspects are similar? Which are different?

4. Make a diorama of a pioneer scene or a scene with characters from the literature book you read for this unit.

5. Would you like to have lived in the mid 1800s? Explain your answer.

6. Using reference materials, find out why the pioneers called warm days in autumn Indian summer.

7. Put on a skit about going to school on the prairie.

8. Make soap and candles the way the pioneers did.

9. Follow prairie recipes for foods such as soda bread, johnnycake, and dried apple pie. Make butter by putting whipping cream in a jar and taking turns shaking it until it turns to butter. Invite visitors to a prairie lunch. Include both Indian and pioneer food.

10. Construct a model of a covered wagon, a pioneer home, (cave, hut, log cabin, dugout home, sod house), or a pioneer or an Indian village.

11. Using reference materials, find out what Illinois is often called (answer: the prairie state).

12. Watch a movie about pioneer life (*Sarah, Plain and Tall,* or *Son of the Morning Star,* or *Dances with Wolves*).

13. Many pioneer clothes were made from calico. The teacher brings in some calico material to show the class.

14. The teacher invites someone to demonstrate whittling for the class.

15. Reproduce a toy used on the prairie (button/string, rag doll), or demonstrate a pioneer game in the gym or outside if possible.

16. Take a field trip to such places as a historical museum, a farm, or an antique shop.

17. One representative from each group reading a Laura Ingalls Wilder book meet together to construct a time line of Laura's life based on the events depicted in the books the various groups have read.

18. Make a Venn diagram (overlapping circles) identifying the jobs girls and boys did on the prairie or do today in this country or another country.

19. Play the computer game Oregon Trail.

20. Gather wild flowers and grasses. Take them home and hang them up to dry. Use them to make a winter decoration. Discuss their uses as sickness remedies.

21. Start a seashell collection.

22. Pretend you are placing an ad in the newspaper for a wife and mother or a husband and father. Write down what you would say. As a class, create an entire newspaper that could have been published in the 1800s.

23. Make a list of some things that are often found where you live but are rare in other parts of the country. Choose one of the items and write a descriptive paragraph about it.

24. Pretend you are a travel agent. Write a travel brochure about the prairie, state, or country you have visited.

25. The teacher invites an artist to come to class to demonstrate how to make Indian or Mexican pottery. Then the teacher arranges to have a pottery wheel and clay in the classroom so that the students can experiment with them.

26. The teacher brings in collections of poetry by Mexican American and Native American poets and shares their poetry through themes such as nature, people, and so on.

27. The teacher assigns a different Native American tribe to each group. Members of each group construct a bulletin board display about aspects of their particular tribe, highlighting famous battles, specific cultural differences, shelter, food, and religious beliefs.

28. Pretend your literature group is an advertising department. Your job is to devise an advertising campaign to promote your book. Present your campaign to other classes. Ask students to choose anonymously which groups' books they would buy on the basis of the campaigns presented to them.

29. Produce a book jacket for the next printing of the book you read for this unit.

30. Make a poster, mural, collage, mobile, TV screen with rolled paper pictures, or bulletin board advertisement for the literature book you read for this unit.

31. The teacher explains to students that many Native American tribes depended on the buffalo for their survival and that the Indians prided themselves on using all of the animal. Then the teacher asks students to research how the Indians used the buffalo and instructs each group to make a drawing of the animal, label the parts, and indicate the use(s) of each part.

32. Make a family tree of the characters in the literature book you read for this unit. How does it compare to your family tree?

33. Make a nine-patch quilt.

34. Make puppets and act out your favorite part of the literature book you read for this unit.

35. Choose your favorite part of the literature book you read for this unit and make it into a "big book." Then share it with another class.

36. Complete your K-W-L chart.

37. Make a sociogram (web of interacting feelings showing arrows from each character to the main character and returning arrows and identifying each arrow with an emotion) for Laura Ingalls or any other main character in the book you read for this unit.

38. Conduct a trial for Custer. Students volunteer for the roles of judge, prosecuting attorney, defense attorney, jury members, witnesses, and the defendant. Attorneys prepare evidence and interview witnesses before the trial begins. Witnesses might view *Son of the Morning Star* or rely on research for data.

39. Write an epilogue to the book you read.

40. Make a "realia" box or time capsule. Collect real items important to the literature book you read for this unit.

41. Write several diary entries that the main character of the literature book you read for this unit might have written.

42. Make a crossword puzzle or word search using the vocabulary of the literature book you read for this unit.

43. Create a cassette of poems to accompany this unit. Make an illustrated book to be viewed while listening to the cassette.

44. Create and illustrate a poem.

45. Write a letter to your favorite author.

Summary

Whole language reflects the effective inclusion of culture in educational instruction. It is a bridge that connects the students and their individual cultures to an understanding of a cross-cultural society. Our national identity is dependent upon successful learning by a culturally diverse population. Good teachers facilitate learning by providing opportunities for active learning by both monolingual and bilingual children. Teachers who appreciate the unique abilities of each student, also recognize the importance of culture in self-development.

References

Acuña, R. (1988). *Occupied America: A history of Chicanos.* New York: Harper & Row.

Baker, O. (1981). *Where the buffaloes begin* (S. Gammell, Illus.). New York: Penguin-Viking.

Banks, J. A. (1991). *Teaching strategies for ethnic studies.* Boston: Allyn and Bacon.

Cummins, J. (1981). *Bilingualism and minority language children.* Toronto: Ontario Institute for Studies in Education.

Cummins, J. (1984). *Bilingual and special education: Issues in assessment and pedagogy.* Clevedon, England: Multicultural Matters.

Farris, P. J., Fuhler, C., & Ginejko, M. L. (1991). Reading, writing, discussing: An interactive approach to content areas. *Reading Horizons, 31*(4), 261–271.

Jacobson, J. M. (1989). Response: An interactive study technique. *Reading Horizons, 29*(2), 86–92.

Kanellos, N. (1990). *A history of Hispanic theatre in the United States: Origins to 1940.* Austin: University of Texas Press.

Keefe, S. E., & Padilla, A. M. (1987). *Chicano ethnicity.* Albuquerque: University of New Mexico Press.

Lim, H. L., & Watson, D. J. (1993). Whole language content classes for second-language learners. *Reading Teacher, 46,* 384–393.

National Council for the Social Studies. (1992). The Columbia Quincentenary Position Statement. *Social Studies and the Young Learner, 4,* n.p.

Porter, R. P. (1990). *Forked tongue: The politics of bilingual education.* New York: Basic Books.

Rigg, P., & Allen, V. G. (Eds.). (1989). *When they don't all speak English.* Urbana, IL: National Council of Teachers of English.

Sutton, C. (1989). Helping the non-native English speaker with reading. *Reading Teacher, 49* (9), 684.

Vsdansky, M. L. (April 28, 1993). Census language not foreign at home. *USA Today* 1A, 11A.

Immersing Learning Disabled Students in History: Traveling Back in Time

CAROL J. FUHLER
NORTH JUNIOR HIGH SCHOOL
CRYSTAL LAKE, IL

Child, teacher, and parent should

celebrate each new learning by focusing

on what is known

rather than what is lacking.

■

DOROTHY S. STRICKLAND
"Emergent Literacy: How Young Children Learn to Read and Write"

Introduction

Like bilingual students, learning disabled (LD) students require additional attention. When a teacher enters an elementary school or junior high social studies classroom, it is unlikely that at first glance he or she could single out a mainstreamed student with a learning disability. For the most part these unique learners do not display an observable collection of symptoms. Since no two LD learners are alike (for that matter, neither are any other two learners), a straightforward, accurate definition remains elusive. More than 50 attempts to pigeonhole this group of learners are currently on the books. It is no wonder that numerous children have been misidentified, swelling the ranks of this catchall category to include a large number of underachievers as well ("Learning Disabilities," 1990).

Underlying the discussion of students with learning disabilities in this chapter is the definition set forth by Congress in the Education for All Handicapped Children Act (PL 94–142). It states that a diagnosed student will have a disorder in the basic psychological processes involved in understanding or using spoken or written language such that it hampers that student's ability to think, speak, read, or do mathematical calculations. If a severe discrepancy between ability and achievement is found, based upon the use of a discrepancy formula, the student is considered to be learning disabled.

While the issue of motivation is not included in the definition, by third and fourth grade it is often a major factor to be considered when creating an exciting, appealing educational program for this population. After years of failure in and out of self-contained classrooms, many students with learning disabilities are reluctant to risk any more. Their battered, fragile egos are buried under a thick, protective coating of feigned indifference and negative or cocky attitudes. One can trace their discouragement by backtracking along a lengthy trail of incomplete assignments. At a time when conformity and peer approval are a number one priority, these students spend an inordinate amount of time and energy proving they are not different from their age-mates. This potent social-emotional overlap to basic cognitive deficits presents teachers and learners with a formidable challenge, indeed.

Smith (1986, p. 51) lays the blame for lack of academic success on the curriculum. His rationale for a learning disabled child's failure is as follows:

> These children may not have experienced reading in an interesting and useful context, or they may have found the instruction confusing or punitive. They may have been intimidated by pressure placed upon all children to succeed in school, or they may actively resent the pressure. Children may be antipathetic to the teacher or just downright cussed and resistant to learning anything adults try to teach them. All these attitudes can cause enormous frustration to parents and teachers, but they are not indicative of anything fundamentally wrong with the child's brain.

Whether a student is labeled as learning disabled or not, segregated or left in the mainstream, the basic question remains—how does one best educate a child who has difficulty learning in the elementary social studies classroom? Despite caring, concerted efforts on the part of a cadre of teachers, it appears that inefficient or ineffective methodology has inhibited this population's academic success. Unfortunately, there is only a meager knowledge base upon which to decide what does constitute effective teaching (Lefstein, 1983; Whyte, 1983).

If the learner is identified as learning disabled and has an individualized education plan, a whole language approach is a viable educational option. Basically, the teacher is looking at a learner with identified strengths and weaknesses that must be considered for instruction to be the most beneficial. Isn't this just highlighting the fact that learning is an intensely personal endeavor? While at first glance, whole language and individualized instruction might seem incompatible, that is not the case. They mesh with a complementary, syncopated beat. While the class as a whole moves forward with a basic rhythm of its own, the educational accent shifts to a different beat, acknowledging specific individual needs that can be met as needed with direct instruction. To maintain a toe-tapping tempo, then, teachers directly teach individual students what they need, when they need it, within the context of their own reading and writing (Hansen, 1987). These teachers maintain a catchy educational rhythm because they have learned to take advantage of those individual and collective teachable moments.

A Look at the LD Learner

Research done with the learning disabled population over the years in terms of writing indicates that this group scored significantly lower than their counterparts in most areas of written expression. While the composing process itself posed difficulties, the more discrepant areas were mechanics, including spelling and punctuation, and word usage (Barenbaum, 1983;

■ For students with learning disabilities, writing poses great challenges and frustration.

Poplin, Gray, Larsen, Banikowski, & Mehring, 1980; Walmsley, 1984; Whyte, 1983). Years of uninspiring, downright boring worksheets and incessant drill have had little effect on the acquisition of these skills. As Smith (1982, p. 202) suggests, "Like baseball bats, many instructional techniques can have a benign and even useful role in school until children are beaten over the head with them" as many teachers have unwittingly done with skill and drill.

In the past, teaching writing skills in special classrooms was delayed until reading, spelling, and handwriting were established. This practice has proved to be an educationally unsound approach in the eyes of current theorists (Barenbaum, 1983; Graham & Harris, 1988; Smith, 1982, 1986). The contemporary belief is that students need to explore the function of language, taking risks as they play with new words and ways of expressing their ideas. Students and teachers weave writing naturally through the social studies classroom, into reading, and through language arts as well (Fountas & Hannigan, 1989; Hansen, 1987; Levstik, 1989).

In regard to reading abilities, middle school and junior high students with learning disabilities are commonly reading three to four years below grade level, plateauing at the fifth- or sixth-grade level late in high school (Whyte, 1983). In addition, short attention spans or auditory memory problems hamper the development of proficient listening abilities. A portion of these learners have difficulty forming thoughts well enough to speak smoothly in front of the class, while others are lacking useful study strategies. The often-segregated skills of reading, writing, listening, and speaking, inherent in successful navigation of the social studies curriculum, need to be addressed in a different way to meet the LD learner's needs. A whole language approach taught by enthusiastic, well-versed educators offers hope to students with learning disabilities who are not currently achieving appreciable success in social studies or many other elementary curricular offerings.

Sound Teaching Strategies

The old adage "Practice makes perfect" ought to be elevated to a whole language golden rule. Its application can improve students' skills and should be kept in mind as learners read, write, think, and integrate knowledge across the curriculum. When addressing the needs of the LD student within a whole language framework, it will be helpful to remember the following premises:

1. Allocate time for practice in reading and writing across the curriculum. Continue to teach critical skills and thinking strategies within the context of the students' reading and writing (Graham & Harris, 1988; Routman, 1991).

2. Whenever new concepts or learning strategies are taught, model, model, model.

3. Expose students to a broad range of reading and writing tasks. Replace contrived writing assignments with more natural writing activities (Poplin et al., 1980).

4. Create a supportive social climate for all learning. Students will need to reestablish confidence so that they can risk without ridicule.

5. Integrate a writers' workshop format into social studies, breaking writing projects into less overwhelming stages.

   Prewrite. Frequently, learning disabled adolescents don't value themselves, what they have done, or what they think. They don't think they know anything to write about or that anyone will be interested anyway, all of which inhibits their ability to write. To overcome this block and encourage idea generation, hold individual conferences. Have students discuss topics they wish to write about, recording ideas on 5" × 7" index cards to be referred to from time to time when writing is to be done. Discuss what students want to do with their topics before beginning to write. This process should ease the transfer of thoughts to paper (Barenbaum, 1983; Graham & Harris, 1988; Hansen, 1987).

Write: Peer editing and brief one-to-one teacher conferences. In dealing with weak mechanics, let the students practice by helping peers edit their work. Ask students to read their draft aloud to several peers. Sometimes hearing the work read highlights errors in continuity. Then ask peers to check for the basics: capital letter at the beginning of every sentence, ending punctuation, proper names capitalized, and questionable words underlined. Fine-tune other parts in a teacher conference.

Rewrite. Encourage students to develop their own personal dictionaries, kept in a permanent writing folder. When spelling is corrected, students keep track of corrected spellings for future use.

Polish and publish. Gradually train students to edit their own work, preparing it for an audience of their choice.

6. De-emphasize mechanics until the final stages of writing. This is an identified area of difficulty for students with learning disabilities. Give students time to build their confidence when expressing their thoughts in writing. Then teach skills in grammar and usage within the context of real writing tasks (Graham & Harris, 1988; Poplin et al., 1980; Routman, 1991; Smith, 1986).

7. Individual conferences have a place in each curricular area. They may be as short as 45 seconds or as long as necessary. It is that concerned, personal touch that counts.

8. Small group work in all three areas promotes constructive peer interaction. Combined efforts, with everyone doing his or her share, yield exciting results.

9. Hold mini workshops—skills still need to be taught directly and reinforced frequently to promote academic success. Take a few minutes to highlight a skill that a number of students need reviewed before starting a new writing project.

    a. Present new information to be learned both orally and in writing, modeling procedures on the chalkboard or an overhead transparency.

    b. Repeat important information a number of times to ensure learning. Begin each day's reading or lecture with a review of previous materials to aid connections with social studies or reading content.

    c. Simplify—don't overwhelm.

    d. Continue to teach skills within the context of literature books and the social studies text such as previewing, questioning, and making predictions to needy students. Urge students to use what they know about language to continually construct meaning from text.

10. Allow for personal choices: there is a greater vested interest in reading a book or poem that a student has selected on the basis of personal interest than one that is assigned by the teacher. That critical element of choice facilitates the development of independence so important for the academic and social growth of students with learning disabilities.

A Case for Children's Literature

In an effort to stretch across the curriculum and integrate subject matter, teaching should infuse their courses with children's literature rather than pallid, remedial fare. A myriad of fiction and nonfiction offerings are available to stimulate a student's personal involvement with history. A judicious match between literature book and LD learner can fill in the gaps left by a social studies textbook's expository, factual approach, providing an opportunity to study a "frozen" slice of history at whatever pace or depth is desired (Cline & Taylor, 1978). Within the pages of a narrative children's book are new worlds, thought-provoking experiences, and interesting people to widen a student's horizons as he or she steps across the years. In addition, nonfiction children's literature provides an "interesting, lively way to share up-to-date information" (Young & Vardell, 1993, p. 405). Such books push back the walls erected by the traditional remedial curriculum and make room in the learner's mind for fascinating historical worlds yet unexperienced.

Such enticing tools of the trade can also extend a teacher's capacity to reach every student in the class. Students' varying reading levels can be accommodated along with their individual interests when a large number of historically related children's literature books and magazines are available to complement the current textbook unit. The more adept reader can travel the streets of Richmond, Virginia, during the Civil War with Susan, gathering beautiful silk dresses to be donated to the construction of a balloon for Southern spying purposes in *The Last Silk Dress* (Rinaldi, 1988). The less able reader can gather some of the same information from the humorous account in *Runaway Balloon* (Davis, 1976). Such options enable the teacher to do what whole language advocates: start where the learner is, progress from there, and create a richer, more diverse educational environment for the entire class.

To overcome flagging motivation often attributed to the student with learning disabilities, lively children's literature books have proved to have a positive impact on students' motivation (Hansen & Schmidt, 1989; Moir, 1992; Wigfield & Asher, 1984). Making an assortment of literature available in both reading and social studies increases the possibility that reluctant learners and inquisitive students alike will become excited about ideas and events in history. Ducking flying bullets with Tillie in *Thunder at Gettysburg* (Gauch, 1990), reacting in horror after shooting a man as Charlie does in *Charley Skedaddle* (Beatty, 1987), or cringing under the crack of the whip as it impacts bare skin in *Runaway to Freedom* (Smucker, 1979) makes history live within the minds of the reader. The magic of reader response is at work here. Readers and listeners are busy people. For instance, they reflect upon what they hear, interpret it in their own unique way, make connections to an accumulation of previous knowledge, and often predict what might come next. This process is the

■ Having students read historical fiction and nonfiction can create
memorable connections between the reader, author, book, and history.

basis of the popular premise that response to a book is a transaction between reader and writer, a personal exploration of meaning (Rosenblatt,
1983, 1991).

The teacher should capitalize on this premise by encouraging
memorable connections between reader, writer, book, and history. The
teacher can facilitate those personal transactions by presenting students
with choices from numerous reading materials beyond the textbook. In
addition to fiction and nonfiction books, poetry, song lyrics, recipes,
maps, and old letters can be included. Their use can heighten enthusiasm,
increase time spent in contact with social studies content, and invite a
variety of written responses. It is highly probable that these efforts will
have a positive impact on learning within the classroom (Cox & Many,
1992). Levstik (1989, p. 183) reminds us of the value of historical fiction:

> It can lead to a richer, fuller, and more empathetic
> understanding of history. Through historical fiction children
> learn that people in all times have faced change and crisis, that
> people in all times have basic needs in common, and that these

needs remain in our time. Children can discover some of the myriad ways in which humans depend on each other, and of the consequences of success and failure in relationships, both personal and historical.

To pique students' interest in a new area of study, the teacher can read an appropriate children's literature book aloud. Reading aloud daily, even briefly, should have a comfortable niche in the social studies regime. There is nothing like a book well read to entice listeners and to tantalize children's imaginations (Evans, 1992; Fuhler, 1990; Markle, 1987). Listening to a book provides an opportunity for readers with disabilities to "taste the delicacy" of well written books regardless of the reading level (Fountas & Hannigan, 1989). As listeners, students are exposed to rich vocabulary and complex sentence structure that would frustrate them if they tackled it on their own.

The descriptive, lengthy sentences in *Johnny Tremain* (Forbes, 1946), for example, will probably be difficult for readers to master independently, but excerpts read aloud will bring pre-Revolutionary War Boston vividly to life. They can take listeners out to the old root cellar, down the damp, earthen steps to emerge in the world of the Civil War with young Rose in *The Root Cellar* (Lunn, 1983). Such excerpts give learners an inside view of the bickering and heated debates that ensued over equal representation and slavery while the Constitution was being written. Students will glean a different perspective while working with Jared as an aide to James Madison in *1787* (Anderson, 1987).

Students can read coordinated titles independently during reading class or as extra reading in social studies. Then the teacher can encourage readers to share their reactions and connections to the read-aloud sessions or text lectures in both large and small group discussions. It is not too much to hope that students will carry their reading right out of the classroom when they walk side by side with a main character, caught up in the tale unraveling within the covers of their book.

No All-Purpose Solutions

The state of American education for adolescents with learning disabilities is looking more promising but has yet to develop concrete solutions to complex learning problems. The best way to teach this challenging population is still in need of refinement based on continued research (Lefstein, 1983; Leigh, 1980). It appears that educational growth remains very modest despite basic skill remediation for the majority of these students. Lefstein (1983) explains that current recommendations for the education of adolescent learners emphasize accommodation rather than remediation. Thus, the focus is on changing the learning environment and/or academic requirements so that students can learn despite their weaknesses. This idea certainly opens the door to whole language premises and offers LD learners some hope via its promises.

One of the potent premises of whole language is that it empowers learners with learning disabilities to take responsibility for their own reading, writing, speaking, listening, and thinking in the process of getting an education. In addition, whole language fits social studies as naturally as it does reading or language arts, so its adaptability is an asset. Furthermore, its emphasis is on the whole child as he or she copes with academic underachievement, inefficient learning strategies, cognitive processing deficits, personality problems, and inhibiting emotional reactions to this entire conglomeration of deficiencies. To deal with all of these is truly an overwhelming task every single educational day. Finally, the whole language approach contrasts with remedial programs that have taught many in this population to survive by inadvertently developing a dependency on others. That in itself is a giant step in the right direction as students acquire skills in how to become independent learners across the curriculum.

Travels Back Through Time

Teachers can invigorate the social studies curriculum facilitated by the whole language approach by mixing and matching the activities suggested in this section to inspire and excite LD learners. Units on the Revolutionary War, the Civil War, and Native Americans are covered here.

The Revolutionary War

Begin study of the Revolutionary War by treating listeners to *Rebecca's War* (Finlayson, 1972), a fast-paced, suspenseful peek at life in Philadelphia in 1777, as one read-aloud experience. Encourage students to predict and problem solve as they combine efforts with Rebecca to outwit British troops and manage the family after the death of her mother. With her father and oldest brother running a privateer and her younger brother with Washington's troops at Valley Forge, Rebecca has to be on her toes, and quick witted she is. In addition to the children's literature books listed at the end of this chapter, you may want to refer students to the following issues of *Cobblestone Magazine:* September 1987 (on forming a new nation), March 1987 (on Alexander Hamilton), and September 1989 (on Thomas Jefferson).

1. Use a Venn diagram to compare and contrast information gleaned via the read-aloud book, student's outside reading choices, or the textbook chapter. Such a diagram enables students to visualize similarities and differences easily. Have students write a paragraph comparing and contrasting the different versions of events during the Revolution.

2. Have small groups of students develop crossword puzzles to review vocabulary words related to the Revolutionary War period. Include words from literature books as well as the textbook. Possible titles could be "American Revolution,"

"Signs of the Times," and "Political Parties." The groups can present their completed products to other classmates to tackle on Crossword Puzzle Day. Puzzles could also be placed in a folder to be done at students' leisure.

3. Have students write a final chapter to the book being read aloud in class or one they are reading independently. The chapter should tell what is happening a year later. Share the completed chapters with the class. Display them attractively, encouraging students to read their peers' work.

4. Discuss the meaning of the word *patriot*, illustrating the term with specific incidents from children's literature books the students are reading and explanations in the textbook. Then have them write a short story about an imaginary Revolutionary War patriot. Compile finished stories into a class volume to be added to the classroom library, useful for both reading and social studies classes. Read the stories to another social studies class.

5. Have students write journal entries for a specified period of time from the viewpoint of a child of the times, of the main character in one of the students' books, or from a secondary character in one of their books. Display journals so that other students can browse through them when time permits.

6. Have students work in small groups to research and then write out an interview with a historical figure of their choice. Have one student in the group assume the role of the figure, while another interviews that person in front of the class. Then open the interview to the class, later researching questions that the historical figure may not have been prepared to answer.

7. Have students write a letter to King George III, taking a stand on whether colonists should be taxed, allowed to govern themselves, or in support of the king's actions. Publish the letters in the school newspaper, inviting reader response.

8. Help students make a chart comparing and contrasting the advantages and disadvantages of being a redcoat and/or one of the minutemen as he prepared for and engaged in battle. A class bulletin board display could be created with illustrations of uniforms and equipment. Paragraphs comparing and contrasting the chances for success could surround the display.

9. As a class project, make an ABC book about the Revolutionary War. Laminate the completed book and keep it in the classroom library for future reference and enjoyment. Students might include key people, places, written works, and events, all attractively illustrated.

10. After a discussion of slavery as it appears in the textbook or literature books, encourage students to walk in another's footsteps. Have them write a paragraph from the viewpoint of a slave, perhaps addressing what it was like to be born into

slavery or a related issue. Suggest other appropriate books (see bibliography of children's books at end of chapter) to deepen the students' understanding of the institution of slavery. Hold a class discussion or arrange a debate on the pros and cons of slavery.

11. Put on a class play. Use authentic music of the period. Write the play or selected scenes as a group or choose one of the following plays: "Patriot and Tory: The Children," *Cobblestone Magazine,* August 1987, pp. 21–27; "Close Call on Nantucket," Cobblestone Magazine, September 1983, pp. 28–35.

12. Although radio did not exist at the time of the Revolutionary War, put on a class-written radio play. Students could also present a 3-minute news story on an event in daily life in a major city such as Boston or Philadelphia. Several students can devise brief commercials for a tradesman or product of the time. Use appropriate background music or sound effects. Present the polished product to other social studies classes.

13. For a complete change of pace, divide the class into small groups to research and prepare a typical meal agreed upon ahead of time by the class as a whole. Prepare recipes of the time, enlisting the help of parents, if possible, or reserve time in the home economics room and prepare the food at school. Print the recipes in a booklet to be distributed to all social studies classes.

The Civil War

Introduce the Civil War period by reading aloud (for about 10 minutes) from *The Root Cellar* (Lunn, 1983), a fascinating book that will quickly capture the students' interest. In this story, young Rose is sent to the northern shores of Lake Ontario to live with Aunt Nan and her rambunctious family after Rose's grandmother and long-time guardian dies. Unaccustomed to the disorganized hubbub of this large family, Rose seeks peace near a hawthorne tree in the far corner of the yard. There she discovers an old root cellar through which she is able to enter the Civil War era. She makes friends with Will and Susan, later traveling through the South with Susan in search of Will, who may be hurt or be a prisoner of war. Life during the aftermath of the war is vividly depicted as listeners travel back in time with resourceful, clever Rose.

In addition to the children's literature books listed at the end of this chapter, you may want to refer students to the following issues of *Cobblestone Magazine:* April 1981 (on highlights of the Civil War), January 1985 (on the making of a newspaper), May 1987 (on Reconstruction), July 1988 (on Gettysburg), January 1989 (on children who influenced history), and February 1989 (on Frederick Douglass).

1. As the read-aloud unfolds, ask the students how events in the book mesh with information in the social studies textbook and class lectures. Have students discuss and then list in their personal journals similarities and differences that they discover. Encourage learners to continue observations on their own. Check their progress periodically.

2. Teach students to analyze the difference between expository and narrative writing. List elements common to each one on the chalkboard, to be transferred later to a poster displayed for easy reference. After modeling the process, invite students in small groups to rewrite a segment of the social studies text in narrative format. Have the students polish the final drafts and publish them by reading copies to the class. Display them on a student-designed bulletin board.

3. Have students keep track of colorful vocabulary words from *The Root Cellar* along with words from literature books they are reading in social studies or reading class. Have them record in their journal words, meanings, and sentences in which each word is used correctly. Share words with the class on a weekly basis, adding the words to a class dictionary along with a pertinent illustration. Dedicate the finished copy to future social studies classes.

4. Choose a historical figure from the social studies textbook. Have students work independently or in small groups to write an episode integrating that person smoothly into *The Root Cellar* or another read-aloud choice. Read finished products to the group as a whole. Perhaps students could dress as the character, videotaping their presentation to be enjoyed by the class or during parent conferences at a later date.

5. Encourage the students to write their reactions to each day's reading of Rose's story in their response journals. Have them predict what will happen next or problem solve solutions to current dilemmas. When periodically checking the journals, be sure to write reactions to what students are sharing. Students will enjoy responding to teacher's comments too.

6. In a large group discussion, ask the class to compare Rose's story to the other literature books they are reading (see bibliography for options). What kinds of information can be learned from literature books? Make a large chart with a catchy title for the classroom wall, listing information acquired from the various literature books. Add to it as new information emerges. Ask students to examine their books for prologues, epilogues, or author's notes to glean the historical facts upon which their books might be based.

7. Make a class time line across one wall. Have each student write the title of his or her book at the appropriate place on the time line and then list the main characters, include a three-or four-line summary, and add an attractive illustration of an event in the story. Be sure someone includes the read-aloud title too.

8. As students finish reading their books, divide the class into groups based on the setting of their stories, the time period covered, or issues such as slavery or the running of the Underground Railroad. Assign a recorder in each group. Ask students to share information that was similar or different in their individual books as you monitor group work. Have students discuss reactions, feelings of the characters, or resolution of war-related conflicts within each story. Have each group write a summary of its findings to be shared with the class. Have the groups compare and contrast their findings to textbook information and/or class lectures.

9. Work across the curriculum in the process of creating an edition of a Civil War newspaper. Provide models for the students to study. Refer to *Cobblestone Magazine's* January 1985 issue entitled "Read All About It! The History of the Newspaper" for some helpful suggestions. Perhaps students would like to do separate issues reflecting the viewpoints of the North and of the South. Students can study and write editorials, want ads, ads for runaway slaves, or upcoming slave auctions. After studying styles of clothing or menus of the times, they should intersperse that information along with daily news and war correspondence. A review of the use of sketches and photography to capture battle scenes might prompt artistic renditions plus articles by correspondents from different parts of the United States. Publish the final editions by displaying them in the learning center.

10. Model a book talk or two. Invite students to give a lively 3-to-5 minute book talk on their fiction or nonfiction book. Their aim is to entice classmates to read it in an effort to deepen an understanding of the human sacrifice and realities of the Civil War.

11. As students finish their books, encourage them to complete a review sheet of each for a loose leaf binder to be kept in the social studies classroom. Students should list title and author, write a summary, include an illustration if they like, add a critique of the book, and conclude with recommendations for their peers. Future readers can then refer to the binder for books to read.

12. Artistic students may enjoy creating illustrated maps showing their character's travels or the area discussed in their book and highlighted by incidents from the story. Laminate the finished products, encourage students to share them briefly with the class, and then display them appropriately.

13. To encourage students to analyze a character in their literature books or a key figure in the textbook, invite them to put themselves into the shoes of a character of their choice. Then have them write an 11-line poem giving the following information about the character:

Character's first name

Son or daughter of

Brother or sister of

Description of a favorite object or activity of the character

What character does routinely

Something character wishes would happen

Another person in the story who is important to the character

A dream the character has

Qualities of people the character likes

Character's general attitude or feelings

Character's full name

Share the poems with the class, and display them appropriately.

Native Americans

The study of Native Americans traditionally falls into the elementary social studies curriculum. The following readings and activities are appropriate for younger students but have strong appeal to the older students as well. It is imperative that students of all ages develop a better understanding of different cultures. One place to begin is right here in America. By meeting American Indians in another time, students may better appreciate the rich heritage that Native Americans have bequeathed to all Americans. In addition, it provides a firm base upon which to study the contemporary life of Native Americans at a later time.

While the study of Native Americans can take many directions, a good place to start is with their myths and legends. There are beautifully illustrated, wonderfully written picture books available that will appeal to readers of all ages and abilities. You may want to choose a sampling of tales from tribes spanning the country or decide to concentrate on one section of the country, highlighting the Plains Indian for example. Since whole language is meant to be used in personally meaningful, purposeful ways, it is wise to gear materials to meet the needs and interests of each student in the class. Following are some "starter" activities.

1. Explain the value of storytelling and its critical role in many cultures since the earliest times in human society (Moir, 1992). It is probably an activity with which elementary students are already quite familiar. Tell them that stories were the way Indian heritage was passed on to the present generation. Help the listeners to consider the value of the spoken word in a different light. To the Indians, the spoken word was sacred because they used it to pass stories, songs, and chants on to the younger generation. Respectful children who revered their

■ Children's literature can heighten students' enthusiasm about a topic of study.

elders retained these messages, regarding them as invaluable (Sneve, 1989). As those children transmitted the words of their elders to their children, a body of knowledge gradually formed, one that future generations would be able to study and to enjoy.

2. Read a selection of chants or poems to the students and discuss their underlying meaning to the Indians. Try some choral reading using *Dancing Tepees: Poems of American Indian Youth* (Sneve, 1989) or *The Sacred Path: Spells, Prayers and Power Songs of the American Indian* (Bierhorst, 1983). Tie in information on masks by using *They Put on Masks* (Baylor, 1974), a poetic description of the importance of ceremonial masks.

3. A natural art activity extending from Baylor's book is to create pictures or papier-mâché masks to be displayed in the room or learning center. Children can write a brief explanation of what their mask represents if it is an original work of art. If it is a reproduction, they can write a short paragraph explaining its origins.

4. After more exposure to the Indian culture, students may want to write their own chants and poetry. Older students might illustrate their writing, with appropriate Indian designs used as a border.

5. Demonstrate the power of the oral tradition by telling an Indian legend that is a personal favorite. Encourage students to discuss why the story might have been passed along over the years. Follow up by reading a selection such as the amusing *Iktomi*

and the Boulder (Goble, 1988), the beautifully illustrated *Legend of Scarface* (Sans Souci, 1978), the pleasing *The Ring on the Prairie* (Bierhorst, 1970), or a selection from *Earthmaker's Tales* (Mayo, 1989). These easily read books will be picked up and reread by young readers as soon as you put them down. Bring storytelling into contemporary times by reading and discussing *Pueblo Storyteller* (Hoyt-Goldsmith, 1991).

6. Older students can research their family background for a story to share with the class. Invite parents of younger students to come to class for a Family Story Sharing Day. While the parent tells the story, the child might hold up an illustration he or she created. The oral tradition is a strong influence in many cultures, a fine lesson for children to learn.

7. Provide a large selection of books of myths and legends for the students to read independently. Give brief book talks on several titles to entice readers to sample the fare. *Where the Buffaloes Begin* (Baker, 1981), *Buffalo Woman* (Goble, 1984), *Annie and the Old One* (Miles, 1971), *The Star Maiden* (Esbensen, 1988a) or *Ladder to the Sky* (Ebsbensen, 1988b) are a few suggestions. *The Adventures of Nanabush* (Coatsworth & Coatsworth, 1980) is an appealing collection of trickster tales that will delight readers and listeners from first through sixth grades. Consult the school librarian or visit the public library in search of other appropriate titles.

8. Discuss the structure of myths and legends, noting the simple plot that usually relates just one incident. Explain that if several events occur in a story, they are usually "chained together" in sequential order rather than one building upon another to create a more complex plot. For example, read *Iktomi and the Boulder* (Goble, 1988) through from beginning to end. Then reread the story, having the students pick out each incident. Work as a class to start an original Indian tale. After the first few incidents are recorded, let the students break into small groups with the task of finishing the story. Read the polished, illustrated versions in class or share them with another class.

9. Investigate the lives of Indian children and their families today. Collura's (1986) *Winners* is a fictional account of Jordy Threebears' life, thought-provoking reading for older elementary students. *Ride the Crooked Wind* (Fife, 1973) describes Po's struggles to successfully blend the past and the present. Ashabranner's (1984) nonfiction account *To Live in Two Worlds* is also a catalyst for further reading that will begin to tie the past and the present together as readers deepen their understanding of Native Americans.

Summary

Social studies becomes more relevant for LD students when they are given a choice of reading materials that they can readily read, write about, and discuss. Thus, whole language activities assist the classroom teacher in facilitating social studies instruction for students.

   With the wide range of narrative and nonfiction children's books currently available, it becomes easier to develop thematic units for social studies. This chapter provided examples of children's literature and whole language activities for the Revolutionary War, the Civil War, and Native Americans. In actuality, social studies can be taught through thematic units because of the vast variety and number of children's literature books and activities that teachers can adopt to accompany them. This enables the LD student to become an engaged learner in the social studies.

Children's Books

THE REVOLUTIONARY WAR

Alden, J. R. (1962). *American revolution, 1775-1783.* New York: Harper & Row. (Reading level not noted)

> Outlines the events leading up to and including the American Revolutionary War.

Alderman, C. (1961). *Samuel Adams, Son of liberty.* New York: Holt. (Ages 11+)

> Illustrating the significant part Sam Adams played in the American Revolution, this colorful biography authentically recreates the man's life while highlighting other political figures of the day.

Anderson, J. (1987). *1787.* Orlando, FL: Harcourt Brace Jovanovich. (Ages 12-14)

> Although this book falls beyond the framework of the American Revolution, it is such an excellent book that it needs highlighting here. As James Madison's aide during the 1787 Constitutional Convention, Jared experiences an eye-opening summer filled with adventure, intrigue, and romance.

Avi (1984). *The fighting ground.* Philadelphia: Lippincott. (Ages 11-14)

> Thirteen-year-old Jonathan gets involved in a battle with Hessians outside his town of Trenton. The action takes place over the span of one day, resulting in conflicting emotions in both Jonathan and the reader.

Bliven, B. (1987). *American revolution, 1760-1783.* New York: Random House. (Reading level: 5.0)

> An overview of the events of the Revolutionary War.

Bulla, C. (1983). *Charlie's house.* New York: Crowell. (Ages 7-10)

> In this story about life as an indentured servant under a mean master, courage and circumstances combine to improve Charlie's life.

Collier, J. L., & Collier, C. (1974). *My brother Sam is dead.* New York: Four Winds. (Ages 14+)

> This Newbery Honor book relates a suspenseful adventure involving the Meeker family as they endure divided loyalties and the resulting turmoil of the American Revolution.

Collier, J. L., & Collier, C. (1976). *The bloody country.* New York: Scholastic. (Ages 14+)

> Two close friends, one a landowner's son and the other a slave, deal with different issues of the war and slavery against the background of the Revolutionary War.

Collier, J. L., & Collier, C. (1981). *Jump ship to freedom.* New York: Delacorte. (Ages 12+)

> From this skillful blend of fact and fiction, the reader learns about Daniel Arabus, a slave and son of a Revolutionary War soldier, and his challenging search for freedom.

Collier, J. L., & Collier, C. (1983). *War comes to Willy Freeman.* New York: Delacorte. (Ages 11+)

> A 13-year-old black girl named Willy finds herself alone when her patriot father is killed by redcoats and her mother is captured. Courage and fortitude enable her to locate her mother and also attempt to free 300 slaves.

Dickinson, A. (1968). *The Boston Massacre.* New York: Watts. (Ages 10+)

> A complete, concise account of the events that led up to the Boston Massacre as well as its aftermath; illustrations include contemporary maps and prints.

Edwards, S. (1985). *George Midgett's war.* New York: Scribner's. (Ages 11–14)

> A special relationship develops between George and his father when they become involved in a treacherous journey through poorly mapped territory in an effort to get two precious barrels of salt to the army at Valley Forge.

Finlayson, A. (1972). *Rebecca's war.* New York: Frederick Warne. (Ages 11+)

> A fast-paced tale in which 14-year-old Rebecca tries to outwit British officers living in her home while her privateer father and brother are away at sea.

Forbes, E. (1946). *Johnny Tremain.* Boston: Houghton Mifflin. (Ages 13+)

> This well-known award winner tells the story of the days in Boston just before the war begins as Johnny, a silversmith's apprentice, strives to overcome his bitterness when his hand is maimed as a result of a practical joke. He regains his self-confidence by serving the American cause.

Fritz, J. (1967). *Early thunder.* New York: Coward McCann. (Ages 11–14)

> In this engrossing novel, 14-year-old Daniel West relates events that will affect his life as he struggles to find a stand he can take proudly in Salem in 1775.

Fritz, J. (1974). *Why don't you get a horse, Sam Adams?* (T. S. Hyman, Illus.). New York: Coward, McCann. (Ages 10–12)

> An amusing biography relating intriguing information about Sam Adams during the American Revolution.

Fritz, J. (1975a). *Where was Patrick Henry on the 29th of May?* New York: Coward, McCann. (Ages 8+)

> The life story of a fine attorney and an outstanding orator who staunchly defended liberty.

Fritz, J. (1975b). *Will you sign here, John Hancock?* (T.S. Hyman, Illus.). New York: Coward, McCann. (Ages 8+)

> An informative, delightfully illustrated biography that outlines John Hancock's contributions to Massachusetts and the new nation while highlighting his flamboyant life-style.

Fritz, J. (1976). *What's the big idea, Ben Franklin?* New York: Coward, McCann. (Ages 8–12)

> An informative and entertaining biography of the eighteenth-century printer, inventor, and statesman who was so influential during the American Revolution.

Fritz, J. (1977). *Can't you make them behave, King George?* New York: Coward, McCann. (Ages 8+)

> An interesting biography the king of Great Britain at the time of the American Revolution.

Griffin, J. (1977). *Phoebe the spy.* New York: Scholastic. (Ages 8–10)

> The fictitious story of Phoebe, daughter of a free black man and owner of Fraunces Tavern, who goes undercover to discover and prevent the assassination of General Washington.

Johnson, N. (1992). *The battle of Lexington and Concord.* New York: Four Winds. (Ages 9–12)

> This book is by photojournalist Neil Johnson. A compelling text is accompanied by color photos of a reenactment of the first battle of the Revolutionary War.

Loeper, J. J. (1976). *Going to school in 1776.* New York: Antheneum. (Reading level: 4.8)

> Describes a typical day in a school in 1776.

McGovern, A. (1975). *The secret soldier: The story of Deborah Sampson.* New York: Scholastic. (Ages 8–10)

> The true and fascinating story of a young woman who disguised herself as a man and fought bravely for American independence during the Revolutionary War.

O'Dell, S. (1980). *Sara Bishop.* Boston: Houghton Mifflin. (Ages 11+)

> Sarah and her family move to the colonies just before the American Revolution. After being scorned by town patriots because her brother and father take different sides during the war, having their farm burned, and seeing Mr. Bishop tarred and feathered, Sarah seeks to rebuild her life.

Phelan, M. K. (1973). *Story of the Boston Tea Party*. New York: Crowell. (Reading level: 7.4)

> Describes events leading up to the Boston Tea Party and its impact on the colonies.

Turner, A. (1992). *Katie's trunk*. (R. Himler, Illus.). New York: Macmillan. (Ages 7+)

> Based on a true story, this book gives insight as to the feelings of a Tory family at the beginning of the American Revolution.

The Revolutionary War: Colonial Life

The four titles listed below are from the *Colonial Craftsman Series* and provide interesting information on the period of the Revolutionary War.

Fisher, L. E. (1986). *Papermakers*. Boston: Godine. (Reading level: 5.8)

> Describes how paper was made during colonial times.

Fisher, L. E. (1986). *Schoolmasters*. Boston: Godine. (Reading level: 5.9)

> Teachers called schoolmasters, in colonial times are depicted not only teaching but also cleaning and maintaining the school as well.

Fisher, L. E. (1987). *Shipbuilders*. Boston: Godine. (Reading level: 5.8)

> Describes shipbuilders of eighteenth-century New England.

Fisher, L. E. (1986). *Tanners*. Boston: Godine. (Reading level: 5.9)

> Describes how hides were tanned and made into shoes and clothing.

The Civil War

Ackerman, K. (1990). *The tin heart* (M. Hays, Illus.). New York: Atheneum. (Ages 8+)

> Mahaley and Flora are best friends who live on different sides of the Ohio River. Traveling back and forth on her father's ferryboat, Mahaley is able to visit Flora frequently. Each wearing one-half of a tin heart, they pledge their friendship forever. As the Civil War erupts, more than the river threatens that pledge.

Beatty, P. (1984). *Turn homeward, Hannalee*. New York: Morrow. (Ages 10–14)

> Twelve-year-old Hannalee and her brother Jem are branded as traitors for making cloth and rope for the Confederacy. When they are sent north to work, Hannalee must serve a harsh employer while Jem is sent to a farm. Hannalee disguises herself as a boy and runs away, finds Jem, and they return to devastated Roswell, Georgia.

Beatty, P. (1987). *Charley Skedaddle*. New York: Morrow. (Ages 10–14)

> A tough New York street kid, member of the Bowery Boys, finds himself a drummer boy in the Union Army. Underneath the tough exterior is a young man who is lonely on the troopship, horrified in battle, repulsed when he shoots a Rebel, and filled with guilt when he "skedaddles" from battle. An old mountain woman teaches him to believe in himself again.

Beatty, P. (1988). *Be ever hopeful, Hannalee.* New York: Morrow. (Ages 11–15)

> This sequel begins where *Turn Homeward, Hannalee* ended. Davey returns from the war without an arm, intent on moving the family to Atlanta to begin a new life. Hannalee's strength of character and optimism still prevail as she works to help her family in this fast-paced historical novel that chronicles the post-Civil War period.

Burchard, P. (1973). *The deserter: A spy story of the Civil War.* New York: Coward, McCann & Geoghegan. (Ages 12+)

> In the dead of the winter of 1862, Levi, a young Yankee spy, travels down the Mississippi aboard the *Essex* to Island Ten. Posing as a Confederate soldier, he gathers important information from the Rebels, which he manages to get to his superiors in Missouri.

Clapp, P. (1986). *The tamarack tree.* New York: Lothrop, Lee, & Shephard. (Ages 12–14)

> An 18-year-old English girl finds her loyalties divided as she and her friends experience the hardships imposed on them during the 47-day siege of Vicksburg in the spring of 1863.

Climo, S. (1987). *A month of seven days.* New York: Crowell. (Ages 9–12)

> Twelve-year-old Zoe Snyder's father is fighting with the Confederates. The family farm is taken over by a Yankee army contingent during their march through Georgia. Frantic to get them away before her father returns, Zoe spends the longest week of her life concocting an elaborate plan to frighten the soldiers off.

Crane, S. (1981). *The red badge of courage.* New York: Watermill Press. (Ages 12–15)

> Young Henry Fleming is skeptical as he and his fellow U.S. Army men prepare to fight Confederate soldiers during the Civil War. Henry thinks of soldiers as heroes one moment and as cowards the next. As a result of his own cowardice, he must face his own worth both as a U.S. soldier and as a human being.

Davis, B. (1976). *Runaway balloon.* (S. Murdocca, Illus.). New York: Coward, McCann & Geoghegan. (Ages 7–10)

> To keep up with Yankee technology and to better defend Richmond, Captain Johnston decides that the Confederates need a balloon too. This humorous and simply written account tells how loyal women surrender their silk dresses, which are pieced together to create a multi-colored, ill-fated balloon.

Davis, P. (1980). *Three days.* (R. Rosenblum, Illus.). New York: Atheneum. (Ages 11–14)

> The battle of Gettysburg is presented through the eyes of Robert E. Lee, following the general from the time he enters Pennsylvania to the disastrous conclusion of the battle. Intertwined with Lee's account is the story of an anonymous Confederate soldier.

Freedman, R. (1987). *Lincoln: A photobiography.* New York: Clarion Books. (Ages 10+)

> The author shapes a vivid portrait of the 16th president from historical photographs, magazine prints, and other pertinent documents. The facts of Lincoln's life, from the growing up years to the turmoil of his presidency, are presented in informative, straightforward text.

Fritz, J. (1960). *Brady* (L. Ward, Illus.). New York: Coward, McCann. (Ages 10-13)

> Brady cannot keep a secret, a fact that worries his parents when he discovers their activities with the Underground Railroad. Brady's resourcefulness in time of need saves the life of a runaway slave and proves he can do a man's work.

Fritz, J. (1979). *Stonewall* (S. Gammell, Illus.). New York: Putnam. (Ages 10-14)

> This biography contrasts Jackson's heroic Civil War battlefield behavior with some interesting personal idiosyncrasies. The narrative is enlivened by personal observations and quotes from Jackson's contemporaries in this carefully researched book.

Gauch, P. L. (1990). *Thunder at Gettysburg.* New York: Coward, McCann. (Ages 9-12)

> Young Tillie is excited as she watches the beginning of the battle from an upper window of her home. Before the battle is over, she has experienced the pain and horror of war as she ducks flying shells and tries to ease the lot of the wounded.

Hickman, J. (1978). *Zoar blue.* New York: Macmillan. (Ages 11-13)

> German immigrants settle in a communal, strongly religious Zoar community in Ohio. Despite bitter family feelings, John Keffer runs away to join the Union Army. Orphaned Barbara also runs away, hoping for a better life with relatives in Pennsylvania. Their stories intertwine as the two young adults nearly meet at Gettysburg and are eventually drawn back to Zoar.

Hunt, I. (1964). *Across five Aprils.* Chicago: Follett. (Ages 12-14)

> The hardship, suffering, and courage of a young farm boy living near Newton, Illinois, is related as nine-year-old Jethro Creighton gradually takes full responsibility for the farm work as a result of tragic home situations caused by brothers and cousins who fight on opposite sides in the war.

Hurmence, B. (1982). *A girl called boy.* Boston: Houghton Mifflin. (Ages 9-12)

> Based on oral histories and plantation records, this book relates the story of a middle-class black girl who is time-warped back into the 1850s when her relatives were slaves of the Yanceys. In the process, she gets a taste of what slavery would really have been like for her.

Keith, H. (1957). *Rifles for Watie.* New York: Crowell. (Ages 12-15)

> A sensitive, naive 16-year-old Kansas farm boy joins the Union Army, becomes a scout, and accidentally, a member of Watie's Cherokee Rebels for a time. Jefferson Davis Bussey is probably one of the few soldiers in the West to see the Civil War from both sides in this 1958 Newbery award winner.

Kent, Z. (1987). *The story of Sherman's march to the sea.* Chicago: Children's Press. (Ages 8–10)

This book describes the havoc wreaked upon the land as General Sherman's Union troops march from Atlanta to Savannah.

Lester, J. (1968). *To be a slave* (T. Feelings, Illus.). New York: Dial. (Ages 12+)

In this Newbery Honor book, the author combines the actual testimony of former slaves with his own commentary in an effort to bring the reality of the institution of slavery to the reader.

Levine, E. (1988). *If you traveled on the Underground Railroad* (R. Williams, Illus.). New York: Scholastic. (Ages 8–12)

A well-concealed railroad helped thousands of slaves escape from owners in the South to freedom in the North. How it worked, what the dangers were, and who helped along the way are explained in this fascinating, easy-to-understand book.

Lindstrom, A. J. (1980). *Sojourner Truth, slave, abolitionist, fighter for women's rights* (P. Frame, Illus.). New York: Julian Messner. (Ages 9–12)

In this biography of a former slave who became one of the best-known abolitionists of her time, the woman's story is told from the harsh days of slavery to a meeting with President Lincoln. The text points out that newfound freedom for Sojourner's people was closer to a nightmare for the majority than it was the long-sought fulfillment of a dream.

Lunn, J. (1983). *The root cellar.* New York: Scribner's. (Ages 11–14)

When her grandmother dies, shy Rose is sent to the northern shores of Lake Ontario to live with her Aunt Nan's lively family. The discovery of a vine-covered root cellar door draws her into a world of over 100 years ago, where she is eventually pulled into the tragedies of the Civil War.

Lyons, M. E. (1992). *Letters from a slave girl: The story of Harriet Jacobs.* New York: Scribners. (Ages 11+)

Harriet Jacobs escaped from slavery in the 1840s and went on to become an author and noted abolitionist.

Meltzer, M. (1989). *Voices from the Civil War.* New York: Crowell. (Ages 12–15)

The author depicts life during the Civil War through the words of people who were there, using such primary sources as letters, diaries, ballads, newspapers, interviews, speeches, and memoirs. The text is highlighted with engrossing photographs.

Murphy, J. (1990). *The boys' war—Confederate and Union soldiers talk about the Civil War.* New York: Clarion. (Ages 9–14)

This book presents a riveting picture of the Civil War through the eyes of boys involved in it. Over 50 archival photographs are included.

Murphy, J. (1992). *The long road to Gettysburg.* New York: Clarion. (Ages 11+)

Firsthand impressions of two teenage soldiers, one a 17-year-old corporal in the Union Army and the other a 19-year-old Confederate lieutenant, of the Battle of Gettysburg.

Perez, N. A. (1984). *The slopes of war.* Boston: Houghton Mifflin. (Ages 12+)

Bekah and Leander see enough fighting during the 3-day battle of Gettysburg to understand the human cost of war. Bekah cares for wounded Union officer Captain Waite upstairs while injured Rebels are tended to in the parlor. This book is filled with authentic information about real officers and battle plans.

Reeder, C. (1989). *Shades of gray.* New York: Macmillan. (Ages 9-12)

Twelve-year-old Will Page regards the Yankees as the enemy because all his family lost their lives as a result of the war. He works the land and hunts the fields in the Virginia Piedmont beside his Uncle Jed, who has offered him a home. Will eventually comes to accept the fact that his uncle refused to fight the Yankees, realizing that good people have different but still acceptable ideas and that all people suffer from war.

Reit, S. (1988). *Behind enemy lines: The incredible story of Emma Edmonds, Civil War spy.* San Diego, CA: Harcourt Brace Jovanovich. (Ages 13-16)

Sarah Emmonds was a feminist long before the word gained popularity. Disguised as a boy, she enlists in the Union Army, frequently acting as a spy for the North. Sarah is a shrewd and courageous heroine.

Rinaldi, A. (1988). *The last silk dress.* New York: Holiday House. (Ages 12-14)

Determined Susan Chilmark longs to do something for the "Cause" during the Civil War despite being hampered by her emotionally unstable mother and the scandalous reputation of her banished older brother. Love, death, and despair stalk her every move as she grows from a naive girl into a wise young woman.

Shore, L. J. (1986). *The sacred moon tree.* New York: Bradbury. (Ages 11-13)

With her father fighting in the North and her mother living with her family in Richmond, 12-year-old Phoebe is left to live on her grandfather's farm in Pennsylvania. She fills her days with wild imaginings until she and her friend Jotham set out on a wild adventure of their own to rescue Jotham's brother from a Southern prison.

Smucker, B. (1979). *Runaway to freedom: A story of the Underground Railway* (C. Lilly, Illus.). New York: Harper Trophy Books. (Ages 9-14)

Twelve-year-old Lilly faces a hard life on Master Hensen's plantation, but Mammy Sally provides a buffer of love and protection. One day mother and daughter are cruelly separated and sold to different masters. A Quaker family, the Underground Railroad, ingenuity, and courage aid Lilly in a successful escape to Canada.

Steele, W. O. (1958). *The perilous road* (P. Galdone, Illus.). San Diego, CA: Harcourt Brace Jovanovich. (Ages 8-10)

Chris Brabson, not quite 12, hates Yankee raiders who steal his family's recently harvested crops, the family horse, and his new deerskin shirt. Seeking revenge, Chris reveals the position of a Union wagon train to someone he believes is a spy. When he discovers his brother might be with that group, Chris is caught in a bitter dawn battle as he tries to warn him.

Tappert, A. (Ed.). (1988). *The brother's war: Civil War letters to their loved ones from the blue and the gray.* New York: Times Books. (Ages 12+)

This collection of memorable letters written by both Union and Confederate soldiers and illustrated with photographs gives readers insight into what the war was like for the soldiers.

Turner, A. (1987). *Nettie's trip south* (R. Himler, Illus.). New York: Macmillan. (Ages 7-11)

The realities of slavery are portrayed in a sensitive manner as seen by a young girl of the North. Nettie writes her impressions of a trip in the pre-Civil War South to a friend. Her comments center on the institution of slavery as it includes the maid at the inn and those at a slave auction.

Weitzman, D. (1975). *My backyard history book.* (J. Robertson, Illus.). Boston: Little, Brown. (Ages 10+)

This is an excellent book to stimulate research about local events that occurred while the Civil War was raging. Cemeteries, cornerstones, old recipes, or photo albums can send sleuths in search of the past right in their own neighborhood.

Native American Literature: Myths, Legends, and Poetry

Ashabranner, B. (1984). *To live in two worlds: American Indian youth today.* New York: Dodd, Mead.

Describes the life-style of contemporary Native Americans and their struggle to maintain their identity.

Baker, O. (1981). *Where the buffaloes begin.* (S. Gammell, Illus.). New York: Viking. (Ages 6+)

A picture book that describes Native American life on the plains.

Baylor, B. (1974). *They put on masks.* (J. Ingram, Illus.). New York: Scribner's. (Ages 6+)

A poetic description of Native American dances.

Bierhorst, J. (1970). *The ring on the prairie: A Shawnee legend.* (L. Dillon & D. Dillon, Illus.). New York: Dial. (Ages 7+)

This books tells about a Shawnee Indian legend.

Bierhorst, J. (1983). *The sacred path: Spells, prayers, and power songs of the American Indian.* New York: Morrow. (Ages 10+)

This book presents a variety of religious traditions of Native Americans.

Coatsworth, E., & Coatsworth, D. (1980). *The adventures of Nanabush: Ojibway Indian stories.* (F. Kagige, Illus.). New York: Atheneum. (Ages 5-12)

A story about an Ojibway Indian child and what childhood is like in the Ojibway tribe.

Esbensen, B. J. (1988a). *The star maiden.* (H. K. Davie, Illus.). Boston: Little, Brown. (Ages 7+)

The retelling of a Native American legend.

Esbensen, B. J. (1988b). *Ladder to the sky.* (H. K. Davie, Illus.). Boston: Little, Brown. (Ages 7+)

A Native American legend about climbing a ladder to reach the sky.

Fife, D. (1973). *Ride the crooked wind.* (R. Cuffari, Illus.). New York: Coward, McCann & Geoghegan. (Ages 10+)

A novel about a young Native American boy.

Goble, P. (1984). *Buffalo woman.* New York: Macmillian. (Ages 7+)

A picture book about the Plains Indians.

Goble, P. (1988). *Iktomi and the boulder: A Plains Indian story.* New York: Orchard Books. (Ages 7+)

A picture book about a humorous Plains Indian legend.

Hoyt-Goldsmith, D. (1991). *Pueblo storyteller*. (L. Midgale, Photo.). New York: Holiday House. (Ages 7+)

A book about a young girl who is the storyteller of her village.

Mayo, G. W. (1989). *Earthmaker's tales: North American Indian stories about earth happenings.* New York: Walker. (Ages 5-14)

Depicts how the earth was created and how it should be cared for by its people.

Miles, M. (1971). *Annie and the old one.* (P. Parnell, Illus.). Boston: Little, Brown. (Ages 6-9)

A young girl befriends an elderly Native American woman.

O'Dell, S. & Hall, E. (1992). *Thunder rolling in the mountains.* Boston: Houghton Mifflin. (Ages 10+)

This book tells of the desperate flight for freedom by the Nez Perce. It describes the wisdom and courage of their leader, Chief Joseph.

Sans Souci, R. (1978). *The legend of Scarface: A Blackfeet Indian tale* (D. Sans Souci, Illus.). New York: Doubleday. (Ages 7+)

The deeds of Scarface, a greatly feared warrior, are presented in this book.

Sneve, V. D. H. (1989). *Dancing tepees: Poems of American Indian youth.* New York: Holiday House. (Ages 4-14)

Poetry written by Native American children.

Yolen, J. (1992). *Encounter.* (D. Shannon, Illus.). San Diego: Harcourt Brace. (Ages 7+)

A Taino boy tells of Christopher Columbus's landing on San Salvador in 1492. Later, Spanish colonization alters the lifestyle, language, and religion of his tribe.

References

Barenbaum, E. M. (1983). Writing in the special class. *Topics in Learning & Learning Disabilities, 3*(3), 12-20.

Cline, R. K. J., & Taylor, B. L. (1987). Integrating literature and "free reading" into the social studies program. *Social Education, 42,* 27-31.

Cox, C., & Many, J. E. (1992). Toward understanding of the aesthetic response to literature. *Language Arts, 69* (1), 28-33.

Evans, K. M. (1992). Reading aloud: A bridge to independence. *New Advocate, 5*(1), 47-57.

Fountas, I. C., & Hannigan, I. L. (1989). Making sense of whole language: The pursuit of informed teaching. *Childhood Education, 65*(3), 133-137.

Fuhler, C. J. (1990). Let's move toward literature-based reading instruction. *Reading Teacher, 43,* 312-315.

Goodman, K. (1986). *What's whole in whole language?* Portsmouth, NH: Heinemann.

Graham, S., & Harris, K. (1988). Instructional recommendations for teaching writing to exceptional students. *Exceptional Children, 54* (6), 506-512.

Hansen, J. (1987). *When writers read.* Portsmouth, NH: Heinemann.

Hansen, M. B., & Schmidt, K. S. (1989). Promoting global awareness through trade books. *Middle School Journal, 21*(1), 34-37.

Learning disabilities: A definitional problem. (1990). *Education of the Handicapped, 16* (21), 5-6.

Lefstein, L. M. (1983). *The learning-disabled student, research and resources: Issues in middle-grade education.* Carrboro: University of North Carolina at Chapel Hill. (ERIC Document Reproduction Service No. ED 256 140)

Leigh, J. (1980). Whole language approaches: Premises and promises. *Learning Disability Quarterly, 3,* 46-53.

Levstik, L. (1989). *A gift of time: Children's historical fiction.* In J. Hickman & B. Cullinan (Eds.), *Children's literature in the classroom: Weaving Charlotte's Web.* Portsmouth, NH: Heinemann.

Markle, A. B. (1987). Developing critical thinking skills through literature. *School Library Media Quarterly, 16,* 43-44.

Moir, H. (Ed.). (1992). *Collected perspectives: Choosing and using books for the classroom* (2nd ed.). Boston: Christopher Gordon.

Poplin, M. S., Gray, R., Larsen, S., Banikowski, A., & Mehring, T. (1980). A comparison of components of written expression abilities in learning disabled and non-learning disabled students at three grade levels. *Learning Disability Quarterly, 3,* 46-53.

Rosenblatt, L. M. (1983). *Literature as exploration.* New York: Modern Language Association of America.

Rosenblatt, L. M. (1991). Literature—S.O.S.! *Language Arts, 68* (8), 444-448.

Routman, R. (1991). *Invitations: Changing as teachers and learners.* Portsmouth, NH: Heinemann.

Sherbenou, R. J., & Holub, S. (1982). The learning disabled adolescent. *Topics in Learning and Learning Disabilities, 2,* 40-54.

Smith, F. (1982). *Writing and the writer.* Hillsdale, NJ: Erblaum.

Smith, F. (1986). *Insult to intelligence: The bureaucratic invasion of our classrooms.* Portsmouth, NH: Heinemann.

Strickland, D. S. (1990). Emergent literacy: How young children learn to read and write. *Educational Leadership, 47,* 18-23.

Walmsley, S. (1984). Helping the learning disabled child overcome writing disabilities in the classroom. *Topics in Learning and Learning Disabilities, 3* (4), 81-90.

Wigfield, A., & Asher, S. (1984). Social and motivational influences on reading. In P. D. Pearson (Ed.), *Handbook on reading research.* New York: Longman.

Whyte, L. A. (1983). The learning disabled adolescent: A review of the research on learning disabled adolescents and its implications for the education of this population. *Mental Retardation and Learning Disability Bulletin, 11,* 134-141.

Young, T. A., & Vardall, G. (1993). Weaving readers theatre and nonfiction into the curriculum. *Reading Teacher, 46,* 396-405.

The Interactive Technology Environment

SUSAN M. COOPER

CALIFORNIA STATE UNIVERSITY, SAN BERNARDINO

The concept that we live on a round planet with large landmasses interrupted by vast oceans is a primary geography learning which is part of any elementary social studies program. At a more sophisticated level of learning, we want elementary students to appreciate the unity and diversity of our world and use technology as a basis for communicating with students in other places.

JOSEPH A. BRAUN

"Connecting the Globe: From Cardboard to Telecommunications"

■

Introduction

The role of technology has changed the American classroom, the responsibilities of the teacher, and the environment in which students can create new knowledge for themselves. Computer-based technology creates an interactive, discovery-based classroom that allows students to access data, question findings, and create new products that reflect the knowledge they have acquired.

In the early 1980s, if you had asked an elementary teacher how he or she was implementing the use of technology in the classroom, the response would probably have been, "I use an overhead projector, a VCR, 16-mm movies and a record player." If that same teacher had the good fortune to obtain a microcomputer for the classroom or had access to a lab of computers in the school, the students would probably have been exposed to a limited variety of software.

During the early to middle 1980s, attention began to turn toward microcomputers in the classroom. The software available at that time included a heavy dose of drill and practice (also known as "drill and kill"), a limited number of tutorials and simulations, and an assortment of games that used graphics and some color. These were all examples of computer-assisted instruction (CAI). This has been traditionally defined as instruction that is assisted through the use of computers and usually includes not only modes of delivery but also modes of interaction. The five generally recognized areas of CAI are tutorials, drill and practice, simulations, educational games, and problem solving (Cooper-Shoup, 1986).

However, a decade ago most teachers did not even have a computer in their classroom. And some of those who had one were not formally prepared to use it. Many teachers took it upon themselves to learn to use computers or obtained skills through the back door by asking their students to teach them. One thing was apparent early on. Children like to work with computers. They are motivated to work with their peers on tasks that can be accomplished with computers. They have fun and receive reinforcement while working with computers. But what was a teacher to do?

Classroom size continued to grow and the amount of resources never kept pace. The idea of using technology was and is appealing because of its ability to address the varied learning styles that students exhibit. Inherent in the use of technology is an ability to stimulate the senses of sight, sound, and touch and the ability to individualize, cooperate, or lead without any incongruence. The use of technology should be fundamental to the successful teaching of social studies. And the integration of technology is essential in a whole language approach to social studies instruction.

While the use of technology has been apparent in the elementary classroom for a long time in the form of radio, television, tape players, movie projectors, overhead projectors, and VCRs, it has taken the use of microcomputers to develop a new level of interactivity between the students and the machines and the students with themselves. Lockard, Abrams, and Many (1990, p. 164) refer to interactivity as "the user engaging in direct and continual two-way communication with the computer, responding to questions and receiving feedback to answers provided." The prior use of technology allowed the learner to be passive until the time came to discuss the movie, sing along with the song, or answer questions based on the video or overhead transparency. Early uses of computers also encouraged this passive mentality by allowing students to respond with simple keystrokes to worksheet-type programs.

The quality of CAI has improved dramatically in the past several years. While early versions of tutorials, drill and practice, and simulations offered little interaction, limited graphics, and a heavy dose of repetitive text, current software has increased the level of interaction and allows students to make a wide variety of choices. This development in software aligns itself neatly with the movement toward treating the learner as an active person capable of creating knowledge.

Tutorial Programs

Tutorial programs are a form of computer-based learning formerly referred to as CAI (computer-assisted instruction). They assume little or no prior knowledge and instruct the student in a new concept or new facts. Usually students are quizzed at appropriate points in the instruction to assure their mastery of the subject matter. A good tutorial allows students to choose their own level of presentation on the basis of what they already know. It allows them to choose the number of examples or problems they want to work with, and the program branches to easier or more difficult information at their request.

Early examples of this type of software include *Famous Blacks in U.S. History* by Frontier Software. This program presents the student with information about many African Americans who have made important contributions to American history and culture. *Dinosaur Dig* by Mindscape presents information related to the types, sizes, and other attributes of

■ Children benefit from the opportunity to use computers as learning tools.

dinosaurs and offers explanations for their disappearance from the earth. When students master the subject matter taught in the tutorial or if the subject matter has already been presented in class, they can go on to tackle a drill and practice program.

Drill and Practice Programs

Drill and practice programs presume prior knowledge of the concepts and drill the student for mastery. The student should be able to choose the number of problems he or she wishes to attempt and the level of difficulty encountered. These programs usually employ a multiple choice format and offer reinforcement for correct answers. Reinforcement may appear in the form of a comment such as, "Great job, Miguel! Keep Working!" or may appear as a choice to participate in an arcade-type game after a predetermined number of correct answers have been given. A good drill and practice program also includes cluing so that students will know whether their choice is correct but perhaps not spelled correctly. An early example of this type of program is MECC's *States.* Students are quizzed on the capitals of states and also on the location of states within specific geographic areas chosen by the student. A good rule of thumb might be to conclude mastery if 90% of the problems are answered successfully 90% of the time.

A good drill and practice program also allows students random choices of problems or situations so that they can repeat the program several times and not encounter the same scenarios each time. An enhancement of this type of program includes a management option that permits the teacher to record the progress of each individual student who attempts the problems.

While tutorial and drill and practice software allow interaction to occur between the student and the computer, simulation software increases this interaction dramatically.

Simulation Software

Simulations are based on sets of concepts and generalizations, called constructs or models, designed to describe real world phenomena (Rooze & Northup, 1989). Simulation software allows students to assume a role in which they are able to make decisions that have future consequences. Some simulation programs allow a limited amount of interactivity. These simulations take the information that the student chooses, and then a subsequent action occurs. The student must react to the new situation and observe how the cause and effect relationship evolves. For example, the MECC program *Odell Lake* assumes that the student is a type of fish and must take action in order not to be eaten by other fish. The program *Lemonade Stand* (MECC) allows students to create their own stand, buy their own supplies, make their own signs, and deal with situations that alter their plans to sell lemonade. In Hartley/Courseware's *Civil War* program, students choose which general they want to be and are then placed in battle scenarios. After they choose whether they want to act offensively or defensively, the action occurs and they must make subsequent decisions based on the battle results.

Students might also take a more active role such as becoming a pioneer on *The Oregon Trail* by MECC, or they might assume the role of a truck driver in *Crosscountry USA* by Didatech Software. Each of these programs requires students to face the decisions that had to be made by the respective pioneer or driver. *The Oregon Trail* allows students to choose the role of banker, farmer, or carpenter while selecting the names of their family members. Their quest includes choosing appropriate supplies to begin their journey from Independence, Missouri, to Oregon. Along the way, the family faces many perils, including illness, a hostile environment, hostile riders, and other situations that would naturally occur on such a journey. Students must decide at what pace they will travel, as well as when to trade, buy additional supplies, hunt for food, and ask for assistance. Students realize that as they progress through the arduous journey, their prior decisions have a direct bearing on the quality of life as well as their ability to complete their trek.

An updated version of this program, retitled *Wagon Train 1848,* allows students to form several independent wagon train teams interacting on a local area network. (A local area network, 'LAN', refers to several computers connected together for the purpose of sharing software or printers.) Each team reports to the trail captain, and the teams are aware of the movement and decisions made by other teams. This increases the interaction within and among the teams tremendously. Not only does this program allow students to assume realistic roles, it also allows student teams to compare the repercussions of their decisions as well as those of their peers.

Crosscountry USA allows the student to travel by truck and assume the role of the driver while reading maps, planning routes to a variety of cities, and solving problems resulting from circumstances encountered on the road. This program is also available in versions specific to Canada, Texas, and California.

The nature of simulations permits students to experience realistic situations and assume roles that normally would not be available to them. For example, historical barriers, safety factors, and the expense of travel can all be overcome through the use of a computer simulation.

The newest varieties of simulation afford students an even more active role. The Decisions, Decisions series by Tom Snyder Productions asks students to assume a position in a scenario and work in teams to decide how to handle a variety of confrontations. Among the individual programs in this series are *The Budget Process, Colonization, Foreign Policy, Immigration, Television, On the Campaign Trail, Revolutionary Wars,* and *Urbanization.* Each program provides students with detailed resources and workbooks to present a variety of viewpoints and then allows them as teams to make informed decisions. Each decision then creates a new scenario to be dealt with later in the simulation. For example, in the program *Colonization,* students must decide as the president how to colonize outer space. They must weigh environmental, budgetary, and political considerations. Similar decisions must be made in the program *Urbanization* when students assume the role of the mayor of a small town that discovers it has a valuable resource. They must decide whether to limit the growth of their town or exploit the value of the resource that has been discovered. The strength of the Decisions, Decisions series lies in its philosophy that students should work in groups cooperatively and use the computer as a resource and tool. The series assumes that only one computer is present in the classroom and that most of the group work will be done off-line (Fernlund, 1993).

Another simulation series that allows a high degree of student interaction and control is produced by Broderbund; its programs are *Sim-City, SimAnt,* and *SimEarth* and *SimLife.* These programs invite students to enter a microworld and make decisions at incredibly detailed and sophisticated levels (Dede, cited in Simonson & Thompson, 1990). Students can position their resources, housing, waste treatment, recreation, and so on at locations that are environmentally correct. They must make decisions that involve current as well as future repercussions at both the local and global levels.

Teachers at the upper elementary and middle school levels have gone so far as to create SimCities that the students work on every day as residents. They form committees and task forces to accomplish goals that include a cross section of subjects contained within the urban theme. Students then become involved in mathematics, science, and writing activities within the context of a social studies environment as they assume their roles as citizens.

This use of a microworld allows total interaction that relies on the computer as a vehicle to present scenarios, quantify data, report results and illustrate repercussions in a graphic and visual manner. Thus the computer is used as a tool rather than as an instructor. The interest that this format generates in students far exceeds that of only reading about the problems of cities or nations in a textbook. This holistic approach encourages students to think of solutions and act on their ideas. It also requires students to take responsibility for their actions within a group setting and further allows each student to assume a role within his or her cooperative group. Moreover, it encourages students to take multiple viewpoints and see the results of acting on them. Such a child-centered approach encourages hands-on activities where students learn best by doing. Oral and written language acquisition increases as students interact with each other, the program, and the teacher as facilitator.

Gerald Bracey (1988) reports on two empirical studies that showed better performance by students using CAI in cooperative groups than by students working alone. In the first study, three groups of eighth graders worked with a social studies simulation program. The cooperative group performed better than the competitive group and the students who worked individually, as evaluated by the number of daily worksheets completed and by final examination scores. The teachers reported that the students in the cooperative group were more goal oriented and task persistent than students in the other groups.

In the second study, conducted with students in Israel, the subjects were divided into two groups, those who studied language with CAI by themselves and those who studied in pairs. The subjects were tested on achievement as well as their attitudes toward classmates. The findings showed slightly higher achievement test scores, more altruistic attitudes toward teammates, and a favorable disposition toward cooperative learning on the part of the pairs when compared to the individuals.

Educational Adventure Games

Another form of computer-based instruction is the educational adventure game. Such games include a level of competition and require the use of logic and problem solving as opposed to rote memory. A student assumes a role and must work against time to achieve a goal.

The Carmen Sandiego series by Broderbund is a popular example of this type of software. *Where in the World Is Carmen Sandiego?, Where in the USA Is Carmen Sandiego?, Where in Europe Is Carmen Sandiego?, Where in Time Is Carmen Sandiego?,* and *Where in America's Past Is Carmen Sandiego?* are examples of "whodunits" in which the student must be the detective who races the clock to find the traveling thieves who leave clues and talk to tipsters. Each time the student enters a city, country, or era, he or she must use the resources available to determine where next to search. These programs include ancillary materials such as *Fodor's USA Travel Guide (1986), Rand McNally Concise Atlas of Europe (1988),* and the *World Almanac and Book of Facts.* Children love the silly names of the culprits in this series and can acquire an amazing amount of useful information about the cities they quickly visit.

Another application of this set of programs includes the use of student-constructed data bases that assemble all the clues and information about the various locales. As students race the clock using the text material provided, they can also use a second computer to search their data base for quick cross-referencing of information. In this way, they have their own crime computer (Greenman, 1990).

Some teachers who use the Carmen Sandiego series regularly, encourage Carmen Sandiego Days. On these days the students dress as the suspects or citizens of the countries to which they have traveled, prepare food from the different countries, and draw or construct examples of buildings and scenery they have observed within the series. This is certainly a way to make geography come alive for children who cannot physically visit many countries. Other programs of this type include the Spy's Adventure series by Polarware. Blue Lion Software's *Ticket to Paris, Ticket to Washington, D.C.,* and so on require students to answer questions about aspects of a culture while trying to reach a destination in a particular city within a time limit.

Other programs that deal with competition in national and international terms also involve the use of reference skills. *National Inspirer* and *International Inspirer* by Tom Snyder Productions encourage group work off-line to accumulate information to form strategies that will enable teams to reach a predetermined goal. Students must move from state to state or country to country and are provided with booklets that contain detailed maps, charts, graphs, and lists of information pertinent to the states or countries. Student groups must then decide which states or countries are appropriate for their movement to the desired final destination. Students are only allowed to move to contiguous states or countries. Inherent in this work is the development of vocabulary, interpretation of

■ Software programs enable children to learn how to become decision makers.

maps and graphs, and collaboration in devising a strategy that will earn a maximum number of points. Students not only enjoy the competitiveness of these games; they also acquire an amazing amount of information about individual locales. These programs can be used with a variety of scenarios that could last from minutes per week to a short period each day for months, depending on the age and abilities of the students.

Problem-Solving Software

Software that deals with problem solving requires students to use logic and deduction to solve problems that are not necessarily linked to a specific subject or curriculum area. This type of software provides exercises in comparing different versus similar objects, recognizing patterns, using rules, and working with attributes and classification. Several excellent Sunburst programs in this category include *Teddy's Playground, Iggy's Gnees, Tip 'N' Flip, Ten Clues,* and *High Wire Logic.*

Computer Literacy

At the same time that many teachers began using CAI in their classrooms, others were teaching computer literacy. This usually included the history of computers, keyboarding, and programming in BASIC. Early efforts at programming stressed the problem-solving aspects of creating software primarily because few schools had good collections of educational software. As the impetus to teach programming waned, the use of application software increased. Today, many educators consider the issue of computer literacy to revolve around a person's ability to use software appropriate to the needed task, as well as to problem solve hardware and software situations.

Application Software

The term *application software* usually refers to programs that allow users to create products or perform tasks. Application software can include word processing, data-base management, spreadsheets and telecommunications programs. Some of these application programs come "bundled" together in an integrated program in which applications are available at the same time. Pogue (1992) believes that the foregoing applications are the minimum that should be included in an integrated package. In addition, he describes packages that also include modules that chart, draw, paint, and outline.

Teachers began to use word processing software to enable their students to write more easily and more enjoyably. One early program that accomplished this goal was *Bank Street Writer* by Broderbund. The simple format presented as a writing square permitted students to easily write, edit, print, and save their work on a data disk. Other examples of word processing software that were and are applicable to the elementary classroom include Computer Using Educators' *FrEd Writer,* and Sunburst's *Magic Slate* and *Muppet Slate* utilizing the *Muppet Learning Keys.* These keys are on a special plastic keyboard where the letters are arranged alphabetically. Children can use the traditional keyboard or the Muppet keyboard.

Today's word processing programs for student use have become much more sophisticated. Routinely, students are able to call up spell checkers, on-line thesauruses and dictionaries, and even grammar checkers to improve the quality of their work. If a teacher wishes young students to incorporate graphics into word processed documents that they create, Spinnaker Software's *KidWriter* in its English or Spanish version would be a good choice. The students can create their own stories and choose appropriate graphics to illustrate them. Children in grades 1 and 2 might use Toucan Pelican's *Big Book Maker* to create their own big books. This program enables them to tell their own stories to the class, and the size of the big books enables all the students to see the stories as well. These programs can also be used to allow very young students to dictate a story from a character's point of view to their teacher. The teacher keys in the story, prints it, and puts it in a class book complete with pictures colored or created by the "author."

Print Shop (Broderbund) is a popular program that enables students to create their own banners, cards, invitations, and T-shirt transfers. Teachers or students can design a class logo and create a transfer by using the *Print Shop* program with a dot matrix printer, printing backward.

The Learning Company's *The Children's Writing and Publishing Center* and the *Writing Center* are two programs that enable students in grades 4 through 8 to use principles of desktop publishing to create documents. These programs include a variety of type fonts, font sizes, and colors. With them, students can create newspaper columns, diaries, journals, and yearbooks. If a lesson plan calls for students to create their own poems, speeches, or political cartoons, these programs would help create professional looking products that the students could create easily and with pride.

The editing feature inherent in application programs allows the teacher to devote more attention to content and the process of writing than to the mechanics of producing paper. Moreover, students who have good ideas and write well are not penalized by a possible inability to produce a clean, neat handwritten paper.

The development of language, spoken and written, is crucial for students in elementary school. Whether a student is writing in the first person or assumes the role or character of another, the opportunity to write for an audience is a necessity. The use of word processing, desktop publishing, and telecommunications can enhance writing efforts. Let's take journal or diary writing as an example. Suppose a student assumes the role of a historical figure such as a soldier in the Revolutionary War or a pioneer girl traveling across the Great Plains. After having read primary source material such as diaries and newspaper articles or children's literature, the student can then create a day-by-day series of journal or diary entries by using a word processing program that is appropriate for his or her age. *Magic Slate* (Sunburst), *KidWriter* (Spinnaker), and *FrEd Writer* (Computer Using Educators) might be good choices for lower elementary school students. *AppleWorks* (Claris), *ClarisWorks* (Claris), and *Microsoft Works* (Microsoft) are appropriate for upper elementary or middle school students.

When students work together in pairs, one can key while the other reads over a rough draft or prepares one. The second student can edit the work of the first, or the two students can create their material together. Peer editing is especially useful with partners who have strengths in different areas. The student who keys well can be paired with a student who reads and edits well. After a designated period of time, the partners can assume the opposite roles.

Another way to increase keyboarding skill and allow students to prepare a neat finished product is to have them write letters to local or state government officials about issues that are of concern to them. The ability to use sophisticated writing aids such as word wrap, delete, a spell checker, an on-line thesaurus, and a variety of type fonts and sizes can help students create professional looking letters that increase their self-esteem as well as get their point across to an audience.

Several useful programs are available for creating a class newspaper or recreating a historical newspaper. *The Newsroom* (Springboard), *The Children's Writing and Publishing Center* (Learning Company), *The Writing Center* (Learning Company), *Publish It!* (Timeworks), *Publish It! Easy* (Timeworks), *Mac Write II, Pro* (Claris) in English and Spanish, and *PageMaker* (Aldus) are all good choices. Each of these programs allows students to create realistic newspaper columns with a variety of headlines and graphics as well as justified text. More sophisticated programs permit students to import graphics from data disks as well as scanned images. Children find it very exciting to choose graphics and pictures to accompany their stories.

Integrated Applications Used as Utility Software

The use of integrated application programs in elementary classrooms began in 1983 with *AppleWorks* (Claris). The earliest edition of this program contained word processing, data-base management, and a spreadsheet, all in one package. It allowed students to integrate their written reports or letters with files from a data base or calculations from a spreadsheet. Needless to say, teachers were able to use this type of program to great advantage as well. It permitted them to create a letter to send home to parents. Within that letter was a record of their child's personal information from the data base and grade book calculations from the spreadsheet, providing an up-to-the-minute assessment of the child's work. The mail-merge function allowed letters and address labels to be printed quickly and easily for a truly personal touch. Newer versions of this type of program include graphics, telecommunications, and page layout components as well. Programs such as *Microsoft Works* (Microsoft), *ClarisWorks* (Claris), *GreatWorks* (Symantec), and *Works for Windows* (Microsoft) allow users not only to merge files from other applications but also to use one application within another.

A different type of application software that is particularly useful in a social studies classroom is a utility program called *Timeliner* by Tom Snyder Productions. This easy-to-use program allows students to create their own time lines in as small or large increments as desired. Students can save their work and revise it later by including additional data. They can create time lines for their own birthdays, historical events, and projects they are working on in simulation activities. Such time lines print out easily in a banner format and can be used by any grade in elementary school.

Data-Base Programs

The use of data-base information is crucial to a social studies classroom. Students can use existing data bases (collections of information) for the purpose of comparing, contrasting and evaluating relationships. On the other hand, students can create their own data bases by means of application programs.

Some of the new geographic data-base software is very useful for making predictions, investigating hypotheses, and compiling reports. MECC's *World GeoGraph* and *USA Geograph* and Comwell Systems' *PC Globe-Plus* and *PC USA* are programs that combine the power of a data base on countries of the world or states of the union with the visual representation of charts, graphs, and data cards in a variety of colors. Students can identify single states or countries, graph characteristics of regions by themes, or arrange countries or states in order according to their position on a certain theme such as number of automobiles, literacy rate, or gross national product. Because of the computer's ability to sort the data so quickly and display it in such a visual manner, students are quickly able to observe comparisons and results.

Other programs such as *Bank Street School Filer* by Sunburst include not only the master program for creating and editing data bases but also individually prepared data bases on colonial times, the United States, and North America. MECC's Dataquest series has a similar format and includes programs on the presidents, the world community, and the fifty states. These programs are especially useful if you have only one computer in the classroom and are using it as a reference, display, or presentation device. Students can query the data base and continue to work in groups or individually at their seats.

The arrival of application software in the classroom signaled an important change in approach and purpose. Prior to this time, computers were looked upon as an extension of the regular classroom activities, including worksheets, teacher-directed and teacher-centered activities, text-based curriculum, and lower-level drill and repetition. In the late 1980s and early 1990s, the emphasis in many classrooms began to shift toward a child-centered curriculum with more meaningful and relevant instruction. In this environment, the child learns best by hands-on activity.

Cooperative Learning

Cooperative learning in its many forms is conducive to the type of experience in which each student makes a contribution that is relevant for group growth. This contributory environment emphasizes active rather than passive participation. This coincides with the movement in technology integration to make active learning the norm, where the child tells the computer what to do rather than the reverse. Arthur Luehrmann (cited in Johnson, 1980, p. 19) refers to computer literacy this way:

> One who is truly computer literate must be able to "do computing"—to conceptualize problems algorithmically, to represent them in the syntax of a computer language, to identify conceptual "bugs," and to express computational ideas clearly, concisely, and with a high degree of organization and readability. Every student should be able to use the computer as an intellectual tool with applications to whatever subject matter is taught.

While this approach was soft-pedaled by some in the middle 1980s, the inherent truth in this statement has returned full circle. Students who are creating knowledge and sharing it with their peers and teachers are not only increasing their own skills but helping those of other students.

Social studies instruction intuitively should be cooperative and active. Some of the goals of social studies instruction in a whole language integrated curriculum should be to develop in the child a positive self-concept, knowledge about the concepts of social studies, feelings of competence, and the ability to work with others. Skill development as well as conceptual development can thrive in an environment of exploration and problem solving. Technology integration can facilitate this exploration.

The use of application software within the social studies classroom can take several forms. When first introduced in the mid-1980s, the components were often used individually. By using a thematic approach, a teacher can utilize the three modules of word processing, data-base management, and spreadsheet to create an exciting unit idea.

The program *Immigrant* was developed at Harvard University as an exercise for middle school students. This disk is distributed as shareware. Shareware is software that users can try out and then pay for later if they choose to continue to use it. *Immigrant* allows teams of students to adopt an Irish family coming to the United States in the 1840s. Using database information on a ship's records, students choose a family and make decisions for them. Other data-base files include information on housing, jobs, and transportation in the 1840s and 1850s. In addition, students examine spreadsheet files to buy clothing, food, and supplies as well as keep a budget. They also use the word processing feature to keep a diary about their lives over a ten to twenty-year period. As students combine imaginary situations with accurate historical data, they must confront the obstacles one faces while trying to make a new home in a foreign country. Low wages, prejudice, and cultural differences weigh heavily in all the decisions the students must make. Students must also grapple with unfamiliar vocabulary, products, and locations. By using maps and other ancillary materials, students in teams interpret and calculate mathematical data, create journal entries, balance budgets, make predictions, and solve problems. This particular program can also be used in a one-computer classroom or with individual groups using one computer per group. *Immigrant* is available in *AppleWorks* and *Microsoft Works* formats.

Telecommunications

Another avenue to explore within application software is the use of telecommunications. Certain equipment is necessary for one computer to talk to another computer in a different location. The computers must be connected to a telephone line by means of a modem. This device translates a computer signal into one that the telephone can transmit. A 2400 baud modem is preferable and can be purchased as an interface card that is inserted into the computer or as an external device. Finally, software such as the communications module in *Microsoft Works, ClarisWorks,* or *Apple-Works GS* is necessary. For this exciting classroom option, a phone line that operates independently of the main school switchboard is preferred.

According to Bernie Dodge (1991), four types of telecommunications experiences are appropriate for children. The first is unstructured and impersonal: children explore the power of telecommunications and go on-line with a bulletin board system. The second is unstructured and personal; students communicate with others such as electronic pen pals. The third type of experience is structured and impersonal; children retrieve data from on-line data bases. The fourth type is structured and personal and involves being video pals or collaboratively setting goals with others in remote locations.

A host of on-line data-base services are available for a fee, either a monthly charge or a per minute charge for access. Among these services are CompuServe, Prodigy, and America On-Line. In addition, teachers can enroll in such subscription services as the National Geographic Kids Network. These provide unit materials that students can use with peers across the country. Current projects include a data base of pets and an acid rain experiment in which students collect, compare, and interpret data as well as communicate with professional scientists and educators across the country.

Other telecommunications projects suitable for social studies classrooms might simply involve communicating with students in another school in the district or across the country as electronic pen pals. On the FrEdMail Network, student work can be sent through local nodes to far destinations. This gives students an audience for their writing, and they get quicker responses than they would receive by traditional mail. Students might also use telecommunications to correspond with retirement home residents, students in schools in foreign countries, or mentor students at the high school level. Such efforts allow students to reach out to a group of people they would normally never meet. Children find it exciting to have a new friend as well as an audience for their writing.

Some classrooms have extended this initiative to include video pen pals after establishing the connection by computer. A classroom of California students became so intrigued by the letters they exchanged by modem with students in Australia that they decided to create a video to see what their Australian counterparts looked like. This deepened the bond between the two groups as they exchanged information about their lives. Teachers should carefully investigate the merits versus the costs of on-line services when choosing the most appropriate alternative for their personal and/or classroom use.

Laser Discs: Videodiscs and CD-ROM

Videodiscs and CD-ROM have the potential to revolutionize the delivery of information. A laser videodisc contains one hour of full-motion video or 110,000 frames of still pictures. Because these videodiscs are read by light, they cannot be worn down and are very difficult to damage (Van Horn, 1987). Access to any frame on a videodisc can be achieved in 2 seconds or less. The quality of the pictures is far superior to that of videotape, and the quality of the sound is superb.

CD-ROM (compact disc, read only memory) is a type of disc that can hold over 150,000 printed pages. The computer treats CD-ROM as an external storage device like a floppy drive. This peripheral allows the student to access immense data bases, music, artwork, photos, and a limited amount of video. Again, because the disc is read by light, there is no wear and tear from magnetic heads (Tanner & Bane, 1988). An entire encyclopedia can be contained on one 5-inch disc. Discis Books (Discis Knowledge Research) allow students to read along with a storybook while the book reads aloud to them. These books are available in English, Spanish, and Cantonese. They can be customized so that the user can click on a word and get a pronunciation, syllabication, definition, or translation of the word. In addition, the user can make a list of chosen words for later reference. The books are presented in color on the computer monitor, and the words are read in a variety of voices (Parham, 1993). The Living Books Series by Broderbund includes "Just Grandma and Me" and "Arthur's Teacher Trouble" which are interactive books on CD-ROM that allow the student to discover how each screen comes alive with hidden buttons.

GTV (National Geographic Society) is a geographic laser disc that allows the learner to access portions of American History through geographic themes. This laser disc combines still photos, artwork, diaries, speeches, full-motion video, and graphics such as charts, maps, and graphs to explain 60 historical themes. Students are able to hear first-person accounts that illustrate the American struggle along with stunning visual effects (Fernlund & Cooper-Shoup, 1991). ABC News Interactive (Optical Data) has produced a series of laser discs that appeal directly to a social studies curriculum. *Martin Luther King and the*

Struggle for Civil Rights, In the Holy Land, The Great Quake of '89, Powers of the President, Powers of the Congress, and *Powers of the Supreme Court* are all examples of still- and full-motion video footage, speeches, and text material that can be used in any order. Students can create a personal lineup of scenes from the laser discs to create their own video term paper. They can determine how long each clip is shown, in what order it is shown, and when to make transitions between lineups.

Multimedia

The implementation of multimedia, also known as integrated media, includes the use of audio, video, text, graphics, and animation. When students use a program such as *HyperCard* by Apple Computer or *Linkway* by IBM, they are creating software to tell the computer what they want it to do. They are including links to other parts of the program that can be linear but can also navigate in nonlinear directions. These programs can be used alone for instructional purposes, or they can be used to interface with videodiscs or CD-ROM. This nonlinear software used with multimedia is known as hypermedia.

Students who use hypermedia to create projects in the social studies are using a holistic approach. The tasks involved in this production include reading, writing, problem solving, and cooperating in groups. Students can choose the path that is most logical to them. They can incorporate text, sound, graphics, video, and speech. They can infuse a multitude of languages and themes by using their own voices and choosing their own areas of interest. The products they create are original and representative of their own talents. This approach to the social studies is a big departure from using a textbook alone. Litchfield and Dempsey (1992) describe the learning environment established with videodisc technology as a healthy one characterized by a success-oriented and risk-free atmosphere where the process is as important as the product created.

Technology can free teachers to allow students to learn in a variety of ways. It can free teachers to express themselves in a way that focuses on the learner's preferred style of learning. It can allow students to create a multitude of projects that are personal, meaningful, and innovative. D'Ignazio (1990) refers to such teachers and students as teams of "knowledge explorers" who translate textbook knowledge into new, exciting multimedia presentations. Those who use an overhead projector, filmstrips and videotape are on the road to bigger and better things. A key to using technology is getting past one's fears that one cannot make it work. Teachers can make it work, and their students will gain a great deal from the experience.

■ Modern technology enables both students and teachers to combine discussion and written reports with scenes from laser discs to further emphasize points and present concepts.

Changing Role of the Teacher

The role of the teacher necessarily changes in a whole language, technologically integrated classroom. He or she becomes the facilitator of activities and the coordinator of group work. Rather than dispensing facts and information, the teacher asks the probing questions that allow students to pursue the answers on their own. The types of programs available to students today are radically different from those introduced in the early 1980s. Giving low-level recall responses has been replaced by using nonlinear approaches to pursue new lines of thinking. The latter activity paves the way for a variety of software programs that were not previously used in the social studies classroom.

Because the teacher's role is changed in this interactive environment, the preparation required of the teacher changes too. Instead of preparing lecture notes, worksheets, or objective tests to evaluate memorization, the teacher must search out activities that allow students, individually and in groups, to take advantage of the variety of technologies available. The teacher must evaluate software (a time-consuming task), choose appropriate tracks from laser videodiscs, contact other teachers to enable their students to correspond electronically, and investigate hardware solutions that will enable students to share software on networks. Many teachers participate in workshops in their own district or take coursework at the local university to learn the curricular uses of technology.

This changing role also requires a different attitude toward student learning. It requires less controlling behavior on the part of the teacher, yet it demands organization and preparation. The role of the student then evolves into that of an active learner—as does the role of the teacher.

Summary

This chapter has described a progression of computer-based technologies from the early 1980s to the present. The role of the teacher as well as the student has changed radically through the effective use of technology in the classroom.

While all classrooms do not have one computer for every student, this should not discourage teachers from making efforts to integrate technology into their curricula. Many lesson ideas, presentation/demonstration efforts, and management functions can be accomplished in a one-computer classroom. The use of cooperative grouping and directed off-line work can allow maximum use of what is available. In the social studies classroom, technology should be a transparent application that is used as naturally as a pencil or pen.

Software

Powers of the President
Powers of the Congress
Powers of the Supreme Court
The Great Quake of '89
Martin Luther King and the
*   Struggle for Civil Rights*
In the Holy Land
ABC News Interactive

OPTICAL DATA CORPORATION
30 Technology Drive
Warren, NJ 07060

PageMaker

ALDUS CORPORATION
411 First Avenue South, Suite 200
Seattle, WA 98104

AMERICA ON-LINE
8619 Westwood Center Drive
Vienna, VA 22182

HyperCard

APPLE COMPUTER, INC.
20525 Marianni Avenue
Cupertino, CA 95014

RSVP Ticket to Hollywood
Ticket to London
Ticket to Paris
Ticket to Spain
Ticket to Washington, D.C.

BLUE LION SOFTWARE
90 Sherman Street
Cambridge, MA 02140

Arthur's Teacher Trouble
Just Grandma and Me
SimAnt
SimCity
SimEarth
SimLife
Bank Street Writer
Print Shop
Where in Europe Is Carmen
    Sandiego?
Where in America's Past Is
    Carmen Sandiego?
Where in Time Is Carmen
    Sandiego?
Where in the U.S.A. Is Carmen
    Sandiego?
Where in the World Is Carmen
    Sandiego?

BRODERBUND SOFTWARE
17 Paul Drive
San Rafael, CA 94903-2101

MacWrite II, Pro
AppleWorks
ClarisWorks

CLARIS CORPORATION
5201 Patrick Henry Drive
Santa Clara, CA 95052

**COMPUSERVE CONSUMER INFORMATION
SERVICE**
P.O. Box 20212
Columbus, OH 43220

FrEdWriter

**FREDMAIL NETWORK
COMPUTER USING EDUCATORS, INC.**
P.O. Box 2087
Menlo Park, CA 94026

PC Globe-Plus
PC USA

COMWELL SYSTEMS INC.
2100 S. Rural Road
Tempe, AZ 85282

Crosscountry USA

DIDATECH SOFTWARE LTD.
3812 William Street
Burnaby, British Columbia
Canada V5C 3H9

Discis Books

DISCIS KNOWLEDGE RESEARCH, INC.
45 Sheppard Avenue East, Suite 410
Toronto, Ontario,
Canada M2N 5W9

Famous Blacks in U.S. History

FRONTIER SOFTWARE
P.O. Box 56505
Houston, TX 77227

The Civil War

HARTLEY COURSEWARE, INC.
133 Bridge Street
Diamondale, MI 48821

IBM Linkway

IBM CORPORATION
P.O. Box 1328-W
Boca Raton, FL 33429-1328

The Children's Writing and Publishing Center
The Writing Center

THE LEARNING COMPANY
6493 Kaiser Drive
Fremont, CA 94555

Lemonade Stand
MECC Dataquest Series
The Oregon Trail
Wagon Train 1848
USA GeoGraph
World GeoGraph
Odell Lake
States

MECC
3490 Lexington Avenue North
St. Paul, MN 55126-8097

Microsoft Works
Works for Windows

MICROSOFT CORPORATION
1 Microsoft Way
P.O. Box 97017
Redmond, WA 98052

Dinosaur Dig

MINDSCAPE, INC.
3444 Dundee Road, Dept. C
Northbrook, IL 60062

GTV: A Geographic Perspective on American History

NATIONAL GEOGRAPHIC KIDS NETWORK
National Geographic Society
Washington, DC 20036

Big Book Maker

TOUCAN PELICAN SOFTWARE
768 Farmington Avenue
Farmington, CT 06032

The Spy's Adventures in South America
The Spy's Adventures in North America
The Spy's Adventures in Europe
The Spy's Adventures in Asia
The Spy's Adventures in Africa
The Spy's Adventures in the Pacific Islands

POLARWARE
P.O. Box 311
521 Hamilton Avenue
Geneva, IL 60134

PRODIGY SERVICES COMPANY
White Plains, NY 10601

KidWriter (English or Spanish)
KidWriter (Golden Edition)

SPINNAKER SOFTWARE CORP.
One Kendall Square
Cambridge, MA 02139

The Newsroom

SPRINGBOARD SOFTWARE, INC.
7808 Creekridge Circle
Minneapolis, MN 55435

Bank Street School Filer
High Wire Logic
Iggy's Gnees
Magic Slate
Muppet Learning Keys
Muppet Slate
Teddy's Playground
Ten Clues
Tip 'N' Flip

SUNBURST COMMUNICATIONS
39 Washington Avenue
Pleasantville, NY 10570

GreatWorks

SYMANTEC CORP.
10201 Torre Avenue
Cupertino, CA 95914

Publish It!
Publish It! Easy

TIMEWORKS, INC.
444 Lake Cook Road
Deerfield, IL 60015-4919

Decisions, Decisions Series
   The Budget Process
   Colonization
   Foreign Policy
   Immigration
   On the Campaign Trail
   Revolutionary Wars
   Television
   Urbanization
International Inspirer
National Inspirer
Timeliner

TOM SNYDER PRODUCTIONS
90 Sherman Street
Cambridge, MA 02140

References

Bracey, G. (1988, January). Two studies show students gain when teaming up. *Electronic Learning,* p. 19.

Braun, J. A. (1992). Connecting the globe: From cardboard to telecommunications. *Social Studies and the Young Learner, 4,* 31–32.

Cooper-Shoup, S. (1986). *The effects of self-paced and group instruction on microcomputer literacy among secondary preservice teachers.* Unpublished doctoral dissertation, Northern Illinois University, DeKalb, IL.

D'Ignazio, F. (1990, September). Integrating the work environment of the 1990s into today's classrooms. *Technological Horizons in Education Journal,* pp. 95–96.

Dodge, B. (1991). *Telecommunications.* Presentation at the Christopher Columbus Consortium, California State University, Dominguez Hills, Carson, CA.

Fernlund, P., & Cooper-Shoup, S. (1991). Hypermedia and social studies. *Social Studies Review, 30*(3), 66–70.

Fernlund, P. M. (1993). Learners, technology and law-related education. *Law Studies,* XVIII (1), 3–5.

Greenman, M. D. (1990, October). A computer based problem solving geography unit. *Computing Teacher,* pp. 22–24.

Johnson, M. F. (1980). Computer literacy: What is it? *Business Education Forum, 35*(3), 18–22.

Litchfield, B. C., & Dempsey, J. V. (1992). The IVD-equipped classroom: Integrating videodisc technology into the curricula. *Journal of Educational Multimedia and Hypermedia, 1,* 39-49.

Lockard, J., Abrams, P. & Many, W. (1990). *Microcomputers for educators.* Glenview, IL: Scott, Foresman/Little, Brown Higher Education.

Parham, C. (1993). CD-ROM storybooks: New ways to enjoy children's literature. *Technology and Learning, 13*(4), 34-44.

Pogue, L. (1992). You get the works with integrated tools. Electronic Learning, *11*(6), 36-37.

Rooze, G. E. & Northup, T. (1989). *Computers, thinking and social studies.* Englewood, CO: Teacher Ideas Press.

Simonson, M., & Thompson, A. (1990). *Educational computing foundations.* Columbus, OH: Merrill.

Tanner, D. F., & Bane, R. K. (1988, August). CD-ROM: A new technology with promise for education. *Technological Horizons in Education Journal,* pp. 57-60.

Van Horn, R. (1987). Laser videodiscs in education: Endless possibilities. *Phi Delta Kappan, 68*(9), 696-698.

Assessing Social Studies in Whole Language Classrooms

MARGARET A. ATWELL
CALIFORNIA STATE UNIVERSITY, SAN BERNARDINO

Let us take social imagination and critical literacy very seriously. As we position our assessment mirrors so that we can view these more clearly, we will find that their reflections will become increasingly part of the stories we tell about ourselves as consequential teachers and the stories children tell about themselves as literate citizens.

PETER H. JOHNSTON
Assessment and Literate "Development"

Introduction

A new instructional paradigm or model requires a new approach to assessment. Over the past few years, much has been written about how to teach "whole language." The methods that are found in these meaning-based, child-centered classrooms have been described in this book and others and are being used in classrooms across the country. Recently, whole language teachers, growing confident in their classroom practices, have become increasingly uncomfortable with and critical of the testing programs and evaluation instruments they must use (Costa, 1989; Goodman, Goodman, & Hood, 1989). Assessing student learning is a difficult task, and if the instructional program does not match the evaluation procedures, scores and grades are not valid. Whole language teachers are pushing for immediate and requisite change. They often feel that the selection of the tools used to measure the outcomes of their students' learning is out of their hands. They feel that the results of the tests they are required to give are of little use to them or, worse, conflict with their own observations and opinions about what their students know. As Worthen (1993, p. 445) writes, "Proponents of alternative assessment prefer it to more traditional assessment that relies on indirect 'proxy' tasks (usually test items). Sampling tiny snippets of student behavior, they point out, does not provide insight into how students would perform on truly 'worthy' intellectual tasks."

Assessment in a whole language classroom requires that the teacher's opinions be highly regarded. It is the teacher's daily observations and interactions with students that are the most informed source of understanding of what and how students learn. Assessment requires that, in addition to knowing the content that is to be taught, teachers must know a great deal about their students' background, experiences, and goals. Whole language teachers are concerned not only with the outcomes or products of their teaching but with the processes in which their students engage as they learn. Evaluation must include indications of not only the quantity that is learned but the quality and depth of information students come to know. Teachers are making changes in the way they assess students, and these changes reflect the methods they use and the goals they have for instruction.

FIGURE 14.1

■

Bloom's taxonomy of educational objectives: cognitive domain.

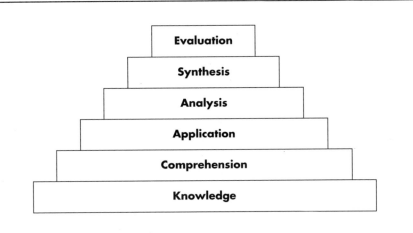

The Traditional Social Studies Classroom

Teaching and learning in a traditional social studies classroom follows a *skills model* of learning. The skills model became popular in the 1950s and 1960s, powered by behaviorism and given structure by the work of learning theorists who believed that knowledge and the learning process are hierarchical. Each of these theorists developed a taxonomy (classification of types of knowledge) of subskills that he or she argued represents the structure of knowledge and provides a plan for instruction and evaluation. Although each taxonomy included different skills in differing order, each followed the same basic design.

In general, according to each taxonomy, thinking begins with basic or low level units such as recognition or recall and progresses upward to the higher levels of synthesis or creativity. These theorists believed that learning is additive and universal, composed of building blocks or steps. According to them, each learner goes through each step in the same order. If a step is missed, the learner must go back and pick it up.

Learning problems were understood to be the result of missing information, and remediation was readily prescribed. By using a taxonomy as a guide, questions could be designed to elicit specific levels of knowledge or thinking skills, diagnose any weakness or misunderstanding, and provide prescriptive profiles for future grouping or instruction. Teachers were led to believe that taxonomies could provide a precise picture of what a student learned. While many theorists devised cognitive taxonomies, others developed affective taxonomies as well. One example of a cognitive taxonomy is Benjamin Bloom's (1956) (see Figure 14.1).

In the traditional skills class or lesson, evaluation follows this model and is most often accomplished by testing. Tests are almost always written and involve objective, multiple choice, true–false, or short-answer questions. This model of evaluation is a poor fit for a holistic classroom, which focuses on the meaning of topics, is child centered, and integrates the curriculum across many subject areas.

The Whole Language Classroom

Whole language is not a method to be followed or a dogma to be believed. Rather, it is a perspective, derived from a constructivist philosophy of learning, that views learning as a natural process (Goodman, 1986). Many people have described whole language (Edelsky, Altwerger, & Flores, 1986; Goodman, 1986; Goodman & Goodman, 1981; Harste, Woodward, & Burke, 1985; Newman, 1985).

Whole language educators believe that the drive for knowledge is one of the most basic and inherent characteristics of all humans. The human mind, starting at birth, categorizes and sorts out the input it receives from the surrounding world and builds complex systems of meaning (Smith, 1989). Whole language educators believe that there is nothing artificial about learning. It is as natural and easy as breathing. Whole language teachers attempt to design their classrooms to support the way that learning naturally occurs and to create environments that allow growth and change through active learning. They avoid artificial or rigid control.

Assumptions About Learning and Teaching

Most whole language educators make certain assumptions about the nature of learning and teaching that have direct bearing on how learning is evaluated.

1. Learning is individual. In really successful situations, each child will learn something different and unique. To a great degree, what children learn is determined by what they already know. Prior knowledge is a potent influence on new knowledge.
2. The goal of testing is to demonstrate knowledge. While group tests and standardized measures can provide some usable information to teachers, alternative means must be available for students to demonstrate their knowledge. Student responses must be considered individually for their logic and content, not necessarily for correctness or the degree to which they match the teacher's expected response.

■ Conferencing with students is a part of the evaluation process.

3. Not all students learn at the same pace, so the opportunities for students to demonstrate their learning need to be flexible. Testing all students only once and at the same time fails to account for all the differences in background and is basically unfair to some students. Any timetable used when measuring knowledge must be flexible.

4. Because they work with students daily, teachers are in the best situation to observe learning in action. Teacher observation or "kidwatching" (Goodman, 1986) is a reliable and valid means of assessment. Those who argue that testing must be pure and scientific and conducted by experts who are totally removed from the classroom environment are incorrect and misunderstand the teacher's role as an informed observer (Bertrand, 1991). Teachers' informal assessments are meaningful and can be systematically recorded and reported.

5. Evaluation is personal. Standardized testing depersonalizes learning and forces teachers to place students in relative status that is not supportive of learning. Many children are actually hurt by their testing program. Just as poor teaching methods are not desirable and ought to be replaced, so poor testing techniques ought to be revised.

As the number of whole language teachers grows, the areas of the curriculum to which the approach applies are also expanding. Although whole language began as a reconceptualization of the nature of language and how reading and writing are best taught to complement the rich natural language learning that goes on throughout a person's life, it has powerful things to say about how other content areas, including social studies, can be taught and assessed. In the classrooms of whole language teachers, literacy lessons extend across the curriculum and are not limited to reading or writing period. According to Edelsky et al. (1987, p. 145),

> Whole language classrooms are rich in a variety of print. Little use is made of materials written specifically to teach reading and writing. Instead, whole language relies heavily on literature [and] on other print used for appropriate purposes. Because language is considered a tool for making sense of something else, the "something elses" (science, social science topics) have prominence. Social science . . . topics receive a big chunk of the school day, providing contexts for much real reading and writing. Assessment is focused on constant kidwatching (Goodman, 1986) and on documenting growth in children's work rather than on comparing scores on work substitutes.

When a teacher extends whole language principles beyond the basic reading and writing and uses them as an appropriate way to teach social studies, the curriculum is understood in a fundamentally different way. No longer are the lines between reading and writing and social studies and mathematics and so on clear, neatly dividing the school day into distinct content areas. Instead, what is learned in one area is seen as supportive of what is learned in another, and all the information combines within the learner's mind. The teacher no longer views himself or herself as a reading or a social studies teacher but as a teacher whose job it is to structure an environment that encourages natural and functional learning. Assessment is no longer a simple matter of objectively testing for a limited set of facts or inferences. The teacher becomes an observer who listens and records evidence that learning has occurred.

In describing the whole language classroom, Cambourne and Turbill (1987), have focused on the qualities that make it natural, functional, and reflective of the learning that goes on outside the classroom. The following conditions must exist to some degree in whole language settings.

1. *Immersion.* From even the earliest grades, students are exposed to a vast array of print: labels, charts, stories, and books of various kinds.
2. *Demonstration.* There are regular opportunities for students to use print and see it being used. Teachers demonstrate how reading and writing are done or apply to their subject area. Students are exposed to the expository writing of textbooks, informational writing of secondary sources and various genres in literature.

3. *Expectations.* Teachers hold and communicate both positive and negative expectations both implicitly and explicitly. These expectations and how they are communicated affect learning outcomes.

4. *Responsibility.* Each student is responsible for his or her own learning and is permitted to decide what will be written, when it will be written, and what will be learned. Inversely, each student is also responsible for determining what will not be learned and what will be ignored. This selection process is a natural part of learning.

5. *Approximation.* Students are encouraged to take risks and try out possible answers. The degree to which the emphasis is on error avoidance or reduction will vary from high to low.

6. *Practice.* Students are given multiple opportunities to use developing skills. There are ample opportunities to engage in reading, writing, and problem solving.

7. *Engagement.* Students are invited to engage with print on the subject matter as the teacher coaches or demonstrates how the print works. The degree to which engagement occurs may vary from high to low, depending on the relevance of the print material and the number and kinds of demonstrations with the learner.

8. *Response.* There are exchanges between experts and novices in this classroom. There is a range in the types of responses to children, but each is centered, nonthreatening, functional, and relevant to the student's needs.

Cambourne and Turbill believe that a natural theory of learning requires a natural form of assessment. If the measurements teachers use do not match the methods they employ, the incongruity will cause discomfort and lack of trust in the evaluations. To be valid, assessment procedures have to be compatible with the foregoing characteristics.

A theory of natural and holistic learning calls for assessment that is less artificial and more authentic than prior means of assessment. In a whole language classroom, students are invited to demonstrate what they learn in a variety of ways. Projects, oral reports, collaborations, portfolios, and other expressions reveal real world knowledge and problem-solving ability.

Characteristics of Authentic Assessment

Grant Wiggins (1989a, 1989b), an expert on assessment and an outspoken critic of standardized testing and evaluation, has popularized the term *authentic assessment* to describe what he contends is the only valid form of evaluation. Although he is not identified as a "whole language educator" and he approaches educational reform from another point, what he says about assessment is highly compatible with holistic instruction.

According to Wiggins, there is little question that testing can be and is a positive part of the learning environment. Teachers should, however, be careful to test for only what they value and not to test for extraneous reasons. Tests should be performance based, and the students' goal in assessment ought to be to find the right questions, not simply to give the expected answers. To be real or authentic, the tasks that are set must be engaging and interesting to students and must be posed in such a way as to make students performers. If a test is measuring what the teacher values, students should be immediately rewarded for displaying qualities of mind such as persistence, perspective shifting, and cooperation.

Assessment in whole language classrooms is done first so that students will understand their own progress, and only after that is it for teachers, administrators, and the public (Harp, 1991). Just as whole language restructures teachers' classroom practices, it requires assessment that rejects traditional evaluation and follows instead a new set of principles. Harp (1991, pp. 36-49) specifies several principles that provide a guide for natural and authentic assessment.

1. Holistic assessment is always meaning centered. In many traditional classrooms, students are tested on small items; they are required to fill in blanks or provide short responses that often fail to tap their potential for problem solving. Outside the classroom, individuals are rarely asked to prove that they understand something by correctly responding to a list of true-false questions. Instead, they will find themselves in situations that demand that they solve real and often complex problems. Instead of using short, controlled items, authentic assessments use larger or "whole" texts that present real problems from a student's background.

2. Holistic assessment is process oriented. Whole language teachers use an inquiry mode of instruction in which students are asked to discover and demonstrate their newfound understandings. What is important in the traditional classroom, on the other hand, is the right answer—the product. In the whole language classroom the emphasis is on the problem-solving process that the students invent in response to a test question. "Failure" in a holistic class is not ending up with incorrect answers but using ineffective strategies or failing to engage in a thinking process.

3. Holistic assessment involves the teacher in a unique way. In the traditional classroom, the teacher is the one who gives information and the student learns the facts and figures. In that setting, the teacher becomes the tester of the knowledge, asking specific questions to discern what and how well the information given out was mastered. In a whole language classroom, the teacher is not the knowledge giver but a coach who sets up the environment so that questions can be raised and students can explore possible answers and outcomes. With students actively engaged in problem solving and discussion, the teacher observes and evaluates their responses. This teacher does not look for "correctness" by calculating the degree of error in the students' answers. Instead, this teacher tries to see the logic in the students' responses and solutions.

■ Whole language classrooms rely less on objective measures of evaluation and more on subjective ones.

4. Holistic assessment does not disrupt the ongoing activity. In the traditional classroom, students are exposed to information, asked to learn it, and required to show evidence that they have learned it. At the end of a specified time set aside for instruction, students are tested. Perhaps most commonly, information that is presented on Monday is tested on Friday. New information is presented the next week and the cycle is repeated. Although some students may wish or need to stay on a topic for a longer period, the curriculum goals and concerns for fairness keep the teacher to the schedule. In a whole language classroom, teaching, learning, and evaluation often merge (Rhodes, 1992; Rhodes & Shanklin, 1993). When a teacher poses a question for discussion, students may share information, learn from each other, and clarify incorrectly held assumptions. Because the process is what is most important, it is often not critical to identify the individual who provided a particular answer if all the group has learned it. The teacher watches to see the process unfold and to see how each student becomes involved. When students learn is not as important as the fact that they do learn.

5. Holistic assessment uses a variety of contexts and samples. In the traditional classroom, students are given one opportunity to show what they have learned. For most students, grades are derived from the Friday morning quiz or the results of a term paper. In the whole language class-room, students are given multiple opportunities to demonstrate what they

have learned. They are asked to engage in written work, oral discussions, whole group activities, small group work sessions, and individually authored work. The teacher and student together evaluate the quality of the aggregate, often put together in a portfolio that stands as evidence of learning.

Assessment Strategies and Activities

Assessment in a whole language social studies classroom should support whole language tenets concerning learning, teaching, and children's development (Harste, Short, & Burke, 1988). Assessment must be based on performance so that the process students go through as they solve problems will be exposed. Questions should be complex, open-ended and somewhat ambiguous, and reflect real life situations. Students must be given the time and resources to identify and complete tasks that will lead to solutions. Their responses may combine individual input with group input and be presented through a variety of formats. Finally, assignments should require students to combine their knowledge of the subject with critical thinking, group cooperation, and oral and written communication.

At times, holistic assessments look very much like the tests and evaluations in traditional classrooms. At other times, the assessment tasks look quite like the ongoing instructional activities in the holistic classroom, and because of this, they have a high degree of validity. The teacher's role is to observe and record the students' responses. "Objective" tests give way to tasks that are structured so that students exhibit proof of learning.

The rest of this section describes five areas of the curriculum and gives examples of alternative ways to assess them. These areas are writing, reading, visual organization, literature extensions, and projects.

Writing

The act of composing and putting one's thoughts in writing is a potent way to clarify what one knows and what one does not clearly understand. It also provides a powerful record for assessment, particularly when considering the various drafts of a piece of work.

Reflective Journals

One way to encourage reflective thinking is to have students keep a journal in which they record what they understand at the end of a reading assignment or unit of study. As they do this, students should be encouraged to think freely about what they have studied and to make connections or interpretations that they feel are important.

Dialectic Journals

Often students have questions about what they read in their textbooks and reading books even though they may not specifically ask for assistance. In a dialetic journal, students record passages that they do not fully

■ Children need to critique and to evaluate their own work if they are to grow as learners.

understand and write comments about what those passages might mean. Intensive reading is an important study skill that can be sustained across time by means of such a record.

Diaries

Developing an understanding of social studies requires the ability to see various points of view and to interpret factual detail in light of opinion. By putting themselves in the time frame or role of the people they study, students can use writing to express what they have learned. For example, at the conclusion of a unit on World War II, students are asked to write two diary entries: one written by a Christian child in Germany and the other written by a Jewish child expelled from Germany. The length of the entries or specificity of detail will provide indications of what the student has learned.

Reading

By the time students enter secondary school, almost all of the information they are asked to learn is presented to them through textbooks and primary sources. Tests on the information learned in this way have traditionally focused on the outcomes or products of the students' reading, that is, on the number of correct answers. The need for strong reading ability is obvious, yet very little assessment focuses on the process of reading, especially in the various subject areas. However, there are several ways to assess the quality of the thinking that students use as they approach written text.

Miscue Analysis

Each time a reader deviates from the written text, the deviation or "miscue" gives us insight into the logic the student is using when he or she reads that material. Miscue analysis begins with the assumptions that readers do not make random guesses but that they do apply logical strategies to help them derive meaning. The number of strategies vary from reader to reader and text to text. For example, a reader who deals deftly with familiar material may bog down when asked to read something about which he or she has little background knowledge.

An analysis of miscues begins by having a student orally read a passage. The teacher asks himself or herself questions about the miscues and the number and types of strategies the reader has applied. The reader who preserves or invents meaning and always tries to make the language of the text sound authentic is a good reader. (Miscue analysis is well documented by Goodman, Goodman, and Hood, 1989, among others.)

The reader selected miscue (RSM) technique (Watson, 1987) modifies the basic reading miscue technique so that it applies to the silent reading typically done in classrooms. Students are given a supply of bookmarks or index cards to indicate any difficulties they encounter when reading the assignment. The teacher instructs the students to read silently and independently. When students encounter a difficult word or passage, they insert a bookmark or index card at the point of the problem, skip the problem area, and continue reading. At the conclusion of the reading assignment, the students are asked to reexamine their trouble spots, or miscues, and to write out any that are still causing problems or that they feel were important to understanding the text. The teacher collects the written miscues and categorizes them. This provides information about individual students and about the appropriateness of the reading material. A student who uses RSM learns that all readers make miscues and that some miscues can be insignificant. If necessary, the teacher groups those students who had similar problems and meets with them briefly to clarify the problems and suggest alternate strategies.

Visual Organization

Sometimes students arrange and present their work through graphics, a powerful means of communication. Often information that is composed visually can later be translated and expanded verbally (Harste et al., 1985).

Diagrams

During a history unit exploring conditions that lead to revolution, a group of students compared conditions in pre-Revolutionary America to those in pre-Revolutionary France. Conditions that occurred in both situations

F I G U R E   1 4 . 2

■

Conditions leading to revolution (based on Quellmalz, 1990).

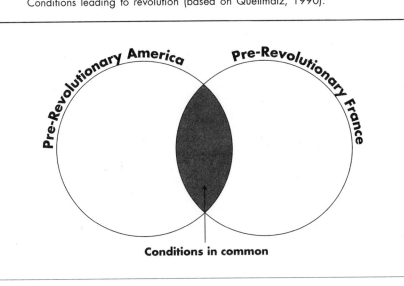

Conditions in common

were depicted graphically as shown in Figure 14.2. Making the diagram helped these students compose a comprehensive comparative analysis and served as a way for their teacher to assess how well they understood the material.

Maps

Vocabulary is often the focus of instruction and tests. However, most tests require students to define terms out of context. In fact, there are two reasons why vocabulary is important. First, the terms themselves provide information that is important to know. Second and often overlooked, terms exist in the textbook in relation to each other. The network that words form provides the bulk of the information students are expected to learn.

In mapping, students are given or asked to list the key terms in a chapter or passage. Then the students are instructed to organize the terms into a diagram that reveals how they are related and to explain the diagram. The teacher reviews this pictorial representation of how the student has related key concepts and can use the map to clarify or expand areas where necessary (See Figure 14.3).

FIGURE 14.3

■

Concept map for the topic of pioneers.

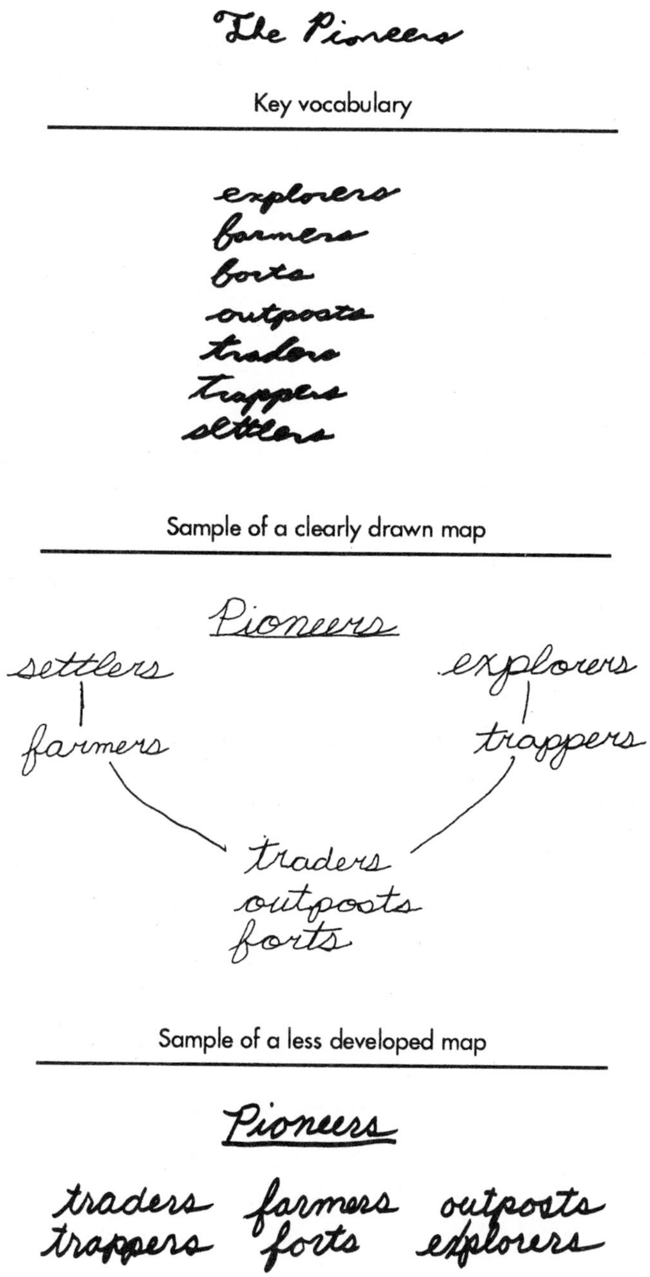

The Pioneers

Key vocabulary

explorers
farmers
forts
outposts
traders
trappers
settlers

Sample of a clearly drawn map

Pioneers

settlers   explorers
farmers   trappers

traders
outposts
forts

Sample of a less developed map

Pioneers

traders   farmers   outposts
trappers   forts   explorers

Literature Extensions

Literature is an excellent means to extend and assess the learning in a social studies class. When assigning a particular piece of literature for analysis, the teacher can ask students to apply most of the concepts they are learning about people and motivation, political systems, cultural diversity, and history to other settings and situations.

For example, at the conclusion of a unit on the Revolutionary War, as an alternative to testing, students might be asked to read *My Brother Sam Is Dead,* (Collier & Collier, 1974), the story of a family torn apart by the war, and to write about or draw a time line specifying the events of the war that actually affected the protagonist and his family. The students might identify the most important events of the war as perceived from the point of view of the protagonist, the father, the brother, the town's constable, and the general.

A unit on western expansion might include the reading of *The Indian in the Cupboard* (Banks, 1982), a novel about a young boy who is able to bring to life toy figures of an Indian, a soldier, a cowboy, and others. As these individuals come together, cultures and history collide. After reading this story the students form groups and assume the roles of the various figures. They review the actual historical events of which these figures should have been aware and compare them to what the figures seemed to have known. Students might also be asked to project what would have happened had the figures been placed in other settings or times.

Projects

Projects are fairly large and complex tasks that require time to develop. Effective projects involve both individual and group tasks and allow some degree of self-selection. Project topics should be engaging and open-ended.

Suppose, for example, the task is this: Imagine what advice former presidents might give to President Clinton concerning the Colombian drug cartel. Students break into five groups, one representing Clinton and the other four representing Theodore Roosevelt, Woodrow Wilson, Franklin Roosevelt, and Jimmy Carter. The students analyze primary and secondary source materials that reflect different points of view. After reading and discussing the materials, each group decides on the position that best represents the president the group is portraying and then reports to the "President Clinton" group. During each presentation, the Clinton group is free to ask questions of the other group about its advice. Following the presentations, each student writes a summary of his or her own advice in telegraph form to be sent to President Clinton. The group representing President Clinton reviews the input and issues a policy statement. This activity can be completed in one class period.

On the second day, following the statement of President Clinton's policy decision, students write an essay supporting or opposing that decision, stating their personal viewpoint, which must be substantiated with facts and examples drawn from their knowledge of history/social science and what they learned from the previous day's group activity.

Each group is evaluated for its success in group and collaborative learning, quality of thinking, ability to communicate ideas effectively, and knowledge and use of history. (This example is based on California Department of Education, 1990, pp. 21–22.)

A similar format and assessment could be used in regard to other contemporary affairs. For example, explore President Clinton's decisions concerning the Baltic states. Should he have invaded? Blockaded? Provided humanitarian aid? What actions do you believe would have been taken by Jimmy Carter? Richard Nixon? Theodore Roosevelt?

Another project could be used as part of a unit on the discovery of the Americas and the role of Christopher Columbus. Was Christopher Columbus's discovery one of the greatest events of civilization or the beginning of a holocaust? Take the perspective of one of the sailors on board *The Niña,* Queen Isabella, the clergy, a North American Indian.

Grant Wiggins (1989a, pp. 42–43) provides an example of a task given as a final examination for ninth-grade history students.

> You must complete an oral history based on interviews and written sources and present your findings orally in class. The choice of subject matter will be up to you. Some examples of possible topics include: your family, running a small business, substance abuse, a labor union, teenage parents or recent immigrants. You are to create three workable hypotheses based on your preliminary investigations and come up with four questions you will use to test each hypothesis.
>
> To meet the criteria, [you] must:
>
> - investigate three hypotheses;
> - describe at least one change over time;
> - demonstrate that you have done background research;
> - interview four appropriate people as sources;
> - prepare at least four questions related to each hypothesis;
> - ask questions that are not leading or biased;
> - ask follow-up questions when appropriate;
> - note important differences between fact and opinion in answers you receive;
> - use evidence to support your choice of the best hypothesis; and organize your writing and your class presentation.

Documentation

To develop an authentic assessment program teachers must find alternative ways to record growth and document the quality of the learning that has been accomplished. Teachers should not rely on the results of Friday morning quizzes, term paper grades, and final examination grades. Assessment records should be extensive and subjective, reflect a variety of assessment tasks, and provide a picture of growth over time.

Portfolios

A portfolio is a record that brings together artifacts or pieces of a student's work so that patterns of growth and development over time become evident (Tierney, Carter, & Desai, 1991). According to Adams and Hamm (1992), teachers need to give consideration to what is being assessed, the design of the portfolio, the intended audience, and the appropriateness of the portfolio's contents to what is being assessed. Portfolios can include tests, completed papers, reports, selected homework assignments, and other work samples that evidence the quality of work produced. The student should always be allowed to select some of the work to be included in the portfolio along with pieces selected by the teacher.

Pieces need not be final drafts or complete products; nor do they have to be graded. The goal of a portfolio is to document growth over time. Initially, teachers tend to include too much in a portfolio. However, it is better to be selective, choosing only those pieces that reveal something about the quality of thinking the student exhibits.

Criteria for evaluating portfolios should include evidence of critical and creative thinking, quality of activities and investigations, variety of approaches and investigations, and demonstration of understanding and skill in situations that parallel previous experiences/activities in the classroom (Adams and Hamm, 1992).

Field Notes

In whole language classrooms, the teacher acts as a coach, raising questions and problems to be addressed and then standing back to observe how students answer and solve them. Field notes or anecdotal records of these observations can become a basic evaluation document (Rhodes & Nathenson-Mejia, 1992). When teachers first begin to keep field notes, they frequently become overwhelmed by the sheer volume of what there is to observe; because they are traditionally trained to focus on the deficits, they begin by recording what the students cannot do. Teachers need to train themselves to observe and record the positive things they see. It is enough to look to simple events or record only single comments. Over time, the record emerges. At first, teachers also find keeping field notes a time-consuming task. To overcome this, teachers can reserve a particular period of time each day, while students are engaged in independent or group work, for writing notes.

F I G U R E   1 4 . 4

■

Sample checklist.

Date _____

Chapter Checklist

Student name _____

Chapter/reading assignment _____

	initiate	novice	expert
1. Predicts logical outcomes			
2. Synthesizes/summarizes key points			
3. Goes beyond the text and applies it to own experience			
4. Questions the text			

Comments:

Checklists

Checklists can provide a systematic means to record specific behaviors or goals (see Figure 14.4). To develop a checklist, a teacher needs to specify two things: goals and levels of attainment. When teachers first begin to develop checklists, they report a tendency to list too many goals (Paradis, Chatton, Boswell, Smith, & Yovitch, 1991), making the system long and unmanageable. Checklists are most efficient when they are focused and limited. Goals that do not prove to be important must be revised because a list that is too long to be helpful will not be used often. The levels of attainment should also be kept brief and should indicate relative degrees of performance that are easily scored. For instance, a choice of "expert," "novice" or "initiate" or simply "high," "moderate" or "low" can provide adequate information concerning progress.

Conferences

When group work is part of the classroom agenda, assessing individual contributions to the team effort becomes a challenge. Periodic student conferences can help the teacher assess the work that individual students are doing. Conferences need only last a few minutes to reveal areas in which a student is experiencing difficulty or success. The literature is filled with examples of the positive effects of individualized attention on student behavior and learning. Making conferences a regular routine is a wise idea.

Tests

Tests have long been the primary means of evaluation, and they can provide some useful information as part of an overall picture. To be valid, a test must reflect what is taught in a manner that is consistent with the goals of the class. In a holistic classroom, the thinking process and creative applications of facts are crucial. Test questions can be constructed in a way to tap levels of knowledge beyond recall and recitation. Students should be asked to project or extend facts to novel situations, summarize and consolidate isolated facts, and take and defend positions. Baskwill and Whitman (1988, p. 32) suggest these challenges:

> Suppose you . . .
> What do you think might happen if . . .
> If the following facts are true, what do you think . . .
> If you found yourself in the following situation, what would you . . .
> In light of what you know about . . . what would you suggest that . . .

Test questions such as these can be multiple choice or short answer or require open-ended essay responses.

Contracts

Some projects or assignments can be evaluated by means of a negotiated agreement or contract. The student, in consultation with the teacher, agrees to accomplish certain tasks by a specified date and in a manner acceptable to both parties. Criteria, frequently grades or points, are established for levels above or below the target that is set. It is important that the teacher serve as a judicious guide in setting standards that are neither too high nor too low for the student.

Summary

Whole language teaching requires an assessment system that evaluates both the processes and products that students learn and create. Unlike some traditional models for learning, whole language is child centered, individualized and performance based. As a result, the means to measure what is learned must be modified. One of the teacher's goals in a whole language classroom is to make the classroom conducive to exploration and discovery. As an evaluator, the teacher becomes a keen observer who listens for and records evidence of what has been learned.

This chapter has described characteristics of appropriate assessment as authentic measures designed to be part of the instructional plan. Ideally, it should be difficult to discern the difference between teaching, learning, and testing. Alternative assessment strategies can include writing (as in journals), reading techniques (miscue analysis), visual displays (maps or diagrams), and extensions of textbook topics through the inclusion of literature and projects. Teachers must develop means to record or document student performance such as portfolios, field notes, checklists, and conferences.

References

Adams, D. M., & Hamm, M. E. (1992). Portfolio assessment and social studies: Collecting, selecting, and reflecting on what is significant. *Social Education, 56,* 103-105.

Banks, L. R. (1982). *The Indian in the cupboard.* New York: Avon Books.

Baskwill, J., and Whitman, P. (1988). *Evaluation: Whole language, whole child.* Ontario, Canada: Scholastic TAB.

Bertrand, J. (1991). Student assessment and evaluation. In B. Harp (Ed.), *Assessment and evaluation in whole language programs.* Norwood, MA: Christopher-Gordon.

Bloom, B. S. (Ed.). (1956). *Taxonomy of educational objectives: Handbook I. Cognitive domain.* New York: David McKay.

California Department of Education. (1990). *California: The state of assessment.* Sacramento: California Assessment Program.

Cambourne, B., and Turbill, J. (1987). *Coping with chaos.* Sydney, Australia: Primary English Teachers Association.

Cambourne, B., & Turbill, J. (1990). Assessment in whole language classrooms. *Elementary School Journal, 90,* 337-350.

Collier, J., & Collier, C. (1974). *My brother Sam is dead.* New York: Scholastic.

Costa, A. (1989). Reassessing assessment. *Educational Leadership, 46,* 3.

Edelsky, C., Altwerger, B., and Flores, B. (1987). Whole language: What's new? *Reading Teacher, 41,* 144-154.

Goodman, K. (1986). *What's whole in whole language?* Portsmouth, NH: Heinemann.

Goodman, K., Goodman, Y., and Hood, W. (Eds.). (1989). *The whole language evaluation book.* Portsmouth, NH: Heinemann.

Harp, B., (Ed.). (1991). *Assessment and evaluation in whole language programs.* Norwood, MA: Christopher-Gordon.

Harste, J., Short, K., and Burke, C. (1988). *Creating classrooms for authors: The reading/writing connection.* Portsmouth, NH: Heinemann.

Harste, J., Woodward, V., and Burke, C. (1985). *Language stories and literacy lessons.* Portsmouth, NH: Heinemann.

Heward, W., & Orlansky, M. L. (1992). *Exceptional children: An introductory survey of special education* (4th ed.). New York: Merrill/Macmillan.

Johnston, P. H. (1993). Assessment and literate "development." *Reading Teacher, 46* (5), 428–429.

Newman, J. (Ed.). (1985). *Whole language: Theory in use.* Portsmouth, NH: Heinemann.

Paradis, E., Chatton, B., Boswell, A., Smith, M., & Yovitch, S. (1991). Accountability: Assessing comprehension during literature discussion. *Reading Teacher, 45,* 8–17.

Quellmalz, E. (1990). Developing reasoning skills. *Proceedings of the Authentic Assessment Fair.* Riverside, CA: Regional Assessment Network.

Rhodes, L. (1992). *Literacy Assessment: A Handbook of Instruments.* Portsmouth, NH: Heinemann.

Rhodes, L., & Nathenson-Mejia, S. (1992). Anecdotal records: A powerful tool for ongoing literacy assessment. *Reading Teacher, 45* (7), 502–509.

Rhodes, L., & Shanklin, N. (1993). Windows into Literacy: Assessing Learners K–8. Portsmouth, NH: Heinemann.

Smith, F. (1989). *Understanding reading.* New York: Holt, Rinehart & Winston.

Tierney, R., Carter, M., & Desai, L. (1991). *Portfolio assessment in the reading-writing classroom.* Norwood, MA: Christopher-Gordon.

Watson, D. (Ed.). (1987). *Ideas and insights: Language arts in the elementary school.* Urbana, IL: National Council of Teachers of English.

Wiggins, G. (1989a). Teaching to the authentic test. *Educational Leadership, 46,* 41–47.

Wiggins, G. (1989b). A true test: Toward more equitable assessment. *Phi Delta Kappan, 70,* 703–713.

Worthen, B. R. (1993). Critical issues that will determine the future of alternative assessment. *Phi Delta Kappan, 74,* 444–448, 450–454.

APPENDIX

Suggested Classroom References

■

Adams, S., Briquebec, J., & Kramer, A. (1992). *Illustrated atlas of world history*. New York: Random House.

Beginning in the ancient world around 30,000 B.C. and ending in contemporary times, this book describes industry, trade, religion, and technology. A helpful time line and index are included.

Black, W. B., & Blashfield, J. F. (1992). *World War II 50th anniversary: D-Day*. New York: Crestwood.

This book describes the Normandy invasion which took place on June 6, 1944.

Fritz, J., Paterson, K., McKissack, P., McKissack, F., Hahy, M., & Highwater, J. (1992). *The world in 1492* (S. Vitale, Illus.). New York: Holt.

This book vividly describes events that were taking place on all the continents as Columbus sailed to the "New World" in 1492.

Grant, N. (1992). *The great atlas of discovery* (P. Morter, Illus.). New York: Knopf.

Double-page presentations with accompanying maps provide short, captivating descriptions of various explorations from 6000 B.C. to today. This is an easy book for children to use.

Perl, L. (1992). *It happened in America: True stories from the fifty states* (I. Ohlsson, Illus.). New York: Holt.

Actual stories from each of the 50 states and the District of Columbia from Colonial times through today provide human interest along with geographical study.

Wagman, J. (1990). *On this day in America: An illustrated Almanac of history, sports, science, and culture*. New York: Gallery Books.

This book gives fascinating information about the United States from 1492 on. Children will enjoy looking up their birthday to learn what special events occurred on that special day.

Suggested Social Studies Magazines

■

Calliope: World History for Young People
Cobblestone Publishing, Inc.
7 School St.
Peterborough NH 03458
(800)821-0115

Published five times during the school year, each issue features indepth information on a single topic. Past topics have included Africa's Carthage, Byzantium, Constantinople, Istanbul, Hinduism, defenders of France, epic heroes, shoguns and samurai of Japan, vanished civilizations, and Vikings. Activities are also included in each issue. This magazine is appropriate for students in grades 4–8.

Cobblestone: The History Magazine for Young People
Cobblestone Publishing, Inc.
7 School St.
Peterborough NH 03458
(800)821-0115

Appropriate for students in grades 4–8, *Cobblestone* is published 10 times a
year. Each issue features a topic of historical interest, such as the antislavery
movement and Theodore Roosevelt.

National Geographic World
National Geographic Society
Dept. 01090
17th and M Streets, N.W.
Washington, D.C. 20036

This magazine is very popular with 8 to 10 year olds. Published monthly, each
issue contains short articles on a variety of social studies topics from around the
world.

Living History Museums

Alabama

Constitution Hall Village
404 Madison St.
Huntsville, AL 35801
(800)678-1819

Located in the same city as the space museum and camp, Constitution Hall
Village is located at the site of the 1819 drafting of the 1819 constitution of
the state of Alabama. Both single-day and five-day programs are available. The
single-day program is "Pioneer Adventures" with the five-day program entitled
"Apprentice Adventures." Children dress in nineteenth century apparel and
participate in a variety of tasks including candle dipping, spinning, open-hearth
cooking, and wooden cooking utensils and toy making.

Alaska

Eklutna Village Historical Park
510 L St., Suite 200
Anchorage, AK 99501
(907)276-5701

Eklutna is over 350 years old. As such it is the oldest continuously inhabited
Athapaskan site in Alaska. The cemetery contains spirit houses which were
colorfully decorated shelters built by loved ones to protect the spirits of the
deceased. The park also has two Russian Orthodox churches, built in the
1830's by missionaries. These churches have the traditional domes which are
representative of Russian Orthodox church architecture.

Native Village of Alaskaland
Fairbanks Native Association
201 First Ave., 2nd Floor
Fairbanks, AK 99701
(907)452-1648

Decendents of Native American Alaskans serve as guides for children. The
village contains a variety of different types of housing used by Native American
Alaskans, including sod dwellings and plank houses.

Arizona

Pioneer Arizona
3901 W. Pioneer Road
Phoenix, AZ 85027
(602)993–0212

Columbus brought horses to North America on his second voyage in 1493. Descendants of those original horses are raised at Pioneer Arizona. This museum includes over 20 authentic and reconstructed buildings of the nineteenth century including adobe and wooden structures. The cultural influences of Native American, Spanish, and Mexican cultures are accurately depicted.

Arkansas

Arkansas Territorial Restoration
200 E. 3rd St.
Little Rock, AR 72201
(501)324–9351

This museum represents frontier life in Arkansas from 1819 to 1870, shortly following the Civil War. Costumed historical interpreters present the actual events based upon memoirs and historic documents of inhabitants of the area during that period of time.

California

El Pueblo de Los Angeles Historic Monument
125 Paseo de la Plaza, Suite 400
Los Angeles, CA 90012
(213)628–0605

Founded in 1781 by 44 settlers as a farming community, El Pueblo de Los Angeles later became known simply as Los Angeles. The museum has 27 buildings, including Avila Adobe which was built in 1818 and is the oldest home in Los Angeles, as well as a 1825 town plaza. Multicultural influences of African American, Chinese, French, Italian, Mexican, and Spanish are all depicted.

Mission San Juan Capistrano
31882 Camino Capistrano # 107
San Juan Capistrano, CA 92675
(714)248–2048

Franciscan padres founded the Mission of San Juan Capistrano in 1776. The Serra Chapel, built in 1777, is the oldest continuously inhabited building in the state of California. The courtyard depicts the Moorish influence. The museum features an exhibit of Native American artifacts. The mission and grounds are preserved as part of an ongoing archaeological excavation. The Mission is also famous for the annual migration of swallows each spring.

Colorado

Bent's Old Fort National Historic Site
35110 Hwy. 194 East
La Junta, CO 81050
(719)384–2596

This is a reconstructed frontier fur trading post. Adobing, blacksmithing, and frontier medicine are featured as part of this museum.

Connecticut

Mystic Seaport and Maritime Museum
50 Greenmanville Ave.
Mystic, CT 06355

(203)572-0711

The Mystic Seaport and Preservation Shipyard on the Mystic River is home to nineteenth century tall ships and schooners. A maritime museum contains antique navigational equipment. The accompanying planetarium has programs explaining how sea captains and their navigators relied upon the stars to determine their location at sea.

Delaware

Delaware Agricultural Museum
866 N. DuPont Highway
Dover, DE 19901
(302)734-1618

Historic activities and demonstrations vary depending upon the season. During the summer months, the "1850s One-Room School-House Program" involved children in schooling from that period of our history. Lessons are taught from the *McGuffey Reader* and Noah Webster's *Blue Backed Speller* with "ciphering" done on a slate. "Summer on the Farm," which runs in July and August, allows the children to dress in clothing of the period and depicts farm life. Children get to churn butter, feed the chickens and cow, and enjoy a storyteller. During the fall through spring, a less intensive program is presented by guides who provide interpretations of rural life in the 1850s.

Hagley Museum and Library
P.O. Box 3630
Wilmington, DE 19807
(302)658-2400

The Hagley Museum and Library preserves the history of one of the most prominent families in the United States, the E. I. du Pont family (founders of Du Pont corporation). The family's role in the nineteenth century Industrial Age is presented. Costumed guides provide tours of the family's 1802 Georgian mansion and gardens, as well as the company's building, workers' quarters, quarries, and hydroelectric plant of the original Du Pont Co. gunpowder mills.

Florida

Historic Saint Augustine Spanish Quarter
P.O. Box 1987
Saint Augustine, FL 32085
(904)825-6830

Saint Augustine was founded by the Spanish over 470 years ago, making it the oldest continuously inhabited European settlement in North America. Life during the Spanish colonial period of the 1740s is portrayed in the Spanish Quarter's restored buildings and gardens. The Castillo de San Marcos, which was used for fortification by Spanish settlers and treasure galleons on their way to Spain, is located close to the Spanish Quarter and may be viewed by children.

Georgia

Agrirama
P.O. Box Q
Tifton, GA 31793
(912)386–3344

This museum consists of nearly 40 restored buildings with the theme of traditional and progressive farming and industrial communities. A one-room schoolhouse provides demonstrations of how children were taught in the 1890s.

Idaho

Pioneer Village and Idaho Historical Museum
610 N. Julia Davis Dr.
Boise, ID 83702
(208)334–2120

This museum village consists of restored and reconstructed log cabins and adobes which may be toured by school groups.

Illinois

Lincoln's New Salem State Historic Site
R.R. #1, Box 244A
Petersburg, IL 62675
(217)632–4000

A young Abraham Lincoln first stopped at New Salem when he and a friend copiloted a flatboat down the Sangamon River to the Ohio and Mississippi Rivers. He later returned there to settle and study law. The recreated village provides demonstrations of activities common to daily living during Lincoln's lifetime.

Naper Settlement
210 W. Porter
Naperville, IL 60540
(708)420–6010

Storytelling, historic games and crafts, candle dipping, lye soap making, and open hearth cooking are all featured in this 1830s–1900 settlement. The underground railroad was quite active in this community as the costumed interpreters point out.

Indiana

Conner Prairie
13400 Allisonville Road
Fishers, IN 46038
(317)776–6000

Conner Prairie consists of 205 acres with three completely different, historically accurate areas. Each area has its own costumed interpreters. Prairietown is an 1836 Indiana village with 29 buildings. A second area is the 1823 brick home of William Conner, a nineteenth century land developer and politician. The third area is the Pioneer Adventure Area. It is in this area where children are encouraged to participate in candle dipping, lye soap making, weaving, wood carving and chopping, and other activities of the period.

Historic New Harmony
506 1/2 Main St.
P.O. Box 579
New Harmony, IN 47631
(812)682–4488

The Harmonie Society fled their native Germany because of religious persecution. In 1814, they developed a self-sufficient, utopian community which later failed. The community was then taken over by Robert Owen and his followers. Interpreters present the history of this unusual community.

Iowa

Living History Farms
2600 N.W. 111th St.
Urbandale, IA 50322
(515)278–2400

Native American agrarian culture from the sixteenth century through to an 1850 pioneer homestead are featured in this museum. It accurately depicts the history of Midwestern agriculture on a 60 acre site.

Amana Colonies
P.O. Box 303
Amana, IA 52203
(800)245–5465

In 1844, a group of separatists from the Lutheran church in Germany initially settled in Ebenezer, Iowa. In 1855, they moved to Amana, where they had 27,000 acres. The community features three furniture factories and several craft shops. A 300 seat theater at the Visitor's Center is used to show a brief film about the history of the Amana Colonies.

Kansas

Old Cowtown Museum
1871 Sim Park Dr.
Wichita, KS 67203
(316)264–0671

Thirty reconstructed buildings recreate a 1865 cowtown of the old west. Buildings range from a log cabin to an elegant Victorian mansion. Interpreters in vintage dress present the educational program of the museum.

Kentucky

Shaker Village of Pleasant Hill
3500 Lexington Rd.
Harrodsburg, KY 40330
(606)734–5411

In the nineteenth century, the Shakers were the largest communal society in America. The Shaker Village has 33 of the original buildings, each furnished with Shaker furniture antiques. A paddleboat for short scenic cruises is available during the late spring and early fall.

Louisiana

Acadian Village
200 Greenleaf Rd.
Lafayette, LA 70506
(800)962–9133

This 10 acre museum site is located in the bayou country. A general store and houses help recreate a nineteenth century Acadiana (who fled Nova Scotia in 1775) village in this French speaking settlement.

Maine

Norlands Living History Center
R.R. #2, Box 3395
Livermore Falls, ME 04254
(207)897–2236

This 400–acre farm site has two programs. One program depicts the post-Revolutionary War period and the first permanent settlers of Maine. The second program portrays the post-Civil War era and the problems Maine farmers encountered in the Reconstructionalist period.

Maryland

Baltimore City Life Museums
800 E. Lombard St.
Baltimore, MD 21202
(410)396–3279

Six different museums portray life in Baltimore during the nineteenth century. Storytelling, historic games and crafts, and open hearth cooking are all featured.

Massachusetts

Hancock Shaker Village
P.O. Box 898
Pittsfield, MA 01202
(413)443–0188

The Hancock Shaker Village is located in a wooded area of the Berkshires. It contains 20 restored clapboard and brick buildings. Craftspeople demonstrate furniture and textile making.

Plimouth Plantation
P.O. Box 1620
Plymouth, MA 02362
(508)746–1622

A replica of the *Mayflower* and a reconstructed village comprises Plimouth Plantation. Guides speaking in old English and Dutch discuss the topics of interest which led to the Pilgrims founding of Plymouth.

Michigan

Colonial Michilimackinac
P.O. Box 873
Mackinaw City, MI 49701
(616)436–5563

Colonial Michilimackinac is located at a former military outpost and fur trading center. *Pe-quod-e-nong,* a 1770s Native American encampment, is recreated with wigwams. Period interpreters provide information.

Troy Museum and Historic Village
60 W. Wattles Road
Troy, MI 48098
(313)524–3570

Children's Chores is a program which allows students to engage in tasks of pioneer families.

Minnesota

Oliver H. Kelley Farm
15788 Kelley Farm Road
Elk River, MN 55330
(612)441-6896

Life in Minnesota in the 1860s is depicted. Interpreters wear period clothing and talk of the agrarian life-style.

Missouri

Arrow Rock State Historic Site
P.O. Box 1
Arrow Rock, MO 65320
(816)837-3330

This nineteenth century village is located near the beginning of the Santa Fe Trail. It includes a restored church, the Old Tavern, the court house, and a newspaper office complete with its antique presses.

Nebraska

Stuhr Museum of the Prairie Pioneer
3133 W. Hwy 34
Grand Island, NE 68801
(308)381-5316

A replica of a Pawnee lodge and a collection of Native American and old west artifacts are available to examine.

New Hampshire

Strawbery Banke
P.O. Box 300
Portsmouth, NH 03802
(603)433-1100

Four centuries of history and culture are depicted. Once a large Colonial seaport, Strawbery Banke provides costumed interpreters who demonstrate scrimshaw and historic boat-building skills and techniques.

New Jersey

Historic Batso Village
Wharton State Forest
Route #9
Batso
Hammonton, NJ 08037
(609)561-3262

Batso was a nineteenth century ironworks and glassmaking center. The Batso Furnace supplied the bullets used in the American Revolution and the War of 1812.

New Mexico

El Rancho de Las Golondrinas
Route 14, P.O. Box 214
Santa Fe, NM 87505
(505)471-2261

This town was founded in 1710 by the Spanish as an overnight stop on the Royal Road to Mexico City. Interpreters dress in the Spanish costumes of the period.

New York

Museum Village
Museum Village Road
Monroe, NY 10950
(914)782-8247

An agrarian community of the 1880s is depicted. Several craftpersons demonstrated such skills as blacksmithing and weaving.

Old Bethpage Village Restoration
Nassau County Department of Recreation and Parks
Round Swamp Road
Old Bethpage, NY 11804
(516)572-8400

Costumed interpreters recreate agricultural, domestic and trade activities from the pre-Civil War period.

North Carolina

Oconaluftee Indian Village
P.O. Box 398
Cherokee, NC 28719
(704)497-2111

Located on the Cherokee Reservation, the history and traditions of the Cherokee Nation are presented.

Ohio

Hale Farm and Village
P.O. Box 296
Bath, OH 44210
(216)666-3711

Rural life in the 1850s is depicted. A variety of architectural styles including Eclectic, Greek Revival, and Federal are available for comparing. Craftspeople demonstrate glassblowing, candlemaking, blacksmithing, and, in season, maple sugaring.

Ohio Village
1982 Velma Ave.
Columbus, OH 43211
(614)297-2439

The problems encountered by African Americans during the early 1800s are portrayed.

Pennsylvania

Historic Fallington
4 Yardley Ave.
Fallsington, PA 19054
(215)295-6567

This 300-year-old village contains six historic structures. Founded as a haven for members of the Society of Friends (Quakers). A garden containing plants common to Colonial America can be viewed in the spring and fall.

South Carolina

Middleton Place
Ashley River Road
Charleston, SC 29414
(803)556–6020

Interpreters in vintage dress tend to woodworking and blacksmithing on this 18th century plantation.

Tennessee

Museum of Appalachia
P.O. Box 0318
Highway 61
Norris, TN 37828
(615)494–7680

During October, the annual Fall Homecoming is staged with goat milking, molasses making, the spinning of dog hair to make thread, storytelling, and bluegrass music being featured.

Texas

Old City Park
1717 Gano St.
Dallas, TX 75215
(214)421–5141

Thirty-five buildings have been restored, including a log cabin and antebellum mansions.

Utah

Ronald V. Jensen Living Historical Farm
4025 S. Hwy. 89–91
Welssville, UT 84339
(801)245–4064

This depicts a Mormon farm in the early 1900s. Interpreters dressed in clothing of the period demonstrate how the family members did the daily chores.

Virginia

Colonial Williamsburg
P.O. Box 1776
Williamsburg, VA 23187
(804)229–1000

Eighty-eight restored and over 50 reconstructed buildings help make Colonial Williamsburg the largest living history museum in the United States. An extensive variety of educational programs are available.

Washington

Fort Nisqually Historic Site
Point Defiance Park
5400 N. Pearl
Tacoma, WA 98405
(206)591–5339

Costumed guides give tours of this former fort and Hudson Bay Company trading post. An education program is available complete with curriculum guides for fourth grade.

Rainier Legacy
Pioneer Farm/Ohop Indian Village
7716 Ohop Valley Road
Eatonville, WA 98328
(206)832–6300

This museum presents a contrast between a native American settlement and that of European pioneers. Native American dwellings for three of the four seasons of the year are depicted. The museum is closed from Thanksgiving through March 1, however, during that time a traveling program visits schools on a reservation basis.

Wisconsin

Old World Wisconsin
S. 103 W. 37890
Hwy. 67
Eagle, WI 53119
(414)594–2116

Nineteenth- and twentieth-century farmsteads are represented, including the following cultures: Danish, Finnish, German, and Norwegian.

State Travel and Tourism Offices

■

Director
Alabama Bureau of Tourism and
Travel
401 Adams Avenue, Suite 126
P.O. Box 4309
Montgomery, AL 36103-4309
205-242-4169, FAX: 205-242-4554

Director
Alaska Division of Tourism
P.O. Box 110801
Juneau, AK 99811-0181
907-465-2012, FAX: 907-586-8399

Director
Arizona Office of Tourism
1100 West Washington Street
Phoenix, AZ 85007
602-542-4764, FAX: 602-542-4068

Tourism Director
Arkansas Department of Parks and
Tourism
One Capitol Mall
Little Rock, AR 72201
501-682-1088, FAX: 501-682-1364

Director
California Office of Tourism
801 K Street, Suite 1600
Sacramento, CA 95814
916-322-2881, FAX: 916-322-3402

Executive Director
Colorado Tourism Board
Broadway, Suite 1700
Denver, CO 80202
303-592-5510, FAX: 303-592-5406

Executive Director
Connecticut Department
of Economic Development,
Tourism Division
865 Brook Street
Rocky Hill, CT 06067
203-258-4286, FAX: 203-563-4877

Director
Delaware Tourism Office
99 Kings Highway, Box 1401
Dover, DE 19903
302-739-4271, FAX: 302-739-5749

Director of Tourism
Washington, DC Convention
and Visitors Association
1212 New York Avenue
Washington, DC 20005
202-789-7000, FAX: 202-789-7037

Director of Tourism
Florida Division of Tourism
Department of Commerce
107 West Gaines Street, Room 511
Collins Building
Tallahassee, FL 32399-2000
904-488-5607 or 9187,
FAX: 904-487-0132

Deputy Commissioner
Georgia Department of Industry,
Trade and Tourism
285 Peachtree Center Avenue
Marquis Tower Two, 19th Floor
Atlanta, GA 30301
404-656-3553, FAX: 404-651-9063

Deputy Director of Tourism
Hawaii State Tourism Office
P.O. Box 2359
Honolulu, HI 96804
808-586-2550, FAX: 808-586-2549

Administrator
Idaho Division of Tourism
Development
Department of Commerce
700 West State Street
Boise, ID 83720
208-334-2470, FAX: 208-334-2631

Director
Illinois Bureau of Tourism
State of Illinois Center
100 W. Randolf, Ste. 3-400
Chicago, IL 60601
312-814-4732, FAX: 312-814-6581

Director
Indiana Tourism Marketing & Film
Division
Department of Commerce
One North Capitol, Suite 700
Indianapolis, IN 46204-2288
317-232-8860, FAX: 317-232-4146

Division Administrator
Iowa Division of Tourism
Department of Economic
Development
200 East Grand Avenue
Des Moines, IA 50309
515-242-4705, FAX: 515-242-4749

Director, Travel and Tourism
Kansas Travel & Tourism Division
400 S.W. 8th Street, 5th Floor
Topeka, KS 66603-3957
913-296-2009, FAX: 913-296-5055

Commissioner
Kentucky Department of Travel
2200 Capitol Plaza Tower
500 Mero Street
Frankfort, KY 40601
502-564-4930, FAX: 502-564-5695

Assistant Secretary
Louisiana Office of Tourism
Department of Culture Recreation
& Tourism
P.O. Box 94291
Baton Rouge, LA 70804-9291
504-342-8100, FAX: 504-342-8390

Director of Tourism
Maine Office of Tourism
Department of Economic
& Community Development
189 State Street, Station 59
Augusta, ME 04333
207-289-5710, FAX: 207-289-2861

Director of Tourism
Maryland Office of Tourism Dev.
Dev. of Economic and
Employment Dev.
217 East Redwood, 9th Floor
Baltimore, MD 21202
410-333-6611, FAX: 410-333-6643

Director of Tourism
Massachusetts Office of Travel and
Tourism
100 Cambridge Street, 13th Floor
Boston, MA 02202
617-727-3201, FAX: 617-727-6525

Director
Michigan Travel Bureau
Department of Commerce
P.O. Box 30226
Lansing, MI 48909
517-373-0670, FAX: 517-373-0059

Director of Tourism
Minnesota Office of Tourism
375 Jackson Street
250 Skyway Level
St. Paul, MN 55101-1810
612-296-2755, FAX: 612-296-7095

Associate Director
Mississippi Department
of Economic Development
Tourism Development Division
P.O. Box 849
Jackson, MS 39205
601-359-3297, FAX: 601-359-2832

Director
Missouri Division of Tourism
P.O. Box 1055
Jefferson City, MO 65102
314-751-3051, FAX: 314-751-5160

Travel Director
Montana Promotion Division
Department of Commerce
1424 Ninth Avenue
Helena, MT 59620-0411
406-444-2654, FAX: 406-444-2808

State Travel Director
Nebraska Division of Travel
Department of Economic
Development
P.O. Box 94666
301 Centennial Mall South
Lincoln, NE 68509
402-471-3794, FAX: 402-471-3778

Director
Nevada Division of Travel &
Tourism
Capitol Complex
Carson City, NV 89710
702-687-4322, FAX: 702-687-6770

Director
New Hampshire Office of Travel
and Tourism Development
172 Pembrooke Road
P.O. Box 856
Concord, NH 03302-0856
603-271-2665, FAX: 603-271-2629

Director
New Jersey Division
of Travel & Tourism
Department of Commerce
and Economic Development
0 West State Street, CN 826
Trenton, NJ 08625-0826
609-292-6963, FAX: 609-292-7418

Cabinet Secretary
New Mexico Department of
Tourism
91 Old Santa Fe Trail
Santa Fe, NM 87503
505-827-7400, FAX: 505-827-7402

Deputy Commissioner
for Tourism Development
New York State Division of
Tourism
Department of Economic
Development
One Commerce Plaza
Albany, NY 12245
518-474-4116, FAX: 518-486-6416

Director
North Carolina Travel & Tourism
Division
Department of Economic
& Community Development
30 N. Salisbury Street
Raleigh, NC 27611
919-733-4171, FAX: 919-733-8582

Tourism Director
North Dakota Tourism Promo.
Division
Parks and Tourism Department
Liberty Memorial Building
04-East Boulevard
Bismark, ND 58505
701-224-2525, FAX: 701-223-3081

State Travel Director
Ohio Division of Travel & Tourism
Department of Development
P.O. Box 1001
Columbus, OH 43266-0101
614-466-8844, FAX: 614-466-6744

Director, Travel & Tourism Division
Oklahoma Tourism
& Recreation Department
Travel & Tourism Division
505 Will Rogers Building
Oklahoma City, OK 73105
405-521-3981, FAX: 405-521-3992

State Tourism Director
Oregon Economic Development
Department, Tourism Division
775 Summer Street, NE
Salem, OR 97310
503-378-3451, FAX: 503-378-3451

Director
Pennsylvania Bureau of Travel
Marketing
Department of Commerce
453 Forum Building
Harrisburg, PA 17120
717-787-5453, FAX: 717-234-4560

Director of Tourism
Rhode Island Tourism Division
Department of Economic
Development
7 Jackson Walkway
Providence, RI 02903
401-277-2601, FAX: 401-421-7675

Director of Tourism
South Carolina Department of Parks
Recreation & Tourism
1205 Pendleton Street, Suite 106
Edgar A. Brown Building
Columbia, SC 29201
803-734-0136, FAX: 803-734-0133

Secretary of Tourism
South Dakota Department of
Tourism
Capitol Lake Plaza
711 E. Well Avenue
Pierre, SD 57501-3369
605-773-3301, FAX: 605-773-3256

Commissioner
Tennesse Department of Tourist
Development
P.O. Box 23170
Nashville, TN 37202-3170
615-741-7225, FAX: 615-741-7225

Director of Tourism
Texas Department of Commerce
Tourism Division
P.O. Box 12728
Austin, TX 78711
512-462-9191, FAX: 512-320-9456

Director
Utah Travel Council
Capitol Hall
300 North State
Salt Lake City, UT 84114
801-538-1030, FAX: 801-538-1399

Director
Vermont Travel Division
Agency of Development
and Community Affairs
134 States Street
Montpelier, VT 05602
802-828-3236, FAX: 802-828-3233

Director of Tourism
Virginia Tourism Dev. Group
Department of Economic
Development
1021 E. Cary Street
Richmond, VA 23219
804-786-2051, FAX: 804-786-1919

Director
State of Washington, Tourism
Development Division
Department of Trade
& Economic Development
101 General Administration
Building Ax-13
Olympia, WA 98504-0613
206-753-5600, FAX: 206-586-1850

Commissioner of Tourism and
Parks
West Virginia Division
of Tourism and Parks
2101 Washington Street, East
Charleston, WV 25305
304-348-2200 or 2286, FAX:
304-348-0108

Administrator
Wisconsin Division of Tourism
Department of Development
123 West Washington Avenue
P.O. Box 7970
Madison, WI 53707
608-266-2345, FAX: 608-266-3402

Director
Wyoming Travel Commission
Division of Tourism
Department of Commerce
Frank Norris Jr. Travel Center
I-25 & College Drive
Cheyenne, WY 82002-0660
307-777-7777, FAX: 307-777-6904

Director, Office of Tourism
American Samoa Government
Office of Tourism
P.O. Box 1147
Pago Pago, AS 96799
684-633-1091/2/3

General Manager
Guam Visitors Bureau
1270 N. Marine Drive
2nd Floor Boon Building
Suite 201-204
Upper Tumon, Guam 96931
671-646-5278 or 5279, FAX:
671-646-8861

Managing Director
Marianas Visitors Bureau
P.O. Box 861
Saipan, MP 96950
670-234-8327, FAX: 670-234-3596

Executive Director
Puerto Rico Tourism Company
P.O. Box 4435
Old San Juan Station
San Juan, PR 00902
809-722-6238, FAX: 809-722-6238

Assistant Commissioner of Tourism
U.S. Virgin Islands
Division of Tourism
Box 6400
Charlotte Amalie
St. Thomas, USVI 00801
809-774-8784, FAX: 809-774-4390

Sample Thematic Units

■

China

Brightfield, R. (1989). *China: Why was an army made of clay?*. New York: McGraw. (Gr. 4–6).

Fisher, L. (1986). *The Great Wall of China*. New York: Macmillan. (Gr. 1–8).

Kendall, C. (1990). *Sweet and sour*. Boston: Clarion. (Gr. 4–7).

Lewis, E. F. (1990). *Young Fu of the Upper Yangtze*. New York: Dell. (Gr. 2–5).

Lobel, A. (1986). *Ming Lo moves mountains*. New York: Scholastic. (Gr. Preschool–3).

Martell, M. H. (1992). *The ancient Chinese*. New York: Macmillan. (Gr. 6–8).

Tan, A. (1992). *The moon lady* (G. Shields, Illus.). New York: Macmillan.

Egypt

Giblin, J. (1990). *The riddle of the Rosetta Stone: Key to ancient Egypt*. New York: Crowell. (Gr. 3–8).

Hart, G. (1989). *Ancient Egypt* (S. Biesty, Illus.). San Diego: Harcourt Brace. (Gr. 3–7).

Koening, V. (1992). *The ancient Egyptians: Life in the Nile Valley*. Brookfield, CN: Millbrook Press. (Gr. 4–7).

Macaulay, D. (1992). *Pyramid*. Boston: Houghton Mifflin. (Gr. 5–9).

Payne, E. (1981). *The pharoahs of ancient Egypt*. New York: Random House Books for Young Readers. (Gr. 5–8).

Stewart, G. B. (1992). *Egypt*. New York: Macmillan. (Gr. 5–9).

Terzi, M. (1992). *The land of the pharoahs*. Chicago: Children's. (Gr. 3–8).

Knights

Bellairs, J. (1992). *The secret of the underground room*. New York: Puffin. (Gr. 5–9).

De Paola, T. (1980). *The knight and the dragon*. New York: Putnam. (Gr. K–3).

Eager E. (1989). *Knight's castle* (N. M. Bodecker, Illus.). San Diego: Harcourt Brace. (Gr. 3–8).

Heyer, C. (1991). *Excalibur.* Nashville: Ideals. (Gr. K–4).

Lasker, J. (1986). *The tournament of the knights.* New York: HarperCollins. (Gr. 3–8).

McAllister, A. (1992). *The battle of Sir Cobb and Sir Filbert.* New York: Crown Books Young Readers. (Gr. Preschool–3).

McKinley, R. (1982). *The blue sword.* New York: Greenwillow. (Gr. 7–10).

Osband, G., & Andrew, R. (1991). *Castles.* New York: Orchard. (Gr. K–8).

Talbott, H. (1991). *King Arthur: The sword in the stone.* New York: Morrow Junior.

Wilde, N. (1984). *Sir Bertie and the wyvern: A tale of heraldry.* Minneapolis: Carolrhoda. (Gr. 2–6).

Winthrop, E. (1985). *The castle in the attic.* New York: Holiday. (Gr. 4–7).

Mississippi River

Butterworth, W. E. (1982). *LeRoy and the old man.* New York: Scholastic. (Gr. 6–9).

Crisman, R. (1984). *The Mississippi.* New York: Watts. (Gr. 4–8).

Fichter, G. S. (1989). *First steamboat down the Mississippi* (J. Body, Illus.). New York: Pelican. (Gr. 4–7).

McCall, E. (1990). *Biography of a river: The Mississippi.* New York: Walker. (Gr. 7–9).

Naylor, P. (1984). *Night cry.* New York: Macmillian. (Gr. 5–9).

Steverner, C. (1992). *River rats.* San Diego: Harcourt Brace. (Gr. 5–9).

Taylor, M. (1992). *The road to Memphis.* New York: Puffin. (Gr. 5–9).

Warner, G. C. (1991). *The haunted cabin.* New York: Whitman. (Gr. 2–7).

Money

Adams, B. J. (1992). *The go-around dollar* (J. A. Joyce, Illus.). New York: Four Winds. (Gr. K–4).

Brittain, B. (1979). *All the money in the world.* New York: HarperCollins Children's Books. (Gr. 3–7).

Caple, K. (1992). *The purse.* Boston: Sandpiper. (Gr. K–3).

Leedy, L. (1992). *The monster money book.* New York: Holiday. (Gr. Preschool–3).

Manes, S. (1991). *Make four million dollars.* New York: Bantam. (Gr. 4–8).

Pfeffer, S. (1982). *Kid power.* New York: Scholastic. (Gr. 4–7).

Viorst, J. (1978). *Alexander who used to be rich last Sunday.* New York: Atheneum. (Gr. Preschool–3).

White, C. A. (1989). *Matthew's allowance.* New York: Winston-Derek. (Gr. K–4).

Williams, V. B. (1982). *A chair for my mother.* New York: Greenwillow. (Gr. K–4).

CREDITS

Chapter 1

Opener: © Michael Newman/Photo Edit; **p. 5, 7:** © Lawrence Migdale; **p. 8:** © James Shaffer; **p. 11, 16, 19:** © Lawrence Migdale

Chapter 2

Opener: © Tony Freeman/Photo Edit; **p. 29, 31, 34, 37:** © Lawrence Migdale

Chapter 3

Opener: © Richard Hutchings/Photo Edit; **p. 45, 52, 54:** © Lawrence Migdale; **p. 61:** © Tony Freeman/Photo Edit

Chapter 4

Opener: © Jeffry Myers/Photo Network; **p. 71:** © Lawrence Migdale; **p. 84:** © Richard Hutchings/Photo Edit

Chapter 5

Opener: © James Shaffer; **p. 102:** © Richard Hutchings/Photo Edit; **p. 103:** © Bachmann/Photo Network; **p. 110:** © Myrleen Ferguson/Photo Edit; **p. 114:** © James Shaffer; **p. 117:** © Richard Hutchings/Photo Edit

Chapter 6

Opener: © James Shaffer; **p. 135:** © Mary Kate Denny/Photo Edit

Chapter 7

Opener: © David Young-Wolff/Photo Edit; **p. 160, 162, 165:** © Martin-Mitchell Museum/Napier Settlement; **p. 169:** © Lawrence Migdale; **p. 175, 182,** (both): © Martin-Mitchell Museum/Napier Settlement

Chapter 8

Opener: © Bachmann/Photo Network; **p. 195:** © Lawrence Migdale; **p. 200:** © Tony Freeman/Photo Edit

Chapter 9

Opener: © James Shaffer; **p. 216:** © Paul Brown/Larado Taft Field Campus/Northern Illinois University; **p. 221:** Courtesy of Northern Illinois University; **p. 224:** Courtesy of Northern Illinois University

Chapter 10

Opener: © James Shaffer; **p. 244:** © Lawrence Migdale; **p. 246:** © Photo Network; **p. 252, 256:** © Tony Freeman/Photo Edit

Chapter 11

Opener: © Mary Kate Denny/Photo Edit; **p. 270:** © Richard Hutchings/Photo Edit; **p. 272:** © Lawrence Migdale

Chapter 12

Opener: © Jeffry Myers/Photo Network; **p. 285:** © Lawrence Migdale; **p. 289:** © James Shaffer; **p. 297:** © David Young-Wolff/Photo Edit

Chapter 13

Opener: © Richard Hutchings/Photo Edit; **p. 315, 320:** © Lawrence Migdale; **Fig. 13.4:** © Amy Etra/Photo Edit

Chapter 14

Opener: © James Shaffer; **p. 340:** © MacDonald/Photo Network; **p. 344:** © James Shaffer; **p. 346:** © Mary Kate Denny/Photo Edit

Children's Books, Authors, and Software Index

SUBJECT AND REFERENCE INDEX